Advanced Criminal Investigations and Intelligence Operations

Tradecraft Methods, Practices, Tactics, and Techniques

Advanced Criminal Investigations and Intelligence Operations

Tradecraft Methods, Practices, Tactics, and Techniques

Dr. Robert J. Girod, JD, PhD

Robert J. Girod Consulting, LLC
Fort Wayne, Indiana, USA

CRC Press
Taylor & Francis Group
Boca Raton London New York

CRC Press is an imprint of the
Taylor & Francis Group, an **informa** business

CRC Press
Taylor & Francis Group
6000 Broken Sound Parkway NW, Suite 300
Boca Raton, FL 33487-2742

First issued in paperback 2020

© 2014 by Taylor & Francis Group, LLC
CRC Press is an imprint of Taylor & Francis Group, an Informa business

No claim to original U.S. Government works

ISBN-13: 978-1-4822-3072-7 (hbk)
ISBN-13: 978-0-367-67014-6 (pbk)

Visit the Taylor & Francis Web site at
http://www.taylorandfrancis.com

and the CRC Press Web site at
http://www.crcpress.com

Contents

**8   Electronic Intelligence and Signals Intelligence:
     Bugs and Taps   127**

9   Emanations Intelligence   153

Preface

"And ye shall know the truth, and the truth shall make you free." John 8:32

~ The Bible (King James Version) ~

I want to dedicate this book to my family—my wife Laurie, sons Bobby and Josh, mother Carolyn (and Bill), mother-in-law Joann, and our siblings, in-laws, and extended family. I want to thank all of my professors, instructors, mentors, comrades-at-arms, brothers and sisters in law enforcement, and all of those who have helped me to prepare this text and serve my country and community. God bless America!

John Wayne once said something that I found very profound and appropriate:

"I won't be wronged. I won't be insulted. I won't be laid a-hand on. I don't do these things to other people, and I require the same from them."

This text is a collection of thoughts based upon my training and experience over more than three decades and upon the notes and handouts that I have collected during thousands of hours of advanced training. I have been trained by law enforcement, the U.S. military, and private-sector sources, including the National Intelligence Academy and numerous other advanced schools in investigations, intelligence, and operations.

In addition to making my own notes over the decades and saving handouts from eminent instructors, I have collected manufacturer specifications and guidelines from vendors of intelligence and investigative equipment that I thought were worth the effort of saving for reference purposes.

This work is a collection of some of the things that I have found useful and interesting in pursuit of my profession. I hope that readers will find them equally useful and interesting.

Take note that laws change often. New statutes are enacted annually by both state and federal legislatures. Case law can change with a decision by state and federal appellant courts. Readers and practitioners are advised (several times in this book) to not only refer to the legal cases and statutes provided, which are current at the time of writing, but to continually seek competent legal counsel and updated legal citations before relying upon them.

Use this information responsibly.

De oppresso liber

Robert J. Girod, JD, PhD

Introduction

"And the man who was standing among the myrtle trees answered and said,
'These are those whom the LORD has sent to patrol the earth.'"

~ Zechariah 1:10 (New American Standard Version) ~

Intelligence gathering has been going on since Moses sent spies into the land of Canaan, and its use was encouraged by military strategist Sun Tzu (*The Art of War*). It has been used in conflicts between nations, in the wars against drugs and terrorism, and in business and industry. Whether using high-tech equipment or agents provocateur (undercover agents), intelligence involves the use of processed information, and information is power. *Tradecraft* is a term that refers to skills acquired through experience in a clandestine trade. The term is used within the intelligence community as a collective word for the methods, practices, and techniques used in espionage.

Chapter 1 provides a discussion of *black bag operational planning* (Chapter 1). The intelligence community refers to covert or surreptitious entry as *black bag operations*. These are operations conducted outside of the United States by intelligence agencies or within the United States by law enforcement agencies with valid search warrants. Most other black bag operations are illegal. While the owner of property may (for some reason) authorize such activities on his or her own property by employees or contracted personnel (like private investigators), even on private property investigators must be cognizant of privacy issues and laws.

The intelligence community also divides intelligence specialties or tasks into what are referred to as the "INTs." Chapters 2 and 3 discuss HUMINT, or human intelligence, the gathering of information from human sources. This can involve surveillance, undercover operations, use of informants or *assets*, etc.

Chapters 4 through 6 deal with defenses against methods of entry (DAME), forced entry into buildings, safes and combination locks, automobile locks, etc. Understanding methods of entry is often necessary in foreign intelligence gathering and DAME is important in security, counterintelligence, and the investigation of burglaries and other forced entry offenses.

Psychological Operations (PSYOPS) and the use of social networks are discussed in Chapter 7. This topic ranges from personal revenge and political dirty tricks to PSYOPS in support of military and diplomatic operations.

Chapter 8 discusses the use of ELINT (electronic intelligence) and SIGINT (signals intelligence). This involves electronic interception of intelligence, *bugs*, wiretaps, and other communications interceptions.

Chapter 9 discusses EMINT (emanations intelligence), which concerns the *emanation* of data, signals, or other intelligence from C4I systems (command, communications, control, computers, and intelligence systems).

Chapter 10 deals with IMINT (imagery intelligence), which involves any intelligence gathered using images, such as photographs, night vision optics, infrared and *forward-looking infrared* (IR/FLIR) devices, satellite and aerial photographs and images, radar images, etc.

Chapter 11 deals with intelligence files and analytical methods. This is the processing, analysis, and dissemination (to end source users) of the intelligence product and may include crime analysis statistics, threat assessments, etc.

Finally, Chapters 13 through 15 discuss legal aspects that are of concern to intelligence officers and investigators in both the intelligence and law enforcement communities, as well as in the private sector. This information is supplemented by four appendices of applicable statutes, as well as one additional appendix on the most commonly encountered languages (for use in HUMINT operations).

NOTE: Statutes and case laws change constantly. Do not rely upon any source of law as being current without conducting legal research or consulting competent legal counsel. Statutes and case law included here are current at the time of research, but should be researched for current and up-to-date law before relying upon them. Always seek competent legal counsel on any legal questions.

This text is for law enforcement and authorized intelligence officers and for legal purposes only. The information contained here is for the academic study of crime and methods and practices of intelligence operations.

Covert or surreptitious entry and associated activities are often conducted to gather information, inspect premises, remove something, or for some other legal or illegal purpose. (Readers are cautioned not to pursue any illegal purposes, as severe criminal penalties may be involved.)

The Select Committee to Study Governmental Operations reported that

Since 1948 the FBI has conducted hundreds of warrantless surreptitious entries to gather domestic and foreign intelligence, despite the questionable legality of the technique and its deep intrusion into the privacy of targeted individuals. Before 1966, the FBI conducted over two hundred "black bag jobs."

(Memorandum from FBI to Senate select Committee; January 13, 1976)

The Select Committee to Study Governmental Operations, Supplementary Detailed Staff Reports on Intelligence Activities and the Rights of Americans, April 23, 1976, reported that

Figure I.1 FBI Director J. Edgar Hoover (left) and Deputy Director Clyde Tolson (right).

> Although several Attorneys General were aware of the FBI practice of break-ins to install electronic listening devices, there is no indication that the FBI informed any Attorney General about its use of "black bag jobs."

It went on to say:

> Surreptitious entries were performed by teams of FBI agents with special training in subjects such as "lock studies." Their missions were authorized in writing by FBI Director Hoover or his deputy, Clyde Tolson (Figure I.1). A "Do Not File" procedure was utilized, under which most records of surreptitious entries were destroyed soon after an entry was accomplished.

(The Select Committee to Study Governmental Operations, p. 1)

"When the strong ones went out, they were eager to go to patrol the earth." And He said, 'Go, patrol the earth.' So they patrolled the earth."

~ Zechariah 6:7

Author

Dr. Robert Girod, Sr. earned a double PhD in criminology and public administration from the Union Institute and University, a postdoctoral certificate in leadership from Harvard University, and a JD (doctor of jurisprudence) from Thomas M. Cooley Law School. He earned an MSc in criminal justice administration from Central Missouri State University, a BA in sociology from Huntington College, a BGS in social and behavioral science and an associate of science in criminal justice from Indiana University, and a diploma in forensic science from the American Institute of Applied Science.

Girod is a graduate of the Indiana Law Enforcement Academy, the Fort Wayne Police Academy, the National Police Institute Command and Staff School, and more than 60 advanced police and instructor schools. He is a graduate of more than a dozen military schools, including the U.S. Naval War College, the U.S. Marine Corps Command and Staff College, and the U.S. Air Force Squadron Officer's School.

Dr. Girod is the president and CEO of Robert J. Girod Consulting, LLC, attorneys-at-law and consulting detectives/private investigators, which provides general law practice and investigative services, litigation support, and management services nationwide, including forensic accounting, computer forensics, accident reconstruction, and linguistic interviewing, translation, and interpretation.

Captain Girod is a command officer with the Haviland-Latty Police Departments (Ohio). He also served as the director of public safety (interim CEO) for the Kanawha Police Department (Iowa).

Sergeant Girod retired from the Fort Wayne Police Department after 23 years as the robbery-homicide supervisor and founding member of the FBI Federal Bank Robbery Task Force. He was also a supervisor over juvenile and auto theft as well as all four detective quadrants and also served as a patrol supervisor. He has served on the Police Reserve Board and the Police Pension Board and has lectured at the Fort Wayne Police Academy/Regional Public Safety Academy.

Girod served as a special deputy for the United States Marshals Service and as a police officer with the Indianapolis Police Department and the Indiana University Police Department. He was a special agent with the Ohio Bureau of Criminal Investigations and an investigator with the Indiana Department of

Insurance and the Wells County Prosecutor's Office, where he began his career in 1979. Prior to this, he was a private detective for Zeis Security Systems.

Major Girod served for 4 years in the Indiana Guard Reserve and for 18 years in the U.S. Army Reserve, attaining the rank of captain. He held command and staff positions in the military police, basic training (infantry), and Special Forces, but served primarily with the U.S. Army Criminal Investigations Command (USACIDC).

Professor Girod has been an adjunct professor or associate faculty member at eight universities: Indiana University, Boston University, Huntington University, Concordia University of Wisconsin, Taylor University, Indiana Wesleyan University, Northcentral University, and the Union Institute and University. He has taught more than 30 subjects in management, criminal justice, public administration, political science, history, and sociology at the undergraduate through the doctoral level in traditional, adult education, correspondence, and Internet programs.

Dr. Girod is a member of numerous professional, political, and civic associations and organizations, including the Fraternal Order of Police, the American Bar Association, and the American Legion, and has served on the board at the Fort Wayne-Allen County Historical Society (The History Center) and First Church of the Nazarene. In addition to his military awards, Girod was awarded the Meritorious Service Medal and the Commendation Medal by the Fort Wayne Police Department and a Letter of Commendation by the director of the Federal Bureau of Investigation. He was listed in the *Who's Who in Law Enforcement* in 1991 and the international *Who's Who in Public Service* in 2000.

Girod is the author of *Profiling the Criminal Mind: Behavioral Science and Criminal Investigative Analysis*; *Infamous Murders and Mysteries: Cold Case Files and Who-Done-Its*; and *Police Liability and Risk Management: Torts, Civil Rights and Employment Law*. He has also authored numerous articles for various professional periodicals, such as *FBI Law Enforcement Bulletin*, *Security Management*, *The Police Marksman*, and *Musubi*.

About Robert J. Girod Consulting, LLC

Run down, my dear fellow, and open the door, for all virtuous folk have been long in bed.

Ambereley excelled at chess—one mark, Watson, of a scheming mind.

He is in my judgment, the fourth smartest man in London, and for daring I am not sure that he has not a claim to be third.

~ **Sherlock Holmes** ~
Sir Arthur Conan Doyle

Robert J. Girod Consulting, LLC is an investigative, legal and litigation support, and management consulting firm. Most of its *consulting detectives* or investigators and expert witnesses are active or retired law enforcement and intelligence officers, university professors, and practicing professionals.

Many of the firm's investigators are still active police detectives and professors, while others are retired from lengthy careers with the CIA, FBI, DEA, IRS, U.S. Secret Service, U.S. Postal Inspectors, and the NTSB (National Transportation Safety Board). Some of the firm's consultants are tenured professors at several universities around the country, including a number of Big Ten universities, while others are adjunct professors at multiple universities. The staff also includes a cadre of expert witnesses that include forensic psychologists, a forensic chiropractor, and physicians (and a former coroner) who are board certified in pain management, orthomolecular medicine (anti-aging), family practice, anesthesiology, and orthopedic and sports medicine.

The firm offers services in a full range of legal and litigation support activities, including computer forensics and security, forensic accounting (auditing) and fraud examination, accident investigation and reconstruction (automobile and interstate transportation, rail road, aviation, and marine, OSHA, industrial and construction, etc.), and auto theft and arson and explosives investigations. The firm also conducts asset protection, loss prevention, internal theft, and risk management investigations and a wide range of litigation support services, such as illustrations, graphics, charts, graphs, diagrams, and analytical and presentation media.

You may visit the firm's web page at RGirodLLC.com for more information or services.

Come, Watson, come! The game is afoot. Not a word! Into your clothes and come!

Chance has put in our way a most singular and whimsical problem, and its solution is its own reward.

I listen to their story, they listen to my comments, and then I pocket my fee.

~ Sherlock Holmes ~
Sir Arthur Conan Doyle

Black Bag Operational Planning

1

Black bag operations, are covert or surreptitious entries for the purposes of intelligence gathering. This may be national security intelligence, military intelligence, law enforcement investigations, or business and industrial intelligence. Domestic *spying* (as opposed to foreign spying) is only legal when conducted pursuant to a valid, legal search warrant, wiretap order, or similar legal requirement (subject to probable cause) and after meeting any other strict statutory requirements. Such operations are subject to very strict laws when conducted domestically.

This point cannot be emphasized enough: Statutes and case laws change constantly. Do not rely upon any source of law as being current without conducting legal research or consulting competent legal counsel. Statutes and case law included here are current at the time of research but should be researched for current and up-to-date law before relying upon them. Always seek competent legal counsel on any legal questions.

Operational Planning

Operational planning involves research, that is, researching the target and target area. The success of the operation depends upon the extent of planning and research. Impromptu operations will produce impromptu results (which are usually bad). Do not skimp on the planning phase. Plan for all possible contingencies; anything that can go wrong probably will. Plan such operations in much the same way as you would plan a surveillance (which you should also plan and may be a part of the *black bag* job). Spend time to determine all that there is to know about the target location. Remember the six *P*s—Proper Planning and Practice Prevents Poor Performance.

The target location may be an obscure, rural, low-tech location or a congested, urban, high-tech, high-rise facility. Floor plans and measurements are essential. These can be obtained from the local agency that approves the building permits. Zoning and building inspection offices may also be a viable source. Maps of the area, especially bounding streets and roads, and aerial photographs are also essential. You should know the type of structure, number of floors (stories), the height, adjacent building information, types of occupants and zoning, etc. You may want to rent the office, apartment, house, or building next to the target.

1

Internal and external lighting systems (including street lights and motion-activated security lights), barriers (fences, windows, doors, access control, etc.), and alarm and other security systems must be determined. The presence of security personnel, dogs, and residents or workers and their schedules is also critical. Even if the entry and operation are legal (and we will assume that it is for our purposes), raising the alarm and summoning the police are not conducive to efficient operations. Do not assume that other law enforcement will know that you are supposed to be doing what you are doing. They probably will not, and such operations are almost always on a *Need to Know* basis, that is, not sharing the information outside of the operation.

Reconnaissance should be conducted, and surveillance photographs and videos should be obtained ahead of time and used in the planning phase. A good cover should also be prepared to conceal your purpose, avoid attention, or explain your presence if detected. Enlisting the unknowing aid of janitors, guards, neighbors, or other tenants may be helpful, but should be done so discreetly and with extreme caution to avoid suspicion and wanton gossiping which will reveal that something is amiss.

Preparation before and debriefing following operations may both involve the use of Periodic Intelligence Reports (PERINTREP). This includes information on the situation, activities (target), order of battle (OB), counterintelligence, weather, terrain, and analysis (see Figure 1.1, FM 30-5 Combat Intelligence, Appendix D-1, Format for Periodic Intelligence Report [PERINTREP], pages 1–3).

Identification and New Identity: Cover Story

A cover story is essential to undercover or *black bag* operations (clandestine operations or investigations). Chapter 4 discusses undercover operations, cover stories, and identity changing in greater detail.

MI9, the British Directorate of Military Intelligence Section 9 and a sister agency of MI5 and MI6, was formed in 1939 and operated throughout World War II to aid resistance fighters and infiltrate POWs who had escaped. MI9 used the advice of the stage magician Jasper Maskelyne to design the hiding places for escape aids: tools disguised in a cricket bat, a saw blade inside a comb, maps in the backs of books and on playing cards and inside gramophone records, boardgame sets that concealed money. Forged German identity cards, ration coupons, and travel warrants were smuggled into POW camps.

The 2012 film *Argo*—adapted from the book *The Master of Disguise* by CIA officer Antonio J. Mendez, in which Mendez led the rescue of six U.S. diplomats from Tehran, Iran, during the 1979 Iran hostage crisis, and from Joshuah Berman's 2007 article *The Great Escape* in *Wired* magazine—provides a dramatic and entertaining view of extraction and exfiltration (Exfil) operations.

Tony Mendez, an artist, illustrator, and tool designer, was an expert in forgery and disguise. The *Canadian Caper* was the popular name given to the joint covert rescue by the CIA with the cooperation of the Canadian government of six American diplomats who had evaded capture during the seizure of the U.S. embassy in Iran on November 4, 1979. The *caper* involved CIA agents Tony Mendez and a man known as *Julio* directing the six diplomats to form a fake film crew made up of six Canadians, one Irishman, and one Latin American used the cover story of "scouting a location to shoot a scene for a

FM 30–5

APPENDIX D

FORMAT FOR PERIODIC INTELLIGENCE REPORT (PERINTREP)

(Classification)

Copy No ....
Unit
Location
Date-time group
Message reference number

PERINTREP NO _____
Period covered: (date and time to date and time).
References: Maps or charts.
Disposal instructions: (if any).

1. GENERAL ENEMY SITUATION

This paragraph contains a brief summary of enemy operations during the period. Amplifying details are furnished in the paragraphs that follow and in appropriate annexes, or both. This paragraph provides a quick briefing on the highlights of the enemy situation and the significance of the enemy's major activities, to include marked changes in morale, strengths, dispositions, tactics, combat effectiveness, and equipment. Data that are lengthy or can conveniently be shown graphically are presented in annexes.

2. ENEMY ACTIVITIES

This paragraph, in conjunction with those following, provides the details of the situation summarized in paragraph 1. Detailed intelligence provided in this paragraph covers all operational activities. Information may be presented graphically by overlays, printed maps, sketch maps, and annexes. Subparagraphs are omitted when appropriate intelligence is not available or is adequately covered by other portions of this report.
(Short title identification)

    a. Ground. (Primarily includes activities of combat arms, reserves, and reinforcements; includes enemy defenses, minefields, fortificaitons, barriers, obstacles, and other defensive works.)

    b. Air. (Includes Air Force activities, such as bombing, close air support, and tactical aerial reconnaissance; air surveillance, and air-supported operations.)

    c. Airborne.

    d. Irregular.

    e. Nuclear, Biological, or Chemical Operations.

    f. Electronic Warfare.

    g. Other. (Normally includes other than combat arms; includes appro-

(Classification)

D–1

Figure 1.1 FM 30-5 Combat Intelligence, Appendix D-1. Format for Periodic Intelligence Report (PERINTREP), pages 1–3.

(continued)

FM 30–5

(Classification)

priate comments not covered in other paragraphs on reserves, reinforcements, new tactics, weapons and equipment, administrative installations, and combat service support. Also includes appropriate technical intelligence.)

3. ORDER OF BATTLE

Frequently, this paragraph will consist only of references to the enemy situation map (or overlay) and to the order of battle annex, which is developed using the format shown below. When desired by the commander, particularly significant order of battle changes may be summarized in this paragraph in addition to being discussed in detail in the order of battle annex. (See Appendix L, Order of Battle Annex to PERINTREP).

   a. Composition and Disposition.

   b. Strength. (Personnel and major weapons and items of equipment.)

     (1) Losses.

     (2) Current strength.

(Short title identification)

   c. Tactics.

   d. Training.

   e. Combat Service Support.

   f. Combat Effectiveness.

   g. Miscellaneous Data.

4. COUNTERINTELLIGENCE

This paragraph, or parts thereof, should be issued as an annex if a limited distribution is required.

   a. General. (A short summary of the counterintelligence situation during the period.)

   b. Espionage.

   c. Sabotage.

   d. Subversion.

   e. Communications and Noncommunications Security.

   f. Miscellaneous.

5. WEATHER

This paragraph gives a summary of the effect of weather on operations during the period.

6. TERRAIN

Use an annex, special maps, and overlays when possible. Include impact on future operations, if appropriate.

7. ANALYSIS AND DISCUSSION

This paragraph lists and discusses briefly enemy capabilities and vulnerabilities. The conclusions present the commander's assessment of the most probable courses of action available to the enemy in order of probability of adoption and vulnerabilities that are exploitable by own, higher, or lower echelons.

(Classification)

D–2

Figure 1.1 (continued) FM 30-5 Combat Intelligence, Appendix D-1. Format for Periodic Intelligence Report (PERINTREP), pages 1–3.

FM 30–5

(Classification)

a. Enemy Capabilities.
b. Enemy Vulnerabilities.
c. Conclusions.
Acknowledge.

Signature

(Short title identification)
Annexes: (Any intelligence document may be distributed as an annex to a PERINTREP. Although annexes are a means of distributing detailed intelligence and information, care is exercised to avoid unnecessary bulk and duplication.)

Distribution:

Authentication:

Note: In joint service operations, the PERINTREP is replaced by the periodic intelligence summary (PERINTSUM). The correct format for the PERINTSUM is contained in Chapter V, JCS Publication 12.

(Classification)

D–3

Figure 1.1 (continued) FM 30-5 Combat Intelligence, Appendix D-1. Format for Periodic Intelligence Report (PERINTREP), pages 1–3.

science-fiction film *Argo*." The ruse culminated on the morning of January 28, 1980, at Mehrabad Airport Tehran. The eight Americans successfully boarded a Swissair flight, escaping to Zurich, Switzerland.

There are three basic forms of new identification (ID) documents: (1) false ID, (2) counterfeit ID, and (3) genuine government-issued ID for a false identity. State-certified birth certificates, driver's licenses, and social security cards with valid correlating numbers are *core documents* from which all other documents come. Identification can be purchased from a variety of mail order companies or manufactured with a good computer and program-providing templates.

Times have changed, and problems develop in the preparation of a cover identity. Older methods for identity changing no longer prove accurate and valid. New legal loopholes may be opened or (more likely) closed, procedures change, and technology evolves.

Somewhere between the official under cover (UC) and the no official cover (NOC), there are other methods for creating an identity. The usual starting place for a cover or new identity is to obtain a birth certificate for a deceased person of the correct gender and approximate age. This is usually a prerequisite to obtaining a social security number (SSN) identification card, a driver's operator license number (OLN), a passport, etc. Birth certificate can be obtained from the county health department (where the clerk may have known the deceased person) or, better yet, from the state bureau of vital statistics (usually the department of health). The county or state health departments or the county clerk's office is usually where birth, marriage, and death records are filed. Usually, an identity of the deceased is obtained from the death records, obituaries, or tombstones in a cemetery.

First, find out what is required to obtain a copy of a birth certificate from the county, state, or country where your subject was born. The date of birth (DOB), place of birth (POB), and both parents' names are generally required. A form and fee are usually required. In some states, such as California, birth and death records are filed together, so this could arouse suspicion. Small towns should be avoided where a clerk may have known the deceased.

Chapter 4 discusses undercover operations, cover stories, and identity changing in greater detail. This should be a part of all operational planning. Planning is critical, yet it is important to remember problems will indeed arise from unexpected sources regardless of how meticulous the plan is. Plan for the worst and hope for the best is a good rule of thumb.

Point of Entry and Exit; Ingress and Egress

Once the planning phase has been completed, rehearsal is always a good idea. Once the plan is ready to be implemented, the entry and exit (ingress and egress or insertion and extraction) are obviously the most important step in the job.

Entry may require obtaining keys or copies of keys. If they are not available, copies may be made using a key impression pad. If access to copies is not possible, lock picks and bump keys may be necessary. This will be discussed in detail later. Security pass cards, access codes, and other devices may be necessary, depending upon the security measures adopted in the planning phase.

Entry and exit should be made in complete silence. Although communications may be necessary, it should be as silent as possible and limited to necessary communications. Command, communications, and control (C3) are essential. Everyone must be in the communications network, and it is best to have one designated communications controller. That person should be responsible for monitoring other communications resources. Law enforcement can disregard the dispatches of other officers who are sent to investigate *suspicious person*, prowlers, or *burglary in progress* calls by patrol officers. Someone outside should monitor what the rest of the team cannot and be aware of what is happening outside. Monitoring security, maintenance, and other facility communications is also extremely useful.

Once egress (exit) or extraction is completed, all personnel should get out of the area of operation (AO) as soon as possible by leaving the surrounding area quickly and undetected or unnoticed. Changing clothing and appearance should be accomplished as soon as away from the immediate vicinity. Discrete vehicle changes may be necessary or simply changing the appearance of the vehicle(s) to avoid detection or notice. (You can be detected, that is, seen or observed, without being noticed, that is, drawing noticeable attention.)

Equipment

All equipment should be light and compact, and only the equipment that is necessary should be carried, without forgetting what may be necessary. This begins with clothing and personal equipment. Clothing that is conducive to concealment (camouflage or low visibility), blends or fits in the environment (looking like everyone else in the area and not standing out), and is part of a cover story or disguise (maintenance, employee, or utility uniforms) should be selected. Do not try to look like a cop or James Bond in a tuxedo at a biker rally. Fit in and be plain and boring; don't try to have any character that makes you noticeable. Dull black or charcoal gray colors show up less than dark black does. Maroon has a lower visibility spectrum than most colors. Broken up patterns are less detectable than solid patterns. Don't forget your face when concealing your identity or avoiding detection or notice. Remember that detection is being seen and notice is taking note of what is seen. Biker clothes at a biker rally are not noticed. Employee uniforms at a business may blend in with the environment.

If keys are not available, key impression pads may be useful in obtaining a copy of keys. Lock picks and pick guns, bump keys, and other access devices are probably a must to gain access to buildings, rooms, safes, drawers, cabinets, vehicles, and other areas that must be accessed.

Communications equipment should be reliable, redundant, compact, and stealthy (as silent as possible). As mentioned earlier, everyone must be in the communications network, and it is best to have one designated communications controller. That person should have access (from a different location) to other communications, such as monitoring police and security. (Law enforcement officers should monitor their own patrol frequencies for possible dispatches of officers to investigate *suspicious activity* or *burglary in progress* calls.)

Illumination equipment, such as flashlights, tactical lights, LED key rings, night vision, heat sensors (infrared or IR), and other optical devices are useful.

Lineman's or cable technician equipment may be useful and a good part of a cover story. Wire ties, electrical and duct tape, and blackout curtains may also be a useful part of concealment, containment, and interruption (emergency detention) kits.

A flaps and seals kit is used to open documents and document containers without detection. Equipment such as cameras, flash drives, keystroke readers, and computer forensics equipment may be necessary to document what you are there for. Bugs, taps, and emissions equipment may be the primary purpose for the operation—to install detection and interception devices for listening or receiving communications or emissions.

Cash is useful. Do not use credit or debit cards on a job. They can be traced, and your identity and purpose will be revealed.

Biometric Security Devices

Carl Sagan once said,

> We live in a society exquisitely dependent on science and technology, in which hardly anyone knows anything about science and technology.

He also said,

> We have also arranged things so that almost no one understands science and technology. This is a prescription for disaster. We might get away with it for a while, but sooner or later this combustible mixture of ignorance and power is going to blow up in our faces.

Finally, Dr. Sagan said,

> Skeptical scrutiny is the means, in both science and religion, by which deep thoughts can be winnowed from deep nonsense.

> (Retrieved from http://www.brainyquote.com/quotes/authors/c/carl_sagan.html on June 5, 2013)

Biometrics is the emerging technology that automatically identifies an individual based on his or her characteristics. It is the science and technology of measuring and analyzing biological data. In information technology, biometrics refers to technologies that measure and analyze human body characteristics, such as fingerprints, eye retinas and irises, voice patterns, facial patterns, and hand measurements, for identification and authentication purposes. Such systems digitally fingerprint people, read the patterns of their irises, measure the unique dimensions of their faces, or verify their voices.

Biometric information can be used for access control and remote identification. Access control is a system that enables an authority to control access to areas and resources in a given physical facility or information systems. There are two classifications of biometric information: physiological and behavioral characteristics. Physiological characteristics include fingerprint, hand geometry, DNA, facial features, and eye (iris) pattern.

Iris recognition uses pattern-recognition techniques based upon resolution images of the irises of an individual's eye (the contractile, circular diaphragm forming the colored portion of the eye and containing an opening, the pupil, in its center). This process is not the same as retina scanning (the biometric use of this scan is used to examine the pattern of blood vessels at the back of the eye). Iris recognition uses camera technology to create images of detailed, intricate iris structures. This information is converted into digital templates that create a mathematical interpretation for positive identification.

Behavioral characteristics that are unique to people include gait, signature, and voice. Anything that is unique to a person can be converted to a digital format that can be used to differentiate him or her from others. Gait is used to authenticate people by the way they walk. The attractiveness of this technique relies in its unobtrusive properties, since individuals are authenticated at certain distances without any need for cooperation. To create a gait signature, some models are based on temporal and spatial metrics of the human motion.

Voice recognition pattern is a combination of physical and behavioral characteristics that are related to the voice signal patterns. The physical pattern of a voice includes characteristics of the vocal tracts, nasal cavity, mouth, and lips. The behavioral pattern of a voice involves characteristics of the speaker's physical and emotional state. The authentication of a voice is divided into two groups: text-dependent and text-independent methods. Text-dependent methods analyze a predetermined phrase.

Facial recognition technology (FRT) uses a digital photograph of an individual's face to take measurements between nodal points, which are locations on every humans face. While there are about 80 different nodal points, an FRT software algorithm requires only 14–22 of these points for comparison.

Postoperational Actions and Debrief

All information should be documented and, if necessary, concealed or kept secret. Once all the personnel are in a safe zone, a debriefing should take place to ensure the objectives were met, no mistakes were made that were not resolved, and the information is disseminated to the recipient(s) or collection is continued (e.g., monitoring).

Make sure no evidence is left behind. This includes equipment, fingerprints, DNA evidence, disturbed items, and security detection (such as video, alarm activations, biometric evidence of intrusion, etc.). The operation will fail if any such evidence is found by the target subject. The information may become useless or obsolete if the target subject becomes aware of it. Once the information has been obtained, it should be analyzed and disseminated among those involved in the operation. These may be someone else's responsibility.

Order of Battle

Order of Battle (OB) is the identification, command structure, strength, and disposition of personnel, equipment, and units of an opposing force participating in field operations. A basic understanding of the units of land, air, and sea forces is useful to understanding the OB of intelligence.

Understanding the identification, command structure, strength, and disposition of personnel, equipment, and units of an opposing force can help determine the tactical and strategic intentions of a force, as well as the composition and capabilities of the force. Special Operations combat support and combat service support may have a different structure. Special operations, for example, usually operate much smaller, but highly specialized, units.

The basic composition of most military forces (army, navy, air force) is illustrated in Figures 1.2 through 1.5.

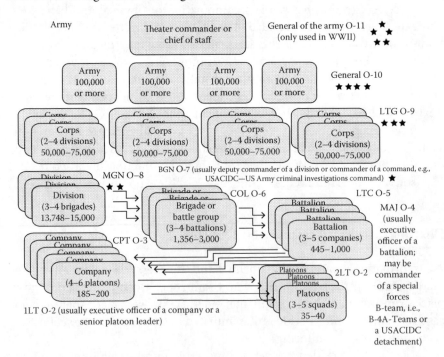

Figure 1.2 Order of battle: table of organization (army).

Order of battle: Army organization

Command	Unit	Strength
• SSG (E-6)	• Squad (2 teams)	11
• 2LT/1LT (O-2/O-1)	• Platoon (3–4 squads)	35
• CPT (O-3)	• Company (4–6 platoons)	184–200
• Maj (O-4)	• (Usually executive officer of a battalion;	
	• May be commander of a Special Forces B-Team, i.e., 3–4 A-Teams or a USACIDC detachment)	
• LTC (O-5)	• Battalion (3–5 companies)	445–1,000
• COL (O-6)	• Brigade or battle group (3–4)	1,356–3,000
• Maj general (O-8)	• Division (3–4 Brigades)	13,748–15,000
• Lt general (O-9)	• Corps (2–4 Divisions)	50,000–75,000
• General (O-10)	• Army	100,000 or more
• General of the army (O-11)	• Theater or chief of staff	(only used in WWII)

Figure 1.3 Order of battle: command structure (army).

Order of battle: Navy

Command	Unit
O-3/LIUET	Patrol or escort
O-4/LTCMD	Destroyer escort, submarine, or small auxiliary
O-5/CMDR	Destroyer, auxiliary ship or Division of destroyers or submarines
O-6/CAPT	Heavy ship, squadron of destroyers or Naval station
O-7/Commodore	Usually commissioned only in time of war
O-8/RADM	Division of heavy ships, Flotilla of lesser ships, Naval district of task force
O-9/VADM	Major division of a fleet or naval district
O-10/ADM	The principal fleet or separate fleets
O-11/Fleet admiral	Theater commander or chief of naval operations (CNO) (only used in WWII)

Figure 1.4 Order of battle: table of organization (navy).

Communications in Unconventional Environments

U.S. Army Field Manual 30-20 Special Forces Operational Techniques says, "The communications system and techniques employed by Special Forces are applicable to both unconventional warfare and counterinsurgency operations." There are times, when conducting *black bag* or clandestine operations, that field-expedient means of covert communications must be relied upon.

One such method is the use of field telephones, which, of course, on not a part of the local telephone system. Field phones are connected

Order of battle: Air force

Command	Unit of establishment
2LT O-1 or 1LT O-2	Flight or detachment (unit)
1LT O-2 or CPT O-3	Flight (4 aircraft or a support detachment) (unit)
CPT O-3 or MAJ O-4	Squadron (2–4 flights) (unit)
MAJ O-4 or LTC O-5	Group (several squadrons) (establishment)
BGN O-7 (establishment)	Wing (up to 4 groups; 30–75 aircraft)
MGN O-8	Air division (2 or more wings or several groups)
LTG O-9	Air force (numbered air force, e.g., 9th air force of the tactical command)
GEN O-10	Major command (e.g., space command, Military Airlift Command [MAC], Formerly Strategic Air Command [SAC], Tactical Air Command [TAC])
General of the air force O-11	Chief of air operations or chief of staff (only used in WWII).

Figure 1.5 Order of battle: table of organization (Air Force).

Figure 1.6 Field-expedient telephone: Ground return circuits using two strands of a fence line. (Adapted from U.S. Army, FM 31-20 Special Forces Operational Techniques, 1971.)

phone-to-phone (or filed switchboard) by filed wire(s). In an unsecured environment where field wire cannot be run or might be detected, operators have *borrowed* fence lines made of wire to use as filed phone-wire lines. Phones are connected to fences, which become the phone lines and go unnoticed, requiring no retrieval upon exfiltration (see Figure 1.6).

Field radios (transmitters, receivers, and transceivers) can also be connected to field expedient antennas using field-expedient (improvised) insulators (see Figure 1.7). Antennas can also be improvised from lengths of wire at appropriate lengths for the band being used (see Figures 1.8 through 1.10).

When encrypted communications are unavailable, an old technique may still be practical. In *the old days*, communications that were subject to unwanted interception were recorded in Morse code, usually in ciphered form (i.e., code other than Morse code, which is merely an International alphabet of dots and dashes). The recorded message was then transmitted at a much higher speed for reception on predesignated frequencies by the

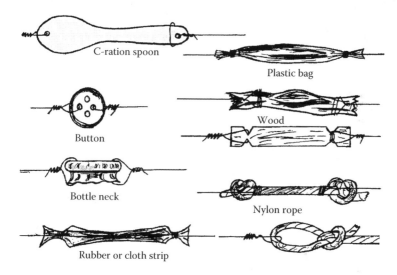

Figure 1.7 Field-expedient insulators. (Adapted from U.S. Army, FM 31-20 Special Forces Operational Techniques, 1971.)

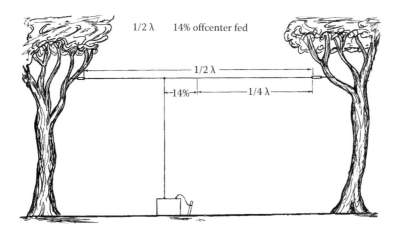

Figure 1.8 Field-expedient half-wave antenna off-center-feed. (Adapted from U.S. Army, FM 31-20 Special Forces Operational Techniques.)

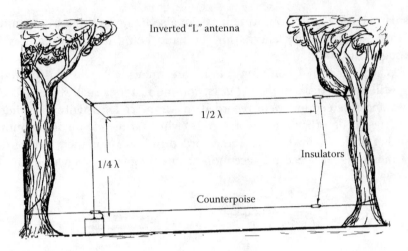

Figure 1.9 Inverted L field expedient antenna. (Adapted from U.S. Army, FM 31-20 Special Forces Operational Techniques, 1971.)

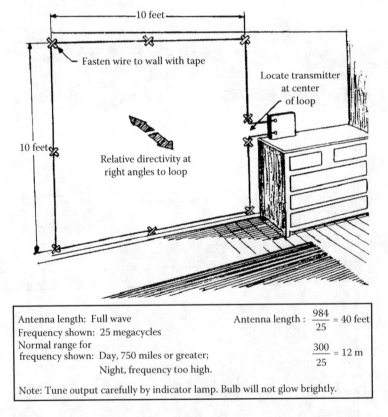

Antenna length: Full wave	Antenna length : $\dfrac{984}{25}$ = 40 feet
Frequency shown: 25 megacycles	
Normal range for	
frequency shown: Day, 750 miles or greater;	$\dfrac{300}{25}$ = 12 m
Night, frequency too high.	
Note: Tune output carefully by indicator lamp. Bulb will not glow brightly.	

Figure 1.10 Indoors, full-wave square-loop antenna. (Adapted from U.S. Army, FM 3-20 Special Forces Operational Techniques.)

intended recipients. These *burst* transmission were sent at, say, 10 times the original speed, received, rerecorded, then played at 1/10 the received speed to play the message at normal speed. Any unwanted monitoring could easily miss the 20 seconds message sent in 2 seconds because the monitors did not know what they were hearing (in 2 seconds), if they hear it at all while scanning thousands of frequencies.

Communications and communications security are important, yet it is limited only by one's imagination, even in the absence of state-of-the-art technology. In fact, with advanced technology, often it is the old and outdated technology that goes unnoticed (more on communications technology in Chapter 8).

Human Intelligence

2

Human Intelligence Operations

Human Intelligence (*HUMINT*) is intelligence gathering by means of inter-personal contact, rather than technical intelligence such as signals intelligence (SIGINT), imagery intelligence (IMINT), and measurement and signature intelligence (MASINT). NATO defines HUMINT as "a category of intelligence derived from information collected and provided by human sources." *Clandestine* HUMINT (*HUMan INTelligence*) involves obtaining information (using *human intelligence* methods) that is considered secret or confidential without the permission of the holder of the information. HUMINT includes a wide range of espionage operations, including the use of spy-professional *assets* or *agents* who collect intelligence, *couriers* who handle secure communications, *access agents* who arrange contacts between potential spies, and *case officers* who recruit them.

Sometimes, the recruiter continues to supervise the recruited agent, but sometimes, the asset may be handed off to a different handler or case officer. Espionage networks may consist of multiple levels of spies, support personnel, and supervisors and are usually organized on a cell system. An operator usually knows the people in his or her own cell, the external case officer, and an emergency method to use to contact higher levels if the case officer or cell leader is apprehended or discovered. They usually have no knowledge of people in other cells.

"I'm with the CIA, but I tell people I'm with the CIC, so they think I'm with the CID"—Colonel Sam Flagg (from M*A*S*H). Typical HUMINT operations consist of interrogations and conversations with persons having access to information. HUMINT is sometimes related to counterintelligence (CI) and sometimes in direct opposition to CI. In one episode of the television show M*A*S*H, intelligence officer Colonel Sam Flagg tells Dr. Hawkeye Pierce, "I'm with the CID. Although I told your boss I was with the CIA. It throws people off who think I'm with the CIC." In another episode, he has a dialog with Major Frank Burns:

Colonel Flagg: I'm in the CIC. (Counter Intelligence Corps)
Major Burns: I thought you were in the CIA. (Central Intelligence Agency)
Colonel Flagg: No I just tell people that so they think I'm in the CID.
(U.S. Army Criminal Investigations Division Command)

(Footnote for M*A*S*H fans: Colonel Flagg was in seven episodes of the popular TV show:

1. Deal Me Out (December 8, 1973)—alias Captain Halloran
2. A Smattering of Intelligence (March 2, 1974)—Colonel Samuel Flagg
3. Officer of the Day (September 24, 1974)—Colonel Samuel Flagg
4. White Gold (March 11, 1975)—Colonel Samuel Flagg
5. Quo Vadis, Captain Chandler (November 7, 1975)—Colonel Samuel Flagg
6. The Abduction of Margaret Houlihan (October 26, 1976)—Colonel Samuel Flagg
7. Rally 'Round the Flagg, Boys (February 14, 1979)—Colonel Samuel Flagg)

The relationship between HUMINT and CI becomes at odds when one side is trying to *turn* agents of the other side, while the other side seeks to detect those turned. Recruiters can run *false flag operations* in which a source of one side believes they are providing intelligence to the other side, when they are actually providing intelligence to a third-party side. For example, a member of the Federation may be recruited to provide information to the Romulans—a culture friendly with the Federation—when in fact they are providing intelligence to the Klingons, which are not friendly with the Federation. (Presumably these examples will not offend anyone in the foreseeable future, regardless of the changing geopolitical environment and relationships.)

Often, the source believes there is no harm in sharing secrets with an ally or neutral state. Sometimes that false assumption comes to reveal that the source is *sleeping with the enemy*—that is, the true identity of the other half of the transactions are a known enemy. That scenario may be further extrapolated when the member of the Federation refuses to continue to provide information and is informed that his or her activities of selling secrets to the opposing Klingons will be revealed if cooperation is not continued. Documentation in the form of financial deposits and audio–video can make a source regretfully fear prosecution for espionage, rather than reveal that he or she has been unwittingly trading in secrets with a known enemy.

Intelligence management begins with a determination of what needs to be known—a needs assessment or determination of the essential elements of intelligence (EEI). Espionage activities often involve accessing places where the information sought is stored or accessing people who know the information. Covert operations may include reconnaissance, sabotage, assassinations, and propaganda or psychological operations, etc. Unless precise objectives are determined, data will be collected unsystematically, and decision makers do not receive the intelligence product that they require for decisions.

Evaluation of intelligence data is critical to determining the reliability of sources and information. A standardized system is used to rate the reliability of sources and the accuracy of the information they provide. Information may be relied upon once it is confirmed by other sources. Sources may be neutral, friendly, or hostile and may or may not be aware of their contribution to the collection of information.

Human Sources: Interviewing and Interrogation

HUMINT operations and activities involve selecting people who may be sources of meaningful *HUMINT*, positively identifying them, and conducting interviews of various types. Properly recording and cross-indexing the results of interviews is essential. Interviews and interrogations with persons having access to information consist of formal, structured conversations with friendly or open sources to elicit information. This includes briefings and debriefings.

Briefings occur before an operation, giving details of the EEI that are critical to accomplishing the mission. Debriefing occurs after the mission and involves getting feedback on intelligence information observed or gathered during the mission that may be exploited afterward. The acronym SALUTE is used by combat units to determine part of the information that can be useful. SALUTE stands for

- *S*ize: How many men in the unit?
- *A*ctivity: What are they doing?
- *L*ocation: Map grid coordinates, if available, or the best description available.
- *U*nit: Identity, uniforms, descriptions, etc.
- *T*ime: When did you see them?
- *E*quipment: Weapons, vehicles, communications, anything else distinctive?

Interrogations differ from interviews in that they usually involve subjects who are unwilling to provide information and may even be hostile, such as prisoners. Obtaining information from unwilling and uncooperative subjects may involve a range of tactics and techniques ranging from persuasion (as in criminal investigations) to coercive (as in enemy combatants and espionage agents). Legal considerations may also be involved.

Interrogation is an interaction, and, even before considering the different attitudes the subject may have, the interrogator needs to know his or her own style, strengths, and weaknesses. The interrogator needs to assess whether he or she needs cultural advice, how to handle language issues, and if he or she needs specialized or technical assistance. (More on this in the section on *Linguistic Skills*.)

Security Clearances

A National Agency Check (NAC) with Local Agency Check and Credit Check (NACLC) is a type of background check required in the United States for granting of security clearances. STANDARD FORM 86, 86A, and 86C are the security questionnaire forms for security clearances. (See also Figures 2.1 and 2.2, Standard Form 312 Classified Information Nondisclosure Agreement.) There are three basic levels of clearance:

- *Confidential (Level 1)*—The screening procedure requires RS checks and screening of foreign employments, immediate relatives, and marriages or common-law relationships.
  - This level of clearance authorizes access to designated and classified information up to *confidential* level on a need-to-know basis.
  - Also known as a *public trust* clearance, this level typically requires a few weeks to a few months of investigation.
  - A *confidential* clearance requires a NACLC investigation, which dates back 7 years on the applicant's record and must be renewed (with another investigation) every 15 years.
  - Applicants are required to complete federal Standard Form 85P.
- *Secret (Level 2)*—The screening procedure is the same as for confidential, and this level of clearance authorizes access to designated and classified information up to *secret* level on a need-to-know basis.
  - A secret clearance, also known as *collateral secret* or *ordinary secret*, requires a few months to a year to fully investigate, depending on the individual's background.
  - A secret clearance requires a NACLC and a credit investigation and it must be renewed every 10 years.
- *Top Secret (Level 3)*—In addition to the checks at the *secret* level, foreign travels, assets, and character references must be given.
  - A field check will also be conducted prior to granting the clearance.
  - A top secret (TS) clearance is often designated following a single scope background investigation (SSBI) and must be renewed every 5 years.
  - This level of clearance authorizes access to all designated and classified information on a need-to-know basis.

Controlled unclassified information is not a clearance, but a level at which information distribution is controlled. It involves information that may be illegal to distribute, is available when needed, but should not

CLASSIFIED INFORMATION NONDISCLOSURE AGREEMENT

AN AGREEMENT BETWEEN   AND THE UNITED STATES

(Name of Individual — Printed or typed)

1. Intending to be legally bound, I hereby accept the obligations contained in this Agreement in consideration of my being granted access to classified information. As used in this Agreement, classified information is marked or unmarked classified information, including oral communications, that is classified under the standards of Executive Order 12958, or under any other Executive order or statute that prohibits the unauthorized disclosure of information in the interest of national security; and unclassified information that meets the standards for classification and is in the process of a classification determination as provided in Sections 1.1, 1.2, 1.3 and 1.4(e) of Executive Order 12958, or under any other Executive order or statute that requires protection for such information in the interest of national security. I understand and accept that by being granted access to classified information, special confidence and trust shall be placed in me by the United States Government.

2. I hereby acknowledge that I have received a security indoctrination concerning the nature and protection of classified information, including the procedures to be followed in ascertaining whether other persons to whom I contemplate disclosing this information have been approved for access to it, and that I understand these procedures.

3. I have been advised that the unauthorized disclosure, unauthorized retention, or negligent handling of classified information by me could cause damage or irreparable injury to the United States or could be used to advantage by a foreign nation. I hereby agree that I will never divulge classified information to anyone unless: (a) I have officially verified that the recipient has been properly authorized by the United States Government to receive it; or (b) I have been given prior written notice of authorization from the United States Government Department or Agency (hereinafter Department or Agency) responsible for the classification of information or last granting me a security clearance that such disclosure is permitted. I understand that if I am uncertain about the classification status of information, I am required to confirm from an authorized official that the information is unclassified before I may disclose it, except to a person as provided in (a) or (b), above. I further understand that I am obligated to comply with laws and regulations that prohibit the unauthorized disclosure of classified information.

4. I have been advised that any breach of this Agreement may result in the termination of any security clearances I hold; removal from any position of special confidence and trust requiring such clearances; or termination of my employment or other relationships with the Departments or Agencies that granted my security clearance or clearances. In addition, I have been advised that any unauthorized disclosure of classified information by me may constitute a violation, or violations, of United States criminal laws, including the provisions of Sections 641, 793, 794, 798, *952 and 1924, Title 18, United States Code, *the provisions of Section 783(b), Title 50, United States Code, and the provisions of the Intelligence Identities Protection Act of 1982. I recognize that nothing in this Agreement constitutes a waiver by the United States of the right to prosecute me for any statutory violation.

5. I hereby assign to the United States Government all royalties, remunerations, and emoluments that have resulted, will result or may result from any disclosure, publication or revelation of classified information not consistent with the terms of this Agreement.

6. I understand that the United States Government may seek any remedy available to it to enforce this Agreement including, but not limited to, application for a court order prohibiting disclosure of information in breach of this Agreement.

7. I understand that all classified information to which I have access or may obtain access by signing this Agreement is now and will remain the property of, or under the control of the United States Government unless and until otherwise determined by an authorized official or final ruling of a court of law. I agree that I shall return all classified materials which have, or may come into my possession or for which I am responsible because of such access: (a) upon demand by an authorized representative of the United States Government; (b) upon the conclusion of my employment or other relationship with the Department or Agency that last granted me a security clearance or that provided me access to classified information; or (c) upon the conclusion of my employment or other relationship that requires access to classified information. If I do not return such materials upon request, I understand that this may be a violation of Sections 793 and/or 1924, Title 18, United States Code, a United States criminal law.

8. Unless and until I am released in writing by an authorized representative of the United States Government, I understand that all conditions and obligations imposed upon me by this Agreement apply during the time I am granted access to classified information, and at all times thereafter.

9. Each provision of this Agreement is severable. If a court should find any provision of this Agreement to be unenforceable, all other provisions of this Agreement shall remain in full force and effect.

(Continue on reverse.)

NSN 7540-01-280-5499
Previous edition not usable

312-102

STANDARD FORM 312 (Rev. 1-00)
Prescribed by NARA/ISOO
32 CFR 2003, E.O. 12958

Figure 2.1 Standard Form 312: Classified Information Nondisclosure Agreement.

be redistributed. An example of this type of information is the operational details of a noncritical system. Similarly, information may be marked *FOUO* or *for official use only*.

Sensitive compartmented information (SCI) clearances are assigned after a single scope background investigation (SCBI) and a special adjudication process for evaluating the investigation. SCI access is assigned only in *compartments*, which are separated from each other, so someone with access to one compartment may not have access to another. Each *compartment* may

10. These restrictions are consistent with and do not supersede, conflict with or otherwise alter the employee obligations, rights or liabilities created by Executive Order 12958, Section 7211 of Title 5, United States Code (governing disclosures to Congress); Section 1034 of Title 10, United States Code, as amended by the Military Whistleblower Protection Act (governing disclosure to Congress by members of the military); Section 2302(b) (8) of Title 5, United States Code, as amended by the Whistleblower Protection Act (governing disclosures of illegality, waste, fraud, abuse or public health or safety threats); the Intelligence Identities Protection Act of 1982 (50 U.S.C. 421 et seq.) (governing disclosures that expose confidential Government agents), and the statutes which protect against disclosure that may compromise the national security, including Sections 641, 793, 794, 798, 952 and 1924 of Title 18, United States Code, and Section 4(b) of the Subversive Activities Act of 1950 (50 U.S.C. Section 783(b)). The definitions, requirements, obligations, rights, sanctions and liabilities created by said Executive Order and listed statutes are incorporated into this Agreement and are controlling.

11. I have read this Agreement carefully and my questions, if any, have been answered. I acknowledge that the briefing officer has made available to me the Executive Order and statutes referenced in this agreement and its implementing regulation (32 CFR Section 2003.20) so that I may read them at this time, if I so choose.

SIGNATURE	DATE	SOCIAL SECURITY NUMBER (See Notice below)

ORGANIZATION (IF CONTRACTOR, LICENSEE, GRANTEE OR AGENT, PROVIDE: NAME, ADDRESS, AND, IF APPLICABLE, FEDERAL SUPPLY CODE NUMBER)
(Type or print)

WITNESS		ACCEPTANCE	
THE EXECUTION OF THIS AGREEMENT WAS WITNESSED BY THE UNDERSIGNED.		THE UNDERSIGNED ACCEPTED THIS AGREEMENT ON BEHALF OF THE UNITED STATES GOVERNMENT.	
SIGNATURE	DATE	SIGNATURE	DATE
NAME AND ADDRESS (Type or print)		NAME AND ADDRESS (Type or print)	

SECURITY DEBRIEFING ACKNOWLEDGEMENT

I reaffirm that the provisions of the espionage laws, other federal criminal laws and executive orders applicable to the safeguarding of classified information have been made available to me; that I have returned all classified information in my custody; that I will not communicate or transmit classified information to any unauthorized person or organization; that I will promptly report to the Federal Bureau of Investigation any attempt by an unauthorized person to solicit classified information, and that I (have) (have not) (strike out inappropriate word or words) received a security debriefing.

SIGNATURE OF EMPLOYEE	DATE
NAME OF WITNESS (Type or print)	SIGNATURE OF WITNESS

NOTICE: The Privacy Act, 5 U.S.C. 552a, requires that federal agencies inform individuals, at the time information is solicited from them, whether the disclosure is mandatory or voluntary, by what authority such information is solicited, and what uses will be made of the information. You are hereby advised that authority for soliciting your Social Security Account Number (SSN) is Executive Order 9397. Your SSN will be used to identify you precisely when it is necessary to 1) certify that you have access to the information indicated above or 2) determine that your access to the information indicated has terminated. Although disclosure of your SSN is not mandatory, your failure to do so may impede the processing of such certifications or determinations, or possibly result in the denial of your being granted access to classified information.

*NOT APPLICABLE TO NON-GOVERNMENT PERSONNEL SIGNING THIS AGREEMENT.

STANDARD FORM 312 BACK (Rev. 1-00)

Figure 2.2 Standard Form 312 (Back): Classified Information Nondisclosure Agreement.

include additional special requirements and clearance process. Information that may require compartmented access includes the following:

- Cryptography (*crypto*)
- Overhead reconnaissance from aircraft, UAVs, or satellite IMINT
- Communications intelligence from SIGINT
- Design or stockpile information about nuclear weapons
- Nuclear targeting

The Department of Energy (DOE) and the Nuclear Regulatory Commission (NRC) have a different designation for security clearances. The need for security clearances became an issue at the end of World War II when the Manhattan Project was transferred to a new entity, the Atomic Energy Commission (AEC). Thousands of civilians were going to be hired, and the newly drafted Atomic Energy Act of 1947 required controls over access to restricted data and nuclear materials. The U.S. Department of Energy has two types of security clearances that it uses:

- *Q clearance* is the DOE equivalent to a U.S. Department of Defense (DoD) TS clearance and Critical Nuclear Weapon Design Information (CNWDI) designation. DOE clearances are for access specifically relating to atomic- or nuclear-related materials (*Restricted Data* under the Atomic Energy Act of 1954) and are issued to nonmilitary personnel only.
  - In 1946 U.S. Army CIC Major Bud Uanna, the first Chief of the Central Personnel Clearance Office at the newly formed AEC, named and established the criteria for the Q Clearance.
  - As of 1993, Q clearances required a single-scope background investigation covering the previous 10 years of the applicant's life by both the Office of Personnel Management and the Federal Bureau of Investigation (which, as of 1998, cost $3225).
- *L clearance* is the DOE and NRC equivalent to a U.S. DoD *Secret* (S) clearance for civilian access relating to nuclear materials and information under the Atomic Energy Act of 1954.
  - The DOE L clearance provides less access than the Q Clearance. L-cleared persons are allowed unescorted access to *limited* and *protected* areas, as well as access to confidential restricted data, confidential and secret formerly restricted data, confidential and secret national security information, and Category III special nuclear material.
  - As of 1989, the NRC required the Q clearance for employees in the most important and sensitive positions, while most employees in positions deemed *noncritical-sensitive* held L clearances.

U.S. Intelligence Community

The U.S. Intelligence Community (IC) is a coalition of 17 agencies and organizations within the executive branch that work both independently and collaboratively to gather the intelligence necessary to conduct foreign relations and national security activities. Their primary mission is to collect and convey the essential information required by the president and members of the policymaking, law enforcement, and military communities to execute their appointed duties. The 17 member agencies of the U.S. Intelligence Community are as follows:

- Air Force Intelligence—Air Intelligence Agency (AIA)
- Army Intelligence—Intelligence and Security Command (INSCOM)
- Central Intelligence Agency (CIA)
- Coast Guard Intelligence (USCG)
- Defense Intelligence Agency (DIA)
- Department of Energy (DOE)
- Department of Homeland Security (DHS)
- Department of State (DOS)
- Department of the Treasury (DOT)
- Drug Enforcement Administration (DEA)
- Federal Bureau of Investigation (FBI)
- Marine Corps Intelligence (USMC)
- National Geospatial-Intelligence Agency (NGA)
- National Reconnaissance Office (NRO)
- National Security Agency (NSA)
- Navy Intelligence—Office of Naval Intelligence (ONI)
- Office of the Director of National Intelligence (DNI)

Members of the U.S. Intelligence Community collect and assess information regarding international terrorist and narcotic activities; other hostile activities by foreign powers, organizations, persons, and their agents; and foreign intelligence activities directed against the United States. As needed, the President may also direct the IC to carry out special activities to protect U.S. security interests against foreign threats.

British Security Service MI5 and Secret Intelligence Service MI6

The *Security Service*, commonly known as *MI5*, was established in 1909 and is the UK's national security intelligence agency. The Security Service plays a vital but secret role in countering the activities of spies and terrorists. The Secret Intelligence Service (SIS), commonly known as *MI6*, evolved from the Foreign Section of the Secret Service Bureau, established by the Committee of Imperial Defence in October 1909. The first head of the Foreign Section, Captain Sir Mansfield Cumming (Royal Navy), wrote his signature as *MC* or *C* in green ink. Thus began the long tradition of the head of the Service adopting the initial *C* as his symbol.

The outbreak of World War I in 1914 brought the virtual integration of the Foreign Section within the Military Intelligence Directorate of the War Office. After the end of hostilities, Cumming returned the Service to the Foreign Office. By 1920 it was referred to as SIS, a title that was used in the Intelligence Services Act 1994. *MI6* has become an almost interchangeable title for SIS, at least outside the Service. The origins of this title are from the 1930s when it was adopted as a convenience. It was used during World War II, especially if distinction needed to be made between *MI5* (the Security Service) and *MI6* (the Secret Service). Although *MI6* fell into official disuse years ago, many writers and journalists continue to use it to describe SIS.

Linguistic Skills (Languages)

One of the most valued skills among intelligence officers and investigators is the ability to speak the indigenous language of the area of operations. This is essential to both HUMINT and Electronic Intelligence (ELINT).

The *List of Official Languages of the United Nations* (by Institution) (UN/ ONU), under the Charter, are Chinese, English, French, Russian, Spanish, and Arabic (added in 1973).

Other common, but not as prolific, languages include Ukrainian, Czech-Slovene, Serbo-Croatian, Bosnian, Tagali, Chaldean, Yiddish, Zulu, and Swahili.

In the Middle East, *Arabic* and *Persian* (*Farsi*) (Afghanistan, Bahrain, Iran, Iraq, Kazakhstan, Tajikistan, Uzbekistan, etc.) are the most widely spoken languages. *Arabic* and *Kurdish* (Iraq and Turkey) are the official languages of the Iraqi government. *Assyrian* (Syriac) (a dialect of Aramaic) and Iraqi Turkmen (a dialect of *Turkish*) are official in areas where the populations are more representative of the respective language. Other languages spoken in the region include Azeri, Berber languages, Circassian, Dimli (Zaza), Gagauz, Gilaki, Greek, Hebrew (in its numerous variations), Kabardian, Luri, Mazandarani languages, Somali, Turkish and other Turkish languages, etc.

Urdu is spoken in many Middle Eastern countries, such as Arab states the United Arab Emirates, Israel, and Qatar, which have large numbers of Pakistani immigrants. It is common to be bilingual in Afghanistan, but the most common languages spoken in Afghanistan are *Dari* (*Eastern Persian*) (Afghanistan) (49%–80%) and *Pashto* (Afghanistan) (35%–50%). Hazaragi, spoken by the Hazara minority, is a distinct dialect of Persian. Other languages spoken include the Turkic languages *Uzbek* (6%) and *Turkmen* (3%), as well as 30 minor languages, including Balochi, Nuristani, Pashai, Brahui, Pamiri languages, Hindko, etc.

Number of Countries with the Same Official Language

This is a ranking of languages by number of sovereign countries in which they are official.

- English: 55 countries: largest—United States, Nigeria, United Kingdom, India
- French: 29 countries: largest—France, Democratic Republic of the Congo, Canada
- Arabic: 24 countries: largest—Egypt, Sudan, Algeria
- Spanish: 20 countries: largest—Mexico, Spain, Colombia, Argentina
- Russian: 10 countries: largest—Russia, Kazakhstan, Belarus
- Portuguese: 10 countries: largest—Brazil, Portugal, Mozambique, Angola
- German: 7 countries: largest—Germany, Austria, Switzerland
- Dutch: 5 countries: largest—the Netherlands, Belgium, Suriname
- Albanian, Italian, Serbian: 4 countries
- Malay, Persian (Farsi), Swahili, Tamil, Urdu, Hungarian, Mandarin Chinese: 3 countries
- Aymara, Bengali, Croatian, Greek, Hindi, Korean, Quechua, Romanian, Sotho, Swati, Swedish, Tswana, Turkish: 2 countries

The thirty most widely spoken languages in the world are listed in Table 2.1, along with their families, scripts used, number of speakers, and regions in which they are spoken.

Learning Languages Fast

HUMINT operations may require the sudden immersion into an environment and culture that is unfamiliar to a mission essential operative. The rapid assimilation of basic language skills may be critical to an operative. The Defense Language Institute (DLI) teaches military, intelligence, foreign service, and other government personnel several languages. Some are more difficult than others, requiring anywhere from 6 to 18 months of step-by-step learning processes. Books, videos, CDs, computer programs, etc., are all good resources, as are watching TV and listening to the radio in the target language. Immersion into the culture by interacting with native speakers is even better.

Language is the capacity for acquiring and using complex systems of verbal, written, symbolic, or other forms of communications and a language is any specific example of such a system. Linguistics is the scientific study of language. Linguistics can be broadly broken into

Table 2.1   Thirty Most Spoken Languages in World, by Number of Speakers

	Language	Family	Script(s) Used	Speakers (Millions)	Where Commonly Spoken
1	Mandarin	Sino-Tibetan	Chinese characters	1051	China, Malaysia, Taiwan
2	English	Indo-European	Latin	510	United States, United Kingdom, Australia, Canada, New Zealand
3	Hindi	Indo-European	Devanagari	490	North and Central India
4	Spanish	Indo-European	Latin	425	The Americas, Spain
5	Arabic	Afro-Asiatic	Arabic	255	Middle East, Arabia, North Africa
6	Russian	Indo-European	Cyrillic	254	Russia, Central Asia
7	Portuguese	Indo-European	Latin	218	Brazil, Portugal, Southern Africa
8	Bengali	Indo-European	Bengali	215	Bangladesh, Eastern India
9	Malay, Indonesian	Malayo-Polynesian	Latin	175	Indonesia, Malaysia, Singapore
10	French	Indo-European	Latin	130	France, Canada, West Africa, Central Africa
11	Japanese	Altaic	Chinese characters and two Japanese alphabets	127	Japan
12	German	Indo-European	Latin	123	Germany, Austria, Central Europe
13	Farsi (Persian)	Indo-European	Nastaliq	110	Iran, Afghanistan, Central Asia
14	Urdu	Indo-European	Nastaliq	104	Pakistan, India
15	Punjabi	Indo-European	Gurumukhi	103	Pakistan, India
16	Vietnamese	Austroasiatic	Based on Latin	86	Vietnam, China
17	Tamil	Dravidian	Tamil	78	Southern India, Sri Lanka, Malaysia
18	Wu	Sino-Tibetan	Chinese characters	77	China
19	Javanese	Malayo-Polynesian	Javanese	76	Indonesia
20	Turkish	Altaic	Latin	75	Turkey, Central Asia
21	Telugu	Dravidian	Telugu	74	Southern India
22	Korean	Altaic	Hangul	72	Korean Peninsula
23	Marathi	Indo-European	Devanagari	71	Western India
24	Italian	Indo-European	Latin	61	Italy, Central Europe
25	Thai	Sino-Tibetan	Thai	60	Thailand, Laos
26	Cantonese	Sino-Tibetan	Chinese Characters	55	Southern China
27	Gujarati	Indo-European	Gujarati	47	Western India, Kenya
28	Polish	Indo-European	Latin	46	Poland, Central Europe
29	Kannada	Dravidian	Kannada	44	Southern India
30	Burmese	Sino-Tibetan	Burmese	42	Myanmar

three categories or subfields of study: language form, language meaning, and language in context. *Forensic linguistics* or *legal linguistics* is the application of linguistics to the context of law, language, crime investigation, trial, and judicial procedure. *Language interpretation* is the facilitating of oral or sign-language communication, either simultaneously or consecutively, between users of different languages. The process is described by both the words *interpreting* and *interpretation* and involves the systematic study of the theory, the description and the application of language interpretation and translation. *Translation* is the communication of the meaning of a source-language text by means of an equivalent target-language text (transforming a source text or document into the equivalent in another language). Translators always risk inappropriate spillover of source-language idiom and usage into the target-language translation.

Transliteration is the conversion of a text from one script to another. The conversion of scripts or writing is a procedure of replacing text written in one script or writing system (such as the Latin alphabet of 26 characters used in English) with the characters of another script or system (such as the 33 Cyrillic characters used in Russian) to make the text (e.g., proper names) legible for users of another language or script.

A quick and effective *head start* to learning any language(s) is to learn the parts of speech. This involves identifying and learning the following parts of speech:

- Nouns—person, place, or thing.
- Pronouns—take the place of nouns or refers to nouns (I, me, he, she, you, it, we, they, his, hers, etc.). (See following list.)
- Prepositions—links between nouns and pronouns (by, to, etc.).
- Adjectives—describe nouns (big, small, tall, short, pretty, ugly, etc.).
- Verbs—action words (come, go, stop, etc.) or links to subjects with other parts of sentences (is, was, am, etc.).
- Present participle (present progressive)—verbs that end in *ing*.
- Tense—present (I go), past (I went), future (I will go), present perfect (I have gone), past perfect (I had gone), and future perfect (I will have gone) (Tables 2.2 through 2.4).
  - Progressive tense forms—I am going, I was going, I will be going. (Note: Some languages distinguish tense differently.)
- Adverbs—describe verbs (quickly, slowly, loudly, quietly, etc.).
- Conjunctions—words that join words (and, or, but, if, etc.); (remember the cartoon jingle "conjunction junction, what's your function?").

Table 2.2 Chart for Language: Present Tense

Present Tense	To Be	To Be (Present Participle)	To Go	To Go (Present Participle)	To Have	To Want	To See	To Be Able	To Make	To Need
I	Am	Am being	Go	Am going	Have	Want	See	Can	Make	Need
You	Are	Are being	Go	Are going	Have	Want	See	Can	Make	Need
You (f, formal)	Are	Are being	Go	Are going	Have	Want	See	Can	Make	Need
You (p, plural)	Are	Are being	Go	Are going	Have	Want	See	Can	Make	Need
He	Is	Is being	Goes	Is going	Has	Wants	See	Can	Makes	Need
She	Is	Is being	Goes	Is going	Has	Wants	See	Can	Makes	Need
It	Is	Is being	Goes	Is going	Has	Wants	See	Can	Makes	Need
She	Is	Is being	Goes	Is going	Has	Wants	See	Can	Makes	Need
It	Is	Is being	Goes	Is going	Has	Wants	See	Can	Makes	Need
We	Are	Are being	Go	Are going	Have	Want	See	Can	Make	Need
They	Are	Are being	Go	Are going	Have	Want	See	Can	Make	Need

Table 2.3   Chart for Language: Past Tense

Past Tense	To Be	To Do	To Go	To Have	To Want	To See	To Be Able To	To Make	To Need
I	Was	Did	Went	Had	Wanted	Saw	Can	Made	Needed
You	Were	Did	Went	Had	Wanted	Saw	Can	Made	Needed
You (f, formal)	Were	Did	Went	Had	Wanted	Saw	Can	Made	Needed
You (p, plural)	Were	Did	Went	Had	Wanted	Saw	Can	Made	Needed
He	Was	Did	Went	Had	Wanted	Saw	Can	Made	Needed
She	Was	Did	Went	Had	Wanted	Saw	Can	Made	Needed
It	Was	Did	Went	Had	Wanted	Saw	Can	Made	Needed
She	Was	Did	Went	Had	Wanted	Saw	Can	Made	Needed
It	Was	Did	Went	Had	Wanted	Saw	Can	Made	Needed
We	Were	Did	Went	Had	Wanted	Saw	Can	Made	Needed
They	Were	Did	Went	Had	Wanted	Saw	Can	Made	Needed

Table 2.4 Chart for Language: Future Tense

Future Tense	To Be	To Do	To Make	To Want	To Be Able	To Need	Fill in the Verb...
I	Will be	Will do	Will make	Will want	Will be able to	Will need	Will...
You	Will be	Will do	Will make	Will want	Will be able to	Will need	Will...
You (f, formal)	Will be	Will do	Will make	Will want	Will be able to	Will need	Will...
You (p, plural)	Will be	Will do	Will make	Will want	Will be able to	Will need	Will...
He	Will be	Will do	Will make	Will want	Will be able to	Will need	Will...
She	Will be	Will do	Will make	Will want	Will be able to	Will need	Will...
It	Will be	Will do	Will make	Will want	Will be able to	Will need	Will...
She	Will be	Will do	Will make	Will want	Will be able to	Will need	Will...
It	Will be	Will do	Will make	Will want	Will be able to	Will need	Will...
We	Will be	Will do	Will make	Will want	Will be able to	Will need	Will...
They	Will be	Will do	Will make	Will want	Will be able to	Will need	Will...

- Articles—designates whether something is specific or general (a, an, the, etc.). (Note: Some languages do not have articles.)
- Synonyms and antonyms—words that are similar and words that are opposites, respectively.
- Interrogatives—question words (like *interrogation*) (who, what, when, where, why, how, because, etc.).
- Numbers—self-explanatory, but useful in addresses, phone numbers, dates, time, age, measurements, money, etc.
- Other parts of language include case, cognates, conjugation (rules for changing a verb to match the pronoun and tense), declension, gender, gerund, imperfection, singular and plural, possession, and syllable (not a part of the word, but a letter or series of a consonant-vowel group making one word mean something different than another).

Key nouns (commonly used):

- Person, place, thing
- Men, women, children, doctor, dentist
- Hotel, house, restaurant, airport, bus station, train station
- Airplane, train, bus, car, bicycle, boat, taxi
- Tree, animal, dog, cat, bird, fish
- Lunch, breakfast, food, water, meat, chicken, beef, pork, egg, coffee, milk
- Morning, afternoon, evening, night, hour, minute, day, week, month, year
- Telephone, radio, air conditioner, bed, chair
- Room, kitchen, bathroom/toilet, table, window, door
- Street, road, highway, map
- Medicine, head, neck, chest, stomach, back, arm, leg, hand, foot, finger, toe, eye, ear, nose, mouth, tooth
- Shirt, pants, coat, shoes, socks, dress, underwear
- Color, black, white, gray, yellow, orange, red, blue, green, gold, silver
- Height, weight, shape, circle, square, rectangle, triangle, etc.

Pronouns:

- I, me, you, he, she, him, her, we, they, us, them
- My, your, his, her, ours, their, mine, yours, theirs
- Myself, yourself, himself, herself, ourselves, themselves
- Someone, anyone, everyone, no one, something, everything, nothing
- These, those, this, that, etc.

Key verbs (commonly used):

- (To) come, go, do, happen, can (able to)
- Work, buy, sell, make
- Eat, drink, rest, sleep, play
- Have, need, want, desire, get (obtain), choose, gather, decide
- Give, take, put (place), borrow, lend, owe, promise, rent, use, cost, send, receive
- Understand, think, believe, know, read, write, learn, study, teach, ask, answer
- See, watch, look, listen, touch, hear, smell, taste
- Break, repair, fix, wash, clean, burn, hit
- Live, die, worry, fear, laugh, cry, dream, try, join, won
- Enter, exit, find, lose, hide, find
- Stop, stay, walk, run, ride, hurry, drive, fly, sail, fall, get up

Conjunctions: and, or, but, however, if, nor, with, unless, until, before, although, as, since, therefore, because, whether, in order that, as soon as, as long as, now that, etc.

Adverbs (commonly used): very, now, later, always, never, perhaps (maybe), probably, possibly, only, more, less, little, some, often, rarely, each, fast/slow (also adjectives), quick, early, late, yesterday, today, tomorrow, here, there, anywhere, somewhere, between, through, about, away, instead, again, together, straight, etc.

Adjectives (commonly used): same, different, good, bad, large, small, thick, thin, short, long, tall, light, heavy, new, young, old, weak, strong, far, near, left, right, light, dark, full, empty, hot, cold, warm, cool, pretty, ugly, many, few, first, last, ahead, behind, above, below, under, over, up, down, high, low, fast/slow (also adverbs), in, out, happy, sad, easy, difficult, soft, hard, wet, dry, smooth, rough, tight, loose, rich, poor, etc.

Prepositions: to, for, from, at, with, within, by, on, in, inside, outside, about, among, around, between, beside, against, through, during, while, except for, instead of, unless, opposite, toward, etc.

Synonyms and *antonyms*: Most of the nouns, pronouns, verbs, adverbs, adjectives, and prepositions have words that mean the same thing (synonyms) and words that mean the opposite (antonyms). Collecting words of the same and opposite meaning can be helpful in expanding your vocabulary.

Past tense (*to be*): I was, you were (male, female, neutral, and formal; singular and plural), he was, she was, it was, we were, they were, etc.

Past tense (to do): I did, you did (male, female, neutral, and formal; singular and plural), he did, she did, it did, we did, they did. (See Table 2.3.)

Past tense (to go): I went, you went (male, female, neutral, and formal; singular and plural), he went, she went, it went, we went, they went, etc.

Past tense (to have): I had, you had (male, female, neutral, and formal; singular and plural), he had, she had, it had, we had, they had, etc.

Past tense (to want): I wanted, you wanted (male, female, neutral, and formal; singular and plural), he wanted, she wanted, it wanted, we wanted, they wanted, etc.

Past tense (to see): I saw, you saw (male, female, neutral, and formal; singular and plural), he saw, she saw, we saw, they saw, etc.

Past tense (to be able): I can, you can (male, female, neutral, and formal; singular and plural), he can, she can, it can, we can, they can, etc.

Past tense (to make): I made, you made (male, female, neutral, and formal; singular and plural), he made, she made, it made, we made, they made, etc.

Past tense (to need): I needed, you needed (male, female, neutral, and formal; singular and plural), he needed, she needed, we needed, they needed, etc.

Numbers, time, and weather: Learning numbers is important in asking or telling time, dates, addresses, money matters, etc. Knowing the months and days of the week is also essential to basic communications. Words used to describe the weather are not only convenient for travel and safety but may be an essential element of intelligence (EEI).

Commands and imperatives: stop, go, shut up, answer, tell me, wait here, do not move, don't do that, take me there, show me, bring me the check (bill), etc.

Expanding Your Vocabulary: Useful Words

As you become more proficient with your language(s), expand your vocabulary by adding words that may be useful in your field and areas of interest and concern. For example, words useful and specific to the military, intelligence, law, law enforcement, public safety, medicine, science, technology, politics, etc. will help round out your vocabulary. Slang words, common expressions, and local dialects will also be useful as you expand your vocabulary.

Danger Words

Danger words and profanity may indicate danger, hostility, or an imminent threat. It is important to know these indicators of danger, as well as how to tell someone that you are in danger or having an emergency. Learn *street slang* for words and phrases that may indicate danger and derision. Some languages use little profanity while others almost punctuate their expressions with it. Know what is common and customary for your environment and know what NOT to say to avoid insulting the indigenous population. Learn the customs with your vocabulary.

HUMINT Surveillance and Undercover Operations

3

Surveillance and Undercover Operations

Operations may require either *fixed* or *moving surveillance* or both. Surveillance may be conducted from stationary or fixed positions, such as a parked vehicle, a room, or by posing under a cover story (often in the open or overtly). Surveillance may also be conducted while moving or *tailing*, such as on foot, in vehicles, or other modes. *Loose surveillance* involves the exercise of caution, preferring to lose the subject rather than risk detection or exposure. *Close surveillance* has the opposite priority, preferring to avoid losing the subject even at the risk of detection or exposure. The latter is often used when the goal is to prevent a crime or learn more about the subject's contacts. Ideally, surveillance should go undetected without losing contact, but often a balance must be made between these competing objectives. (See Figures 3.1 and 3.2 for common surveillance methods.)

Surveillance involves two broad categories: (1) *passive surveillance*—just watching (possibly electronically tracking a vehicle or using electronic communications devices, closed-circuit television monitoring of an intersection, or watching a location through a thermal imaging device); and (2) *interactive surveillance*—surveillant interaction with the surveillance target (e.g., an undercover [UC] operation tape recorded by a body wire or video recorded by a covert camera). Interactive surveillance has different technology, tactical considerations, and legal requirements than passive surveillance (Foster, 2005, p. 311).

In an undercover (UC) operation, an investigator or intelligence officer operates under an assumed identity, seeking out and making direct contact with the suspect(s) or target(s). As discussed in Chapter 1, a cover story and identity must be planned for as part of the most clandestine operations and covert investigations. The UC officer must adapt his or her identity, appearance, actions, language, habits, and cover story to gain the confidence of the suspect(s) or target(s). The cover and disguise must be convincing and must withstand scrutiny and checks by those who may become suspicious or are necessarily cautious. The UC officer must be able to step out of real life and into the cover role he or she has assumed. Alertness is essential.

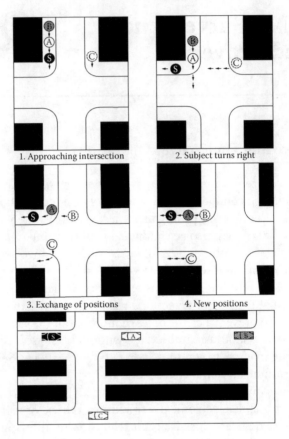

1. Approaching intersection

2. Subject turns right

3. Exchange of positions

4. New positions

Figure 3.1 ABC method of surveillance. (Adapted from U.S. Army, FM 30-17 Counterintelligence Operations, p. 4-19, 1972.)

Be familiar with the techniques used to find fugitives, missing persons, etc. Olympic bomber Eric Rudolph lived for 5 years in the Smokey Mountains without being seen, despite a massive effort on the part of law enforcement and professional bounty hunters to find him. If he had not wandered into a small town to raid dumpsters, he may still be free.

Disguise

There are numerous disguise variations to adapt to various scenarios and environments, ranging from the obvious to the subtle. A disguise may be a physical cover-up designed to make the wearer unrecognizable. This may camouflage the wearer or conceal his or her true identity. The psychology of disguise is the art of making someone *invisible* in a particular environment or situation. The *disguise artist* seeks to blend in with his or her surroundings and become a part of the background. The goal is to NOT stand out, be different, be out-of-place,

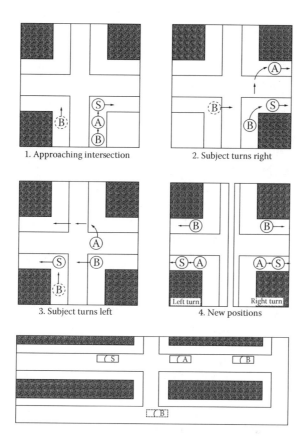

1. Approaching intersection   2. Subject turns right

3. Subject turns left   4. New positions

Figure 3.2 AB method of surveillance. (Adapted from U.S. Army, FM 30-17 Counterintelligence Operations, p. 4-20, 1972.)

or be noticeable. The objective is to become a part of the pattern of the environment. This is often referred to as *getting small* or *not being*.

The psychology of disguise recognizes that people are attracted to some stimulus or stimuli. To limit or eliminate stimuli that will make you noticeable, start by calming yourself, clearing your mind, and having confidence in your ability to be a part of the scenery. Avoid furtive movements or suspicious activity that may attract attention. Many novice surveillance or UC operatives make the mistake of, perhaps unconsciously, wanting those they believe are not the subject of their investigation to know that they are *undercover* or *on surveillance*. They may create clues to reveal this to bystanders and in so doing arouse suspicion. Don't! You will not impress anyone (with your skills or position) and may blow your cover by having additional attention paid to you by a police officer on a *suspicious person* call who knows nothing (and should know nothing) about your presence or mission.

Eliminate noise, do not move quickly (unless everyone else is), and do not take up too much space (*be small*).

Avoid eye contact. Staring at a target from behind them may alert an *intuitive* sense that activates their instinct to look for who is watching them. Whether you call this a *sixth sense*, intuition, the hackles on the back of your neck, a *feeling*, or your *spider senses tingling*, research indicates that people often sense someone is staring at them. Be aware that others may have this sense to varying degrees and develop it yourself to avoid countersurveillance.

Getting small or *not being* works when you are not in disguise and can enhance your disguise when you use one. The key to disguise and camouflage is to conform, adapt, and blend in with the crowd (if there is one) and the environment. Try to be plain and not have character or stand out. You are not a TV character, so don't try to look like one. Be the stereotypical *John Doe* with the goal that *we all look alike*. Be so *invisible* that you are the guy in the room that nobody notices. Be what people expect to see and you will be given little notice. (Practice by looking for people that nobody notices.)

Context is the principle of seeing someone in an everyday situation, but when you see them in a different environment (context) than usual, you cannot place them. We have all said, "Where do I know you from?" (or some less Midwest form of the same query). Context involves unconscious stereotyping. Do not *make an impression* on your target.

Disguise preparation begins by honing your own powers of observation and intuitive sense of being watched or followed. Observing others who are unnoticeable will help become *invisible*. Develop your skills as a *trained observer* with technical training such as *flash recognition* training. Develop impersonation skills by watching characters in movies, on TV, or in person (but do not try to become a *character* that will stand out).

Get to know yourself critically and see how others see you. What are your disguise handicaps (height, weight, hair, etc.)? Can you change these into advantages at times? Or instance, if you are uncommonly short, you will be noticed as an adult, but you may not be noticed at all if you are perceived as a child.

Vehicle Disguise

Your vehicle should also be plain and generic. Your objective is not to draw attention with your Aston-Martin DB-5 spy car, but to be unnoticed. Some cars are so common that they become *invisible*. Light colors are sometimes less noticeable. Do not have bumper stickers, personalized plates, or other identifiers that will mark you unless they are a part of a planned *disguise* for your car. Dust or poster paint (nonacrylic) can be used to change the car color. Other techniques such as having switches that turn on and off head lights and brake lights, etc., can also be used.

Physical Disguise

A physical disguise should be generic and commonly available. It should cover your presence or conceal your identity. It should camouflage your individual features or characteristics, yet be easy to put on, take off, and dispose of. Such features include facial features, hair, facial hair, height, weight, etc. Do not draw attention to yourself by hiding or obscuring your face (this is too obvious). This may result in fear or suspicion by others, which in turn results in heightened scrutiny and vigilance.

Physical disguise involves the use of clothing, accessories, and makeup. Makeup is used for cosmetic, theatrical, and disguises purposes. The third type (disguise makeup) is what should be used. Makeup includes mascara (eyelash darkener), eyebrow pencil, foundation (skin-colored makeup base), blemish cover, blush (rouge), eye shadow, etc. Wigs, fake facial hair, and hair color are also elements of a disguise. Scars, marks, tattoos, bruises, etc., can also be simulated using makeup.

Long-Term Disguise

Longer term disguises are more involved than shorter term or one-time cover disguises. Long-term disguises require sustaining a *personality* or *persona* rather than merely concealing a true identity. This is often the case when working in an UC mode, particularly when in *deep cover*. Such cover disguises require skills in disguise, acting, observation, practice, and calm nerves. Part of an identity change requires a lifestyle change. Changes in habits, patterns, and customs are necessary. This requires not only a change in appearance but also a change in mannerisms, expressions, speech, and a credible cover story.

Some disguise experts and experienced and expert UC operatives opine that many amateurs or inexperienced operators try too hard to be convincing about the reality of their disguise character. Because of their insecurity in their adopted disguise and giving too much credit to their audiences' discernment, they often give too much information to support their *cover story*.

Permanent Disguises

When one chooses to change their identity permanently, they often adopt a permanent *disguise* or change in appearance, which usually includes new identification documents to support their new identities. Creating a new identity for an *official cover* may be as simple as the issuing agency creating the UC identity through official channels. There are occasions when it is preferable to have no *official* trail of the UC identity, for instance, when an investigator is investigating the agency or employee of an agency that issues identity documents or covers or where there must be no way to reveal the intelligence officer's UC identity. There may also be occasions where an operative cannot receive official sanctions or support, such as when a POW is escaping from captivity or an intelligence officer is in sudden and unexpected need of egress, extraction, or exfiltration. Where there is *no official cover* (NOC), forgery may be the only way to create cover identity documents. This is risky and illegal in most countries (perhaps not only forgery, but espionage).

Identity Theft: Protection and Exploitation

To steal your identity, an identity thief must know something about you. With little more than your name, date of birth, address, and your SSN (the key), a criminal can assume your identity. An identity thief may assume your identity on a long-term or a short-term basis when you are not using credit, maintaining a bank account, or making investments.

A short-term identity thief will take over a portion of your identity, run up bills in your name, and then disappear. The thief may take your wallet and use your credit cards until they are denied because you have reported them stolen or the cards are *maxed out*. The thief then abandons them. The thief may cash checks from your checking account. Many businesses will cash checks with little or no ID or without looking at the ID.

A long-term identity thief may assume your identity for months or years. He or she is using your identity to hide his own and will take actions in your name to obtain credit cards, open accounts, and/or make major purchases (such as automobiles), and then default on these debts.

While the short-term identity thief takes over your established accounts, a long-term identity thief establishes new accounts in your name.

Birth Certificates

Birth certificates are usually considered the first document creating identification; this is because birth is the first step in the creation of an identity and because nearly all other identification documents are procured using a birth certificate. The registry or bureau of vital statistics in each state is a clearinghouse for birth, marriage, and death records. County clerks offices are another option. There are more than 7000 different forms of birth certificates in the United States. A certified copy of a birth certificate is often what is required to obtain a social security card and driver's license. Sample *uncertified* birth certificates can be obtained from state bureau of vital statistics or county offices and state stamps, available from stationary stores, can be used to authenticate documents.

Social Security Numbers and Cards

A social security card with an assigned social security number (SSN) is usually the second most important document; this is usually required to gain employment, pay taxes, obtain a driver's license, and for many other purposes. It has become a de facto *national identification number*. The Social Security Administration (SSA) uses the SSN to track quarterly earnings. The Internal Revenue Service (IRS) uses the SSN for taxpayer identification (more on this as you read).

In Canada, the equivalent to the SSN is the SIN—the Canadian Social Insurance Number (SIN), issued by Human Resources Development Canada (HRDC). Do not disclose your SSN to anyone unless it is absolutely necessary. Even revealing a portion of your number may be the key an identity thief needs to obtain your number and identity. Your last four digits Disclosing the last four digits only of your SSN does nothing to protect you and may be exactly what an ID thief needs to steal your identity. You will see how to piece together a number as you read.

There are three methods of obtaining an SSN: (1) apply for a valid card and number under a new identity, (2) procure someone else's identity and obtain a valid copy of their SSN, and (3) create an SSN and forge a card. If you are investigating an identity theft, you should be familiar with these techniques. If you are an intelligence officer creating a cover identity, you should still be familiar with the laws covering such documents, including, but not limited to the following:

42 U.S.C. 301 and 208(g) The Social Security Act of 1981
18 U.S.C. 1028 The False Identification Crime Control Act of 1982

If one chooses option #1 (apply for a valid card and number under a new identity), it will be necessary to have a legal name change (discussed further along). If option #2 (procure someone else's identity and obtain a valid copy of their SSN), there are a few facts that need to be known.

An option to *creating* an SSN is to actually apply for a valid SSN under your new identity. This may have fewer risks and hassles and actually provide social security benefits. Most identity changers (unless in a government relocation program) are too old to apply for a new SSN without being conspicuous.

Children less than 5 years of age are usually issued mail order SSNs with few questions. A birth certificate and one piece of collaborating documentation are required (a doctor's or hospital bill, a baptismal certificate, a government bond, etc.). (Again, there are more than 7000 different forms of birth certificates in the United States.) Anyone over 45 who applies for a social security number and card will attract scrutiny.

If the person applying for the SSN is under the age of 18 years, application may be made by mail. The SSA requires (1) a birth certificate and (2) some identification (driver's license, passport, medical record, government employee ID card, school record, report card, or ID). A birth certificate used to obtain a new identity SSN would have to be from someone who died young, did not have an SSN, and would be only 16 or 17 years old. (Note: This information often changes.)

Even a *valid* SSN may not pass scrutiny because most data banks are tied together, for example, BMV, IRS, NCIC, and SSA. The IRS and the SSA indexes *retired* SSNs to prevent unauthorized reuse of them. Quarterly circulars are made available to banks so they can detect bogus SSNs.

If someone chooses option #3 (create an SSN and forge a card), there are a few facts that must be understood about this modus operandi (method of operation).

Take care in choosing a new SSN. Credit reporting agencies use the Social Security Death Index (SSDI) to cross-reference SSNs of deceased individuals with existing credit profiles. If the SSN belongs to a deceased person, it may be flagged for fraud. Banks also receive bulletins from the SSA that indicate the most recent SSNs. The IRS also issues watch lists of fraudulent SSNs to banks and other entities to search accounts and safe deposit boxes.

SSNs are for social security benefits, though the IRS and many other government agencies also use it as a national identification number. An employer identification number (EIN) may be used by an entity and a taxpayer identification number (TIN) may be sued for tax purposes in lieu of an SSN, but no benefits are accrued.

The SSN is made up of nine numbers (000-00-0000): area—block—serial. The first three numbers (area) of the SSN indicates the area of the country where the card was issued (except the 700 series, which was reserved for railroad retirement use). This is the *area segment*.

The middle two digits (block) is the *group* or *block* segment and gives an idea of when an SSN was issued. *Odd* groupings (01–09) were used first (probably before 1940). *Even* groupings 10–98 were used next, then *even* groupings 02–08, then *odd* groupings 11–99. It is important to know in which year a particular block of numbers was issued in the target area.

The last four digits (serial) are used to serialize 0001–9999 numbers within each group and is the *serial number* or the *segment*.

You may also get a new ID using a police report as proof of your stolen ID, with a certified copy of a birth certificate. Applicants for an SSN who are over the age of 18 must appear in person for an interview and usually must provide SSNs for both parents, unless they are aliens or foreign visitors. The SSA may issue a new SSN if one can show that they have been the victim of identity theft. This must be under the old name, not the new one. A juvenile application can be made by mail with one parent's SSN.

Illegal immigrants in the work force (or anyone) can get an Individual Taxpayer Identification Number (ITIN), which is a nine digit number like the SSN. This allows a worker to file tax returns but not to receive social security benefits. Many banks will accept an ITIN in lieu of an SSN to open accounts. A *W-7 Application for IRS ITIN* may be used for this.

Insurance companies offer plastic social security cards with their information packages, as well as bulk junk mail at your mail drop.

Driver's Licenses

Most states issue a paper or temporary driver's license until the regular one arrives by mail. Some of these temporary IDs have no expiration date or photograph. A Canadian driver's license, or one from virtually any country, may be a viable alternative. You may be required to have an *International Driver's Permits* or *International Motorist Qualifications* (IMQ) (issued by the AAA) with a foreign license.

A homemade *International Driver's License (Permit)* may not be recognized by anyone who has never seen one. They do not include an SSN and verification is virtually impossible on short notice. Using an international driver's permit and other ID documents may make it possible to get a driver's license in a state that does *not* require an SSN to get a license. The American Automobile Association issues standard international driving permits. One may purchase a legitimate permit using a valid state license as a validating document. (The permits were issued on Wasau Royal Fiber Cover Sheet Recycled Pewter with red AAA seals.)

The National Commercial Motor Vehicle Safety Act of 1986 stopped those getting multiple driver's licenses by mandating that all states issue and enforce a *national commercial motor vehicle license* called a commercial driver's license (CDL). These state licenses are all linked in one *info sharing* computer system. It may be possible to obtain multiple legal driver's licenses using a valid SSN attached to an alias, using a pretext for why you are getting a license at this time (age), for example, you have been in Canada for the last 8 years. It is even better if you are asked for a birth certificate, rather than an SSN.

Vehicles must also be licensed, that is, have a license plate or *tags*, and a registration. Most states also require that proof of insurance coverage be carried in the vehicle while operated. Register vehicles to your company name and mail drop address.

Military ID and Ancillary Documents

Military identification includes an Armed Forces Identification Card. An honorable discharge may be some evidence of military service, but a *DD214* (*Report of Separation*) is the form that is the standard for verification of military service. Military personnel records can be used for proving military service, or as a valuable tool in genealogical research. A DD Form 214/215 is prepared in eight copies and distributed as follows:

- Copy 1—Service Member
- Copy 2—Service Personnel File
- Copy 3—U.S. Department of Veterans Affairs
- Copy 4—Member (if initialed in Block 30)
- Copy 5—U.S. Department of Labor
- Copy 6—State Director of Veteran Affairs
- Copy 7 and 8—Distributed in accordance with Military Service Department directions

Most veterans and their next of kin can obtain free copies of their and other military and medical records by completing a *Standard Form 180* and submitting it to

National Personnel Records Center
Military Personnel Records
1 Archives Drive
St. Louis, MO 63138 (314) 801-0800

School IDs (student and faculty) are easily manufactured and difficult to detect. Most have photos and an SSN or other ID number. Student IDs are useful when used with a birth certificate to acquire an SSN. Fake numbers used on fabricated documents may arouse suspicion.

Baptismal certificate—The SSA has accepted a *church membership or confirmation record* (if not used as evidence of age).

Library cards—Known as *ancillary documentation*, such documents can be helpful, so it may be worthwhile to obtain several library cards under several names so your checkouts are not tracked by a database.

Checkout counter cards are used for discounts and for credit coupons. These cards make records of your buying habits and how much you are willing to spend for certain items. *Data Resellers* use databases track last known addresses, mail forwarding addresses, magazine subscriptions, motor vehicle information, buying habits, income, marital status and number of children, court filings and judgments, etc. Magazine subscriptions and *junk mail* can be useful for establishing a *history* at a certain location.

Other Ancillary ID cards:

- ID from video rental stores or *preferred customer* cards become *secondary ID*
- U.S. Coast Guard Merchant Mariner Card
- Native American tribal document
- Basque identification card (e.g., Mina Brookie and 1/8 Miami Indian from north central Indiana)

- Voter registration card
- Work ID cards—name, DOB, hire date, issue date, height, weight, description, ID#, signature, expiration, and photo

There are several web pages that claim to offer fake or *novelty* IDs (driver's licenses and other ID). A couple of these include:

- www.phonyid.com
- www.novelty-ids.com
- www.qualityids.com

Fingerprints

Once you have your new identity, do *not* (ever) be fingerprinted as this will link back to your old identity.

New Passports

Passports are very difficult to obtain (even your own with proper identification). If you are an intelligence officer, your host agency will no doubt expedite obtaining not only your passport but also UC or camouflage passports.

Passports from other countries may be legitimately obtained in some circumstances. Guatemala, Costa Rica, Honduras, Venezuela, Paraguay, Nicaragua, Dominican Republic, etc., may be the easier countries to obtain them from. Some identity changers also suggest contacting

PT Shamrock Ltd.
EBC House
Townsend Lane
London NW9 8LL
Great Britain
ptshamrock@ptshamrock.com

Camouflage passports. A *camouflage passport* is a counterfeit document designed to be carried by Americans (or others) who could be in danger in certain areas because of their nationality. Obtaining dual Irish citizenship has been another option. *Changers* sometimes suggest contacting the FINOR Organization: http://www.finor.com, www.theidshop.com, or

The Freebooter	Quester Press Ltd.
P.O. Box 489	6-8 High Street
St. Peter Port	Bishops Watham
Guernsey GY1 6BS, Channel Islands	Hampshire SO32 IAB United Kingdom
www.freebooter.com	

Document Security Devices

Access control security systems use a variety of high-technology solutions for determining identity: fingerprints, retinal scans, voice prints, heart beat patterns, and brain activity patterns. Identification documents themselves may contain a variety and combination of security features, such as

- One-piece ID (photo not laminated on).
- State registration system—*not on file.*
- Lamination—USI, Inc., 33 Business Park Drive, Suite 5, Branford, CT 06405-2944.
- State seal and signature overlap.
- Background design—color, pattern, line (usually for bank checks and credit card signatures). Erase the signature and the *squiggle lines* on the checks or cards. If it cannot be duplicated, erase the entire *squiggle* area.
- Soundex—a method of encoding the driver's name and other identifying information into the driver's license.
- UV Ink—Incite Technologies Corp., 10059 E. Washington Street, Indianapolis, IN 46229; www.my-secret.com.
- Hologram.
- Machine-readable technologies—bar codes and mag strips (PVC).
- Ghost Image—half-tone duplication.
- Optically variable device (OVD)—an image that shifts positions, changes into another object, or appears to be moving as you hold it at different angles to the light.

Mail, Mail Drops, and Remailing Services

The operative or *changer* may receive mail by placing a mail box in a line of rural route boxes on a country road. The carrier will leave forms to be completed, probably without ever seeing a house associated with the box. (Boxes at abandoned farm houses may also work.)

Mails drops (such as mailboxes) are common for forwarding mail. In addition to mail forwarding, mail drops usually offer private mail box rentals, shipping and receiving packages for UPS and Federal Express, money orders, photocopying, desktop publishing, 24-hour access, etc. For a higher level of security, rent another box at a mail drop near the place where you relocate to and have mail from the first mail drop forwarded to the second drop.

Remailing services receive mail from you and remail it from its location to wherever you designate. Some mail drops offer this service as well.

Be cautious about accepting oddly shaped or colored packages that you are not expecting, as these may be used to *mark* you by someone surveilling your pickup.

Credit bureaus and government agencies maintain databases of known mail drops and routinely compare these to credit applications and credit profiles. If your address matches one of these known mail drops, your application or credit report may be flagged for fraud. Using published drops could lead pursuers to your new or cover identity. Check mail drop directories and use one that is NOT published.

A mail drop facility that allows its *tenants* to use its full street address may add the mailbox number as a *suite* or *apartment* number. This is better than using a *box number*. Mail drops may also be used to forward mail (for a fee) to another address or another mail drop. Some mail drops have 24-hour access. (You might consider having someone else pick up your mail for you.) The government, insurance companies, and credit bureaus maintain databases of mail drops to detect fraud. A commercial address could also be used temporarily.

Storage Facilities and Real Estate Trusts

There are three things that you can do with the *stuff* that you don't take with you and don't want to throw away: store it, sell it, or give it away. The storage option usually involves renting a storage building by the month and storing your stuff there while you are gone. Usually you must pay the first month's rent with a small deposit and an agreement giving the storage facility owner permission to confiscate your possessions if you fall behind in the rent.

You must either visit the storage unit during the operating hours or, at an additional charge, you may be able to get a private access code to disarm the security system to enter at any time. These units can range from $50 to $200 per month in most areas.

Real estate can be purchased by a business trust. In a trust with undisclosed beneficiaries, a statement called a Schedule of Beneficiaries is filed with the trustee. In some states this does not need to be filed with the registrar of deeds. Some states allow land trusts. You may create a corporation to act as the trustee.

Utilities, Pay-as-You-Go Phones, and Answering Services

When relocating under a new identity, having utilities turned on using your new name helps establish your new identity. Having a phone in your name helps establish credit and serves as proof address. Utility bills may serve as proof of address when opening a bank account.

Prepaid cell phones can be purchased without credit cards, names, etc. Having a basic ID, an identity thief may set up cell phone service using some-one else's SSN.

Caller ID or *CLID* (calling line ID) is used to identify the name, address, and/or phone number of the caller on either landline phones or cellular phones. *Spoofing* software can help conceal the caller's identity or even falsely identify the CLID information.

Line blocking prevents your name, number, and address from showing up on caller ID and indicates either PRIVATE, BLOCKED, or RESTRICTED. You will be unable to connect to phones equipped with *Anonymous Call Rejection* (ACR), *unless* you subscribe to *per-call unblocking* (*82), which you must pay for in most cases. *Per-call blocking* (*67) blocks outbound Caller ID on a per-call basis.

Neither line blocking nor per-call blocking prevents your number from being displayed at toll-free (800/888/877) or pay-per-call (900/976) numbers, which use automatic number identification (ANI). Emergency numbers (911) are also unaffected by CLID blocking. Large private branch exchanges (PBX) with extensions show up at a single billing number.

Telephone service codes:

TelCo Service	DTMF Code (Tone)	Pulse Dialer Code
Call trace	*57 (number, date, and time)	1157
Call cue	*66 (redials busy)	1166
Per-call blocking	*67	1167
Dial last caller	*69	1169
Call waiting OFF	*70 (On a per-call basis)	1170
Call forwarding ON	*72	1172
Call forwarding OFF	*73	1173
Activate ARC	*77 (Anonymous Call Rejection)	1177
Per-call unblocking	*82	1182
Deactivate ARC	*87	1187

Internet and Internet Privacy

Spam is a scam (usually). Source Socket Layer (SSL)—secures information *in transit*. Encryption of data files—PGP (Pretty Good Privacy) is FREE from MIT:

- http://web.mit.edu/network/pgp.html
- www.pgpi.org
- www.pgp.com

Remove your name from the data file created during setup (e.g., Internet Explorer or Netscape Navigator). Using Netscape, click on OPTIONS, then MAIL NEWS AND PREFERENCES, highlight your name, and delete it. You may replace it with a *handle* or a first name.

Cookies were introduced by Netscape. They are or it is a small file placed by the remote server on the client side of the network interface (your computer). The first time you visit a site, you get a JavaScript or CGI script message asking for your name. The JavaScript message box results from unseen programming code embedded in the HTML (hypertext markup language) of the web page. Once you enter your name, another unseen code snippet writes that information to a file on your computer. When you log on to that website again, another JavaScript routine looks for the cookie and retrieves your name and information stored in the cookie. If your browser does not allow cookies or you disable them, you will be prompted for your name on each subsequent visit. Cookies can track information, such as buying and spending habits, time spent viewing page screens, etc.

In *Microsoft Internet Explorer*, cookies will usually be found in the Windows subdirectory *Cookies*. Open Windows Explorer and open the subdirectory to find them. In *Netscape Navigator*, go to the Program Files directory or the subdirectory to find *cookies.txt*. If either of these fails, click *Start/Find/Files or Folders* and type in *cookie*.** (cookie*.*) and click *Find Now* or do a File Manager search.

To have your browser warn you before setting Cookies, set the *switch* in your *Options* menu. For Navigator, click *Options/Network/Protocols*, then check *Accepting a Cookie* in the *Show an Alert Before* box. You may also click *Options/Mail and News Preferences/Identity*. Go to the *Your Name* box and type in a made-up name, anonymous name, or none at all. Below that, in the *Your E-Mail* and *Reply-to Address* boxes enter an alias e-mail address. Microsoft Internet Explorer users should click on *View/Options/Advanced* and then click *Warn before accepting Cookies*. (Use this restriction sparingly for your convenience.)

E-Mail Privacy

Most browsers allow you to change the *Reply to* e-mail address. To increase Internet privacy, avoid e-mail accounts provided by your Internet service Provider (ISP), as they often allow marketers, bill collectors, and even private investigators to discover your location. An option is to use *FREE e-mail addresses*, which allow to access e-mail from any computer with Internet access, such as

- Yahoo.com
- hotmail.com
- gmail.com
- geocities.com

Use a computer at a library or other location to access your e-mail without being traced to an Internet Service Provider (ISP). When you apply for these, you will be asked to provide personal information in exchange for the free service. You can use an alias and make up the rest.

Prepaid Internet service is another option. Such service can be purchased with no credit agreement or personal information and used virtually anywhere. These companies usually ask for your name, address, and phone number for initial sign-up. You can use an alias. If you do not have an ISP, you can login to your free e-mail anywhere in the world using a library, university, or company computer.

Anonymous remailers are another option. When you route your e-mail through an anonymous remailer, the server replaces your e-mail address with one it makes up. It then forward your message to its original destination. Any replies from that destination automatically pass back through the remailer, which then recalls your e-mail address and forward it back to you. (There is a distinction between anonymous and pseudo-anonymous remailers. Neither is recommended and you can usually tell that they are anonymous.)

Pretty Good Privacy (PGP), created by Philip Zimmerman in 1991, is a *pretty good* encryption option. It is a data encryption and decryption program that provides cryptographic privacy and authentication for data communication. It is commonly used for signing, encrypting, and decrypting texts, e-mails, files, directories, and whole disk partitions to increase the security of e-mail communications.

Education and Employment (EIN and TIN) and Doing Business

Working to secure income is essential. It is estimated that taxes consume up to 35%–45% of a person's income, making *off-the-books* employment desirable. Service industries (plumbing, repairs, cleaning, locksmithing, gunsmithing, computer repair, etc.) are often in demand and often pay in cash. Farming, gardening, and selling firewood are also low-key endeavors. Pastors and monks (who live in monasteries) often make a cash income while living by some of the *church* resources. Many participants in the underground economy keep a foot in both worlds. They engage in off-the-books cash enterprises and report enough income to attract little attention. Some *underground economy entrepreneurs* can't have bank accounts or stay in one location or with one employer for long. It is best to work for private individuals rather than companies, which file 1099s. Temp services and employment agencies can help someone find a *job*.

Your new identity must create a factious work history that represents your actual skill sets, experience, and knowledge (but not so close as to leave tracks or a nexus between your old and new identities). You will also need *references* that will check out. You can use an answering service for your *old boss* and *previous employer*. You can FAX letters of reference or use a remailing service (which also offers FAX services).

Self-employment is also a viable option. Some businesses require a retail merchant permit, usually issued by the city clerk, county treasurer, or state department of revenue (or their equivalents). Some regulated professions require a license issued by the state or, in some cases, a federal agency. Incorporation offers several advantages, especially the limited liability company (LLC). You may also need to file a DBA (Doing Business As) certificate with the county recorder, particularly if you are doing business under a name other than the one the incorporation is filed under.

Some states have strict requirements for incorporation and others are much easier to do business in. Nevada, Wyoming, and Delaware are often considered good options for filing for incorporation. In Nevada, for example, the fee is usually about $125 and nominal annual fees. There are no state corporation taxes or personal income taxes, and there is minimal reporting and disclosure and total privacy of shareholders and only the names of officers and directors are on public record. This requires a resident agent or manager and a nominee to serve as officer(s). A *TIN* is required and *IRS Form SS-4* requires the nominees SSN. There are companies that will serve as the resident agent and provide nominee services, such as Laughlin Associates, Inc. (Carson City, NV) and Val-U-Corp. Services, Inc.

Form SS-4 is the IRS form a business entity uses to apply for an *EIN* or a *TIN*. The EIN is the business entity's equivalent to an SSN and is required by banks and creditors to conduct business. Even a sole proprietorship may apply for an EIN. The IRS requires the person filling out *Form SS-4* to furnish their SSN. Be sure to file for a TIN, file tax returns, and pay taxes for employees.

Self-employment is an alternative to a *job front*. By establishing a business identity, the identity changer can appear to own, be associated with, or be employed by a business.

Traveler's Checks, Money Orders, and Prepaid Credit Cards

Checks leave an obvious paper trail. Carrying cash to buy what you need (food, hygiene, etc.) is a good idea, but you can also pay bills with money orders as another alternative to using checks. However, ID is required to purchase *traveler's checks*. Any post office will cash postal *money orders*, but they also require ID.

Using credit cards or debit cards leaves a paper trail, but this can sometimes be used to good advantage to mislead pursuers. It is often preferable to use *cash* or *prepaid charge cards* to buy what you need (food, hygiene, etc.). Prepaid *credit cards* with the VISA or MasterCard logo can be purchased anonymously, with no name, credit references, proof of income, or identification because they are prepaid. Their value is equal to the amount you pay for them, minus a modest processing fee.

Credit card companies often solicit *secured accounts*, even from people with poor or no credit. After establishing credit you will be added to *secured* credit card mailing lists (for more credit cards). Use your *new identity* address and phone number for these. When you activate the new card(s), you are usually required to call a toll-free (800) number, which will ask for the phone number on the account or a computer system answering the phone will try to verify the number using caller ID. You are also prompted to enter your SSN or other identifiers.

Another way of obtaining a credit card is to add a cardholder to an existing account (usually your own), but this links the *new* identity to your *old* identity. This also establishes your credit history with credit information services, such as TRW, Equifax, Transunion, etc. After 6–8 months, you will start receiving preapproved credit card offers.

When applying for credit or credit cards, avoid using mail drops that may be in a database. Rather than using mail drops, look for someplace that does not specialize as such, but just happens to have a few mail boxes to rent. They usually require you to fill out a form for the post office, who may sell or trade this information.

Credit Cards and Credit Bureaus

1-888-5OPT-OUT   1-888-567-8688

Keep a list of all credit cards with the phone numbers used to report them lost or stolen. Use low-limit cards for daily use and high-limit cards for traveling. Limit the number of cards that you carry (usually one or two). Do *not* provide *supplemental identification* when using credit cards. The signature on the back is all that is required.

- Equifax   www.equifax.com
- Trans Union   www.transunion.com
- Experian   www.experian.com

Banking Privacy and Offshore Money

Privacy, cover identities, and identity changing are perpetually evolving issues. Vigilance is the key! Since 1970 the IRS has required banks to file a report for each customer transaction of $10,000 or more and on any person making cash transactions over $10,000. This includes their SSN.

With a business account you do not need to endorse deposit checks with a signature, only a stamp with the name of the business, the account number, and/or the words *For Deposit Only*. When writing checks, a signature stamp may be used. Print the post office street address along with your post office box number on checks when you are required to have a street address.

Sending a *sucker check* (a check of a nominal amount payable to the target of an investigation) may be used to see where checks are deposited or what account numbers are, such as when a party is attempting to attach an account (following a judgment) or identify the location of assets.

Taking over a personal account involves having someone else open an account with an authorized user who then *takes over* the account. Opening an account under an assumed name may be discovered by an SSN database check and probably violates several State and/or federal laws. Opening a business account may be a preferable option. The bank representative will probably ask for

- Corporate resolutions—corporate directors meeting
- EIN or TIN—applied for using *IRS Form SS-4*
- DBA certificate—a *Doing Business As* form filed with the city or county clerk
- Business address—a mail drop, residence, or other address
- Business telephone—an answering service, voice mail, prepaid cell phone, or *MagicJack* type phone
- Declaration of trust—recorded at the deeds registry (for real property); an assertion by a property owner that he or she holds property or an estate for the benefit of another person or for particular designated objectives

Offshore banking is another alternative for personal privacy, identity changing, or an UC operation. Such accounts are often associated with criminals, but are also used by the rich and famous, corporations and businesses, privacy seekers, and government and intelligence agencies. Often they require a minimum deposit and balance (sometimes as little at $5000). Countries that are known for strict banking privacy laws include Switzerland, the Bahamas, Canada, Panama, and the Caymans. Some banks that have been reported with good reputations include the following:

- Robecco Bank, Geneva, Switzerland
- Anker Bank, Lausanne, Switzerland
- Standard Chartered Bank (House), St. Helier, Jersey
- Piazza Financial Services, LTD, London, United Kingdom

For more information on such services, try checking privacy@privacyworld.com (fiscal tax shelters or *havens*). *Caveat*: The Swiss have been cooperating on a regular basis with agencies like the IRS, where it is believed the money on deposit came from criminal activity.

It is illegal for U.S. citizens to have more than $10,000 in foreign banks without reporting it to the U.S. government. It is not illegal to move money to another bank or investment. It may, however, be illegal to move assets into offshore accounts without declaring their existence to tax authorities. (Taxes must be paid on income from any source, no matter where it comes from.) However, protection of assets from litigation or seizure may be a privacy advantage to such accounts.

Few, if any, banks still offer purely *numbered accounts*, where no name is required and deposits or transfers are only made using a code number. Most banks will not bother with small accounts and the transfer charges will soon deplete a small account. The cost of setting up an account ranges from $750 to $1500. It may be prudent to consider creating a *corporation* in a haven country to keep the money out of your name and avoid the problem of being a foreign account holder.

It is also possible to open an *offshore credit card* or *ATM card* (VISA, MasterCard, etc.), allowing one to withdraw funds anywhere in the world with minimal record keeping. Most will want a secured deposit. Carefully choose both the country and the bank to make sure they are trustworthy. A reputable attorney in that country may be helpful. Other overseas investments, such as Swiss annuities, may be another option.

There is nothing illegal about moving funds outside the United States. The U.S. economy is dependent upon international trade. Since all U.S. global trade is transacted in U.S. dollars, there would be no imports or exports without such transfers. Most U.S. banks accept deposits from persons overseas and often invest in foreign stocks and hold accounts with foreign banks. The IRS, however, wants to keep track of everyone's liquid assets.

INTER-FIPOL (International Fiscal Police) has been described by tax avoidance advocates as an Orwellian "super-national police force." It is a European organization for "mutual assistance for the recovery of tax claims" and the "international exchange of fiscal and other data." Little is known about this "secret financial police force."

Legal avoidance: Many tax evaders open accounts in fictitious names and use mail forwarding and pickup drops for privacy. In some cases an account may be opened for as little as $100 and may draw higher interest than in U.S. banks or credit unions. They usually only allow a liquidity factor (insurance) of around 10% of the public deposits and many are self-insured.

The IRS requires a *Treasury Form 90.22-1 Report of Foreign Bank and Financial Accounts* to be completed and submitted to the IRS by June 30 of each year for any foreign accounts. The U.S. Treasury Department's *Currency and Foreign Transactions Reporting Act* outlines which monetary instruments (checks, money orders, etc.) must be reported. You may not be required to report personal checks or money orders payable to you, if it is *restrictively endorse* (made payable to the order of the bank) or checks or money orders payable to an offshore bank. Most countries (except the United States and the Philippines) do not tax income earned outside of their countries.

The investigator, intelligence officer, or one hoping for financial privacy should be familiar with *methods of finding hidden assets.*

- Passports evidencing travel to destinations such as Switzerland, the Cayman Islands, the Bahamas, Isle of Man, the Netherlands Antilles, and other banking and tax havens.
- Telephone, cell phone, and FAX phone record to undisclosed business connections and contacts.
- Credit card statements indicating travel, products purchased, and who one does business with.
- Using mail covers to identify those one has a relationship with.
- Bank transactions—withdrawals of $3000 or more must be reported to the federal government by your bank, whether by cash, check, or electronic transfer.
- Checking private courier logs (UPS, DHL, FedEx, Airborne Express, etc.).

Court-Ordered (Legal) Name Change

Changing identity is not illegal, but many of the methods of documenting a new identity are. It is possible to legally change one's identity while retaining at least some of the covert benefits. The objective is to create a *paper trip* that leaves no connection between the old and new identity. A legal name change creates a nexus between the old and new identity, but there are methods to help obscure this link.

One method is the *use* method in which one simply starts using a new name in everyday business and becomes generally known by that name in the community.

- Some states require a notarized *declaration of name-change form.*
- Most states require a *legal* name change in order to receive a driver's license and/or voter registration card. This usually requires a petition to be filed with the court having jurisdiction. If no objections are made, a name-change order is usually issued.
- Other states have a residency requirement of anywhere from 6 weeks to 6 months and some proof of residency.
- Still other states require name changes to be published in a local newspaper or record.

Once you have a court order for a new name change, you can establish your new identity by *registering to vote* and getting a *driver's license* or *State ID card.* You will need the name-change order and a certified copy of your original *birth certificate*. If you want to avoid a link to your old identity, you may want to get only a State ID card, and then go to another State using the new ID to get a driver's license. Immediately surrendering your old license for a new one creates a link (nexus) to your new identity. Obtaining a new SSN or a passport will, however, create a nexus.

Half the states require less than half the trouble to get a legal name change than the other half does. In other words, half the states have very stringent requirements for a name change. States that have the least problems involving name changes include Alabama, Alaska, Arkansas, California, Colorado, Delaware, Idaho, Indiana, Kansas, Kentucky, Maryland, Massachusetts, Missouri, Montana, Nebraska, Nevada, New Hampshire, North Dakota, Ohio, South Carolina, Tennessee, Texas, Utah, Washington, West Virginia, Wisconsin, and Wyoming.

In the United Kingdom and other countries, you may be able to have a legal name change without going through any legal procedures, but you will need to complete a legal *deed-poll name change* by downloading an application from the Ministry of Justice.

The key to a new or cover identity is planning and vigilance to detection. You must have a credible cover story and live it.

Appendix: Indiana Name Change Statute (IC 34-28-2, Chapter 2, "Change of Name")

An example of state name change statutes is the Indiana statute. This statutes reads in part:

IC 34-28-2-1 Petition to Circuit Court

Sec. 1. Except as provided in section 1.5 of this chapter, the circuit courts in Indiana may change the names of natural persons on application by petition. *As added by P.L.1-1998, SEC.24. Amended by P.L.18-1998, SEC.1.*

IC 34-28-2-1.5 Incarcerated Persons May Not Petition for Change of Name

Sec. 1.5. A person may not petition for a change of name under this chapter if the person is confined to a department of correction facility. *As added by P.L.18-1998, SEC.2.*

IC 34-28-2-2 Filing Petition; Procedure for Change of Name of Minor

Sec. 2.

(a) The petition described in section 1 of this chapter must include the following:
   (1) If applicable, include the information required by section 2.5 of this chapter
   (2) In the case of a petition filed by a person described in section 2.5 of this chapter, be subscribed and sworn to (or affirmed)
      (A) Under the penalties of perjury
      (B) Before a notary public or other person authorized to administer oaths
   (3) Be filed with the circuit court of the county in which the person resides.
(b) In the case of a parent or guardian who wishes to change the name of a minor child, the petition must be verified, and it must state in detail the reason the change is requested. In addition, except where a parent's consent is not required under IC 31-19-9, the written consent of a parent, or the written consent of the guardian if both parents are dead, must be filed with the petition.
(c) Before a minor child's name may be changed, the parents or guardian of the child must be served with a copy of the petition as required by the Indiana trial rules.

As added by P.L.1-1998, SEC.24. Amended by P.L.61-2010, SEC.1.

IC 34-28-2-2.5 Contents of Petition

Sec. 2.5.

(a) If a person petitioning for a change of name under this chapter is at least 17 years of age, the person's petition must include at least the following information:
   (1) The person's date of birth
   (2) The person's current
      (A) Residence address
      (B) If different than the person's residence address, mailing address
   (3) The person's valid
      (A) Indiana driver's license number
      (B) Indiana identification card (as described in IC 9-24-16) number
   (4) A list of all previous names used by the person
   (5) Proof that the person is a U.S. citizen
   (6) A statement concerning whether the person holds a valid U.S. passport

      (7) A description of all judgments of criminal conviction of a felony under the laws of any state or the United States that have been entered against the person.

  (b) A petition under subsection (a) is subject to Indiana Rules of Court Administrative Rule 9.

As added by P.L.61-2010, SEC.2.

IC 34-28-2-3 Notice of Petition

Sec. 3.

  (a) Upon filing a petition for a name change, the applicant shall give notice of the petition as follows:

      (1) By 3 weekly publications in a newspaper of general circulation published in the county in which the petition is filed in court.

      (2) If no newspaper is published in the county in which the petition is filed, the applicant shall give notice in a newspaper published nearest to that county in an adjoining county.

      (3) The last weekly publication shall be published not less than 30 days before the day the petition will be heard as indicated in the notice.

  (b) In the case of a petition described in section 2(b) of this chapter, the notice required by this section must include the following:

      (1) The name of the petitioner

      (2) The name of the minor child whose name is to be changed

      (3) The new name desired

      (4) The name of the court in which the action is pending

      (5) The date on which the petition was filed

      (6) A statement that any person has the right to appear at the hearing and to file objections

  (c) Except as provided in section 1.5 of this chapter, in the case of a person who has had a felony conviction within 10 years before filing a petition for a change of name, at least 30 days before the hearing the petitioner must give notice of the filing of the petition to

      (1) The sheriff of the county in which the petitioner resides

      (2) The prosecuting attorney of the county in which the petitioner resides

      (3) The Indiana central repository for criminal history information

(d) The notice given to the Indiana central repository for criminal history information under subsection (c) must include the petitioner's full current name, requested name change, date of birth, address, physical description, and a full set of classifiable fingerprints

(e) The Indiana central repository for criminal history information shall forward a copy of any criminal records of the petitioner to the court for the court's information

(f) A copy of the court decree granting or denying such a petition shall be sent to the Indiana state police

(g) A person who violates subsection (c) commits a Class A misdemeanor

As added by P.L.1-1998, SEC.24. Amended by P.L.18-1998, SEC.3; P.L.1-1999, SEC.72; P.L.61-2010, SEC.3.

IC 34-28-2-4 Proof of Publication; Time of Hearing; Notice Requirements; Determination on Petition

Sec. 4.

(a) Proof of the publication required in this chapter is made by filing a copy of the published notice, verified by the affidavit of a disinterested person, and when proof of publication is made, the court shall, subject to the limitations imposed by subsections (b), (c), and (d), proceed to hear the petition and make an order and decree the court determines is just and reasonable.

(b) In the case of a petition described in section 2(b) of this chapter, the court may not hear the petition and issue a final decree until after 30 days from the later of
   (1) The filing of proof of publication of the notice required under subsection (a)
   (2) The service of the petition upon the parents or guardian of the minor child

(c) In the case of a petition described in section 2(b) of this chapter, the court shall set a date for a hearing on the petition if
   (1) Written objections have been filed
   (2) Either parent or the guardian of the minor child has refused or failed to give written consent as described in section 2(b) of this chapter

The court shall require that appropriate notice of the hearing be given to the parent or guardian of the minor child or to any person who has filed written objections.

(d) In deciding on a petition to change the name of a minor child, the court shall be guided by the best interest of the child rule under IC 31-17-2-8. However, there is a presumption in favor of a parent of a minor child who

    (1) Has been making support payments and fulfilling other duties in accordance with a decree issued under IC 31-15, IC 31-16, or IC 31-17 (or IC 31-1-11.5 before its repeal)

    (2) Objects to the proposed name change of the child

(e) In the case of a person required to give notice under section 3(c) of this chapter, the petitioner must certify to the court that he or she has complied with the notice requirements of that subsection

As added by P.L.1-1998, SEC.24. Amended by P.L.61-2010, SEC.4.

IC 34-28-2-5 Court Decree as Evidence; Copy Sent to Health Department, Clerk of Circuit Court, or Board

Sec. 5.

(a) A copy of the decree of the court changing the name of any natural person, certified under the seal of the court by the clerk of the court, is sufficient evidence of the name of the person, and of a change having been made, in any court of Indiana.

(b) In the case of a petition described in section 2(b) of this chapter, the court shall send a copy of the final decree to the state department of health and to the local health department of the county.

(c) In the case of a petition filed by a person at least 17 years of age, the court shall send a copy of the final decree to the clerk of the circuit court or board of registration of the county where the person resides.

As added by P.L.1-1998, SEC.24.

Defenses against Methods of Entry

4

The U.S. military and law enforcement communities do not teach surreptitious entry or methods of burglary (which would be wrong). What they do teach is defenses against methods of entry (DAME) or how to prevent, detect, and investigate burglaries. Obviously, to know how to prevent, detect, and investigate burglaries and provide security and counterintelligence services, it only makes sense to understand how unauthorized, covert, or surreptitious entry is accomplished by spies, burglars, thieves, and others.

There are three common types of locking systems: (1) the pin tumbler system, (2) the wafer tumbler system, and (3) the side bar system. Warded locks are also commonly used on door locks using skeleton keys, padlocks, and handcuffs.

Neutralization of locks and locking devices can be accomplished in a clandestine manner, leaving no trace, and entry gained by covert means. In addition to locks and windows and doors with locking devices, DAME may be achieved by other methods of target hardening through a variety of security technologies and access control hardware. These include, but are not limited to, lighting, barriers (such as fencing and walls), and alarms and other early warning systems (such as sensors, video cameras, enhanced vision surveillance devices, etc.).

Harry Houdini became famous as *The Handcuff King* because of his ability to escape from handcuffs. He later became famous as an *escapologist* and a magician. He is rumored to have worked undercover as an operative for the U.S. Secret Service, the London Metropolitan Police Force Criminal Investigation Division (CID or Scotland Yard), and other law enforcement and intelligence agencies in the United States and Great Britain. He was also a close friend of Dr. Sir Arthur Conan Doyle, the author of the *Sherlock Holmes* mystery novels. (See *Infamous Murders & Mysteries* by Dr. Robert Girod.)

There are various methods of picking locks on handcuffs that are used by locksmiths, magician-escapologists, and criminals. Many begin by using a common *bobby pin* with the plastic tip removed. Bend the end that had been concealed and put it into the key hole. Take it out and bend it the other way making an angle shape having two bends. Then insert it into the keyhole of the handcuffs. Bend the edge of the bobby pin down and release the latches that will open the jaws of the handcuffs. If you have a double lock, put the bobby pin in the keyhole on the other side and turn it around to release the double lock latches and open the jaw. Use care, as the pick may break while you are working on the double lock because of the additional force needed, causing you to be in worse shape than before.

Basic Lock Picking

Lock picking is one method of locksmiths and a method that is shared by law enforcement and intelligence agents. Even if never used to gain lawful entry, such methods are useful to know in the investigation and prevention of burglary crimes and for security of facilities.

Locksmithing, naturally, requires knowledge of locks (and a lot of practice). We will discuss pin cylinder and disc tumbler locks here. Safes and automobile locks will be discussed later.

Practice Preparation

To begin practicing locksmithing and lock picking, a few items are standard fare:

- *Pin cylinder lock* (common night latches found in hardware stores and locksmith supply stores) (Figures 4.1 and 4.2)
- Plug follower (found at a locksmith supply store or made from a 1/2 inch diameter wooden dowel) (Figure 4.3)
- Large tweezers (for removing and inserting tumbler pins) (Figure 4.4)
- Lock picks and torsion (tension) wrench (approximately 0.025 inch thick) (Figure 4.5)
- Vise, such as a table vise (for holding the cylinder when practicing) (Figure 4.6)

Once you have your basic supplies and equipment, it is time to practice. A table light and/or other lighting and a small tray to hold pins and other parts would also be useful. Figure 4.7 shows a *cutaway view* of a common pin tumbler lock. Take the cylinder apart by removing the retaining screws and retaining plate (at the right side, but not pictured, in the illustration in Figure 4.7). If the cylinder has a key, insert the key, raising the pins to the shear line.

Use the key or plug follower (Figure 4.3) to prevent the springs and pins from flying. The plug will turn now and, with the retainer removed, the plug can be pulled out of the shell or case. As you pull the plug out (from the front) follow it from the rear (back) with the plug follower. The bottom pins will remain with the plug while the top pins and springs remain in the shell, held there by the plug follower.

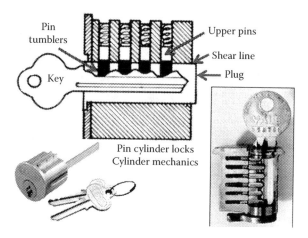

Figure 4.1 Pin cylinder lock (Yale).

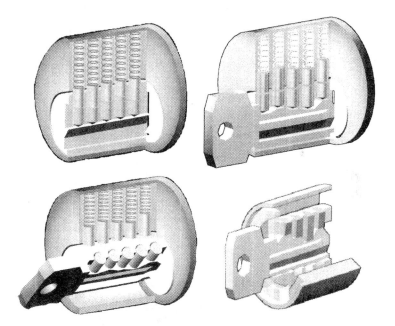

Figure 4.2 Cut away view of pin tumbler lock. (Reprinted http://en.wikipedia.org/wiki/File:Pin_tumbler_no_key.svg.)

Slowly and carefully remove the plug follower to remove the top pins and springs (one at a time) from the shell. If some of the top pins are preceded by a short pin, this indicates that the cylinder was master keyed. The master pins can be discarded.

If you have a cylinder without a key, disassemble it using a shim, a narrow piece of thin steel, or a feeler pick (feeler gauge), illustrated in Figure 4.8.

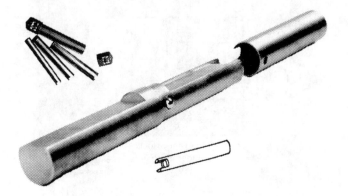

Figure 4.3 Key followers.

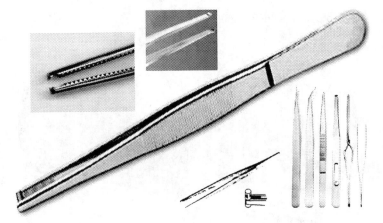

Figure 4.4 Locksmith tweezers.

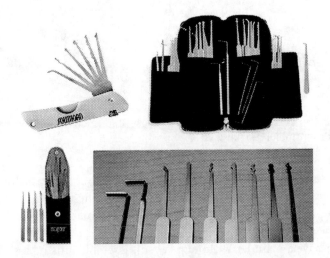

Figure 4.5 Lock pick and torsion (tension) wrench tool sets.

Figure 4.6 Common table or bench vises.

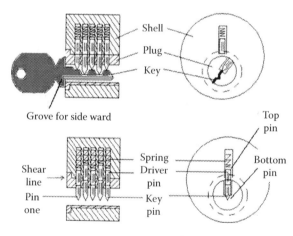

Figure 4.7 Cutaway view.

After the retaining screws and plate are removed, insert the shim between the plug and the shell from the rear (back). Start with the rear pin and use a feeler pick to raise each pin consecutively until you feel the shim go between the top and bottom pins. Continue until the shim is between the shear line and all the pins. The plug can be removed now, as described earlier.

When you reassemble the cylinder, follow the earlier process in reverse. The springs and top pins should be loaded into the shell (one at a time) and retained by inserting the plug follower (Figure 4.3). The bottom pins should be loaded into the plug and inserted from the front while the follower is pushed out of the rear.

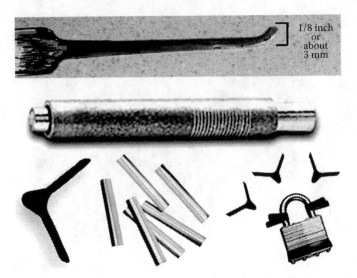

1/8 inch
or
about
3 mm

Figure 4.8 Feeler and shim.

Lock Pick Practice

Once you are ready to practice picking, remove the plug from the shell. Remove all the pins and springs, except one or two. Insert the torsion (tension) wrench (Figure 4.9) into the keyway without blocking the keyway from accepting the pick. Use light turning tension with the torsion or tension wrench while lightly lifting the bottom pin with the *feeler pick* (Figure 4.8). When the shear line is reached, the lock should turn and open. If you pass the shear line, it will not open, and you must release the tension on the tension wrench to allow the spring to bring the pins back into original position.

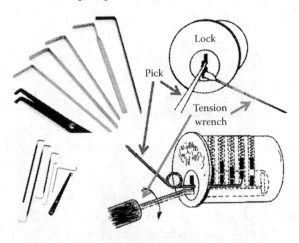

Lock

Pick

Tension
wrench

Figure 4.9 Tension wrenches (torsion wrenches).

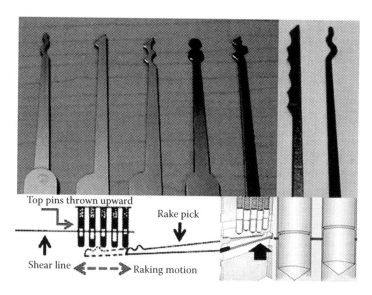

Figure 4.10 Rake picks. From left to right: offset diamond pick, ball pick, half-diamond pick, short hook, medium hook, saw or *L* rake, snake or *C* rake.

Then start again. The lock usually opens clockwise, but with the plug turning the lock will open in either direction.

Next, try using the *pick rake* (Figure 4.10). The rake pick is used similarly to the feeler pick, but it requires less tension on the torsion (tension) wrench. Insert it past the pins and quickly rake it outward. The most common problem is using too much tension or torsion pressure. The pick rake can also be used to *rake* the pick in and out quickly. Practice using varying amounts of tension pressure, until you feel the proper amount for each method.

Once you feel comfortable with both the feeler and rake picks, using only one or two pins, add one or two more pins and springs to your practice lock. Practice each technique again until you feel proficient in each method. You may notice now that, while using the feeler pick, one of the pins will catch on the shear line before the others. You will feel the plug turn slightly. When the last pin reaches the shear line, the lock will open. Cheaper locks are usually master-keyed, which means more shear lines and are easier to pick. Continue this process until you replace all the pins and feel proficient in picking them. Some locks, obviously, will be easier than others.

Pin Cylinder Lock

We have been discussing and working with the *pin cylinder* or *pin tumbler lock* (also known as a Yale lock), which is a lock mechanism that uses pins of varying lengths to prevent the lock from opening without the correct key

(Figures 4.1 and 4.2). Pin tumblers are most commonly employed in cylinder locks, but may also be found in tubular pin tumbler locks (also known as radial locks). The pin tumbler is commonly used in cylinder locks. If you can master the pin tumbler lock (as discussed earlier), other types of locks will be easier.

Warded Pad Locks

One of the derivatives of the warded lock is the warded padlock. *Pick keys* are used for simple *warded locks* and will open most padlocks (Figure 4.11). The basic warded lock uses a set of obstructions, usually consisting of concentric plates that protrude outward. When the wrong key is inserted, the edge hits one or more of the obstructions, preventing it from rotating. When the correct key rotates, it will either push against the bolt or activate a latch, opening the drawer or padlock. Warded locks cannot be picked with tension wrenches and picks because there are no pins in the lock. However, warded locks are basic in design and relatively simple to pick. A set of skeleton keys will open most warded locks.

Disc Tumbler Locks

Tumbler key locks or *tubular key locks* (also known as *disc tumbler locks* and *axial pin tumbler lock*) are commonly found on vending machines and things using similar locks. The *pin tumbler lock* has the pins radially situated around the axis of the plug. Special picks are available for these locks and provide turning force that allows each tumbler to be worked until reaching the shear line (Figure 4.12). Tubular key locks are sued on vending machines, file cabinets, pay phones, gun safes, and a variety of other containers (Figure 4.13).

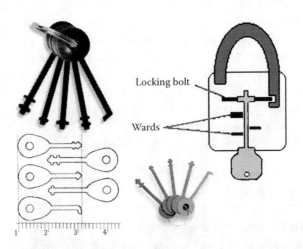

Figure 4.11 Warded pick keys and cutaway of a warded padlock.

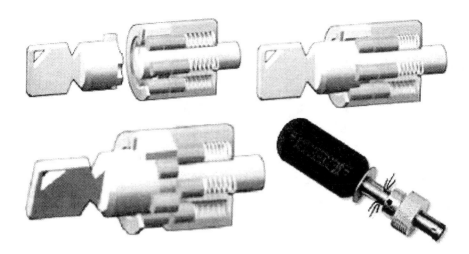

Figure 4.12 Tumbler key locks (disc tumbler locks or tubular key locks). (Used with permission (public domain): http://en.wikipedia.org/wiki/Tubular_pin_tumbler_lock.)

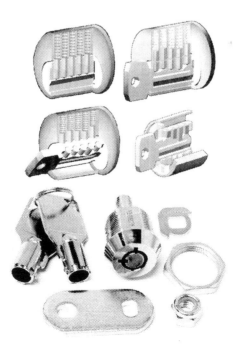

Figure 4.13 Tubular key locks are used on vending machines, file cabinets, pay phones, gun safes, and a variety of other containers.

Pick Guns and Snap Picks

Electric pick guns or *mechanical pick guns* (Figure 4.14) use the same principles as picking locks by hand. The pick extends slowly forward and, once it reaches its full forward travel, it snaps back out of the lock, raking all the pins as it extracts itself. The amount of force is often adjustable. When the *snapping pick* (Figure 4.15) hits the bottom pin the force is transferred to the top pin, causing it to move up and away from the bottom pin. When the top and bottom pins are apart at the same time, the slight turning pressure or torsion force applied with a tension wrench (Figure 4.9) will open the lock.

Snap picks (Figure 4.15) can be purchased or made from 0.025 × 0.125 inch steel strips by grinding the end to fit various keyways. It is then inserted

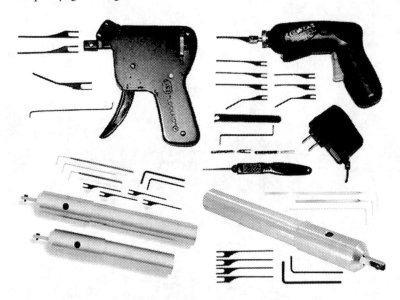

Figure 4.14 Electric pick guns or mechanical pick guns.

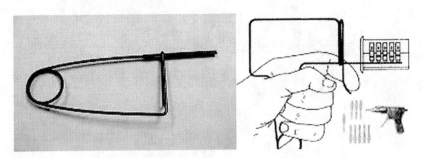

Figure 4.15 Snap picks.

into the keyway (the same as the pick gun), just touching the bottom pins. The spring is compressed. When the spring *springs* upward, it raps the pick end. A tension wrench provides light tension for turning force. The top pins should pop upward, making the shear line free to turn.

Schlage™ Disc Tumbler Lock

There are two types of keyway plugs or units in *disc tumbler* locks (Figure 4.16), each requiring a different cut on the *key blank* tip (ingeniously referred to as Type 1 and Type 2) from the same basic key blank (Figures 4.17 through 4.19). There are three different keyway types: (1) one *master tumbler* (always farthest tumbler in the plug), (2) three *series tumblers*, and (3) four *combination tumblers*.

Figure 4.16 Disc tumbler lock. (Used with permission (public domain): http:// en.wikipedia.org/wiki/Wafer_tumbler_lock#Types_and_Wafer_Arrangements.)

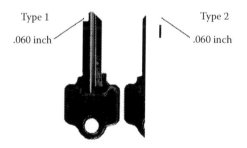

Type 1   Type 2
.060 inch   .060 inch

Figure 4.17 Type 1 and Type 2 key blanks.

.000   .000

Figure 4.18 Sketch of Type 1 and Type 2 key blanks.

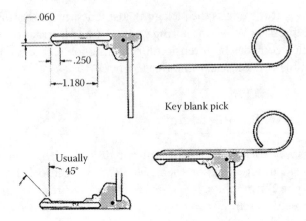

Figure 4.19 Key blanks pick.

The *master tumbler* (always farthest tumbler in the plug) and the three *series tumblers* are spring loaded to extend from the plug and prevent it from turning. When the proper key blank is inserted, the master tumbler *withdraws* into the plug. When an uncut key blank is inserted into the keyway, the master and three series tumblers are *withdrawn* into the plug. The four *combination tumblers* are spring loaded so that they are normally withdrawn into the plug. If an uncut key blank is inserted into the keyway, the tumblers *extend* from the plug. This becomes clearer once you begin to practice on these locks. To pick these locks, you need a set of picks designed for these types of locks.

First, you can make a set of *pick keys* by altering the *key blanks* (as shown in Figure 4.19) with a 0.060 inch deep cut on both sides. On the side of the tip cut, the entire key is removed to the same level as the tip cut, and on the opposite side, a 0.060 inch deep cut is made. A short piece of material (2–3 inches) is soldered or otherwise attached to the remaining portion of the bow to provide turning force to the plug during picking. Second, a *wire pick* can be made from a 0.060 inch diameter wire with a beveled tip (tapered to a point on one side).

You will not be able to determine from exterior observation whether the lock is a Type 1 or Type 2 lock. You will need to insert one of the two picks into the keyway. The correct pick key will withdraw the master tumbler and the combination tumblers. Holding the *pick key* in place, slide the *wire pick* into position. The resistance encountered while inserting the pick is the series tumblers withdrawing into the plug. If you feel resistance near the end of the travel of the pick toward the rear, the master tumbler indicates that you have chosen the wrong pick key. Repeat this step using the correct (the other) pick key. (See also Figures 4.20 through 4.27.)

Once you have the correct *pick key*, inserting the *wire pick* withdraws the series tumblers into the plug. The plug would turn now, but the wire pick

Figure 4.20 Cutaway view of a locking device.

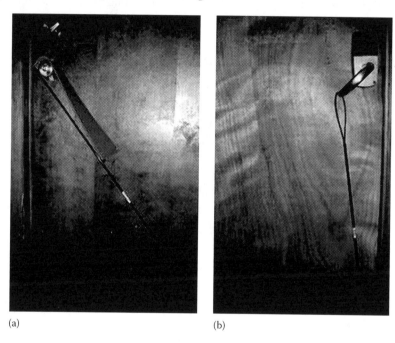

(a)   (b)

Figure 4.21 Knob tool (a) and lever tool (b) for door entries.

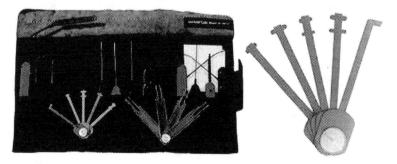

Figure 4.22 DAME lock pick set and close-up of warded key set.

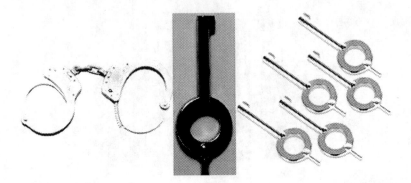

Figure 4.23 Handcuffs and handcuff keys (note the double-lock tab at one end).

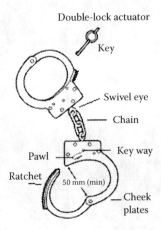

Figure 4.24 Anatomy of swivel-chain handcuffs.

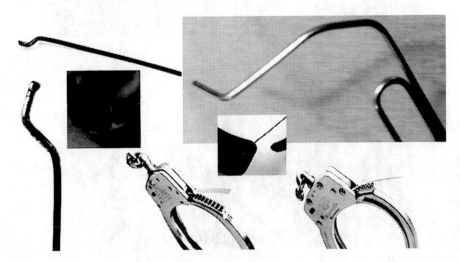

Figure 4.25 Illustration of picking handcuffs.

Figure 4.26 Handcuff shim pick and hinged cuffs.

Forced entry

Figure 4.27 Forced entry.

withdraws the series tumblers and forces the combination tumblers out of the plug. Exert slight clockwise turning tension to the *pick key* with the soldered lever and withdraw the wire pick. Slowly reduce the turning force until you hear the combination tumblers click back into the plug. The plug will now turn clockwise and open the lock.

How do you get to Carnegie Hall? Practice, practice, practice!

Forced Entry into Buildings

5

Aside from picking the locks, expedient forced entry into building can be accomplished by *jimmying* or *shimming* the door. If done well and with some luck, no marks will be detectable. Otherwise, the door, door frame, or nearby windows may be broken or marked.

Door Jimmy

The *jimmy* method involves prying the door jam or jacking it apart far enough (about an inch with mot locks) that the lock bolt no longer engages the striker plate. If a pry bar is used, the door stop is pried or slit away. A small auto jack may also be used by placing short pieces of 2 × 4 wood across the door, near the knob, and jacking the frame apart.

Door Shimming

Shimming is a method that uses a steel blade, wire, shim, or other tool to work the bolt back from the frame and striker plate enough to free the door. A curved linoleum knife or putting knife can work well. Once the dead-latch plunger is no longer engaged, the bolt can be forced back. The bolt plunger can be depressed ¼ inch or more, enough to move the bolt back and allow opening. Spreading can be done with a pry bar, but will probably leave marks. Simple wooden wedges leave less scarring and detection of entry. Wider wedges spread the force over a larger area and leave some marks. Commercially available wedges may also be used (Figures 5.1 through 5.3).

Inward opening doors usually have a spring latch bolt that can be opened with a Z-wire tool, which can be made from a piece of 0.062 wire. Hold the tool flat against the door and slide it under the stop and weather stripping (if any). When the 2-inch end of the Z wire is under the stop, it can be rotated back toward you at the top. The 2-inch end will rotate between the door and the jam to contact the beveled edge of the bolt. The bolt must not be binding in the striker plate. It may be necessary to apply pressure on the knob and to force the door up, down, in, and out. If the bolt is free and not bound, the Z wire will retract the bolt enough to allow the door to open.

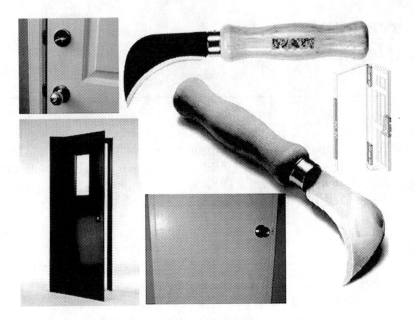

Figure 5.1 A common linoleum knife and door jam.

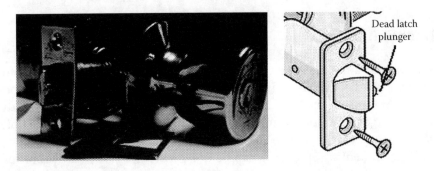

Figure 5.2 Door lock and dead-latch plunger.

Figure 5.3 Door wedge and door lock.

Cylinder Drill

If jimmying and shimming are not practical or possible, another method is to either drill or wrench out the cylinder. These methods will cause damage and are either last resorts or used for expedient forced entry. There are three common ways to drill the cylinder.

- First, drilling out the entire cylinder with a drill bit of that size (usually ½ inch).
- Second, drilling down the shear line (with a 1/8-inch drill bit) to drill through the pins.
- Third, inserting an uncut key blank into the keyway and lifting all the pins to the top, then drilling a 1/32-inch hole about 1/8 inch above the shear line. The hole must be perpendicular to the front surface and pass through all the top pins. A small wire can be inserted into the hole to hold the top pins when the key blank is extracted. When the bottom pins drop down, the shear line is unpinned and the cylinder will turn using a screwdriver.

Cylinder Wrench

The other method of expedient forced entry is wrenching. Again, this will cause damage and is a last resort. A rim cylinder is usually held by two screws, and a twisting force will shear off the screws or wrench off the cylinder, allowing the retaining plate to rotate and operate the lock. Large pliers, channel locks, or wrenches may be used to twist the cylinder. If a wrench-resistant steel collar is used, drill two 3/16-inch holes 7/8-inch apart on the face of the cylinder. Drive in two 3/16-inch by 1½-inch dowel pins. With about 1 inch protruding out, use a large pry bar or screwdriver between the dowel pins for leverage to wrench them.

Window Entry

Breaking glass is quick, but not very covert. However, in older windows with wooden frames, glass may be removed after chiseling away the putty and replacing the pane after completing the mission. Latches may be unlocked using a knife, putty knife, or similar tool between the upper and lower panes. Drilling a hole up, at an angle, through the wood frame, allows a wire or thin rod to be inserted through the hole to work the latch. A glass cutter can cut a hole in the glass and duct tape or suction cups can be used to remove the piece, allowing you to reach through. It can then be replaced, but is likely to be discovered eventually.

Office Equipment and Furniture

Office equipment and furniture, such as file cabinets and desks, may require surreptitious entry. If the filing cabinet is empty, it may be able to be unlocked by turning it upside down to release the locking mechanism. This is usually only practical if it is empty, but if it is empty, there would be little reason for covert entry.

There are many types of locking mechanisms for file cabinets and furniture, but most are similar. The locking bar is either moved up or down to engage vertical or horizontal *ramps* on the drawers. The locking bar is coupled to the lock by a link mechanism or cam. The locks usually have a spring-loaded bolt that engages when pushed in. The bolt is retracted by turning the cylinder in the lock. The primary difference in such locks is the position of the bolt. Some are up, some down, and some to the side. This can be determined by inserting a shim, feeler pick, or 1/8-inch diameter rod along the side of the lock (Figures 5.4 and 5.5).

Figure 5.4 File cabinet locking systems vary greatly.

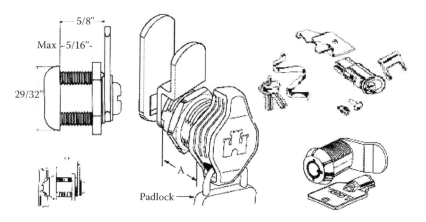

Figure 5.5 File cabinet locks also vary greatly.

Once you determine the position and distance of the bolt, you can bend the rod so that it can push the bolt in and pop the lock out into the unlocked position. However, some cabinets have brackets designed to prevent this method of covert access. An 18 inches tool that is ½–1 inch wide and 0.020 inch thick, made of flat spring stock, can be made so that the end will fit between the drawer ramp and the locking bar, allowing the ramp to ride over the locking bar.

If the bolt is in the top position and cannot be reached with a hooked tool, you may try drilling a hole downward through the top of the cabinet over the bolt. A thin rod or stiff piece of wire can be inserted through the hole to retract the bolt. A 0.025 inch by 3/16 inch wide flat spring stock with a beveled end can be used to access the bolt through the cylinder's keyway. The beveled end is used to engage the bolt and, with slight upward manipulation, should be able to retract the bolt enough to pop it out.

Most office desks, other furnishings, and home furniture with locks have conventional disc tumbler locks and can best be opened by traditional lock picking, as described earlier. Sometimes, the locks will actually have a code number stamped on the face identifying the key code. (How convenient!) If the lock on any of these is damaged, the drawers may have to be jimmied or the bolt may need to be sawed off. This, of course, is not very clandestine, but then neither is a cabinet or piece of furniture with an inoperable locking mechanism. Finally, the lock can be drilled. This is even less covert, but by this time stealth and secrecy may not be an option.

If you encounter a lock or locking mechanism that is beyond your skill level, you may seek advice or contract the services of someone (like a professional locksmith) who is more skilled. Auto dealers, apartment managers, and hotel managers may be able to supply keys to what you need to gain entry to. Keep in mind that they may want to share this adventure by telling someone (everyone) and may not be as confidential as you need. If the dealer or apartment complex has a security officer (often an off-duty police officer) or the hotel has a *house detective* (hotel detective who is often a retired cop), they may be bit more reliable and eager to help. We stayed at the Watergate Hotel once and one of the bellhops from the days of the infamous Watergate break-in scandal was still employed there. You might be surprised to find how eager some of the folks will be to share stories (and information) with you. Store detectives and mall security may be equally helpful. (It pays to have contacts.)

Oh, while we are on the topic of Watergate and history (at least while I am), it may be appropriate to provide at least one sobering reminder of the gravity of clandestine operations and the consequences of failing to comply with all the legal requirements of such operations. During the infamous Watergate scandal, when I was very young, I wrote a note to President Richard Nixon. He wrote back a very congenial letter, which I did not have the foresight to save. To avoid what he called a *constitutional crisis*, he wrote another letter not long after that. A copy is included here (Figures 5.6 and 5.7).

Figure 5.6 The infamous and still luxurious Watergate Hotel. (This book just would not be complete without mentioning the Watergate.)

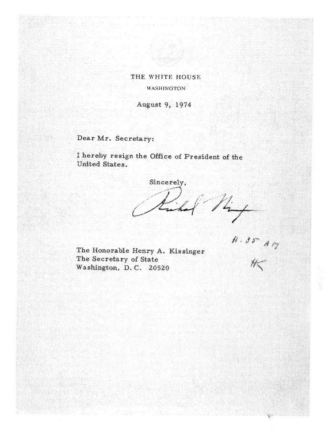

THE WHITE HOUSE
WASHINGTON

August 9, 1974

Dear Mr. Secretary:

I hereby resign the Office of President of the
United States.

Sincerely,

[signature: Richard Nixon]

11.35 AM

The Honorable Henry A. Kissinger
The Secretary of State
Washington, D. C. 20520

Figure 5.7 President Richard M. Nixon's letter of resignation following Watergate (initialed by Secretary of State Henry Kissinger).

Impressioning

Before discussing *lock bumping* it may be appropriate to take a moment to mention *impressioning* as an alternative. Impressioning can take two forms. The first is the use on a *key impression pad*, used to press a key to reveal the key pattern and copy it (Figure 5.8).

Key-based (copying) impressioning focuses on obtaining a key for a lock to duplicate it. A negative image of the key is created in a soft material, usually clay or silicone, and a duplicate key is cast using the negative image. The casted key can be used to open the lock or duplicated further into a stronger material (Figure 5.9).

The second type of impressioning involves impressing a mark on a key blank by twisting it firmly in the *plug* and moving it up and down to cause the mark on the blank. This action causes the marks to show on the top edge of the key blank blade. It is helpful to use a C-clamp, vise grips, or similar device to hold the key blank firmly. These impression marks are made by

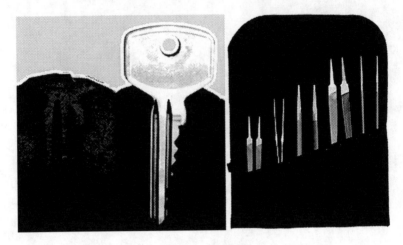

Figure 5.8 Key impression pad and impressioning tools.

Figure 5.9 Master key to the White House (on display in Key West, Florida).

binding the pins in the chamber as you twist the key side to side. The points of the *bottom pins* dig into the top edge of the key blank blade when moved up and down. Then the marks are filed down two or three strokes at a time, using a Swiss number four file. Be sure not to cut too deep, keeping the cuts smooth and only where the marks show. If the marks disappear, the pin is no longer binding and you look for where the next bind occurs. Continue the file cuts as each mark appears until the key is completed and works. This takes considerable time. Do not make the cuts too narrow or the pins may rest on the slope of the notch instead of the bottom (Russell, 1979, pp. 11–12).

Lock Bumping

Lock bumping is a lock picking technique for opening a pin tumbler lock using a specially crafted *bump key*. Bump keys are easy to make and can be created very quickly. They are keys in which all the cuts are at the maximum depth (999). They can be cut for standard pin tumbler type locks as well as *dimple* locks. The bump key pushes the pins up for a split second so that the plug can turn and the lock is opened. One bump key will work for all locks of the same type. With a bump key it will take only 1 minute or less for intruders to turn the lock and open the doors.

A 29-key *complete bumping set* (Figure 5.10) is available from various vendors, such as Bump-J (see http://bumpj.com/shop/product_info.php?products_id=62&osCsid=b3d3737c9f0914017e3978877595cd65) for about $50–$90. The vendor's ad (on the mentioned web page) says as follows:

> This is the Complete 29 Bump Key set. This bump key set has been cut slightly deeper then the factory deepest specs, and uses the pull back method. This set includes all keys listed on www.bump-j.com. Keys included: Schlage SC1 Bump Key Schlage SC4 Bump Key Schlage SC20 Universal Keyway Bump Key Arrow AR1 Bump Key Arrow AR4 Bump Key Kwikset KW1 Bump Key Kwikset KW10 Titan Bump Key Ilco IN3 Bump Key Ilco IN33 Bump Key Corbin-Russwin RU46 Bump Key Dexter DE6 Bump Key Yale Y1 Bump Key Lockwood L1 Bump Key Master M10 Bump Key Segal SE1 Bump Key National NA6 Bump Key S22-6 Bump Key S31 Bump Key WK2 Bump Key Weiser WR5 Bump Key Weiser WR4 Bump Key Master M1 Bump Key Best BE2 Bump Key Master M16 Bump Key American AM3 Bump Key American AM7 Bump Key National NA12 Bump Key Master M2 Bump Key Yale Y11 Bump Key.

From the earlier 29-key list (which is a little difficult to read, as is), the set includes the following:

1. Schlage SC1 bump key
2. Schlage SC4 bump key
3. Schlage SC20 universal keyway bump key
4. Arrow AR1 bump key

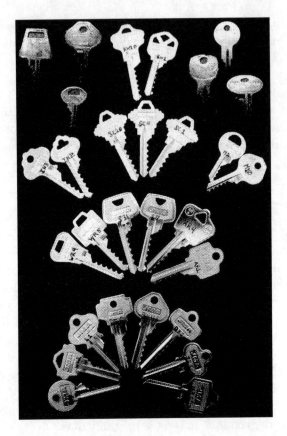

Figure 5.10 Twenty-nine (29) key set of bump keys.

5. Arrow AR4 bump key
6. Kwikset KW1 bump key
7. Kwikset KW10 Titan bump key
8. Ilco IN3 bump key
9. Ilco IN33 bump key
10. Corbin-Russwin RU46 bump key
11. Dexter DE6 bump key
12. Yale Y1 bump key
13. Lockwood L1 bump key
14. Master M10 bump key
15. Segal SE1 bump key
16. National NA6 bump key
17. S22-6 bump key
18. S31 bump key
19. WK2 bump key
20. Weiser WR5 bump key
21. Weiser WR4 bump key

22. Master M1 bump key
23. Best BE2 bump key
24. Master M16 bump key
25. American AM3 bump key
26. American AM7 bump key
27. National NA12 bump key
28. Master M2 bump key
29. Yale Y11 bump key

Bumping is not difficult, but as with most locksmith skills, it takes practice. Here are the four (or so) basic steps to follow:

- First, get a key blank or a spare key for the type of lock you want to bump, making sure the key you choose fits the lock you are attempting to defeat. If the key fits in the lock, there's a good chance it will work for this purpose.
  - Most locks of a particular model will accept all keys from that model because only the teeth of the keys are different.
  - That is, when you have a bump key for a lock manufactured by ABC, it may well open all other ABC-model locks.
- Second, choose a bump key. You have two options:
  - Buy the type of key for the model lock you are attempting to defeat and have a locksmith (or yourself, if you are skilled and have a lathe) lathe a 999 key, where all the valleys are at the deepest possible setting.
    - Asking for a 999 key might be a little obvious to an attentive locksmith.
  - Cut your own bump key.
    - Start with a copy of the key in question and use a metal file to create your own bump key by filing all the valleys down so that they are even with the lowest point in the teeth.
    - This homemade bump key may not necessarily open all locks for the model in question because a different lock may need a key with even lower valleys.
- Third, insert the key into the lock and pull it out one *click*, so it is almost in all the way, but not quite.
- Finally, push or pull on the edge of the key (applying tension or *torsion*) in the desired turning direction and strike (*bump*) the back end of the key with something solid (a tool or something handy).
  - The amount of tension required is equal to the amount of tension required to open the lock.

If done correctly, the key will turn in the direction it is being pushed or pulled in and the lock can then be opened. If not, repeat this procedure until it works.

Garage Door Openers: High-Tech Burglary

Most *garage door openers* are controlled by switches on the garage wall or remote controls. The electric overhead garage door opener was invented by C.G. Johnson in 1926 in Hartford City, Indiana. The first garage door opener controls were simple and consisted of a very simple remote and receiver, which controlled the opener mechanism. The transmitter transmitted on a designated frequency and the receiver received the signal and opened or closed the garage door.

The second generation of remote (wireless) garage door openers had a shared frequency problem, so multicode systems were developed which required the operator to preset a digital code by switching 8–12 DIP switches on the receiver and transmitter. While these switches provided garage door systems with $2^8 = 256$ to $2^{12} = 4096$ different codes, they were not designed with high security in mind. The intention was to avoid interference with similar nearby systems. Criminals were able to defeat the security of this system by trying different codes on a transmitter. They could also make code grabbers to record and retransmit a signal or use code scanners that would try every possible combination in a short time. Multicode openers became unpopular in areas where security was an issue, but due to their ease of programming, such openers are often still used to operate gates in gated apartment complexes and similar environments.

The third generation of garage door opener uses a frequency spectrum range between 100 and 400 MHz, and most of the transmitters/receivers rely on *hopping* or *rolling code* technology to prevent burglars from recording a code and replaying it to open a garage door. Because the signal is supposed to be significantly different from that of any other garage door remote control, manufacturers claim it is impossible for someone other than the owner of the remote to open the garage. When the transmitter sends a code, it generates a new code using an encoder. The receiver, after receiving a correct code, uses the same encoder with the same original *seed* to generate a new code that it will accept in the future. Because there is a high probability that someone might accidentally push the open button while not in range and desynchronize the code, the receiver generates look-a-head codes ahead of time. Rolling code is the same method of security used on the car remotes and with some Internet protocols for secure sites.

The fourth generation of garage door openers is similar to third generation, but is limited to the 315 MHz frequency. The 315 MHz frequency range avoids interference from the land mobile radio service (LMRS) used by the U.S. military. (Some sources report that ELSIMA units use 27.145 MHz narrow band FM, but this information is vague and uncorroborated.) (See Table 5.1.)

Many of garage door opener remote controls that use fixed-code encoding use DIP switches or soldering to do the address pins coding process and

Table 5.1 Garage Door Remote Opener Frequencies

Dates	System	Color of Programming Button (on Chamberlain Manufactured Units)
1984–2004	8–12 DIP switch on 300–400 MHz	White, gray, or yellow button with red LED
1993–1997	Billion code on 390 MHz	Green button and green or red LED
1997–present	Security+ (rolling code) on 390 MHz	Orange or red button with amber LED
2005–present	Security+ (rolling code) on 315 MHz	Purple button with amber LED
2011–present	Security+ 2.0 (rolling code) on 310, 315, and 390 MHz	Yellow button with amber LED and yellow antenna wires

they usually use pt2262/pt2272 or compatible ICs. These fixed-code garage door opener remotes can be cloned using a self-learning remote control duplicator (copy remote), which can make a copy of the remote using face-to-face copying. *Cloning* garage door remotes involves three key points:

1. The *operating frequencies* of both the copy remote and the original remote must be the same.
2. Only *fixed-code models* can be cloned; *rolling-code models*, which is also used on car remotes, is not supported.
3. The *code* of the copy remote must be cleared before the cloning procedure.

How to Change the Frequency for a Garage Door Opener (Instructions)

Genie Openers

1. Look for a small *black* button behind the lens light of the head receiver on the door opener, near the antenna. Press and hold this button until the light stops blinking.
2. Point the door opener remote toward the head receiver (2 feet or closer) and press the *Learn Code* button three times, then Pause.
3. Press the remote button once to test the new code.

Chamberlain, Sears, or LifeMaster Openers

1. Find a button labeled *Smart* or *Learn* on the motor unit of the door opener. Press it and then release it.
2. Press and hold the *Learn* button on the door opener remote within 30 seconds.

3. Release the *Learn* button when the motor unit light blinks or clicks twice, then Pause.
4. Press the remote button once to test the new code.

Garage door companies have created *rolling code* technology for better security. With this technology, the remote doesn't rely on a frequency only: A new code is generated every time you press the remote. To change the frequency and rolling code digits, look for a button on your remote labeled *Learn* or *Learn Code*. You may also need to access the motor head unit of the opener itself.

Levels of Security

Security against forced entry (burglary) follows three models: (1) The Five Ds (deter, detect, delay, deny, and destroy), (2) lines of defense (target hardening), and (3) internal and external threat identification (see Figure 5.11 and Table 5.2). Barriers, access control, lighting, alarms, surveillance cameras and monitors, etc. are all a part of denying access to a premises or structure.

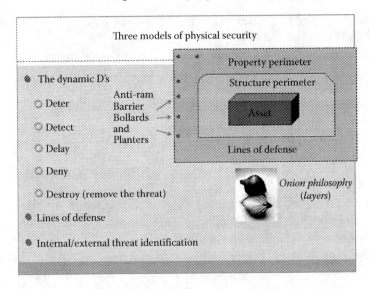

Figure 5.11 Three models of physical security.

Table 5.2   In-Car Camera Microphone Frequencies

MHz frequency range	2404.8–2475.0 MHz
GHz frequency range	2.4048–2.4750 GHz
Physical range	Approximately 1200 feet (line-of-sight)

Safes, Combinations, and Automobile Locks

6

Two common methods for opening safes are (1) by forced entry, such as drilling a hole through the door above the *fence* to examine and align the tumbler positions, and (2) by manipulation. The first method is not stealthy at all and leaves clear indication of entry (or attempted entry). The second method is more covert and leaves little or no trace. Safes are not the only artifacts that use combination locks. Luggage (such as brief cases or attaché cases), padlocks, furniture, and a variety of items use combination locks.

Forced Entry

The *rip job* or *peel job* is sometimes used for lightly constructed safes. A hole is drilled in the upper left corner of the front plate, which is usually riveted to the casing door. A long jimmy is inserted in the hole, and the tip of the plate is pried away from the casing. Once the plate is ripped or peeled away from the casing, the bolts are accessible and can be opened.

The *punch job* can be used on older insulated safes. The dial and ring are cut or chiseled off. A punch, smaller than the spindle, is driven through the door to punch out the spindle by driving the curb and tumblers from their seat in the lock case. Once the tumblers are removed, the fence drops to the unlocked position, and the safe can be opened. Newer and more expensive safes are designed to defend against this type of attack.

The *can opening* method involves turning the safe upside down and drilling a hole through the bottom. A 5 foot steel tool, resembling a big can opener, is inserted and used to cut out the light sheet metal bottom of the safe.

The *torch job* requires knowledge of the construction of the target safe. An oxyacetylene torch is used by the *burner* on *burglarproof* safes, but requires a great deal of skill and the equipment required is not easily concealable or conducive to covert action. Some burglars use this method.

Use of *explosives* is probably the most extreme and least covert method of attacking safes or vaults. In most cases, it should be considered a last resort and resorted to only by someone fully qualified to handle explosives. Extreme caution is required. One technique is to drill a hole above the dial and insert a glove finger (or similar delivery device) containing dynamite or nitroglycerine. When detonated, the lock mechanism is destroyed.

An antiburglar device is often used in safes to deter this method. A dynamite trigger is sometimes installed to jam the door by deadlocking the door when the lock is destroyed. This is only one drawback of this method. The danger and skill required are not the least of the other drawbacks. Again, stealth is not a characteristic commonly associated with this method. Explosives, particularly nitro, can also be used to fill the seams and blow the door off of the safe. The drawbacks are still pretty much the same.

Manipulation

Manipulation is the method of opening a combination lock using sight, sound, and touch and without the combination number. Sometimes, this is aided by a stethoscope or an electronic listening device (Figure 6.1). As with the lock-pick practice exercises, a combination lock should be set up for practice by mounting it on a stand of some type. First, it is important to know how a safe combination lock operates. The driving mechanism of a combination lock is made up of the dial, the spindle, and the driving cam.

To practice manipulation, begin with the cover plate removed from your practice lock. Pull the spline key out and unscrew the drive cam

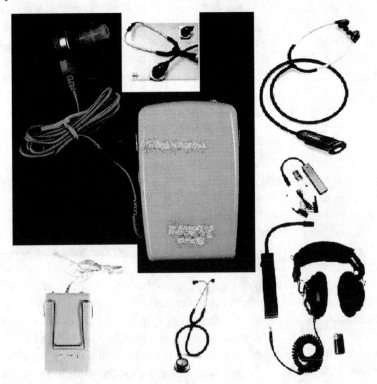

Figure 6.1 Electronic stethoscopes.

from the spindle. Pull the dial and spindle assembly out and set it aside for now. Remove the tube nuts and dial ring. Mark the removed tube and cut off 1/16 inch past the tube nut and file the cut end smooth, then mount the lock on your stand. Mount the dial ring with the remaining tube nut. Reinstall the dial and spindle in the tube, screw on the drive cam, and measure the length of the spindle that protrudes past the drive cam and cut it off (Anonymous, 1978, pp. 5–6).

As the dial is turned, the *driving cam* moves in the same direction as it is keyed to the spindle. Once the cam sets the last tumbler in place, the dial is rotated slowly to the left until the *gate* of the cam reaches the same position as the gates of the tumblers. Continued movement of the dial to the left draws the *fence* down and moves the bolt to the open position. Turning the door handle releases the bolts and opens the safe.

When turning the dial one complete turn, the *drive cam* contacts the *third wheel* and it starts turning. Another complete turn causes the third wheel to contact the *second wheel* and it starts turning. On the third complete turn, the second wheel contacts the *first wheel* and all three wheels, the drive cam, and the dial all turn as one unit.

Looking at only the dial, turn it (at least) four times to the right and stop on 0 (zero). Next, turn back to the left to 90 and then turn quickly past 0. As you pass 0, you should hear and feel the *drive cam* as it contacts the *third wheel*. Continue to the left to 90 and then turn quickly past 0 (again). You should feel the third wheel contacts the second wheel. Repeat this once again, and you should feel the second wheel contacts the first wheel. If you repeat this procedure a fourth time, you should not feel or hear anything as the dial passes 0 if the lock is a three-wheel lock. Repeating these steps of passing 0 until no more wheels are detected is important because it reveals how many wheels the lock has.

Once you feel competent with this, replace the cover plate on the lock and reset the combination (or have someone else do so), following the changing instructions given here or that come with your lock. Using graph paper, you can now chart a graph of each number in the combination. Note that the *drive cam* can be keyed to the *spindle* in four different positions (each 90° apart on the dial) and the dial may read one of the four different numbers.

- Turn the dial left at least four times, until all the wheels are turning, and stop at 0.
- Turn to the right to the contact point and record the dial reading.
- Turn back to the left, past 0, and stop at 2½.
- Turn to the right to the contact point and record that reading.
- Turn left again, past 2½, and stop at 5.
- Turn right to the contact point and record that reading.
- Repeat this until you move the wheels to the left and record contact points every 2½ numbers.

When you pass the contact point you will have only a short distance to turn right for a contact point reading (Anonymous, 1978, p. 25).

The next step is to make a *magnifying graph* to get more precise in each particular area. To find which wheel is *indicating*, use this process of elimination:

- Turn the dial left at least four times, stopping at your first reading (from your first graph).
- Turn right one turn, picking up the third wheel at your reading and past about 10 numbers.
- Turn left to the contact point and take a reading.
- Repeat this process after picking up the third wheel, turning one more revolution to the right to pick up the second wheel.
- Turn back left to the contact point and take a reading. (A high reading would indicate that the second wheel is indicating and a low reading would indicate that the first wheel is.)
- Make another graph to plot the readings of the first and second wheels (Anonymous, 1978, p. 26).

With the *third wheel* now set to the combination number determined with the graph, read the first and second wheels every 2½ numbers.

- Turn right (at least) four times and stop at 0 (zero).
- Turn left one turn, picking up the third wheel at 0 and stop at the previously recorded reading.
- Turn right to the contact point and record the reading of the second number.
- Repeat this process until you complete a graph of every 2½ numbers around the dial.

Do another *magnifying graph* of this area for the second number (if the reading is low, wheel one is indicating; if the reading is high, wheel two is indicating).

- Turn the dial (at least) four times to the left, stopping at the previously recorded reading.
- Turn the dial one turn right, picking up the *third wheel*, and continue right one more turn to pick up the *second wheel* at the previously recorded number.
- *Wheel two* is carried past that point approximately 10 numbers (lower).
- Turn left one turn to pick up the *third wheel* (at that lower number) and continue to the number determined for *wheel three*.

- Turn right to the contact point and take a dial reading (determining the second combination number) (Anonymous, 1978, pp. 29, 31).

Now that the third and second numbers are known, the first number can now be determined by trying every 2½ numbers, using the known numbers for the second and third numbers.

- Turn the dial (at least) four times to the left, stopping at 0.
- Turn right past the third known number two turns and stop on the third known number the third time.
- Turn left past second known number and stop on that number the next time.
- Turn back right to the drop-in position and quickly turn the dial between the two contact points. (In cases where the combination is close, but not exact, this may work the *fence* into the *gates*.)
- Repeat this process, setting the number on 2½.
- Continue dialing this combination, but advancing the first number 2½ numbers each time until the lock opens (Anonymous, 1978, p. 31).

Manipulation resistant locks (usually called *manipulation proof* by manufacturers) may be indicated by the addition of a pointer knob in the center of the dial. The manufacturer has tightened up the tolerances and added mechanical features that (1) prevent the reading of contact points and/or (2) provide false sound or feel readings. Such measures make it more difficult to manipulate these locks and make the process much longer. This is a part of the process of *target hardening*. While it may not be impossible to defeat, the security measures make the process more difficult and time-consuming, thus increasing the chances of failure and detection.

In such locks, the *drive cam* is often altered by making it a two-piece moving part (the inner and outer slide) with a spring. These slides are actuated by a shaft extending through the center of the spindle to a small pointed knob in the center of the dial knob. The lock is normally opened using the combination and turning the dial to 0, the drop-in position, and turning the pointed knob to the right. The inner slide is withdrawn and exposes the drop-in opening in the *drive cam*. The *fence* drops into the *gates* and allows the *lever nose* to engage the *drive cam*. Turning the dial CLOCKWISE withdraws the bolt (Anonymous, 1978, p. 34).

The lock has all the features for contact point reading, but they are concealed by the inner cam slide. The outer slide has a tab that matches the radial groove in the cover plate, which restricts the actuation of the cam slide. To expose the drive cam and contact points, you must return to 0 and withdraw the inner cam slide with the pointed knob in the center of the dial. Now if you turn the dial COUNTERCLOCKWISE you should *feel* a contact point, but the radial groove in the cover plate restricts dial rotation with the tab on the outer slide. This does not permit the lever nose to touch the contact points (Anonymous, 1978, pp. 35–36).

Combination Dial Lock

Combination locks are used on everything from padlocks and luggage to safes and vaults. They may use a simple series (three to five) of wheels (Figures 6.2 through 6.4) or a dial (Figures 6.5 through 6.9). Padlocks and luggage may use a simple set of wheels that can be defeated with a little effort and patience. If you have the time and patience, a rotary combination lock with three dials (each side) can be opened simply by dialing in all 1000 possible combinations (000–999). This takes about a half hour of perseverance.

Figure 6.2 Sesame combination locks.

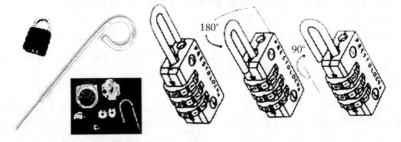

Figure 6.3 Combination locks and change pin.

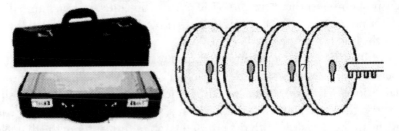

Figure 6.4 Many items of luggage use rotary combination locks.

Figure 6.5 Most combination locks use a wheel pack like this.

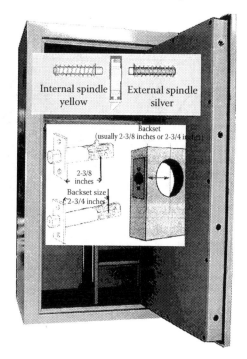

Figure 6.6 Spindle safe.

Figure 6.7 Digital and dial lock safes.

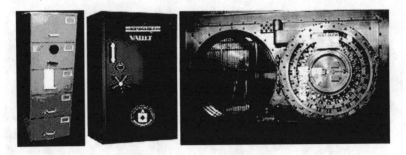

Figure 6.8 Dial lock file cabinet, safe, and vault.

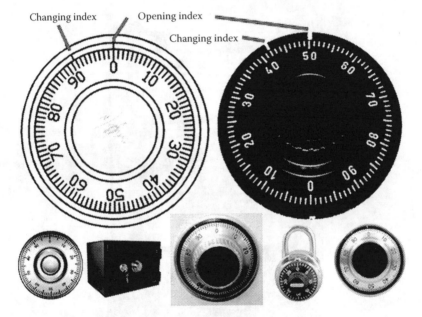

Figure 6.9 Combination lock dial.

Safes and Vaults

Safe and vault panels earn UL (Underwriters Laboratories) approval by withstanding severe torch and tool attacks and meeting insurance standards. They are rated as follows:

- Class M—15 minutes
- Class I—30 minutes
- Class II—60 minutes
- Class III—120 minutes

A cutaway view of a dial combination lock (Figure 6.10) shows the key parts and functions of such a lock. When the combination has been dialed in and the dial is returned to the drop in position, the *lever nose* drops into the *cam gate*. With the three wheels lined up, the *fence* drops into the *cam gate* and the *lever nose* engages the *cam drive*. With the fence dropped in and the drive cam engaged, a clockwise turn of the dial will retract the *lock bolt*, unlocking the lock (note: If the cover is removed from your practice lock, you may need to manually disengage the *relock lever* before retracting the bolt) (Figure 6.11).

To manipulate the lock (with the cover plate still removed), first, move the dial and wheels so that all of the *gates* are away from the *fence*. The *lever nose* contacts the *drive cam* and holds the *fence* from contacting the wheels (*wheel pack* and *wheel combination gate*). Second, rotate the dial and *cam*

Figure 6.10 Dial combination lock.

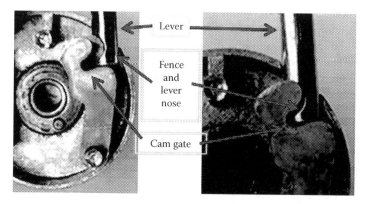

Figure 6.11 Fence lever and gate.

drive (without moving the wheels) until it reaches the drop-in position. The *lever* is now lower and the *fence* makes contact with the wheels.

Any variation in the wheel diameters will vary the degree to which the *lever nose* protrudes into the opening of the *drive cam*. The variance in *lever* travel can be read on the dial by turning it to the contact point and taking a reading (Anonymous, 1978, p. 15).

The *lever* pivots on the shoulder screw or *lever screw*. To pivot freely there must be some clearance in the diameter between the hole in the lever and the screw, also giving the lever a little sideways *wobble*. To demonstrate this, set up the practice lock again, with the *gates* away from the *fence*, the *lever nose* in the drop-in position of the *drive cam*, and the *fence* resting on the wheels. Take a reading on both contact points and record the readings. Rotate the third wheel only until its *gate* aligns with the *fence*. You should see the *lever wobble* enough to allow the nose to drop a little more into the cam opening. Take another set of readings on the contact points and compare them with the first set. One will be lower and one higher. The contact point is usually the best to use for manipulation (Anonymous, 1978, pp. 15–16).

Changing the Combination of a Dial Combination Lock

Caution: *Never* insert the *Changing Key* in the lock when the cover is removed. Make certain that the *wing* of the *Changing Key* is entirely in the lock before turning the key (Figure 6.12).

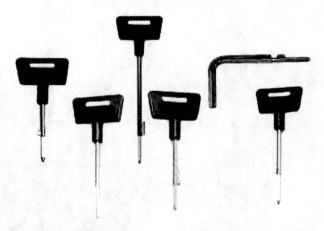

Figure 6.12 Change keys.

First, refer to the *opening index* and the *changing index* on the dial (Figure 6.9). Extreme precision must be used in aligning the combination numbers with the index. (Note: If, after turning the dial the correct number of revolutions, any of the numbers is turned beyond the *opening index*, the entire series of combination numbers must be redialed. Do NOT turn back the dial to try to regain the proper alignment with the numbers.) Each time a correct number is aligned with the *opening index*, one revolution is counted.

To unlock the factory settings (often set on 50 at the factory), turn the dial to the left four full revolutions and stop when the factory setting (e.g., 50) is aligned with the *opening index*, then turn slowly to the right until it stops. *To unlock a three-number combination* (e.g., 36–24–34)

- Turn the dial left until 36 is aligned with the *opening index* after the fourth revolution.
- Turn the dial right until 24 is aligned with the *opening index* after the third revolution.
- Turn the dial left until 34 is aligned with the *opening index* after the second revolution.
- Turn the dial slowly to the right until it stops.

To lock again, turn the dial to the left at least four full revolutions.

To change the combination you, obviously, start by choosing the new numbers in the combination. Do NOT select numbers between 0 and 20 for the last numbers. A more secure combination does NOT use numbers ending in 0 or 5 and does NOT use numbers in ascending or descending sequence (e.g., 25, 50, 75 or 50, 40, 30).

- Using the *changing index*, dial in the current combination numbers (as explained earlier in the unlocking sequence).
  - Locks leave the factory with all three numbers set, usually all three at 50.
  - When setting the combination for the first time, turn the dial left and stop at the preset number (e.g., 50) after the fourth revolution.
- Hold the dial with the last number at the *changing index*, and insert the *changing key* in the hole in the back of the lock until the wing is entirely inside the lock and it comes to a stop.
- Turn the key a quarter turn to the left and with the *changing key* in this position
  - Turn the dial to the left
  - Stop at the *changing index* upon the fourth revolution.

- Turn the dial to the right and stop when the second number is aligned with the *changing index* after the third revolution.
- Turn the dial to the left and stop when the third number is aligned with the *changing index* after the second revolution.
  - Holding the dial in this position, turn the *changing key* back to the right and remove it.

The new combination is now set. *Before closing, try the new combination several times* using the *opening index* to ensure it works correctly before closing the door (and locking yourself out).

If an error is made, contact a certified locksmith or, if one is not available or practical, try the following:

- Remove the two screws on the back of the lock and remove the cover.
- Using a tool or straightened paperclip, insert the tool into the square keyways or the square slots in the wheels.
- Rotate each wheel until all the slots are in alignment and the square keyways are over the small hole in the bottom of the case.
- Replace the cover and screws and insert the *changing key.*
- Repeat the last three steps in the steps described earlier for changing the combination (Figures 6.13 and 6.14).

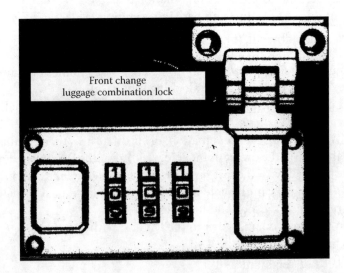

Figure 6.13 Front change luggage combination lock.

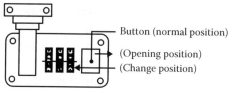

Button (normal position)
(Opening position)
(Change position)

OPERATING INSTRUCTIONS
FRONT CHANGE COMBINATION LOCK
The locks are set at the factory to open at O-O-O. They will, however, close on any setting.

TO SET YOUR OWN COMBINATION
(1) Choose 3 digits which you can recall easily—address, phone, birthday, etc.

(2) Press the button in a direction toward the dial with your thumb and holding with your other hand (use point of ball pen) rotate the dials to the desired setting. Then, release the button.

(3) Your lock is now set to open on the three digits engaged at the time you release the button.

CAUTION
(4) Your locks are equipped with SCRAMBLE FEATURE for ADDED SECURITY. They are designed to CLOSE on ANY SETTING.

(5) Rotating the dials (scrambling) after having opened the lock will prevent others from recognizing your set combination while your case stands open.

(6) You need not recall your combination to close the lock.

(7) Accordingly, NEVER rotate the dials with the button held open UNLESS you make careful note of the dial setting upon release of the button.

(8) The manufacturer is not responsible for damage resulting from misuse, abusive handling, or failure to follow instructions.

Figure 6.14 Directions for changing front change luggage combination lock.

Locking System for Automobiles

Locking mechanisms on motor vehicles did not change or evolve much from their inception through the 1950s. After that, door locks were either (a) push button on the window sill, (b) a lever on the door panel, or (c) a reverse movement of the inside door handle. Windows were either (a) vent and frame windows, (b) one-piece front windows, (c) door post windows (front and rear), or (d) front and rear windows separated by a weather strip. Doors could often be opened with a mere coat hanger. Trucks had locks that were keyed with the door lock keys and were often punched.

Today, door locks are *automatic*, windows are usually power operated, and even the trunks have remote control access. Many door locks have combination and keyless entry devices. Some have antitheft mechanisms designed to prevent keyless entry. Since the 1970s steering columns have added security measures to prevent unauthorized operation and steering wheel locks and GPS trackers have added to automobile security systems (not to mention the constantly annoying car alarms).

A variety of tools are available for entry into automobiles and other vehicles. *Slim jims* and other devices are used to open door locks through windows. Others are used to open the locks themselves. Still others are used on the trunks and ignitions or to disable alarms and other access control devices.

Key Codes

Key code information identifies the keys that go with a particular motor vehicle. Sometimes you can easily find the key codes on the first or second page of the owner's manual or *warranty book*. Key codes may be obtained from the title clerk of the dealership where the vehicle was purchased. By providing the title clerk with the name of the purchaser, the date of purchase, and the serial number (*vehicle identification number* or *VIN*), the clerk should be able to obtain the key codes from the purchase contract. Used cars are little harder. It may be necessary to locate the original dealer through the Bureau of Motor Vehicles or DMV (Russell, 1979, p. 62).

Ignition Locking Systems

In popular media, it is common to *hot-wire* vehicles by twisting two wires together causing ignition. Most vehicles today have antitheft devices making this less practical. Most car thieves simply pop the column next to where the key is inserted (Figure 6.15) and use a screwdriver to activate the ignition like a switch (Figure 6.16). Hot-wiring generally involves connecting the two wires, which complete the circuit when the key is in the *on* position (turning on the fuel pump and other necessary components), then touching the wire that connects to the starter (Figure 6.17). The specific method of hot-wiring a vehicle is dependent on the particular vehicle's electrical ignition system. You may want to experiment with different types of vehicles (perhaps in a salvage yard or tow lot). Reviewing manufacturer's manuals

Figure 6.15 Typical ignition and door locks and keys.

Figure 6.16 Auto door locks, keys, and a remote.

Figure 6.17 Ignition system.

and replacement parts or catalogs at auto parts stores may be helpful to update your knowledge as things change (such as keyless entry).

Doors and Trunks

Doors may be opened without manipulating the locks. There are various opening devices, *slim jims*, wedges, and other tools for entry (Figures 6.18 and 6.19). *Caution*: Use of *slim jim* type devices may activate air bags in modern vehicles. Bladder and wedge kits may be the preferred method. Different manufacturers of automobiles use various types of locking systems. Volkswagen, for example, has commonly used *wafer tumbler locks*, while Ford and Chrysler have commonly used *pin tumbler locks*. General Motors (GM) and American Motors (AM) have traditionally used *side-bar locks*.

Figure 6.18 Auto locksmith tool kits (including *slim jims*).

Figure 6.19 Auto window bladder, wedges, and shutter tool set.

Pin Tumbler Locks for Autos

Pin tumbler lock systems have been used by Ford and Chrysler ignition and trunk locks for decades. There are some exceptions to this, depending on the year and model. The pin tumbler has a *plug* or *cam* and an outer cylinder or *shell*. A series of two-piece tumblers (as many as five) extend into the plug and have a bottom pin and a driver pin (top pin). The springs rest on the top of the driver pin and are held in place by a spring retainer clip (Figure 6.20).

Side-Bar Locks for Autos

Side-bar lock systems have been used by GM and the now-defunct AM. These too have a *plug* and a *shell*. The side-bar lock is a modified wafer system of wafer tumblers or side-bar discs (five in the AM and six in GM products).

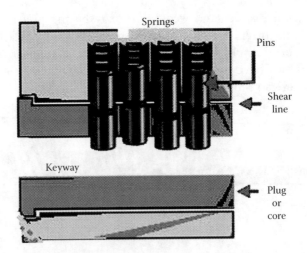

Figure 6.20 Pin tumbler system.

These side-bar discs are mounted in the plug of the locks and are also spring-loaded and have a spring retainer. The sidebar is also mounted in the plug. When the key is inserted into the keyway, the side-bar discs or wafers are raised or lowered, allowing the sidebars to hold the discs in a straight line so the plug can turn (Figures 6.21 and 6.22). (Please note that with time, technology and designs change. Newer models of autos may not be equipped with these types of locks.)

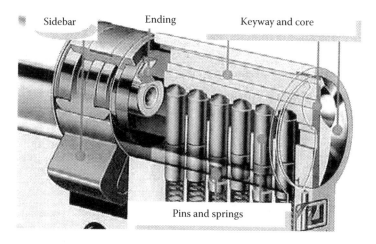

Figure 6.21 Side-bar locking system.

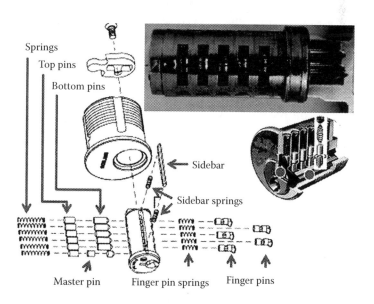

Figure 6.22 Sidebar locks.

Wafer Tumbler Locks for Autos

The wafer tumbler system has rarely been used for automobiles, except Volkswagens. This lock system, however, has been discussed elsewhere in this work.

Hacking Car Keyless Entry Systems

Researchers discovered how to break into cars that use radio frequency technology to open the doors and start it. By stringing a piece of cable between the car and the car's key fob, they were able to open a car and start it, because the cable acts as an antenna and retransmits the signal from the key.

A more sophisticated method involved setting up a radio receiver near the key to pick up the signal the fob transmits or emits. The computer, along with an antenna and of course special software, was able to extract a code that was transmitted by a radio frequency identification (RFID) chip located in the key. Converting the signal to one of higher frequency (to boost its range) enables transmission to another receiver near the car. That receiver retransmits the open command to the car. This method does not rely on breaking the encryption in the transmission between key and car. All that the thief has to do is retransmit it.

The problem is that the radio signal, the key, and the car use is at a frequency of 130 kHz (kilohertz) (about the middle of the *AM* radio dial) and it is short range because it is generated by an *induction coil* rather than a regular radio transmitter. This is because constant transmitting would drain the car's battery and the car makers didn't want the range to be too far. The short range of the signal offers some security. In order for the car to open, the key has to be able to pick up the signal and the car must be able to hear the key's answer. For that to happen, the car and keys must be within a few yards or less of each other. Security is compromised because there is no way to turn it off; the key and car are always transmitting to each other. The range on the key signal, however, was great enough that the team was able to open a car from a key left on a kitchen table inside the house.

Psychological Operations and Social Networks

7

Psychological Operations

Psychological operations (PSYOPs) are planned propaganda operations to convey purposeful information to designated audiences. It is the application of social psychology, sociology, and political psychology to influence individuals, groups, organizations, and governments in their motives, reasoning, emotions, and behavior. It is the deployment of the power of persuasion, use of motivation, and manipulation of communications sciences to influence an agenda.

U.S. Army Field Manual 31-20, Special Forces Operational Techniques, says,

> Basically, psychological operations is [sic] concerned with persuading people, or groups of people, to take actions favorable to one's interests. In an insurgent situation, psychological operations can be called upon to persuade the people of the area to actively and willingly cooperate with the local government, disrupt the efforts of the insurgent, and assist in separating the insurgent from other elements of the nation's population.

It goes on to say that,

> In an unconventional warfare role psychological operations are designed to achieve just the opposite effects: disassociation of the people with the government in power, creation of shared goals for the resistance movement and the population, and mutual help and cooperation between the guerrillas and the people to disrupt the efforts of the common enemy. (FM 31-20, 1971, p. 19)

The purpose of military PSYOPs is to induce or reinforce behavior that is favorable to military objectives. PSYOPs are also a critical part of the diplomatic, informational, and economic activities available to the government, particularly military, intelligence, and diplomatic agencies. They are utilized in both peacetime and during conflicts and have three perspectives: strategic, operational, and tactical. *Strategic PSYOPs* include informational activities conducted by government agencies outside of the military arena.

Operational PSYOPs are conducted in support of military operations, including during peacetime, in a defined operational area to promote the effectiveness of the joint force commander's (JFC) campaigns and strategies. *Tactical PSYOPs* are conducted in the area assigned to a tactical commander to support the tactical mission against OPFORS.

PSYOPs promote discontent with the opposition's leadership by combining persuasion with a credible threat and degrade an adversary's ability to conduct or sustain its own operations. PSYOPs disrupt, confuse, and protract the adversary's decision-making process and have the potential to lower OPFORS' morale, efficiency, and will to fight. PSYOPs include *information operations* (IOs), such as electronic warfare, computer network operations, deception, and operations security (OPSEC) to influence or disrupt OPFORS decision making.

PSYOPs use carefully crafted and disseminated *product messages.* There are three types of *propaganda* used to create these messages. White, gray, and black do not refer to the propaganda's content, but the methods used to carry out the operation. (1) *White* propaganda is (a) true and factual, (b) used in overt operations, and (c) acknowledged as an official statement or act and reflects an official viewpoint. (2) *Gray* propaganda is of a source that is deliberately ambiguous; the true source is not revealed to the target audience and the activity appears to plausibly emanate from a nonofficial source, an indigenous, nonhostile source, or no attribution is made at all. (3) *Black* propaganda is used in covert PSYOPs and appears to emanate from a source (government, organization, group, or person), which is concealed or denied. Covert PSYOPs are used in special operations and are politically sensitive.

In order for PSYOPs to be successful, they must be based in reality and all messages must be consistent and not contradictory. A *credible truth* must be presented, which is consistent to all audiences. Counter information can be used defensively and in support of special operations, unconventional warfare, and counterinsurgency (COIN) operations. They include strikes and raids, counterterrorism operations, enforcement of sanctions and maritime interception operations, peacekeeping operations, and noncombatant evacuation. The PSYOP process (usually) involves (at least) 10 steps (Figure 7.1):

1. Clearly define the mission and objectives.
2. Prepare an estimate of the situation.
3. Prepare a plan of operations.
4. Determine the available and best suited media.
5. Develop a message product.
6. Pretesting to determine the probable impact on the target audience.

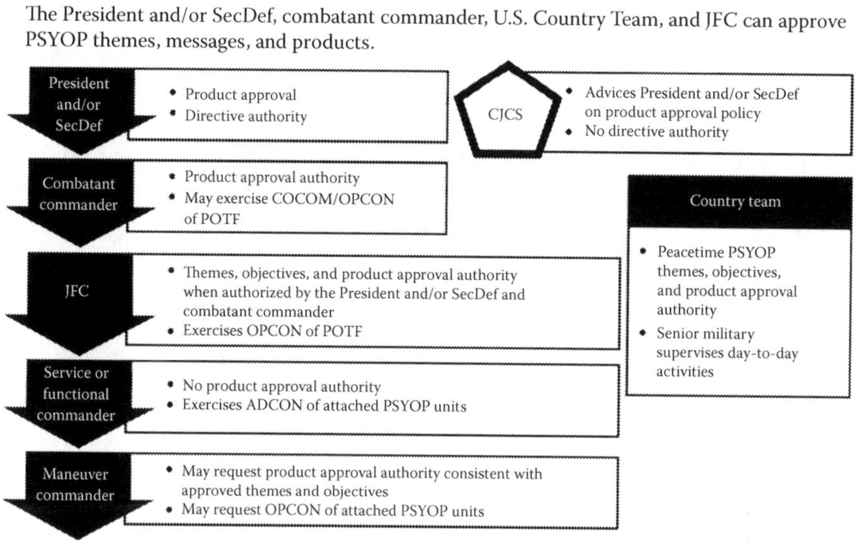

The President and/or SecDef, combatant commander, U.S. Country Team, and JFC can approve PSYOP themes, messages, and products.

Figure 7.1 U.S. army FM 3-05.30 psychological operations. (Available at http://www.fas.org/irp/doddir/army/fm3-05-30.pdf, 2005.)

7. Production and dissemination of PSYOP material (propaganda).
8. Implementation of the plan and operation.
9. Posttesting to evaluate audience responses.
10. Debrief and analyze feedback to determine any modifications to be implemented.

Military PYSOPs: Psychological Warfare

Psychological warfare has been used since the wars of ancient Asia, the Bible, Alexander the Great, and before. They were prominent in WWII and typified personas, such as *Tokyo Rose*. It involves the use of military, political, and economic means to a tactical or strategic advantage. Sun Tzu said that the best kind of victory was one in which you never have to fight.

Social psychology is the scientific study of how people's thoughts, feelings, and behaviors are influenced by actual, imagined, or implied social or behavioral factors. *Social psychology* is an interdisciplinary field combining psychology and sociology. Social psychologists explain human behavior in terms of the interaction of psychological and social factors. During the years immediately following WWII, there was frequent collaboration between psychologists and sociologists, particularly in the areas of motivation, communications, and persuasion.

Motivation is the driving force by which we achieve our goals. It is the intrinsic or extrinsic causes for behavior. According to behavioral science theories, motivation may be based on a basic need to minimize physical pain and maximize pleasure and may include (1) specific needs, such as eating and resting; (2) a desired object, goal, state of being, and ideal; or (3) less-apparent factors, such as altruism, selfishness, morality, or immortality. Motivation should not be confused with volition or optimism; although related to emotion, it is distinct from it.

Communications is the articulation and sending of a message, by verbal or nonverbal means. Communication is the process by which any message is given or received through talking, writing, or gestures. It can be defined as the process of interaction, the act of passing information, and the process by which meanings are exchanged so as to produce understanding.

Persuasion is an active method of influence that attempts to guide people toward the adoption of an attitude, idea, or behavior by rational or emotive means. Persuasion relies on *appeals* rather than strong pressure or coercion.

Propaganda and Counterpropaganda

Black propaganda purports to emanate from a source other than the true one and is used most often to support strategic plans. *Gray propaganda* does not identify and cannot be identified with a source. Clandestine radio is a major medium for disseminating both black and gray propaganda. Both are also tools for the use of tactical deception, that is, the dissemination of information that supports or confirms the deception story and its objectives. Behavior factors that are important include perception, motivation, frustration, and attitude. Communications can arouse needs and emotions to persuade a target audience to change attitudes and behavior.

Propaganda is the *sales pitch* or the message (point of view) that involves the deliberate spreading, by any means of communication, the doctrine, ideas, facts, argument, information, allegations, or appeals to advance a proponent's cause or inure an opponent's cause. Propaganda must (1) be based in reality, (2) be credible and not contradictory, (3) gain attention immediately, (4) awaken awareness, and (5) reinforce and give permanence to actions.

Counterpropaganda is designed to counteract an opponent's propaganda and exploit its vulnerabilities. Techniques include (1) conditioning (education and information), (2) forestalling (counteracting), (3) minimizing the subject (emphasizing the favorable aspects, insinuating that the entire story cannot be told at this time, and/or briefly mentioning the story and dropping it), (4) direct refutation (point by point), (5) indirect refutation (introduction of new, relevant themes), (6) diversionary propaganda (divert attention), (7) imitative deception (alteration of the opponent's propaganda to give a different slant that appears to be from the same source), (8) silence (ignore it), and (9) restrictive measures (isolate or deny access to the target audience).

Political PYSOPs

Political psychology is an interdisciplinary field that studies the relationship between psychological factors and political factors, with an emphasis on human thought, emotion, and behavior in politics. It is the analysis of political issues and factors.

Political warfare is the use of political means to compel an opponent to do one's will. The term *political* refers to the calculated interaction between a government and a target audience, including another country's government or general population. Governments use a variety of tactics and techniques to coerce actions and gain an advantage over an opponent. *Psychological manipulation* is a type of social influence with the goal of changing the perceptions or behavior of others through deception.

Lawfare is the use of domestic or international law to harass or damage an opponent, such as winning a public relations victory, depleting an opponent's finances, or manipulating the opponent's time so that they are distracted from implementing their opposing objectives. One example of *lawfare* involved former U.S. Secretary of State Henry Kissinger when he faced questioning and possible prosecution in France, Brazil, and England (initiated by Spanish magistrate Baltasar Garzón) because of Kissinger's involvement as a Nixon administration official with a South American program of abductions, torture, and assassinations known as Operation Condor. Kissinger warned that *universal jurisdiction* risks "substituting the tyranny of judges for that of governments."

Techniques of Harassment and Revenge: The Dirty Tricks Department

The Kennedy Administration used the CIA to plan an operation to cause Cuban dictator Fidel Castro's beard to fall out as a *dirty trick* designed to embarrass Castro and eliminate his symbol of personal charisma. A decade later, the Committee to Re-elect the President (CREEP) effectively used techniques of harassment to distract members of the DNC in the 1972 election (until the Watergate affair erupted). CREEP followed opposing candidates around to implement distracting harassment techniques, such as canceling hotel reservations, ordering pizzas to be delivered and billed to opponents, and putting controversial bumper stickers on cars at rallies.

In the 1970s, there was a series of books on techniques of harassment and revenge (by those titles), which outlined various tactics for exactly that: harassment and revenge. Many of the techniques employed could be referred to as the *poor man's PSYOPs* and could rank right up there with those employed by Kennedy's CIA experts and CREEP. While many of the techniques are outdated, with the evolution of society and technology, many are timeless and are worth knowing, especially if you are an intelligence officer, law enforcement investigator, security consultant, political advisor, or anyone who wants to defend themselves from such *tricks*.

A college acquaintance I once knew initiated an action against one of his former *friends* (a professor). It was a devious and brutal plan and the target was miserable for months. I think he even lost his job and moved away. Oh, and the instigator... he's dead. He died at home alone and lonely. Moral of the story: tend toward the side of the morally right. If in doubt, choose righteousness over revenge. I will not take this opportunity to lecture on morality, ethics, or the righteousness of anyone's cause. Hopefully, each reader has a moral compass that discerns right and wrong. Choose the high road and do not involve innocent people (such as family members or persons who will lose something without being involved). I am also going to save a lecture on the legality of such tactics for another lecture. You should always consult competent legal counsel for any legal questions. If your objective is to disrupt the elections in Columbia or Iran, well, you better talk with someone at a higher pay grade. Our objective here is awareness, that is, awareness of the techniques of harassment and revenge available from the *dirty tricks department*.

Experts from the *dirty tricks department* will tell you that the objective is to create as much distraction and cause as much harassing disruption to the target as possible without being discovered as the source. Aside from civil and possibly criminal litigation, discovery could expose the source of these tactics to have them turned against him or her—perhaps even worse. So, a few preliminaries are advisable. First, make a plan beforehand and be as complete and careful as possible; a chronological, written plan or chart may be in order. Second, assemble a dossier of information and intelligence on the target; know home and business addresses and phone numbers, e-mail addresses, schedules and patterns, vehicle descriptions and information, etc., which are vital. Third, avoid contact with the target yourself; you do not want to be seen or your voice recognized and give your identity away (refer back to the first two sentences of this paragraph). Fourth, use other sources to *multiply the effect* of your plan by arranging for others to do your work without tying up your time. (You will see what this means as we elaborate.)

Dirty Tricks: Nasty Pranks

Every teenager remembers a few little pranks like dipping a sleeping person's hand in a pan of warm water to make them wet themselves or putting shaving cream in their hand and running a feather under their nose to get them to rub the shaving cream in their own face. Well, that's not really spy tactics (like debearding Castro for the Kennedy Administration was). There is always Nair, Neat, or similar *hair removal* products in the shampoo or cream rinse bottles. (This is a little closer to the CIA Castro beard caper.) What about *Ex-Lax* chips in the cookies or *Milk of Magnesia* in the milk? I once knew a detective (we'll just call him *Ralph*) who was called to Internal Affairs and took *syrup of ipecac* before reporting with his attorney. He threw up on the Internal Affairs investigator. (Let's make that "Ralph!!!!!") I have been told that eyedrops in drinks have a similar effect. Oh, by the way, that former detective is also dead now (note that this is an emerging theme of some kind). OK, let's file these under juvenile, but sometimes effective, little cheap tricks.

Utilities and Life's Little (Planned) Inconveniences

The *utilities* are important in most people's lives for comfort and convenience. Disrupt these and you have created a major disruption, distraction, and inconvenience. By notifying the water, power, gas, phone, and other utilities that you (actually your target) will be out of town for a period of time, you can temporarily disable the target's household. This can be further complicated if you notify the utilities that you (your target) are moving and will not need service at the current address and to please forward your bills to your new address where you will be establishing service. Meanwhile, your target is in the shower full of soap and shampoo when the water stops. As he or she reaches for a towel, the lights go out and he or she fumbles in the dark wondering why it is getting so dog-gone chilly as the gas furnace stops. By the time he or she realizes a phone call to the utilities companies, the phone has gone dead, along with his or her DSL Internet connection, unless he or she uses the cable company for Internet access, but that is gone too. It is like something out of *War of the Worlds*. If you haven't been able to discontinue his or her cell phone service, he or she may be able to get to the utilities companies within a few hours and arrange to have service restored sometime that week (or next). Don't forget, the target may have utilities at his or her business too. Again, this is an example of a *multiplier*, so should not occur during the telephone phase(s). (See "phone tag," discussed later).

Credit bureaus and *collection agencies* can be a source that destroys the target's ability to get credit (and buy things or pass a background check) and become an unwitting ally in annoying the target. (See *sleep deprivation*.) You should become familiar with the laws on credit reporting and use them to protect yourself from this technique.

Let Your Fingers Do the Walking: Yellow Pages and Telephones

The *yellow pages* are a source to use (both the paper pages and the Internet pages). Start from the beginning and go to the end and look for goods, services, and rental items that can and will deliver to the target's home or place of business. Just as with the pizzas that CREEP had delivered to the DNC, many businesses will deliver and expect payment upon delivery or bill the recipient later. Others may simply annoy the target by scheduling and showing up for *free estimates* or quotes. (You can also sign up for these at fairs and trade shows.) Contractors and home repair services are persistent. Pest control companies can be a pestilence. What about having a load of manure delivered to his or her lawn or a load of gravel to him or her at his or her neighbor's address?

While we are on *the telephone* (phone tag), remember those annoying little *phone pranks* we all played when we were kids? (Come on; you know you did it too.) You know, calling someone and asking, "Do you have Prince Albert in a can? Yes? Well, you better let him out!" How about asking, "Is your refrigerator running? Well, you better catch it!" (This is an oldie, but a *goodie*.) Oh, they were hysterical when we were about 9 years old and didn't have to worry about caller ID. OK, we all got a little scared when the guy recognized our voices as the neighbor kids and answered the phone "city morgue." (At least that's how it happened for us.) Well, the dirty tricks guys suggest that if you get off of work late (or can't sleep and have a phone that won't show up as yours on caller ID), take the opportunity to share your sleepless night or make your own *wake-up call* on the way home. OK, a little childish, but sleep disrupting nonetheless. If the target has an unlisted phone, there are ways of getting that too, or you can use the target's work number, which cannot be disconnected or changed.

You can create further *sleep disruption* by scheduling estimates or demonstrations by salesmen (or women) at unusual hours. You can tell them that you work late and need an early or late appointment. If they call ahead, they have still interrupted your target.

On the job is where the target can receive a lot of calls that will annoy both the target and his or her employer, who may want to make the target scarce. If the target owns the business, this ties up the phone for potential clients and businesses. Calling an employer about an employee about a job reference or even as a bill collector or credit bureau can create havoc. Arranging for or canceling deliveries and shipments can also disrupt the target's business.

The books and other writings on revenge and harassment from the 1970s were big on *telegrams*. This is much less commonly used today, so take that for what it is worth. Not so much used, or even known, in the 1970s was *the Internet*. No, not the Al Gore "I invented the Internet" Internet, but the real dub, dub, dub (www) Internet. This is better than the yellow pages (which can also be found on the Internet) and telegrams together. This is limited only to my one's imagination and resources.

Car Tricks

There are also *dirty car tricks* (no the car does not have to be dirty or get dirty). If you have a good vehicle description and know where the target parks, you may be able to have his or her car towed, perhaps for repairs. Some revenge seekers go for damaging their target's vehicle in the night. Leave the vandalism to the vandals.

The Pervert Next Door

Creating *the pervert next door* can be entertaining. Expert and committed harassers (like some politicians) have been known to find prostitutes of both genders in dirty magazines or the local vice district and then make house calls. (This has happened at national political conventions on more than one occasion.) That may not be as big a deal as it once was, but even in this millennium, the neighbors still talk. A variation of this is to simply have someone impersonate of these *oldest profession* professionals. The serious revenge experts suggest that you do not waste time writing the target's phone number on bathroom walls, as these are rarely taken seriously and called.

Mail Misery

Snail mail or the postal system is another avenue, but make sure that you are not committing any illegal acts of mail fraud or disruption. This can have serious consequences. Disruption of personal and business mail can be disabling and costly to a deserving target. Again, timing is important, so time this not to interfere with the magazine subscriptions and book or record club memberships (discussed later). Mail can be held when the target *goes on vacation* and can be forwarded to another address with a change of address. Bills go unpaid and business can be lost, not to mention the trouble of getting the mail back and reestablished. Mail drops or so-called accommodation addresses can be used to receive mail and then forward it to yet another address. Using no return address can be arranged, which cause the mail to be permanently *lost*. Again, be cautious about committing any violations of postal laws. (This is one tactic that is included to warn you against your own risks of harassment.)

Signing the target up for *magazine and book clubs* creates a nuisance, annoying bills, and maybe even an adverse credit report. You can collect subscription cards and membership applications in most magazines at your local bookstore, dentist's office, library, etc. This can also support the previous tactic (creating *the pervert next door*) if they are for pervert magazines. You can have these delivered not only to the target's residence but also his or her place of business or the neighbor's address (maybe a few doors down), where the occupant will be reluctant to bring the seedy mail down to the addressee. (Remember the little note earlier? Neighbors talk.)

Another scheme that you should be cautioned about is *the smear letter*, which is a variation or combination of *the pervert next door* and the *handbills and circulars* techniques. In fact, once the perpetrator has established that there is a *pervert next door*, letters and handbills are often used to continue this technique. I include this here because each word in the following *letter* has significant meaning and this tactic has serious consequences for both the perpetrator and the target. One revenge practitioner described this *technique of harassment* as distributing letters around the neighborhood and at the target's (victim's) place of employment that anonymously accused him or her of being a child molester. The contents read something like this:

> A child molester in this neighborhood molested my child. His name is Chester D. Molester and he lives at 1234 Elm Street (the brown house on the corner). He works at the Cheetum Department Store as the clothing department manager. His work phone is (999) 555-1234 and his home phone number is (999) 555-5678.
>
> I am not using my name or my child's (for obvious reasons) because I have been told that Molester will sue us if we tell the truth about him. By revealing him this way, he will know who it is (unless he has too many victims to guess), but he will not be able to sue us for revealing his perverted acts.
>
> We threatened to go to the police, but Molester said that it will be his word against our child's and he will win, leaving our child publicly humiliated. Obviously, Molester has thought this out and may have experience in such matters.
>
> Molester molested our child at least five times and threatened our child not to tell. Talk to your children and make sure he did not do the same to them. If your child comes forward, maybe mine can too, but we need to protect our children from this perverted freak.

As with all of these techniques of harassment, the moral implications should be weighed carefully, as well as the legal ramifications. What is a *PSYOP* to one may be *criminal harassment* to another.

Ads, Handbills, and Circulars

Political *PSYOPs* practitioners, revenge freaks, and criminal harassers often employ free advertising, handbills, and circulars in the campaigns. Yes, even distinguished political advisors and members of the intelligence community have used these methods.

Free ads are a great tool, not only for buying used stuff cheaply but for placing ads for good, no great deals, and listing the target's phone number. Slightly used 70 inches HDTV with 3D for only $200? Call 555-1234. Free baseball cards and comic books from the 1950s, 1960s, and 1970s? What a deal! Call 555-1234. This is what it means to *multiply the effect* of your plan by arranging for others to do your work without tying up your time. This is also known as letting someone else's fingers do the walking... well, you get the point. Feel green? Do the environment a favor and have all of those cans, plastics, and other recyclable items delivered to, yes, you guessed it—the target. At work or at home... why not both? An ad was once placed by a U.S. intelligence agency asking for stray cats to be delivered to the address of a known foreign intelligence service, offering to pay a nominal fee. The results were that the target was overwhelmed and kept busy by dozens of drop-offs. This is another example of *multiply the effect*.

For sale by owner and other *real estate ads* can also be annoying. Calls not only from potential buyers (for that great deal you have listed) but from realtors hoping to sell that house and turn a nice profit can be draining. Make sure that you have not had the target's phone disconnected at this point (that comes at a different time and timing is critical).

Handbills and circulars are posted on every tree, telephone, Starbucks bulletin board, boards at the colleges and places of employment, etc. There are even virtual bulletin boards on the Internet. Posting free ads, wants, classifieds, etc., is as close as the nearest keyboard or copy center. If you post paper, be sure to include several of those unsightly little tear-away tabs for the target's phone number so everyone can share the opportunity to avail themselves of the opportunity that you have created for the target to share with the mass-calling (or e-mailing) public (*multiply the effect*).

Composite Photography, Audio–Video Recordings, and Plants

While film is still an option for the hard-core photographers, digital photography opens up the world of Photoshop® or Photoshop Elements® and other digital editors for what is known as *composite photography* or *trick photography*. This tactic involves two techniques.

Figure 7.2 Controversial photo of Lee Harvey Oswald, reputed assassin of President John Kennedy. (Courtesy of the Warren Commission.)

The first is to take real photographs that appear to depict one thing, when they really are not what they seem. This is referred to as *circumstantial photographic evidence* (not to be confused with the legal term *circumstantial evidence*). An example of this would be taking a photo of a woman putting her arm around a man as she passes by (as if to say "excuse me, I'm coming through") to give the circumstantial appearance that they are together. Any other type of setup would be of this type.

The second is *composite photography*, which involves *tricks* employed to combine parts of one photo with another to give a false impression. This is known as *merged* or *fused* images in digital photography. An expert can usually examine a photo and determine whether or not it is authentic, but this is not always the case and not every photo is worth examining. One famous and controversial photo is the Lee Harvey Oswald photo taken before the Kennedy assassination (Figure 7.2).

Historical footnote: According to the Warren Commission report, the *backyard photos*, allegedly taken by Marina Oswald sometime in 1963 using a camera belonging to Oswald, show Oswald holding two Marxist newspapers and a rifle and wearing a pistol in a holster. After his arrest, Oswald insisted they were *forgeries*, but Marina testified in 1964 that she had taken the photographs and she reaffirmed her testimony repeatedly over the decades. These photos were labeled CE 133-A and CE 133-B. CE 133-A shows the rifle in Oswald's left hand and newsletters in front of his chest in the other. In CE 133-B, the rifle is held with the right hand. Oswald's mother testified that on the day after the assassination, she and Marina destroyed another photograph with Oswald holding the rifle with both hands over his head. (For more on the Kennedy assassination, see *Infamous Murders & Mysteries* by Dr. Robert J. Girod.)

There are two basic techniques used in composite photography today. The first uses a black background, which does not record at all on the film, such as black velvet or electrostatically coated black flock paper. The image is then made by making two separate exposures, both against black backgrounds, and printing the negatives sequentially or together on one sheet of paper. The second technique makes two exposures of the whole scene, with and without the *ghost* element.

The *tape recording* technique is quite simple. Everyone says something at some time that they wish they hadn't said or could rephrase. *Tape* can mean an audio tape or CD or a video recording. Today, everybody has their *Rodney King* camcorder handy and every cell phone has an audio recorder, camera, or video recorder (or all three). Let's leave this one at that and leave the rest to one's imagination. The ironic part of this one is that the target does almost all the work for you (embarrassing himself or herself) and all that is left is distribution or dissemination.

Finally, there is *the plant*. This ranges from the highly unethical to the highly illegal. DO NOT DO THIS! Be aware that it can be done to you. Fake photos or real photos that give a false impression and letters can be sent to the target's address giving a false impression (or maybe a true one if you *get the goods* on the target, but be aware of potentially innocent persons and collateral damage). Drugs and other contraband or evidence of crimes can also be planted. This should not even be considered unless it is officially sanctioned as government operation outside of the United States. What does that mean? If it is not apparent, it does not apply to you, so do not do it! Stay on the high ground!

Internal Disruption: The Coin-Tel-Pro Technique

The *Coin-Tel-Pro* is a tactic or technique used by both intelligence PSYOPs and political *dirty tricks department* professionals. It was allegedly a favorite of the Watergate black-bag crowd, as well as the left-wing subversive groups, to disrupt and confuse communications by sending false messages back and forth, supposedly from within the organization. An *open letter* is sent from (allegedly) one department, faction, or organization to others (widely circulated) denouncing another department, faction, organization, or an individual, creating hostility between one side and the other. Even if the letter is proven to be false, a lot of time and resources have been expended proving or correcting this and the animosity may never be alleviated. Imagine the chaos this creates within a political campaign. The objective of this technique is to create and maintain animosity between allies to divide and conquer or waste their time, resources, and energy.

Be Aware of the Implications

The psychological aspects of these *dirty tricks* can be devastating. Use common sense and always seek the moral high ground. The lives you interfere with may not only be those of a petty dictator, crooked politician, thieving assailant, etc. Always consider the collateral damage and ethical implications of your actions. Do not fail to recognize the potential civil litigation and criminal prosecution that violations of law can precipitate.

Social Media

Social media has become a great tool for investigative purposes, as well as a significant social force of great influence. Social media networks such as Facebook, MySpace, Twitter, and LinkedIn and video-sharing sites such as YouTube are being used by millions of people daily.

YouTube is a video-sharing website created by three former PayPal employees. Created and launched in February 2005, YouTube lets you upload and view videos using Adobe Flash and HTMLS technology, which is common on all computers and portable electronic devices such as phones, iPods, and iPads. It is used to display a wide variety of user-generated video content, including movie clips, TV clips, music videos, and personal home videos. Anyone can view these videos but only registered users can upload videos.

Facebook was launched in 2004 by the Harvard students Mark Zuckerberg, Eduardo Saverin, Andrew McCollum, Dustin Moskovitz, and Chris Hughes. By 2013, Facebook had reached its one billion user mark. That means that one billion people are sharing information back and forth and putting videos, comments, and photos for their friends and families to see. Registered users create profiles and they can add pictures, interests, place of work, contact information, and other personal information. You can then ask friends and family to join the network and you can link them to your profile. You can then share that information with friends and family that are in your network. Once you select those friends and family, they will be able to see those pictures, comments, videos, and anything else you post on your profile. You will also be able to view their information, video, pictures, and comments. Now that you are linked with someone, you can now see some of the comments from your friends' friends that you don't even know.

MySpace is similar to Facebook, as it is another social media network site. It was launched in 2003, before Facebook. It allows registered users to post pictures, videos, and messages. Your selected friends and family can view the content on your page and they can communicate with you. There are differences between MySpace and Facebook. MySpace allows you to link music to your webpage and allows you to customize your page to set you apart from other users. One fundamental difference between the two is that MySpace does not require you to use your true personal information where Facebook does.

Twitter is a real-time information network that connects you to the latest stories, ideas, opinions, and news about what you find interesting. Simply find the accounts you find most compelling and follow the conversations or create your own. Once you have an account, you will be able to follow or post your own comments. Every time you post something, it's called a *tweet*. If someone is following your account they can see what you posted and you can answer. Unlike Facebook and MySpace, anyone can see your tweets if they follow your account.

Tweets are publicly visible by default, but senders can restrict message delivery to just their followers. Users can tweet via the Twitter website, compatible external applications (such as for smartphones) or by short message service (SMS) in certain countries. While the service is free, accessing it through SMS may result in phone service provider fees.

Users can group posts together by topic or type by use of hash marks— words or phrases prefixed with a "#" sign. Similarly, the "@" sign followed by a user name is used for mentioning or replying to other users. To repost a message from another Twitter user and share it with one's own followers, the *retweet* function is symbolized by *RT* in the message.

LinkedIn is a social network site for people in professional occupations for professional networking.

Instagram is a social network site for sharing pictures and videos. These can be shared via Facebook, MySpace, Twitter, and Tumblr.

Tumblr is a microblogging platform and social networking website that allows users to post multimedia and other content to a short-form blog. Users can follow other users' blogs, as well as make their blogs private.

All of these sites have privacy settings that you can adjust to your preference, but the whole purpose of these sites is to share information with your friends and family. These companies also share your information with vendors and advertisers. That's how they make their money so they can exist.

Privacy and Security

Twitter messages are public, but users can also send private messages. Twitter collects *personally identifiable information* about users and shares it with third parties. The service reserves the right to sell this information as an asset if the company changes hands. While Twitter displays no advertising, advertisers can target users based on their history of tweets and may quote tweets in ads directed specifically to the user.

In 2007, a security vulnerability was reported when Twitter used the phone number of the sender of an SMS message as authentication. Malicious users could update someone else's status page by using SMS spoofing. The vulnerability could be used if the *spoofer* knew the phone number registered to their victim's account. Within a few weeks of this discovery, Twitter introduced an optional personal identification number (PIN) that users could use to authenticate their SMS-originating messages.

In 2009, 33 high-profile Twitter accounts were compromised after a Twitter administrator's password was guessed by a *dictionary attack*. Falsified tweets were sent from these accounts.

Twitter launched the beta version of their *Verified Accounts* service on June 11, 2009, allowing famous or notable people to announce their Twitter account name. The home pages of these accounts display a badge indicating their status.

In May 2010, a bug was discovered that allowed Twitter users to force others to follow them without the other users' consent or knowledge and often changed to receive nearly malicious subscriptions.

On December 14, 2010, the U.S. Justice Department issued a subpoena to Twitter to provide information for accounts registered to or associated with WikiLeaks. Twitter decided to notify its users and said in a statement, "…it's our policy to notify users about law enforcement and governmental requests for their information, unless we are prevented by law from doing so."

A *MouseOver* exploit occurred in 2010 when an XSS worm became active on Twitter. When an account user held the mouse cursor over blacked-out parts of a tweet, the worm within the script automatically opened links and reposted itself on the reader's account. The exploit was then reused to post pop-up ads and links to pornographic sites.

Electronic Intelligence and Signals Intelligence
Bugs and Taps

8

Bugs and Electronic Surveillance

Two similar devices for the electronic surveillance of *open areas* (areas outside of structures, vehicles, etc.) are the *parabolic reflector microphone* (*mic*) or *big ear* and the *shotgun mic* (Figures 8.1 and 8.2). A *parabolic mic* is a mic that uses a parabolic to collect and focus sound waves onto a receiver, in much the same way that a parabolic (like those used for a satellite dish) does with radio waves. The purpose of the parabolic reflector is to reflect sound to a centralized point, which is where the mic element is located. A parabolic reflector is used to collect and focus sound waves to a mic receiver (Figures 8.3 and 8.4).

Shotgun directional mics reduce the *receiving range* in which the mic is pointed rather than increase the gain (Figure 8.5). One can be built from 3/8-inch (some recipes say *1*) OD aluminum tubing (like old TV antennas) and cut from 1 to 36 inches (a total of 36 tubes). They are bundled together, held with epoxy, and then connected to a small aluminum funnel and a mic element (Figures 8.6 through 8.8).

A *spike mic* is similar to a contact mic but has a metal spike or probe that is driven into a wall to pick up voice or sound vibrations on an attached mic. If these vibrations are caused by room conversations, the electrical signal will correspond to those conversations (Figures 8.9 through 8.11).

Bugging involves concealing mics to pick up sound. A related, but not synonymous, technique is tapping. *Wiretapping* is the interception of telephone communications, usually wired telephone service, and other wired intercepts.

DTMF and ANI Decoders

DTMF and ANI decoders are used to decode *dual-tone multifrequency* touch-tone beeps and automatic number identifiers (received over phones, radios, and scanners).

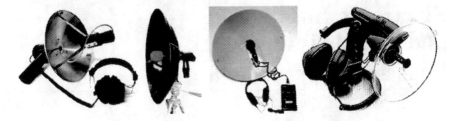

Figure 8.1 Examples of parabolic reflector mic or *big ear* mics.

Figure 8.2 More examples of parabolic reflector mic or *big ears*.

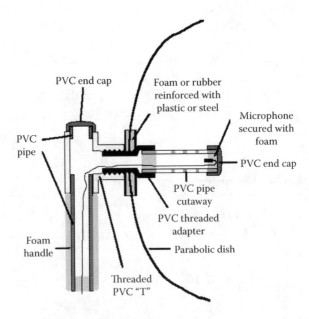

Figure 8.3 A diagram of a parabolic dish.

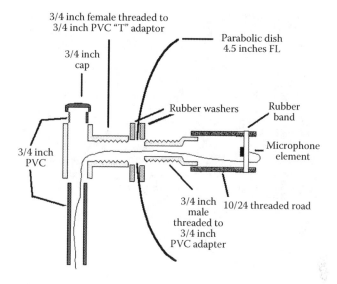

Figure 8.4 Another diagram of a parabolic dish.

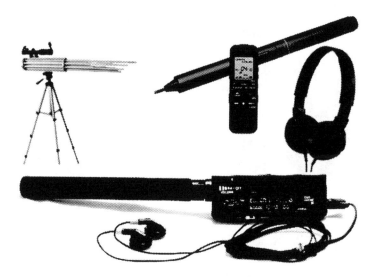

Figure 8.5 Example of a commercially available shotgun mic.

Pirate and Underground Radio

Just a quick word on *pirate* or *underground* radio stations is worth mentioning. These stations are often propaganda stations and may be used in psychological operations or for other similar purposes. These stations are commonly
found at 6950–6960 kHz (6955 kHz is common and MI6 uses 6959 kHz) and
7425–7415 kHz.

Figure 8.6 Example of a homemade shotgun mic.

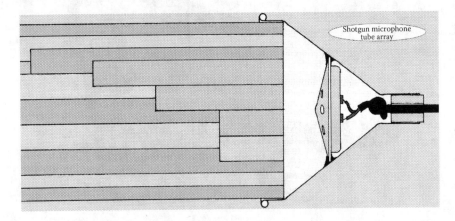

Figure 8.7 Shotgun mic tube array (side view).

Laser Surveillance Laser Listening

Laser surveillance listeners consist of a highly focused light transmitted at a distance and beamed onto the surface of a window of a building, structure, etc. This highly focused laser light or IR light receives a series of microvibrations on the window's surface. These vibrations of windows from conversations and other sounds inside the targeted room enable

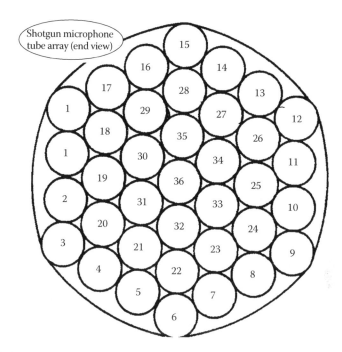

Figure 8.8 Shotgun mic tube array (end view).

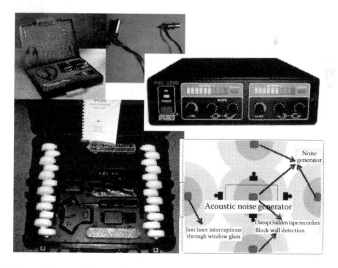

Figure 8.9 A spike mic kit and acoustic noise generator to counter spike mics.

laser listening to occur. The window vibrations are caused by oscillating frequencies from sound waves that emanate from speech and conversations of the people in the room.

Just like a diaphragm of a mic, the window vibrates and the laser surveillance system picks it up or receives the *signal*. The IR light of the laser listener

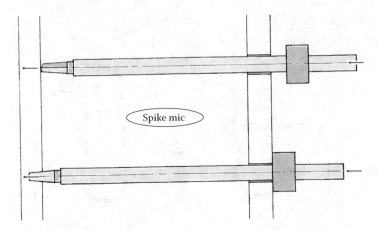

Figure 8.10 Spike mic insertion.

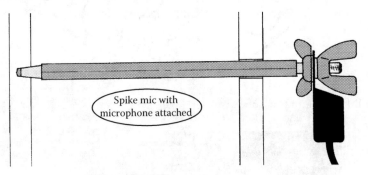

Figure 8.11 Spike mic with mic attached.

reflects off of the surface of the window and back to an optical receiver. The optical receiver is connected to an electronic demodulation system that converts the optical signals from the IR light into sound waves. These sound waves are filtered and made available for listening in real time or recorded.

Telephone Taps

While bugging, as mentioned, involves the interception of sound by mics, tapping involves interception of wired communications. *Wiretaps* are commonly associated with telephone taps of wired lines but can involve other taps of wired communications, including wired Internet and cable television, FIOS, and other wired data and communications lines. Primarily, we will discuss telephone taps here, but the same principles and techniques may apply to a certain extent.

It is a common misconception among laymen that clicks and odd sounds on their telephones are *wiretaps*. A properly installed tap by a competent technician will be virtually undetectable. A *trap and trace device* is an electronic device used to record and trace communication signals from a telecommunication system. This functions very similarly to a common caller ID feature. A trap and trace device is similar to a pen register. A *trap and trace* device can show the *incoming* phone numbers that called a specific telephone, while a *pen register* shows what *outgoing* numbers a phone had called. The term has come to include any device or program that performs similar functions to an original pen register for telephones but now includes programs that monitor Internet communications. (Refer to 18 U.S.C. Chapter 206 for statutory purposes.)

Internet Phone Services

The *Internet* is a global system of interconnected computer networks that use the standard IP suite (*transmission control protocol* and *Internet protocol* [TCP/IP]) to serve several billion users worldwide, with its origins in the 1960s from the military and academic communities. It is a network of networks that consists of millions of private, public, academic, business, and government networks, of local to global scope, which are linked by a broad array of electronic, wireless, and optical networking technologies. The Internet provides an extensive range of information resources and services, such as the interlinked hypertext documents of the World Wide Web (WWW) and the infrastructure to support e-mail. The *WWW* is a system of interlinked hypertext documents accessed via the Internet. Using a web browser, one can view web pages containing text, images, videos, and other multimedia and navigate between them via hyperlinks. The web was developed between March 1989 and December 1990.

There are ways to *capture* wireless signals. One way is to simply intercept cordless phone signals. It's easy to record calls using a freeware application called *Cain* if a trespasser has access to your local area network (LAN) (through an insecure wireless network). Internet phone service is an alternative to wired or hardwire service (a *plain old telephone service* [POTS] line from the TelCo), but the network used must also be secured. MagicJack® is one of these service providers, but there are others. You can also get a *free Google Voice number* (go to voice.Google.com and use your Gmail account information to login) (Figures 8.12 and 8.13).

MagicJack is a device that plugs into a USB port on the user's computer (or, in the case of MagicJack Plus®, plugs directly into a router) and that has a standard RJ-11 phone jack to plug in any standard phone, proving Voice over Internet Protocol (VOIP) service (Figure 8.14). MagicJack works exclusively with the company's captive landline supplier and competitive local exchange carrier (CLEC), YMAX. Voice mail is stored on the MagicJack servers and is delivered via direct telephone access and e-mail with WAV audio file attachments.

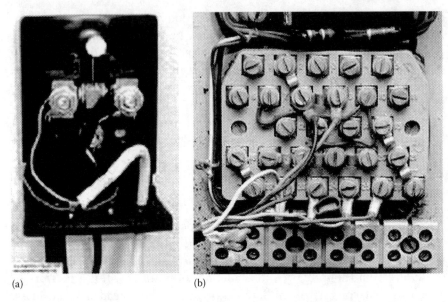

(a)   (b)

Figure 8.12 Telephone terminal block (a) and a main terminal block (b).

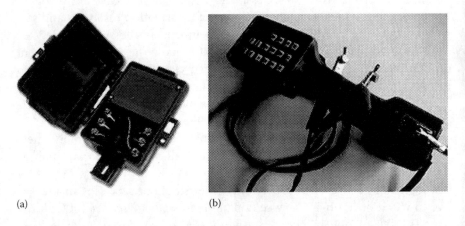

(a)   (b)

Figure 8.13 The Telco's terminal box (a) and lineman's handset (b).

Free *Google Voice number* (www.voice.google.com) includes many services such as voice mail, free text messaging, call history, conference calling, call screening, call blocking, and voice transcription of voice-mail messages to text that are available to users in the United States. Transcribed and audio voice mails, missed call notifications, and text messages can optionally be forwarded to an e-mail account of the user's choice. Text messages can be sent and received via the familiar e-mail or instant messaging (IM) interface by reading and writing text messages in Gmail or by adding contact's phone

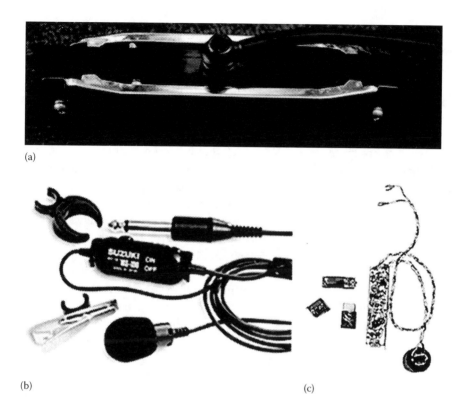

(a)

(b)   (c)

Figure 8.14 Harmonica mic (a) and infinity mic (b and c).

numbers in Google Talk (PC-to-phone texting). Google Voice multiway videoconferencing (with support for document sharing) is now integrated with Google+ with Hangouts.

For *VOIP* calls, you have to snoop on the *user datagram protocol (UDP) packets* and then convert to *real-time transport protocol (RTP)*. So someone connecting to your unsecure wireless router would be able to do this. The *UDP* is one of the core members of the IP suite (the network protocols used for the Internet). With UDP, computer applications can send messages, in this case referred to as datagrams, to other hosts on an IP network without prior communications to set up special transmission channels or data paths. The *RTP* defines a standardized packet format for delivering audio and video over IP networks.

Such services are not available through Wi-Fi and must be hardwired through a computer with an Ethernet connection (using the users' IP address and router IP). An *IP address* is a numerical label assigned to each device (e.g., computer, printer) participating in a computer network that uses the IP for communication. An IP address serves two purposes: (1) host or network interface identification and (2) location addressing. A *name* indicates what we are looking for, an *address* indicates where it is located, and a *route* indicates how to get there.

Security is usually provided by some type of scrambler like those used for IPs to protect Internet activity. One suggestion for added security is to run it on a dedicated machine (e.g., an older Dell Dimension 4500, XP Pro Sp3 with a 1.7 gigahertz [GHz] Intel and 1 GB of RAM) running as a *headless server* (a computer system or device that has been configured to operate without a monitor, i.e., the missing *head*, a keyboard, or a mouse). A headless system is typically controlled via a network connection.

Since you have to first register your new *MagicJack* (MJ) via your PC, protection against a *trojan* or a *key logger* on the PC (which may reveal the MJ *nimer*) should be used. This means antispyware, malware, virus protection, etc. It is also possible to open an e-mail attachment or visit an infected web page and allow something to be put on your PC. There are also commercially available spying programs that monitor keystrokes and allow spies to see IMs on both sides of the conversation. Once a trespasser gets into a network, he/she may be able to give commands to the target computer to bypass regular *proxies* and substitute others.

In computer networks, a *proxy server* is a server (a computer system or an application) that acts as an intermediary for requests from clients seeking resources from other servers. A client connects to the proxy server, requesting some service, such as a file, connection, web page, or other resource available from a different server, and the proxy server evaluates the request as a way to simplify and control its complexity. Today, most proxies are *web proxies*, facilitating access to content on the WWW. If you know the trespasser's IP address, there may be ways to prove who is trespassing by contacting your ISP or the trespasser's ISP (if you know it).

Change any and all passwords (including your router's *admin* account). Many people never change their *admin password* from "admin."

Packet Sniffing on the VOIP Data

Packet sniffing is used within a network in order to capture and register data flows. Packet sniffing allows you to discern each individual packet and analyze its content based on predefined parameters. Packet sniffing is a form of wiretap applied to computer networks instead of phone networks. It came into vogue with Ethernet, which is known as a *shared medium* network. This means that traffic on a segment passes by all hosts attached to that segment. Ethernet cards have a filter that prevents the host machine from seeing traffic addressed to other stations. Sniffing programs turn off the filter and thus see everyone's traffic.

Packet sniffing, or packet analysis, is the process of capturing any data passed over the local network and looking for any information that may be useful. Most of the time, we system administrators use packet sniffing to troubleshoot network problems (like finding out why traffic is so slow in one part of the network) or to detect intrusions or compromised workstations (like a workstation that is connected to a remote machine on port 6667 continuously when you don't use IRC clients), and that is what this type of analysis originally was designed for. But that didn't stop people from finding more creative ways to use these tools. The focus quickly moved away from its original intent—so much so that packet sniffers are considered security tools instead of network tools now. Tools like Wireshark, Ettercap, or NetworkMiner give anybody the ability to sniff network traffic with a little practice or training. These tools have become increasingly easy to use and continue to make things easier to comprehend, which makes them more usable by a broader user base.

Steps for Sniffing:

1. *Identify your operating system and network structure to determine what kind of packet sniffer to use.* Some packet sniffers work across various platforms, but most are written for a specific operating system.
2. *Determine if you can capture the traffic that you are concerned about, based upon your network structure.* On wired networks, you can sniff packets across the network, depending on the hub or switch that's being used. Check your switch and network setup, since some switches may prevent sniffing from another network subnet. On wireless LANs (WLANs), you can only monitor traffic on a specified channel.
3. *Find out whether the sniffer supports promiscuous mode.* It is necessary to set the network adapter on the computer that will do the sniffing to *promiscuous mode* to capture all types of network traffic, not just traffic being sent to the machine or a group that the machine belongs to.
4. *Decide how much you want to spend on a packet sniffer.* There are several options to choose from: free shareware (like Ethereal), sniffers that are bundled with other software (like Microsoft Network Monitor), and fee-based systems (like LANWatch).
5. *Research product options from various vendors to determine which is best for your needs.* Make sure they have documentation, manuals, FAQs, and other types of technical support.
6. *Download the packet sniffing software and install it according to the manufacturer's instructions.*
7. *Configure the software.* This varies by application, but generally you will need to set up addresses to capture and choose an interface from the menu. For wireless networks, you will have to set the channel to be monitored.

8. *Hit the "Start" button or other command to start monitoring.* Choose the "advanced options" to filter incoming results.
9. *Select "Stop" to stop the session and "Save" to save the results* (pretty self-explanatory).
10. *View the results.* You will see each packet's time, source, destination, protocol used, and general information.
11. *Filter the display or select individual entries.* This varies by the type of software but usually shows the results on part of the screen (while the entry is highlighted) or in full screen (by double-clicking the entry). Most systems allow you to filter the results based on values in fields, comparisons between fields, and other options.
12. *Get help from books, online resources, or user forums to learn more about how to sniff packets and interpret the results.* The results you see on-screen may not be immediately clear until you have some experience in learning to decipher them.

Packet sniffing is a passive technique. No one actually is attacking your computer and looking through the files. It is more like eavesdropping, in that one computer is just listening in on the conversation that another computer is having with the gateway. Typically, most people think that network traffic goes directly from their computers to the router or switch and up to the gateway and then out to the Internet, where it routes similarly until it gets to the specified destination. This is accurate except that the computer isn't directly sending the data anywhere. It broadcasts the data in packets that have the destination in the header. Every node on your network (or switch) receives the packet, determines whether it is the intended recipient, and then either accepts the packet or ignores it.

Packet Sniffers: Carnivore and Magic Lantern

Carnivore and Magic Lantern are methods of intercepting Internet-based information, primarily e-mail. The FBI developed Carnivore (referred to as DCS1000 by the FBI), a software tool designed to facilitate the interception of electronic communications on the Internet. Internet messages travel in digital packets that contain a destination, protocol instructions, and a message. Carnivore uses an IP packet *sniffer* that can select and record a defined subset of the traffic on a network. Packets to be examined by Carnivore can be selected based on IP address, on protocol, or, in the case of e-mail, on the user names in the TO and FROM fields (Foster, 2005, p. 304).

A *sniffer* is a program used by network managers to monitor and analyze traffic to detect problems. A sniffer can also be used to capture data being transmitted on a network. A network router analyzes each packet of data passed to it. The router must determine where to send the information; it may stay on its own network or be passed to the Internet. A router with a sniffer, however, may be able to read the data in the packet. A sniffer can also be a program used to analyze information on a database (Foster, 2005, p. 304).

In some cases, packets can be selected based on their content. Whenever an investigation seeks to intercept the TO and FROM lines, IP address, or user names of an Internet e-mail message, the investigation is "acting much like a pen register in that it is intercepting device-identifying information." This is referred to as the *pen mode*. However, the Internet transmission can be intercepted in what is called *full mode*, so the content of the message is also intercepted (Foster, 2005, p. 304).

Magic Lantern is a computer virus developed by the FBI that is sent to and infects a target computer. Once the program has manifested itself, every tap of the target's fingers on the keyboard is recorded and forwarded to the FBI. This software was developed in order to defeat an offender's use of encryption technology (Foster, 2005, p. 304).

Field Expedient Radios

A *crystal radio receiver* or *cat's whisker receiver* is a simple radio receiver that does not need a battery or power source (Figure 8.15). It runs on the power received from radio waves received by a long-wire antenna. Its most important component is a crystal detector (a diode), originally made with a piece of crystalline mineral such as galena (the natural mineral form of lead sulfide). Reduced to its essentials, it consists of four components:

1. An *antenna* to pick up the radio waves and convert them to electric currents.
2. A *tuned circuit* to select the signal to be received, out of all the signals received by the antenna. This consists of a coil of wire called (a) an *inductor* or *tuning coil* and (b) a capacitor connected together.

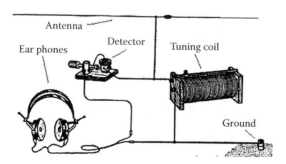

Figure 8.15 Crystal radio set.

One or both are adjustable and can be used to tune. In some circuits, a capacitor is not used, because the antenna also serves as the capacitor. The tuned circuit has a natural resonant frequency, which allows radio signals at this frequency to pass while rejecting signals of other frequencies (Figure 8.16).

3. A *semiconductor crystal detector* that extracts the audio signal or *modulation* from the radio-frequency carrier wave by only allowing current to pass through it in one direction and blocking half of the oscillations of the radio wave. Some sets used a *cat's whisker detector* or a fine wire touching the surface of a pebble of crystalline mineral such as galena.

4. An *earphone* or some type of speaker substitute to convert the audio signal to sound that can be heard. The low power produced by crystal radios is insufficient to power an unamplified speaker, so earphones are usually used.

A field expedient radio receiver may be made using some basic components from commonly found items (Figure 8.17):

- Something for a base (such as a piece of wood)
- Lacquer or glue
- Tacks or screws for fastening components
- Razor blade
- Cardboard toilet paper tube
- Large safety pin
- Lead from a wooden pencil

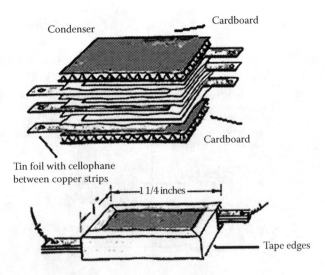

Figure 8.16 Homemade capacitor or condenser.

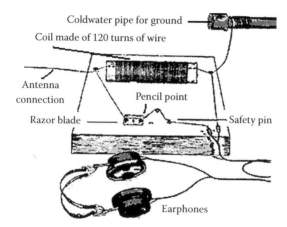

Figure 8.17 Field expedient radio receiver.

- #22 AWG (or so) wire
- Wire coat hanger or other strip of workable metal
- Headphones or earphone (2–4 kΩ)

4G Broadband Public Safety Communications

The latest version mobile *broadband* communications is *4G*, and it represents a significant increase in speed and capacity for the exchange of mobile data. 4G is the fourth generation of mobile phone and communications technology standards. 5G (fifth-generation mobile networks or fifth-generation wireless systems) is a term used to denote the next major phase of mobile telecommunications standards beyond the current 4G/IMT-Advanced Standards.

Broadband wireless technology enables police agencies to use pocket-sized handheld devices that have capabilities to stream live on-scene video of an incident to the nearby EOC. Increased bandwidth can turn a patrol car on-scene into a Wi-Fi hotspot. For police video, the 3G experience of 100 ms *of latency* wasn't good enough for real-time streaming. The new mobile broadband system can deliver about 30 ms *latency*, a 70 ms difference.

Future-proof devices are ruggedized communication devices with capabilities in the public safety band spectrum and the ability to operate as vehicular modems for devices that are portable and multifaceted and have reasonable battery life.

Band 14 refers to the frequency spectrum allocated for public safety use. In July 2007, the Federal Communications Commission (FCC) revised the 700 MHz band plan and service rules to promote the creation of a nationwide interoperable broadband network for public safety and to facilitate the availability of new and innovative wireless broadband services for consumers.

The commission designated the lower half of the 700 MHz public safety band (763–768 and 793–798 MHz) for *broadband* communications. The commission also consolidated existing *narrowband* allocations to the upper half of the 700 MHz public safety block (769–775 and 799–805 MHz). Further, in order to minimize interference between broadband and narrowband operations, the commission adopted a *one megahertz guard band* (768–769 and 798–799 MHz) between the public safety broadband and narrowband segments. Finally, the commission established a single nationwide license—the Public Safety Broadband License—for the 700 MHz public safety broadband spectrum.

Since broadband is broadband, local network control can be done at the end-user level. If multiple units from multiple jurisdictions are responding to an incident, the net controller can isolate the incident. End users will still be on the same network, and it really won't look any different to the end user.

Band 14: 700 MHz Public Safety Band

- *763–768* and *793–798 MHz broadband* communications (lower half of the 700 MHz public safety block)
- *769–775* and *799–805 MHz narrowband* allocations (upper half of the 700 MHz public safety block)
- *768–769* and *798–799 MHz—one megahertz guard band* to minimize interference between broadband and narrowband operations

Routers

A standard modem allows you to connect one computer to the Internet at a time. A router allows you to connect one or more computers at a time. It is called a router because signals are being routed back and forth. Routers are manufactured by various companies, such as Linksys, Belkin, D-Link, and Netgear.

Routers intended for ISP and major enterprise connectivity usually exchange routing information using the Border Gateway Protocol (BGP). The main purpose of a router is to connect multiple networks and forward packets destined either for its own networks or other networks. Another function a router performs is to decide which packet should be processed first when multiple queues exist. Routers also perform what is called *policy-based routing* where special rules are constructed to override the rules derived from the routing table when a packet forwarding decision is made. These functions may be performed through the same internal paths that the packets travel inside the router.

Computers can be connected to the router either with a wire called an Ethernet cable or without wires, in the case of a wireless router. Some wireless routers have two antennas; most have at least one. The antennas can be unscrewed and replaced by bigger, more powerful antennas. Data from the Internet will travel through the router and then transmitted through the antenna(s) and broadcast to the wireless adaptor on the computer, laptop, or any other wireless adaptor in range (whether it is yours or not). So the wireless signals are radio waves from a wireless router at between 2.4 and 2.5 GHz.

Other electric devices known to clash with your wireless signals are digital phones, baby cot monitors, Bluetooth devices, other wireless routers, etc. To solve this problem, change the frequency of the radio waves by changing the channels. The changes you are permitted to make are from 2.4 to 2.5 GHz. You make these changes from the router's control panel (called the configuration page). So *Channel 1* will mean 2.41 GHz, *Channel 2* will mean 2.42 GHz, *Channel 3* will mean 2.43 GHz, and so on.

The first step in setting up a router is usually to set up the router with a direct cable connection, that is, an Ethernet or network cable. The setup or installation wizard should then take you through the steps to get you connected to the router and onto the Internet. Before you do this, contact your ISP and get any router setting they may have. You will need your broadband user name and password. Once you have a wired connection set up, you can then set up a wireless connection, and when you have your wireless connection up and running, you can unplug the network cable.

External networks are an important part of the overall security strategy. Separate from the router may be a firewall or VPN handling device, or the router may include these and other security functions. Many companies produced security-oriented routers, including Cisco Systems' PIX and ASA5500 series, Juniper's Netscreen, WatchGuard's Firebox, and Barracuda's variety of mail-oriented devices.

A lot of wireless routers don't have security turned on by default. Your configuration pages will allow you to turn it on, and there is usually a Help menu that explains the various security settings. You may need to go into the *config* pages to set up *wireless security*. If you don't have security switched on, anyone within range of your wireless router will be able to connect to it. There are two types of security that most wireless routers use: Wired Equivalent Privacy (WEP) and Wi-Fi Protected Access (WPA), which encrypt your signals with a key. With the wireless security turned on, the router needs your key before it will allow access and any traffic through it.

WEP is an older form of security and is not as safe as WPA. There are programs around that hackers can download to crack WEP. Once they have WEP cracking software, they may be able to gain access to your router and get a free ride on the Internet or worse. The WEP key will be either

64 bits or 128 bits in length (128 bits is 26 characters and will be mixture of the numbers 0–9 and the letters A–F.) When setting up the router for a wireless connection, you have to type out all 26 characters correctly or it won't connect.

WPA security is really an updated WEP, using different and stronger encryption that is harder to crack. It is easier to set up because you only need to set up a short pass phrase instead of typing out 26 letters and numbers. WPA is better than WEP.

Here are a few steps you can take to make your home network a less inviting target: (1) In your router security settings, make sure you've changed any default user names and passwords. These will be the first things any hacker tries, much the way a burglar jiggles a doorknob to see if it's unlocked. (2) Disable wireless access to your router's management console, which allows you to manage its settings by pointing a web browser to an address such as 192.168.1.1. Disabling wireless access means you will have to be physically plugged into the router in order to manage it, making it far more difficult to hack. (3) Consider replacing your router's internal software with an open-source alternative such as DD-WRT, Tomato, or OpenWRT. While these options aren't particularly consumer friendly, their firmware is less likely to contain obvious vulnerabilities. (4) If you haven't already done so, you should consider enabling your wireless router's built-in firewall. Enabling the firewall can help to make your network less visible to hackers looking for targets on the Internet. Many router-based firewalls have a *stealth mode* that you can enable to help reduce your network's visibility.

Routers and Wi-Fi: How to Access Router Settings

A *router* is a device that forwards data packets between computer networks, creating an overlay *internetwork* (a computer network that is built on the top of another network). A router is connected to two or more data lines from different networks. When a data packet comes in one of the lines, the router reads the address information in the packet to determine its ultimate destination. Then, using information in its routing table (a table that lists the routes to particular network destinations) or routing policy (decisions based on policies set by the network administrator), it directs the packet to the next network along its route.

Routers perform the *traffic directing* functions on the Internet. A data packet is typically forwarded from one router to another through the networks that constitute the internetwork until it reaches its destination node. Small home and office routers simply pass data, such as web pages, e-mail, IM, and videos between the computers and the Internet. An example of such routers is the owners' cable or DSL modem that connects to the Internet through an ISP. More sophisticated routers, such as enterprise routers, connect large business or ISP networks to powerful core routers that forward data at high speed along the fiber-optic lines of the *Internet backbone*. Though routers are typically dedicated hardware devices, use of software-based routers is increasingly more common.

The IP address is the address used for identifying a device on the Internet. The correct router default IP address (IP address) is the one specific to the router manufacturer that is connected to the computer being used. The internal router settings can only be accessed if the computer that is searching the IP is connected to that router. To access router settings (security, firewall, passwords, etc.), enter the correct default IP address into the address bar on any search engine (see Figure 8.18). Different brands have different default addresses that apply to those specifically, for example,

- Belkin: 192.168.2.1
- Linksys: 192.168.1.1
- Netgear: 192.168.0.1

To get to Command Prompt, go to Start (on your computer), then use the search bar for "search programs and files" to search for "command prompt" or just "cmd." Under Command Prompt (cmd), enter "ipconfig." This shows a user all of the current IP configurations on his computer (Figure 8.19).

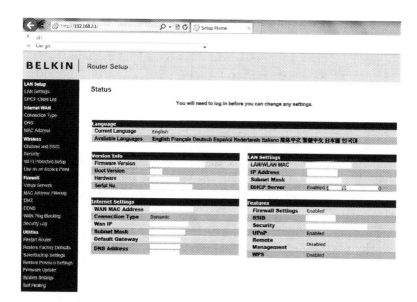

Figure 8.18 Router setup.

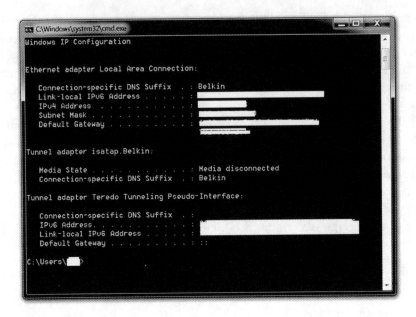

Figure 8.19 IP configuration.

Using Wi-Fi Technology

Wi-Fi technology allows an electronic device to exchange data wirelessly, by any WLAN. A device that can use Wi-Fi, such as a personal computer, video game, smartphone, tablet, and digital audio player, can connect to a network resource such as the Internet by a wireless network access point or *hotspot*, having a range of about 20 m (65 feet) indoors and a greater range outdoors. Hotspot coverage can involve an area as small as a single room with walls that block radio waves or as large as several square miles, using multiple overlapping access points. They transmit at frequencies of 2.4 or 5 GHz. The higher frequency allows the signal to carry more data.

802.11a transmits at 5 GHz and can move up to 54 megabits of data per second. It also uses *orthogonal frequency-division multiplexing* (OFDM), a more efficient coding technique that splits that radio signal into several sub-signals before they reach a receiver. This greatly reduces interference. *802.11b* is the slowest and least expensive standard and transmits in the 2.4 GHz frequency band of the radio spectrum. It can handle up to 11 megabits of data per second and it uses *complementary code keying* (CCK) modulation to improve speeds. *802.11g* also transmits at 2.4 GHz like 802.11b, but it is faster and can handle up to 54 megabits of data per second, because it uses the same OFDM coding as 802.11a. *802.11n* is the most widely available of the standards and is backward compatible with a, b, and g. 802.11n can achieve speeds as high as 140 megabits per second and transmit up to four streams of data, each at a maximum of 150 megabits per second, but most routers only allow for two or three streams.

802.11ac is the newest standard as of early 2013 but has yet to be widely adopted. 802.11ac is also backward compatible with 802.11n (and therefore the others, too), with *n* on the 2.4 GHz band and *ac* on the 5 GHz band. It is sometimes called *5G Wi-Fi* because of its frequency band, sometimes *Gigabit Wi-Fi* because of its potential to exceed a gigabit per second on multiple streams, and sometimes *very high throughput* (*VHT*) for the same reason. Wi-Fi radios can transmit on any of three frequency bands. Or they can *frequency hop* rapidly between the different bands. Frequency hopping helps reduce interference and lets multiple devices use the same wireless connection simultaneously (Tables 8.1 and 8.2).

Public Wi-Fi hotspots normally require a paid subscription. The sign-up process involves providing credit card information online or by phone and choosing a service plan. Some service providers offer plans that work at thousands of hotspots throughout the country. A few pieces of technical information are also required to access Wi-Fi hotspots. The network name (also called service set identifier [SSID]) distinguishes hotspot networks from each other. Encryption keys (a long series of letters and numbers) scramble the network traffic to and from hotspots and businesses. Service providers supply this *profile* information for their hotspots.

Computers can scan for hotspots within range of their wireless signal and identify the network name (SSID) of the hotspot allowing the computer to initiate a connection. Users can also use a small *Wi-Fi finder* device, used

Table 8.1   Wi-Fi Frequencies 2.4G Band

Channel	Lower Frequency	Center Frequency	Upper Frequency
1	2.401	2.412	2.423
2	2.406	2.417	2.428
3	2.411	2.422	2.433
4	2.416	2.427	2.438
5	2.421	2.432	2.443
6	2.426	2.437	2.448
7	2.431	2.442	2.453
8	2.436	2.447	2.458
9	2.441	2.452	2.463
10	2.451	2.457	2.468
11	2.451	2.462	2.473

Note: In the United States and Canada, there are 11 channels available for use in the 802.11b 2.4 GHz Wi-Fi frequency range. This standard is defined by the IEEE.

Table 8.2   Wi-Fi Frequencies 5G Band (5.180–5.825 GHz)

Channel	U-NII Band	Frequency (MHz)	U.S. (40/20 MHz)	Europe (40/20 MHz)
36	1	5180	Yes	Yes
38	1	5190	No	No
40	1	5200	Yes	Yes
42	1	5210	No	No
44	1	5220	Yes	Yes
46	1	5230	No	No
48	1	5240	Yes	Yes
52	2	5260	Yes	Yes
56	2	5280	Yes	Yes
60	2	5300	Yes	Yes
64	2	5320	Yes	Yes
100	2e	5500	Yes	Yes
104	2e	5520	Yes	Yes
108	2e	5540	Yes	Yes
112	2e	5560	Yes	Yes
116	2e	5580	Yes	Yes
120	2e	5600	No	Yes
124	2e	5620	No	Yes
128	2e	5640	No	Yes
132	2e	5660	No	Yes
136	2e	5680	Yes	Yes
140	2e	5700	Yes	No
149	3	5745	Yes	No
153	3	5765	Yes	No
157	3	5785	Yes	No
161	3	5805	Yes	No
165	3	5825	Yes	No

scan for hotspot signals, and many provide an indication of signal strength to help pinpoint their exact location. Before traveling, the location of Wi-Fi hotspots can be found using online wireless hotspot finder services. With the profile (network name and encryption settings) applied on the wireless network adapter, you initiate the connection from your computer operating system (or software that was supplied with the network adapter). Paid or restricted hotspot services will require you to log in with a user name and password the first time you access the Internet.

Taking basic precautions help ensure reasonable safety when using Wi-Fi hotspots. First, choose only reputable public hotspot service providers and ones who use strong security settings on their networks. Second, be aware of your surroundings and watch for suspicious individuals in the vicinity who may be reading your screen or planning to steal your computer. Third, ensure you do not accidentally connect to *nonpreferred* hotspots by checking your computer's settings. Although not normally enabled, most computers have a setting available allowing these connections to happen automatically without notifying the user. This setting should not be enabled except in temporary situations with the user's awareness. To verify whether automatic connections to open Wi-Fi networks are allowed, check the computer's wireless configuration settings. For example, for Windows XP:

1. From the Start menu, open Windows Control Panel.
2. Inside Control Panel, click the "Network Connections" option if it exists; otherwise, first click "Network and Internet Connections" and then click "Network Connections."
3. Right-click "Wireless Network Connection" and choose "Properties."
4. Click the "Wireless Networks" tab on the Properties page.
5. Click the "Advanced" button in this tab.
6. Find the "Automatically connect to nonpreferred networks" setting. If checked, this setting is enabled; otherwise, it is disabled.

Wi-Fi can be less secure than wired connections (such as Ethernet) because an intruder does not need a physical connection. Web pages that use *SSL* or its successor, *transport layer security (TLS)*, to encrypt the data of network connections are more secure, but unencrypted Internet access can easily be detected by intruders. Because of this, Wi-Fi has adopted various encryption technologies. Because the early encryption, *WEP* (a security algorithm for wireless networks), was proven easy to break, higher-quality security protocols and security certification programs *WPA* and *WPA II (WPA2)* were added later.

The *man-in-the-middle attack* (abbreviated *MITM, MitM, MIM, MiM, MITMA*) in cryptography and computer security is a method of active *eavesdropping* in which the attacker makes independent connections with the victims and relays messages between them, to make them believe that they are talking directly to each other over a private connection, when the entire conversation is actually controlled by the attacker. The attacker is able to intercept messages going between the two victims and inject new ones (e.g., an attacker within reception range of an unencrypted Wi-Fi access point).

A man-in-the-middle attack can succeed only when the attacker can impersonate each endpoint user by attacking mutual authentication or lack thereof. Most cryptographic protocols include some form of endpoint authentication to prevent MITM attacks. SSL can authenticate one or both parties using a mutually trusted *certification authority.*

To connect to a Wi-Fi LAN, a computer has to be equipped with a wireless network interface controller. The combination of computer and interface controller is called a *station*. All stations share a single radio-frequency communication channel. Transmissions on this channel are received by all stations within range. A carrier wave is used to transmit the data in packets, referred to as *Ethernet frames*. Each station is constantly tuned in on the radio-frequency communication channel to pick up available transmissions.

Piggybacking refers to access to a wireless Internet connection by bringing one's own computer within the range of another's wireless connection and using that service without the subscriber's explicit permission or knowledge. Piggybacking often occurs unintentionally, since most access points are configured without encryption by default and operating systems can be configured to connect automatically to any available wireless network. A user who happens to start up a laptop in the vicinity of an access point may find the computer has joined the network without any visible indication. A user intending to join one network may instead end up on another one if the latter has a stronger signal.

Using Bluetooth Technology

Bluetooth is a wireless technology standard for exchanging data over short distances, using short-wavelength radio transmissions in the *industrial, scientific, and medical (ISM) radio* band from 2400 to 2483.5 MHz (including guard bands) from fixed and mobile devices, creating personal area networks (PANs) with high levels of security. Each channel has a bandwidth of 1 MHz. The first channel starts at 2402 MHz and continues up to 2480 MHz in 1 MHz steps. It usually performs 800 hops (1 MHz step changes) per second, with adaptive frequency hopping (AFH) enabled. Bluetooth provides a secure way to connect and exchange information between devices such as digital cameras, FAXes, GPS, laptops, mobile phones, personal computers, printers, telephones, and video game consoles.

Any Bluetooth device in *discoverable mode* will transmit the following information on demand:

- Device name
- Device class
- List of services
- Technical information (e.g., device features, manufacturer, Bluetooth specification used, clock offset)

Any device may perform an inquiry to find other devices to connect to, and any device can be configured to respond to such inquiries. However, if the device trying to connect knows the address of the device, it always responds to direct connection requests and transmits the information shown in the aforementioned list if requested. Use of device's services may require pairing or acceptance by its owner, but the connection itself can be initiated by any device and held until it goes out of range. Some devices can be connected to only one device at a time, and connecting to them prevents them from connecting to other devices and appearing in inquiries until they disconnect from the other device.

Every device has a unique 48-bit address. However, these addresses are generally not shown in inquiries. Instead, friendly Bluetooth names are used, which can be set by the user. This name appears when another user scans for devices and in lists of paired devices.

Prior to Bluetooth v2.1, encryption is not required and can be turned off at any time. Moreover, the encryption key is only good for approximately 23.5 hours; using a single encryption key longer than this time allows simple XOR attacks to retrieve the encryption key. Turning off encryption is required for several normal operations, so it is problematic to detect if encryption is disabled for a valid reason or for a security attack.

Bluetooth v2.1 addresses this in the following ways: (1) encryption is required for all nonservice discovery protocol (SDP) connections; (2) a new encryption pause and resume feature is used for all normal operations requiring encryption to be disabled, enabling easy identification of normal operation from security attacks; and (3) the encryption key is required to be refreshed before it expires. Link keys may be stored on the device file system, not on the Bluetooth chip itself. Many Bluetooth chip manufacturers allow link keys to be stored on the device; however, if the device is removable, this means that the link key will move with the device.

Bluejacking is the sending of a picture or a message from one user to an unsuspecting user through *Bluetooth* wireless technology. Common applications include short messages, but do not involve the removal or alteration of any data from the device. Bluejacking can also involve taking control of a mobile device wirelessly, etc. (There's always something new!)

Emanations Intelligence 9

Emanations Intelligence

Emanations intelligence (EMINT) involves the investigation and study of *compromising emissions* (CEs), also known as TEMPEST. *Compromising emanations* are unintentional data-related or intelligence-bearing signals, which, when intercepted and analyzed, may disclose the information transmitted, received, or processed by any information-processing equipment. Emanations may consist of (1) electromagnetic emanations or emissions (space radiations, stray magnetic fields, conducted signals, and power-line modulation) and (2) acoustic emanations or emissions. An example of this is the reading of emanations generated by the key strokes of a computer (sound waves produced by mechanical motions and striking parts in a functional relationship to the information being processed).

Early discovery and technology of this source was known as *van Eck phreaking*. In 1985, Wim van Eck published the first unclassified technical analysis of the security risks of emanations from computer monitors. His findings created a stir in the intelligence and security community, which believed that such monitoring was a highly sophisticated and technologically advanced attack methodology. Van Eck demonstrated that he could successfully eavesdrop on a computer system from hundreds of feet away, using a television set and $15 worth of electronic equipment. Such emanations are still referred to as *van Eck radiation* and the eavesdropping technique as *van Eck phreaking*. The term *compromising emanations* rather than *radiation* is used because the compromising signals can and do exist in several forms, such as magnetic and electric field radiation, line conduction, or acoustic emissions.

Government researchers were already aware of the danger of such emanations, as Bell Laboratories reported this vulnerability to secure TTY communications as early as WWII and was able to produce 75% of the plaintext being processed in a secure facility from a distance of 80 feet. The NSA published *Tempest Fundamentals, NSA-82-89, NACSIM 5000, NSA* (Classified) on February 1, 1982.

Compromising emanations consist of electrical, mechanical, or acoustical energy intentionally or unintentionally emitted by sources within equipment and systems that process information. This energy may relate to encrypted messages or to information being processed in such a way that it can lead to recovery of the plaintext. *CE* can be propagated through space and through available conductors. The interception and propagation ranges and analysis of such emanations are affected by a variety of factors, such as the functional design of the information-processing equipment, system and equipment installation, or environmental conditions related to physical security and ambient noise.

Computers and other electronic equipment emit interference into the surrounding environment. For example, by placing two video monitors close together, the images will behave erratically until you space them apart. Any electrical or electronic circuit that carries a *time-varying current* will emanate electromagnetic signals with the strength of the emission proportional to the current amplitude and its time rate of change. These signals propagate from the source as *free space waves* and *guided waves* along conductors connected or close to the radiator. If time variations of the source currents are related in any way to the information content of the signals, the emanation will also have some relationship to the data, making it possible to reconstruct the original information into intelligence through analysis of these emissions.

The term TEMPEST, coined in the late 1960s and early 1970s, refers to the field of Emissions or Emanations Security (EMSEC) and is a code-name for NSA operations to secure electronic communications equipment from eavesdroppers and to intercept and interpret those signals from other sources. The term TEMPEST is not an acronym and does not have any particular meaning, although it is sometimes referred to as

- Transmitted Electro-Magnetic Pulse/Energy Standards & Testing
- Telecommunications Electro-Magnetic Protection, Equipment, Standards & Techniques
- Transient Electro-Magnetic Pulse Emanation Standard
- Telecommunications Electronics Material Protected from Emanating Spurious Transmissions

Insiders even jokingly refer to it as "Tiny Electro-Magnetic Particles Emitting Secret Things."

Measurement and Signature Intelligence

MASINT is scientific and technical intelligence information obtained by quantitative and qualitative analysis of data (metric, angle, spatial, wavelength, time dependence, modulation, plasma, and hydromagnetic) derived from specific technical sensors for the purpose of identifying any distinctive features associated with the source, emitter, or sender and to facilitate subsequent identification and/or measurement of the same.

Things That Are Vulnerable to Hacking

Automobiles. Car thieves can unlock your car and start it by sending it a text message or two. Many automotive systems, such as OnStar, use the same type of cellular technology as a common cell phone. The same hack could potentially affect infrastructure like power grids and traffic systems.

Baby monitors. Baby monitors have been around for a long time, and video-equipped versions have become popular. What most users probably don't realize is that the dozen or so wireless channels that these helpful devices use can often be picked up by anyone with a similar device or a wireless receiver. Newer baby monitor models feature *frequency hopping* technology that changes channels randomly to ensure privacy.

Garage door openers. Hackers can easily modify a standard door opener to accept a USB port, and software is available on the web to modify how it operates. This vulnerability is typically an issue only for older garage door systems, and newer openers use a more secure rolling code that changes each time it is used.

Medical implants. High-tech medical devices like pacemakers and insulin pumps that use a wireless signal for easy tweaking are vulnerable to anyone with the correct reprogramming hardware. Unfortunately, the signal they use is not encrypted, meaning that anyone who finds a way to obtain such a device could literally manipulate the heart of a patient, causing cardiac arrest or even death. Insulin pumps are apparently even more susceptible to outside interference and may be vulnerable from distances of up to a half mile. Using radio antennas, hackers can hijack a pump's wireless signal and cause it change the rate insulin, with potentially lethal results.

Human brain. Because of the immense amount of data that the human brain can hold, scientists have been attempting to crack our internal hard drives for quite some time. Researchers have begun to translate the trillions of impulses that go on in our heads into readable data. DARPA has been funding a program to reverse engineer the human brain in an effort to mine its computational abilities.

Computer Anonymity, Privacy, and Security

There is a difference between computer anonymity, privacy, and security. Anonymity is merely concealing one's identity, for example, the concealment of masking of an e-mail address. Privacy involves more than mere masking, but complete concealment or invisibility, even from your system administrator, for example, through codes or encryption. Security involves active countermeasures to prevent threats from succeeding. Anonymity and privacy (cover and concealment) are the first steps to take (by depriving the threat of knowing of your existence or whereabouts).

E-mail is like dropping a post card in the e-mail. Without an envelope, it is subject to observation. An *anonymous* e-mail remailing system (a pseudo-anonymous server) is much like an electronic mail drop. Users are given an anonymous e-mail address to which other people can send e-mail to them. That e-mail is then forwarded to their real e-mail address. It can also post or mail the user's e-mail without a trace of their real e-mail address. To add *privacy*, encryption is a good idea. A few potential sites include

- http://www.cs.berkeley.edu/~ralph/remailer-list.html (University of California at Berkeley)
- http://www.compulink.co.uk/~net-services/jd.htm (re-mailer and encryption software)
- http://www.anonymizer.com (keeps your web browsing anonymous)
- http://www.micros.hensa.ac.uk/gci-bin/msg2html/path=micros/ mac/finder/g/g119 (automatically deletes *cookies* from the *Preference folder* after each web session)
- http://www.emf.net/~mal/cookiesinfo.html
- http://www.simtel.net/pub/simtelnet/win3/inet/ns-demo2.zip
- http://www.shareware.com
- http://java.sun.com/sfaq/index.html (removes *applets*, which is a Java program that runs from inside a web browser; a *hostile applet* exploits and monopolizes a computer system's resources inappropriately and is a threat to security)

Encryption is hiding information behind a façade of nonsensical code. The key to encryption and decryption is the use of two *keys*: one to encrypt (by the sender) and one to decrypt (by the receiver). The *sender* encrypts an encoded or encrypted message using the receiver's (recipient's) *public key*. The recipient then uses his or her *private key* to decode or decrypt the message received. The public key encryption program PGP was designed by Phil Zimmerman in 1991 and was considered the encryption standard. Most of the websites I checked were out of date. (Note: Encryption programs are considered *munitions* and are subject to export restrictions under the *International Traffic in Arms Regulations* or *ITAR*; refer to 15 C.F.R. 734.2(b) (1997) and 15 C.F.R. 744.9 (1997).)

Steganography, the technology of hiding files within files, is the science of communication that obscures the existence of the communication by hiding (in a virtually undetectable manner) messages within *surplus* space within picture and sound files.

Cryptonomics is the marriage of cryptography and economics to provide secure transactions online through *digital cash* (electronic currency) or *virtual cash*. One web page on this is http://www.clickshare.com/clickshare (which tracks and monitors online digital cash purchases for the purchaser).

Security is the final phase of *privacy, anonymity, and security*, and it begins with a good password. Computers connected to a network for communicating with each other use a protocol or *language* called TCP/IP. It should be obvious that when choosing a password, users should select one that is not obvious or easily guessed. Crackers identify users' passwords and can use them to access files and data, read, or send e-mail and attachments, and access other parts of networks.

Passwords are only where security begins. A word on deleting files is warranted. Merely deleting a file does not completely eliminate it. Deleted files are still on the hard drive and are recoverable with *undelete programs* and forensic programs. To eradicate a file, users must *overwrite* it using a *file wipe utility*.

Firewalls monitor traffic from inside and out to ensure that selected communications are allowed to cross the threshold in either direction. (This is *not* protection against viruses.) Firewalls are custom made either to allow traffic in or to block traffic, based upon access control policy for the network involved. *Kerberos* is a network security that protects against internal threats from attempts to login to another host in the network. *Security Administrator Tool for Analyzing Networks* (SATAN) is a tool that probes for and analyzes computer system vulnerabilities. (It can also be used by crackers to probe victims for weaknesses.)

Cell Phone Baseband Hacking

Smartphone hacks on iPhones and Android phones have been on the rise, and in 2011, a new threat was identified—hacking the cell phone signal itself or *baseband hacking*. Ralf-Philipp Weinmann of the University of Luxembourg showed off a pretty neat proof-of-concept hack at the Black Hat D.C. conference in Washington, DC.

Previously, mobile hacking involved phone's operating systems or other software. This new threat involves breaking into the phone's *baseband processor*, which is the hardware that sends and receives radio signals to and from cell towers. *Baseband* is the component in the iPhone that manages all the functions that require an antenna, notably all cellular services. The baseband processor has its own RAM and firmware in NOR flash, separate from the core resources and functions as a resource to the main CPU. The Wi-Fi and Bluetooth are managed by the main CPU, although the baseband stores their MAC addresses in its NVRAM.

In a presentation, he set up his own cellular base station and was able to message all the iPhones in the room, asking them to join his new network. Had the iPhones' users accepted his invitation, Weinmann would have been able to inject a firmware update into the chips used to run the basic radio signals (baseband) in and out of the phones. That firmware would have switched on the phones' autoanswer feature, which would have let Weinmann silently dial into the phone and remotely listen to anything nearby.

It's not just iPhones that are vulnerable. Most phones, smart or not, running on the AT&T Wireless or T-Mobile networks in the United States are vulnerable, as are most European mobile phones. The Global System for Mobile Communications (GSM) standard that governed second-generation (2G) communications on those networks is more than 20 years old and wasn't designed to guard against base station attacks. Third-generation (3G) signals are unaffected, but almost all 3G mobile phones automatically drop down into 2G mode when 3G is not available. Anyone carrying it out this type of hack must set up a cellular base station and know the technical workings of the various baseband chips used in mobile phones. Open-source software has reduced the cost of setting up a fully working base station to less than $2000, putting the hack within the budget of anyone who really wanted to eavesdrop.

Cell Phone Data Retrieval

There are GPS data (if the phone is GPS capable), photographs and videos, text messages, phone logs, notes, and websites that were visited. Everything the cell phone does is tracked and logged somewhere. *Cellebrite* has developed a *Mobile Forensics and Data Transfer System*, called the Universal Forensics Extraction Device (UFED), which extracts all the information from a cell phone to aid in investigations. There is a mobile unit that can be used in the field, but there is also a device that is in a Pelican case that is a little less mobile but has the ability to charge the phone just in case the battery of the phone you are holding for evidence is dead. The Cellebrite device hooks up to cellular telephones to extract information, including call history logs, text messages, contact information, and photographs. It works on 3000 phone models and can even defeat password protections. Once the information is extracted from the cellular phone, the Cellebrite creates an easy-to-read report, which investigators can add to their reports.

Visual malware, for example, *PlaceRaider*, allows someone to view a smartphone camera remotely. *Sur Tec's APParition* is a smartphone application that allows an undercover officer to stream high-quality audio and at the same time to provide global positioning (GPS) locating. The application called *Casper* and the monitoring component called the *Fog* are not limited by distance.

The proliferation of new technology has made getting a quick wiretap more difficult. Facebook, Twitter, MySpace, BlackBerrys, Android, iPhones, iPads, and other mobile devices have diminished law enforcement's ability to tap. The Justice Department calls this phenomenon *going dark*. Criminals can now communicate using wireless devices and anonymous avatars. For example, in 2009, a pimp used a social networking site to entice children into prostitution. Although there was enough evidence to obtain a wiretap, one was not obtained because there were no means to conducting electronic surveillance of the particular website. While wiretaps are still useful, the advancement in technology is exceeding developments in electronic surveillance.

IMSI Catchers and Cell-Site Simulators: The StingRay

Computers are not the only electronic devices that *emanate* signals that can be exploited into intelligence data. *International Mobile Subscriber Identity* (IMSI) *catchers* are tools being used in Europe and the United States. They are advanced pieces of hardware that can be used to send out a signal, tricking mobile phones into thinking they are part of a legitimate mobile phone network. *Cell-site simulators* are a sophisticated surveillance system to scoop up data from cell phones and other wireless devices to track suspects.

The IMSI is used to identify the user of a cellular network and is a unique identification associated with all cellular networks. It is stored as a 64-bit field and is sent by the phone to the network. It is also used for acquiring other details of the mobile in the *home location register* (HLR) or is locally copied in the visitor location register (VLR). To prevent identifying and tracking the subscriber on the radio interface, the IMSI is sent as rarely as possible and a randomly generated Temporary Mobile Subscriber Identity (TMSI) is sent instead.

The TMSI is the identity that is most commonly sent between the mobile and the network. TMSI is randomly assigned by the VLR to every mobile in the area the moment it is switched on. The number is local to a location area, so it has to be updated each time the mobile moves to a new geographical area. The network can also change the TMSI of the mobile at any time and normally does so to avoid the subscriber from being identified and tracked by eavesdroppers on the radio interface. This makes it difficult to trace which mobile is which, except briefly, when the mobile is just switched on or when the data in the mobile become invalid for one reason or another. At that point, the global IMSI must be sent to the network.

IMSI catchers, such as the one purchased by the London Metropolitan Police, allow authorities to shut off targeted phones remotely and gather data about thousands of users in a specific area. They can force phones to release their unique IMSI and IMEI identity codes, which can then be used to track a person's movements in real time. They can be slipped into a suitcase and used almost anywhere to spy on mobile phone communications. IMSI catchers are high-tech portable devices used by law enforcement agencies across the world to secretly intercept conversations and text messages.

Meganet is a vendor of these devices and they are based out of Washington, DC. They have several government contracts including the DoD and NSA. There are also several websites that give detailed instructions on how to make your own IMSI catcher. But you can buy units from China-based websites for around $1700–$2000.

The device, known as a *StingRay*, simulates a cell phone tower and enables agents to collect the serial numbers of individual cell phones and then locate them. The Justice Department has generally maintained that a warrant based on probable cause is not needed to use a *cell-site simulator* because the government is not employing them to intercept conversations, but some judges around the country have disagreed and have insisted investigators first obtain a warrant.

Geotagging

A photo taken by a *smartphone* contains an image embedded with metadata that reveals the exact geographical location where the photo was taken. So by simply taking and posting a photo on the Internet, one may reveal the exact location where the photo was taken, such as one's home, place of employment, school, or other location. Data usually consist of latitude and longitude coordinates but can also include altitude, bearing, distance, accuracy data, and place names (see Figure 9.1).

Because iPhones embed geodata into photos that users upload to Flickr, Picasa, or similar web pages, iPhone shots can be automatically placed on a map. A map search can then be conducted. Clicking through the user's photo stream and adjusting the settings to view only those of interest on the map may reveal a cluster of images in one location. This may give clues as to the exact location of a home, place of employment, or other important target location. With advancements in technology, such as enhanced GPS capabilities and smartphones with built-in GPS, emanation of geodata becomes both a source of intelligence and a challenge to privacy and security.

Geotagging is the process of adding geographical identification to photographs, video, websites, and SMS messages. It is the virtual addition of a 10-digit grid coordinate to everything you post on the Internet. Geotags are automatically embedded in pictures taken with smartphones. When loaded to the Internet, they have been geotagged. Photos posted to photo sharing sites like Foursquare, Facebook, Twitter, Flickr, and Picasa can also be tagged

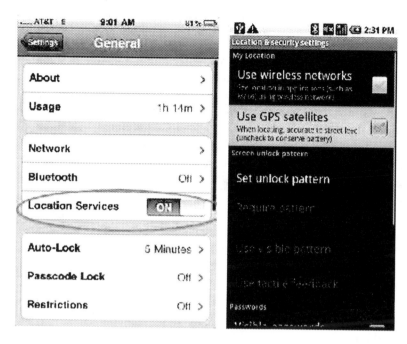

Figure 9.1 Disabling geotagging functions.

with the location, but it is not an automatic function. Foursquare currently has iPhone, Android, webOS, Windows Phone 7, and BlackBerry applications.

Facebook *Places* is similar to Foursquare in that it gives an individual's location when users post information using a mobile application. This feature is available when using the Facebook application for iPhone, touch.facebook.com, and Android. This function is automatically active on Facebook accounts until disabled (http://www.facebook.com/places/). Most location-based social networks have *checking in* applications at various locations to "earn points, badges, and discounts" and other geo-related awards. The popularity of these network applications has changed the way our emerging digital culture must view intelligence, security, and privacy.

Gowalla is another location-based social network with functions similar to Foursquare and Facebook Places. Users can build a passport that includes a collection of stamps from the places users have been. Gowalla users can also post photos and submit tips at various locations (http://gowalla.com/). SCVNGR is a location-based social network with a *checking in* application that allows companies, educational institutions, and organizations to build *challenges* inside the platform. Users are encouraged to complete the challenges in order to earn points, badges, or real-life discounts and coupons (http://www.scvngr.com/).

Formats like the JPEG format allow for geographical information to be embedded within the image and then read by picture viewers. This shows the exact location where a picture was taken. Most modern digital cameras do not automatically add geolocation metadata to pictures, but that is not always the case. Camera users should check their camera's operating manual and determine how to turn off GPS functions.

Even if a camera does not have a GPS function, a photo can be tagged with a location and added to photo sharing sites. A simple search for "Afghanistan" on Flickr reveals thousands of location-tagged photographs that have been uploaded. Tagging photos with an exact location on the Internet makes it possible to track locations and correlate it with other information to give valuable intelligence on classified areas of operation or the location of particular individuals of interest. These dangers can be avoided by removing geotags with a metadata removal tool for photos before publishing them on the Internet.

By tracking movements and aggregating information, where someone lives, works, or otherwise frequents, can be revealed. Services, like MotionX and other location-based social network applications, allow tracking user movements and establishing patterns. When watched long enough, a pattern emerges of when and where to find a targeted individual. A geotag readout for a photo might look like the following:

```
GPS Latitude     : 57 deg 38' 56.83" N
GPS Longitude    : 10 deg 24' 26.79" E
GPS Position     : 57 deg 38' 56.83" N, 10 deg 24' 26.79" E
```

or the same coordinates could also be presented as decimal degrees:

```
GPS Latitude     : 57.64911
GPS Longitude    : 10.40744
GPS Position     : 57.64911 10.40744
```

Metadata removal tools or a *metadata scrubber* is a privacy software designed to protect the privacy by removing privacy-compromising metadata from files before they are shared (e.g., by sending them as e-mail attachments or by posting them on the web). Metadata can be found in audio files, documents, images, presentations, and spreadsheets. Metadata can include information such as the file's author, file creation and modification dates, document revision history, and comments. Since metadata is not visible or clearly obvious in applications, there is a risk that the author will be unaware of its existence or will simply forget about it. If the file is shared, private or confidential information may inadvertently be exposed to intelligence collection. Metadata removal tools minimize the risk of such data *emanations*.

There are four groups or types of metadata removal tools: (1) *integral metadata removal tools*, which are included in some applications, like the *Document Inspector* in Microsoft Office 2007; (2) *batch metadata removal tools*, which can process multiple files; (3) *e-mail client* add-ins, which are designed to remove metadata from e-mail attachments just before they are sent; and (4) *server-based systems*, which are designed to automatically remove metadata at the network gateway.

Barcode Scanners and Magnetic Stripe Reader/Programmer

A *barcode reader* (or *barcode scanner*) is an electronic device for reading printed barcodes. It consists of a light source, a lens, and a light sensor translating optical impulses into electrical ones. Most barcode readers contain *decoder* circuitry to analyze the barcode's image data provided by the sensor and send the barcode's content to the scanner's output port (see Figure 9.2).

A *magnetic stripe reader* or *magstripe reader* reads information encoded in the magnetic stripe on the back of a plastic badges and cards. Since the 1970s, magnetic stripe readers have been used for access control and transaction processing, such as ATM and credit cards. Magnetic stripe readers can read data using a computer program through a serial port, USB connection, or a keyboard wedge. *Insertion readers* require that the badge be inserted into the reader and then pulled out. *Swipe readers* require that the badge pass completely through the reader. The magnetic stripe on the back of a card is composed of a bar magnet of iron-based magnetic particles encased in plastic-like tape (see Figures 9.3 and 9.4).

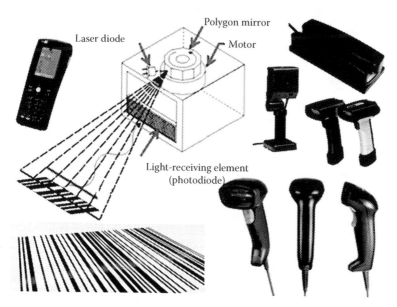

Figure 9.2 Barcode readers.

Figure 9.3 Logic controls MR 3010U, magnetic card reader, USB, external (left), and Unitec MS240, magnetic card reader, USB (right).

Figure 9.4 Blank USB MSR605 MSR206 magnetic stripe card reader writer encoder + 20PCS card offer a reading and writing solution of high- and/or low-coercivity cards.

When the bar magnets are polarized in the same direction, the magnetic stripe is blank. Information is written on the stripe by magnetizing the bars in either a *north* or *south* pole direction with an electromagnetic writer, called an *encoder*. The writing process, called flux reversal, causes a change in the magnetic field that can be detected by the magnetic stripe reader, much like the binary system used by computers. The magnetic stripe reader reads the information by detecting the changes in the magnetic field caused by the flux reversals on the card's magnetic stripe.

Smart cards are a newer generation of card containing an integrated circuit chip. The card may have metal contacts connecting the card physically to the reader, while *contactless cards* use a *magnetic field* or RFID for proximity reading. Hybrid smart cards include a magnetic stripe in addition to the chip, so the cards are also compatible with payment terminals that do not include a smart card reader. Cards with all three features, magnetic stripe, smart card chip, and RFID chip, are also becoming common as more activities require the use of such cards.

Stripe Snoop is a suite of commercially available research tools that captures, modifies, validates, generates, analyzes, and shares data from magstripe cards. The data are captured through different hardware interfaces (or stdin), the contents are decoded into the correct character set, and a CDDB-like database attempts to figure out what the contents mean.

Magstripe Forgery and Skimming

Magstripes have become a favorite tool of identity thieves. By altering the magstripes of authentic bank gift cards, the suspect bypasses the difficult and risky step of fabricating fake credit cards. Instead of having to make fake cards, data harvesters can load up bank gift cards with stolen data obtained from people online and use them like cash. Identity thieves have to defeat a security code on the magstripe, as well as automated systems that watch for and alert the credit-issuing bank to suspicious transactions. Every Visa transaction that goes through their network, for example, is rated for fraud potential in real time. Data hacked from retail sources, in the hands of data harvesters, identity thieves, and forgers, are embedded into the magstripes of counterfeited credit cards.

Gift cards issued by Visa, MasterCard, and American Express have emerged as attractive fraud targets because they are widely available and can be used in more places than merchant gift cards. Acquiring a bank gift card is easy at grocery stores or by ordering online. Thousands of banks, credit unions, supermarkets, drugstores, and convenience stores offer them; they can be picked up at a checkout line or ordered from online banking websites or sites such as iCardGiftCard.com and work at millions of restaurants and shops, using exactly the same magstripe-driven payment system used for credit and debit card transactions.

Bank gift cards are flat, with no embossed numerals and no individual's name anywhere on the card. No proof of identity is required to use them. Altering the magstripe to convert a bank gift card into a credit card is a way to convert low-value cards into high-value ones. It takes thousands of dollars of equipment to create counterfeit credit cards from scratch, but a generic Visa gift card, with an altered magstripe, no name on it, and no way to trace it, is easier. Visa, MasterCard, and American Express have started producing payment cards that use a computer chip to speed transactions and make it more difficult to compromise than a magstripe.

Credit and ATM card skimming is on the rise worldwide. It relies on data-reading electronics to copy the magnetic stripe information from your credit card or debit card. It can capture both your credit card number and the PIN at restaurants, gas pumps, ATM machines, and almost anywhere where cards are used. ATMs are vulnerable for the same reasons that gas pumps are. They are exposed and unattended.

An identity thief or skimmer merely needs to place an electronic magnetic strip reader over the existing ATM card slot or a point of sale device. When you slide your card in, the skimming device reads it first, and then the actual card reader does, at which point the transaction proceeds as expected. Now a skimmer has an exact copy of your card data. Older card-skimming devices required data harvesting thieves to return and collect the information periodically, exposing them to risk of discovery. But newer skimmers can transmit data to thieves by either short-range Bluetooth or by GSM cellular. This enables the thieves, who may be sitting in a car nearby or in a building on the other side of the planet, to capture the account numbers live as the account holder makes a purchase or a withdrawal.

Collecting credit card data is a relatively simple matter of capturing the account number. But debit cards are even more desirable to thieves because the bad guys can plunder a bank account quickly and completely without the account holders realizing what is happening. The card networks monitor credit card usage and have rigorous risk- and fraud-prevention policies in place, whereas debit cards are linked directly to a bank account, though obtaining the PIN associated with a debit card is somewhat more difficult.

The most common high-tech ways to steal PINs are with tiny cameras mounted within a fish-eye mirror or with an electronic mesh overlaid on the keyboard. But data harvesting thieves have found a less obvious and risky way to steal PINs. PINs may be four or six digits long. When you key in your PIN, software at the ATM or point of sale automatically converts it into a one-way algorithm called a *hash*. Then, if someone captures the data steam, they will see only the resulting hash value, not the original four or six digits. By itself, a hashed PIN is a useless string of numbers. You can't type in the hashed PIN as it appears on your debit card or within a database inside a bank network, because those digits will be converted into yet another value. Instead, you have to find a way to generate that hash value.

Data harvesting attackers located the PIN data in a data breach, analyzed and decrypted the algorithm used, and generated a table of all the possible four- and six-digit PIN codes that the algorithm might produce, called a *rainbow table* in cryptography. Thieves do not have to match a PIN exactly, only the four or six digits that would produce the same hash value.

In a related story in Rhode Island, magnetic keyboards were used to *turn on* the pumps at a closed gas station. This illustrates the constant innovation of high-tech thieves in our ever-increasingly high-tech society.

RFID

RFID is a wireless noncontact system that uses radio-frequency electromagnetic fields to transfer data from tags attached to objects, for automatic identification and tracking. Some tags require no battery and are powered and read at short ranges via magnetic fields (electromagnetic induction). Others use a local power source and emit radio waves (electromagnetic radiation at radio frequencies). Unlike a barcode, the tag does not need to be within line of sight of the reader and may be embedded in the tracked object. The tag contains electronically stored information that can be read from several feet away.

Active RFID tags also have the potential to function as low-cost remote sensors that broadcast telemetry back to a base station. Applications of tagometry data could include sensing of road conditions by implanted beacons, weather reports, and noise-level monitoring.

Passive RFID tags can also report sensor data, for example, the *Wireless Identification and Sensing Platform* is a passive tag that reports temperature, acceleration, and capacitance to commercial Gen2 RFID readers:

- *Low-frequency* (LF 125–134.2 and 140–148.5 kHz) (LowFID) tags and *high-frequency* (HF 13.56 MHz) (HighFID) tags can be used globally without a license.
- *Ultrahigh-frequency* (UHF 868–928 MHz) (Ultra-HighFID [UHFID]) tags cannot be used globally as there is no single global standard.

See Table 9.1 and Figures 9.5 and 9.6, RFID tag frequencies and readers.

Other Frequencies

Other frequencies of interest include invisible fence and dog training collar frequencies:

- Invisible fence frequencies—7.5–10.8 kHz with a 30 Hz modulation frequency.
- Training collar frequencies—216.0, 433.825, 915.0 MHz.

Table 9.1 RFID Tag Frequencies

Band	Range	Data Speed	Remarks	Tag Cost
120–150 kHz (LF)	10 cm	Low	Animal identification and factory data collection	$1
13.56 MHz (HF)	1 m	Low to moderate	Smart cards (MIFARE, ISO/IEC 14443)	$0.50
433 MHz (UHF)	1–100 m	Moderate	Defense applications (active tags)	$5
865–868 MHz (Europe) 902–928 MHz (North America) UHF	1–2 m	Moderate to high	EAN, various standards	$0.15 (passive tags)
2450–5800 MHz (microwave)	1–2 m	High	802.11 WLAN, Bluetooth standards	$25 (active tags)
3.1–10 GHz (microwave)	Up to 200 m	High	requires semiactive or active tags	$5 projected

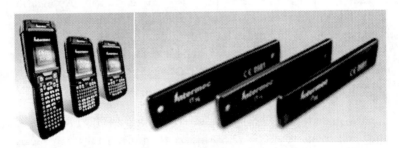

Figure 9.5 Intermec RFID scanners and tags.

- Automobile door lock and starter remote frequencies are covered in *automobile locks*.
- Garage door frequencies (see Table 9.2 Garage Door Opener Frequencies).

Remote Electromagnetic Sensors

Magnetic sensors can detect objects composed of ferrous metals (containing iron), such as equipment or vehicles. Magnetic intrusion detection systems (MAGID) can detect vehicles from 60 to 80 feet away and personnel from 10 to 15 feet away. They can transmit warnings up to 1000–2000 yards away or further, suing buried cable transmission lines. They are used for perimeter security or for surveillance in an area of operation.

Figure 9.6 Motorola RFID scanners–readers.

Table 9.2 Garage Door Opener Frequencies

Dates	System	Color of Programming Button (on *Chamberlain* Manufactured Units)
1984–2004	8–12 DIP Switch on 300–400 MHz	White, gray, or yellow button with red LED
1993–1997	Billion Code on 390 MHz	Green button with green or red LED
1997–present	Security+ {rolling code} on 390 MHz	Orange or red button with amber LED
2005–present	Security+ {rolling code} on 315 MHz	Purple button with amber LED
2011–present	Security+ 2.0 {rolling code} on 310, 315, and 390 MHz	Yellow button with amber LED and yellow antenna wires

Seismic sensors detect vibrations and can be used to detect earthquakes, atomic energy tests, and, on a smaller scale, intrusion into security perimeters or areas of operational surveillance. Disposable seismic intrusion detector systems can remain in place for 7–60 days, until the batteries expire, and can detect vehicles from 100 yards and personnel up to 30 yards away. The U.S. Army's Patrol Seismic Intrusion Device (PSID) can detect movement up to 130 yards away and transmit warnings up to 21,000 yards away. They are affected by *background clutter* or the natural vibrations of the earth surface.

Acoustic sensors are basically mics that detect sounds up to 300–400 feet away and transmit them back to receivers. Acoustic buoys can be hidden, can be suspended from tree foliage, and are concealed in other manners.

Disturbance sensors transmit warnings when moved or stepped on, interrupting the electric current. They are also concealed or disguised as natural objects in the area.

IR sensors monitor changes in heat or temperature to detect intrusion, usually in areas 50 × 100 feet.

The *AN/TRS-2* is the platoon early warning system (*PEWS*) (Figure 9.7) and was used throughout the 1980s (operating approximately between 139.250 and 141.100 MHz). These systems will detect either seismic or magnetic disturbances within 10 m of the transmitter detector and report to the receiver up to 1500 m away with either a *P* for personnel intrusion or *C* for vehicle intrusion, along with the transmitter's ID for the location of the intrusion. The receiver will cache alerts received (with the most recent first) and has an audio alert tone that can be enabled or disabled. It can also be hardwired to the transmitters. All components use standard 9 V batteries (each transmitter takes one and the receiver takes two). Each transmitter detector is programmed with an area code and an ID code (1–5). The receiver can monitor up to 10 transmitter detectors in each of up to 8 areas. It can only monitor 1 area of up to 10 detector transmitters at a time and is switch selectable on the receiver.

Figure 9.7 The AN/TRS-2 PEWS.

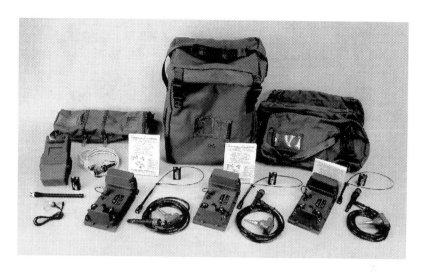

Figure 9.8 The AN/PRS-9 BAIS or PEWD II.

The AN/TRS-2 PEWS was replaced by the *AN/PRS-9* battlefield anti-intrusion system (BAIS), or platoon early warning device (PEWD II) (Figure 9.8) is the U.S. Army's standard unattended physical security system, providing early warning, intrusion detection, and threat classification at the platoon and higher levels. It is both a *seismic* and an *acoustic* detection system, which can be supplemented by *IR* and *magnetic* sensors.

The AN/GSQ-159 is a disposable seismic intrusion detection system and the AN/GSQ-160 is an electromagnetic detection system, both used by the military. The DT-515/GSQ is another detection device that has been used. The PEWS was in wider use and the BAIS/PEWD II is the current standard and state of the art.

Explosives Trace Detectors (Vapor Detectors)

Explosives trace detectors (ETDs) (vapor detectors) are security equipment able to detect explosives of small magnitude, using ion mobility spectrometry, thermo-redox technologies, and chemiluminescence and amplifying fluorescent polymer. The detection can be done by sniffing vapors as in an explosive vapor detector or by sampling traces of particulates or by utilizing both methods depending on the scenario. Most explosive detectors in the market today can detect both vapors and particles of explosives. Devices similar to ETDs are also used to detect narcotics. The equipment is often used in airports and other high-security areas considered susceptible to acts of unlawful interference. These are related flammable gas and vapor detection systems (see Figure 9.9.).

Figure 9.9 Thermo-redox detector (*sniffer*) Sintrex/IDS EVD-3000.

Imagery Intelligence 10

Imagery and *remote sensing* are the use of technology that ranges from simple film and digital cameras, to IR (night vision) and thermal imaging, to satellite images and mapping. *Looking through the keyhole*, as satellite imagery is often called, has made great advances since the days of the Cuban missile crisis when film canisters had to be retrieved, developed, analyzed, interpreted, and distributed. Ground imagery includes photography, IR imaging and viewing (such as *forward-looking IR* or FLIR), thermal imaging and viewing, and radar. Satellite imagery and remote sensing include aerial photography, mapping and geological data, digital data, radar, and meteorological and climatological images and data.

Before satellites, aerial photography was the source of high-level imagery. Film, rather than digital photos or real-time video, was the state of the art in intelligence imagery (Figures 10.1 through 10.9).

Night Vision Devices

Night vision technology consists of two major types: *light amplification imaging* (or intensification) and *thermal imaging* (IR) (Figure 10.10).

Most commercially available night vision products are *light-amplifying devices*. This technology takes the small amount of light from the surrounding area (moonlight, starlight, or streetlights) and converts the protons that make up the light energy into electrons or *electrical energy*. The electrons are then directed through a thin disk that can be as small as a quarter. This disk has millions of channels through which the electrons pass. As the electrons pass through the channels, they bounce around, and when they strike the walls of the channels, they release even more electrons. By turning the light energy into electrical energy, the technology is in a position to increase the amount of electrical energy. The increased amount of electrons bounces off a phosphor screen and turn them back into protons or *visible light energy* (Foster, 2005, pp. 324–325).

Thermal imaging devices work by using the upper portion of the IR light spectrum. This portion of the light spectrum is emitted as heat instead of as light, so the hotter an object is, the more heat it will radiate. This radiated heat can be seen as IR light. Thermal imagers take the IR light that is emitted

Figure 10.1 Japanese aerial photograph of *Battleship Row* in Pearl Harbor on December 7, 1941.

Figure 10.2 Satellite (NASA). (Available at http://en.wikipedia.org/wiki/File:2001_mars_odyssey_wizja.jpg.)

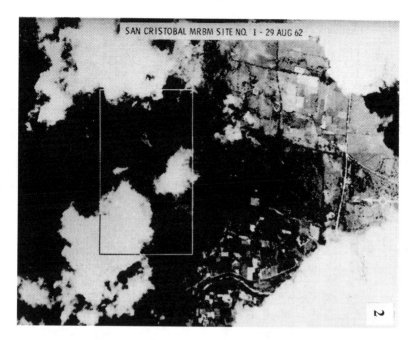

Figure 10.3 Cuban missile crisis: August 29, 1962, U-2 photograph showing no construction at San Cristobal.

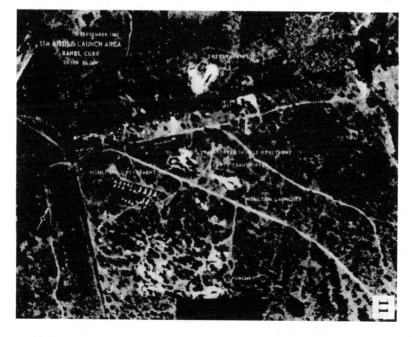

Figure 10.4 Cuban missile crisis: September 26, 1962, U-2 photograph showing surface-to-surface cruise missile (named *Kennel* by the United States and FKR in Soviet plans) launch area at Banes.

Figure 10.5 Cuban missile crisis: October 23, 1962, U.S. Navy low-level photograph of San Cristobal MRBM site No. 1 (mission led by Commander William Ecker).

Figure 10.6 USGS satellite photo. (Landsat data, acquired by the U.S. Geological Survey on March 20, 2011, shows the Sendai, Japan region. (Available at http://www.usgs.gov/blogs/features/2011/03/28/preliminary-magnitude-8-9-near-the-east-coast-of-japan/.)

Figure 10.7 The seals of the NGA and the NRO.

Figure 10.8 Serum and Vaccine Institute in Al-A'amiriya, Iraq, as imaged by a U.S. reconnaissance satellite in November 2002.

by objects and focus it on an array of IR light detectors. These detectors are used to create a thermogram or a temperature pattern image. The thermal imager takes the information from the thermogram and converts it into electrical data. These data impulses are sent to a microprocessor that creates an image for display. Thermal imagers are significantly more complex than light amplification devices (Foster, 2005, p. 325).

Figure 10.9 Satellite image of Kuwait dust storm April 13, 2012 (NASA). (Available at http://www.ncdc.noaa.gov/sotc/hazards/.)

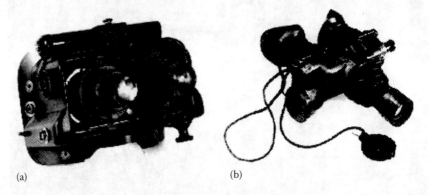

(a)   (b)

Figure 10.10 Night vision devices. NVG-500 double-tube night vision goggle (a). AN/PVS-7B third-generation monotube goggles (b).

Satellite Imagery

Satellite imagery and *remote sensing* (detecting something from a distance) are complex applications of several scientific and technological disciplines, including orbital mechanics, physics, and optics. It involves the application of how light reacts with the target package, how the image is received, and how the data are manipulated and interpreted (Hough, 1991, p. 37).

Satellite imagery utilizes still photography, video feed, and mapping technology. Resolution from such distances (space, the final frontier) can be critical. The smallest element in conventional film is the silver halide grain and, in high-resolution films, can be as small as 0.05 µm. The charge-coupled devices (CCDs) in intelligence grade *recon sats* are probably thirty times larger and, therefore, of greater resolution (Hough, 1991, p. 40). Conventional film, however, is not only *real time* deficient, but photos can only be interpreted using conventional methods unless converted to a digital format. Therefore, digital photography and computer enhancement and interpretation are more suitable (Hough, 1991, p. 42).

One of the first uses of real-time television images was the application of a return beam vidicon (RBV), but the resolution was inadequate for most intelligence applications. Multispectral scanners were developed to scan various parts of the electromagnetic spectrum because different types of light provide different types of information about targets (Hough, 1991, p. 43). The information from CCDs is passed to a controller, which labels the position of *each of the charges in the overall picture* and measures the *electrical charge on a scale of 0–255*, and transmits stored images back to earth. CCDs cannot capture as many bands of energy as multispectral scanners. They are limited to visible or near IR. They are also sensitive to low-level current, called a *dark current*, which can interfere with electrical signals and change images. This is countered by liquid gas or thermoelectric cooling (Hough, 1991, p. 47).

Radar can *see* through haze and clouds that hinders other viewing and is not dependent upon natural or independent light sources. Microwaves can provide data on the terrain, its electrical characteristics, and the physical characteristics of vegetation. Radar can even *see* some subsurface features, including submerged submarines and structures (Hough, 1991, pp. 48–49). Passive radar is related to radio astronomy (sensing stellar objects with radar receivers), sensing the difference between incoming signals and reference signals. It can detect hot, high-conductivity objects (e.g., aircraft and vehicles) and can see through thin layers of soil, revealing underground structures. While passive radar is itself nearly undetectable, it has the potential of detecting even stealth craft (Hough, 1991, pp. 53–54).

Mapping and Geographical Data

Aerial and satellite photos and maps are available from several open sources, not the least of which is the U.S. Geological Survey (USGS), which has a web page at http://www.usgs.gov/. The USGS defines its mission as "a science organization that provides impartial information on the health of our ecosystems and environment, the natural hazards that threaten us, the natural resources we rely on, the impacts of climate and land-use change, and the core science systems that help us provide timely, relevant, and useable information."

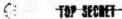

TOP SECRET

(S) NATIONAL RECONNAISSANCE OFFICE
WASHINGTON, D.C.

THE NRO STAFF

15 March 1977

MEMORANDUM FOR MR.
COL...

SUBJECT: DCI Briefing to the President

Dr. Cook was informed yesterday that Admiral Turner plans to
brief the President on intelligence collection. As an input to that
briefing he would like the NRO to prepare a 10 minute presentation
on the capabilities and limitations of our imagery systems. This
briefing should include the management of imagery, i.e., response
to and satisfaction of requirements and flexibility of the systems.
Under capabilities the briefing should include resolution and different imagery modes. In the limitations area, we should stress

Our proposed briefing to Dr. Cook should be around 20 minutes
to permit editing down to the final version. Please provide me a
proposed briefing by noon, Friday.

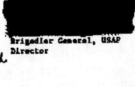

Also wants to discuss our
organization and management
philosophy, with reference to the
advantages gained in flexibility,
and efficiency.

Brigadier General, USAF
Director

TOP SECRET

CONTROL NO.
COPY ____ OF ____ COPIES
PAGE ____ OF ____ PAGES

Figure 10.11 Declassified briefing document to the president from the NRO
(note the handwritten comments).

The NGA is a DoD combat support agency and a member of the national intelligence community (IC). NGA develops imagery and map-based intelligence solutions for U.S. national defense, homeland security, and safety of navigation. The NGA applies a wide range of geospatial intelligence (GEOINT) capabilities, including imagery and geospatial and targeting analysis, with image sciences to produce imagery intelligence (IMINT) products.

The NRO is the U.S. government agency in charge of designing, building, launching, and maintaining America's intelligence satellites. Since 1961, the NRO has provided the reconnaissance support to the IC and DoD. Formed in response to the Soviet launch of Sputnik, the NRO was secretly created on September 6, 1961, to oversee *all satellite and overflight reconnaissance projects, whether overt or covert.* The existence of the organization is no longer classified today, since its declassification was made public in 1992. As its mission states, the NRO is relentlessly working to foster "Innovative Overhead Intelligence Systems for National Security" and remains unwavering in its dedication to its vision and motto: "Vigilance From Above" (Figure 10.11).

GEOINT means the exploitation and analysis of imagery and geospatial information to describe, assess, and visually depict physical features and geographically referenced activities on the earth. GEOINT consists of imagery, IMINT, and geospatial (e.g., mapping, charting, and geodesy) information. Information collected and processed by NGA is tailored for customer-specific solutions. By giving customers ready access to GEOINT, NGA provides support to civilian and military leaders and contributes to the state of readiness of U.S. military forces.

Processing and Consuming Imagery Intelligence

Once images are returned from space as a stream of digital signals, these signals tell receiving stations the value of each pixel in the image (usually between 0 and 255, with 0 representing black and 255 representing pure white). Once data are processed and displayed, images are sharpened by edge enhancement (making important objects easier to notice) or smoothing (eliminating sudden changes in intensity to make images less confusing and easier to see) (Hough, 1991, pp. 59–60). Spectral enhancement involves interpreting the light absorbed or reflected to reveal shape, for example, through a color composite (Hough, 1991, p. 62). Other processing may include coordinate transformations, ratio image generation, and temporal enhancement (Hough, 1991, pp. 64–70).

Once IMINT is processed, analyzed, and interpreted, it can be disseminated to consumers or end users of intelligence. While *spy* satellites have been critical in such *Cold War* missions as verifying arms controls agreements and tracking strategic weapons, real-time surveillance remains essential in locating and identifying weapons of mass destruction (WMDs) such as nuclear, biological, and chemical weapons (NBC). Real-time applications also provide timely tactical information and intelligence to military units, monitoring of political events of significance (such as riots), tracking terrorist movements and installations, and economic intelligence (such as industrial and agricultural information). IMINT can also support law enforcement and surveillance operations, as well as a variety of non-security-related civil functions.

Surveillance Target Acquisition and Night Observation

The term surveillance target acquisition and night observation (STANO) was first coined by General Westmoreland and represented his perspective of technological innovations in tactical intelligence for the electronic battlefield. The type of equipment included in this field are night vision devices; intrusion detection devices; portable surveillance radar; laser aiming, ranging, and detecting devices; and specialized optical systems (stabilized optical monoculars and binoculars). Photography, of course, is an integral part of surveillance and photo intelligence (PHOTINT) is an important part of intelligence operations.

Pinhole Cameras

Alternative photography is the practice of any process of photography, where the worker has to make his or her own light-sensitive materials because these are not produced by factories or manufacturers (Figure 10.12).

A *pinhole camera* is a homemade camera without a lens and with one small aperture. It is basically a *light-proof box* with a small hole in one side. Light passes through the aperture hole and projects an inverted image (upside down) on the opposite side of the box, much as the human eye does. The smaller the hole, the sharper the image, but the dimmer the projected image is. Optimally, the size of the aperture should be 1/100 or less of the distance between it and the projected image. Because a pinhole camera requires a lengthy exposure, its *shutter* may be manually operated, as with a light-proof door or cover to cover and uncover the pinhole. Typical exposures range from 5 seconds to several hours.

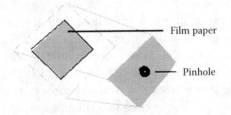

Film paper

Pinhole

Figure 10.12 Pinhole camera.

The image may be projected onto or exposed to photographic film or a CCD. Pinhole cameras with CCDs are often used for surveillance because they are difficult to detect. Photographic film is a sheet of plastic (cellulose acetate, nitrocellulose, polyester, or PET) coated with an emulsion containing light-sensitive silver halide salts (bonded by a gelatin) with variable crystal sizes that determine the sensitivity, contrast, and resolution. When the emulsion is sufficiently exposed, it forms an invisible image. Chemical processes are applied to develop the visible film image. A CCD is a device for the movement of electrical charge and is a major technology for digital imaging.

Pinhole cameras can be handmade and consists of a light-tight box with a pinhole in one end and a piece of film or photographic paper (photo paper) at the other end. *Photo paper* is paper coated with light-sensitive chemicals for making photographic prints. A flap of cardboard with a tape hinge can be used as a shutter. The pinhole may be punched or drilled using a sewing needle or small diameter bit through a piece of tinfoil or thin metal. This piece is then taped to the inside of the light-tight box behind a hole cut through the box.

Coat paper with KI solution and mix with spent fixer (drying at each stage, the second stage taking place in subdued lighting) and use as printing-out paper. KI is a precursor to silver iodide (used in photography). KI is a component in some disinfectants and hair treatment chemicals. KI is also used as a *fluorescence quenching* agent in biomedical research. It is also used as a nutritional supplement in animal feeds and the human diet as the most common additive used to *iodize* table salt. Water color paper coated with silver emulsion works, if silver emulsion is available. Leaves, flowers, and fruit juices have been used to make photo paper. Kitchen salt, alcohol, and a sodium bicarbonate or prune juice have reportedly worked (although I have not tried this yet). Each of these takes days to develop.

Biometrics

Biometrics is the new and emerging technology that automatically identifies an individual based on characteristics. It is the science and technology of measuring and analyzing biological data. Location data can be created, linked, stored, and analyzed through the formation of *geographic information systems* (GIS), GPS, and *automatic vehicle locator* (AVL) systems. In information technology, biometrics refers to technologies that measure and analyze human body characteristics, such as fingerprints, eye retinas and irises, voice patterns, facial patterns, and hand measurements, for identification and authentication purposes.

The demand for greater security at borders, government buildings, public transportation facilities, public venues, and other locations has created greater demand for biometrics—technologies that measure biological traits to identify individuals. Systems that digitally fingerprint people, read the patterns of their irises, measure the unique dimensions of their faces, or verify their voices are expected to quadruple over the next 5 years.

There are two classifications of biometric information: (1) physiological characteristics and (2) behavioral characteristics. Physiological characteristics include fingerprint, DNA, facial features, eye pattern, and hand geometry. Behavioral characteristics that are unique to people include gait, signature, and voice. Anything that is unique to a person can be converted to a digital format that can be used to differentiate individuals from others. Biometric information is categorized by use as either (1) access control or (2) remote identification.

Another word for eye pattern is iris recognition. Iris recognition uses pattern-recognition techniques based on his resolution images of the irides of an individual's eye. This process, not to be confused with retina scanning, uses digital technology to create detailed images of the intricate structures of the iris. This information is converted into digital templates that create a mathematical interpretation for positive identification.

One of the most controversial biometric applications is FRT. FRT can acquire digital photographs of an individual's face to take measurements between nodal points, which are locations on every human's face. While there are about 80 different nodal points, an FRT software algorithm requires only 14–22 points for comparison. Gait is also used to identify individuals by the way they walk. Digital images can be taken by imagery collection devices (fixed cameras, aerial photographs, satellite imagery, etc.), analyzed, and compared for digital patterns.

Voice is a combination of physical and behavioral characteristics that are related to the voice signal patterns. The characteristics of a voice include the vocal tracts, nasal cavity, mouth, and lips. The behavioral characteristics of a voice deal with the speaker's physical and emotional state. The authentication of a voice is divided into two groups, text-dependent and text-independent methods. Text dependent is when the speakers speak a predetermined phrase. Text independent does not have any conditions and can be done with any statement.

License Plate Readers

License plate readers (LPRs) can record license plates at about one per second at speeds of up to 100 mph, and they often utilize IR cameras for clarity and to facilitate reading at any time of day or night. The data collected can either be processed in real time, at the site of the read, or it can be transmitted to remote center and processed at a later time.

Internet and Database Open Sources $\quad$ 11

Open-Source Intelligence

Open-source intelligence (OSINT) is derived from the Internet, newspapers, journals, radio and television, etc. Source reliability is one of the major issues of concern with this method of collection. Here, I am providing, among other things, a collection of websites with databases and other useful information. While I have tried to access these recently and have found them to be sound, web pages come and go daily, so a source I cite may no longer exist when you pull this book off of your crowed shelf a couple of years down the road. Happy hunting!

Intelligence Research Sources

Here are some open sources of intelligence data and research that are very useful. You should probably save these in your Internet *favorites*:

> https://www.cia.gov/library/publications/the-world-factbook/ (*the Central Intelligence Agency World Fact Book*)
> https://www1.nga.mil/GEOINTOnline/Pages/default.aspx (the National Geo-Spatial Intelligence Agency GEOINT On-Line)
> http://www.nro.gov/ (the National Reconnaissance Office web page)
> http://intelweb.janes.com/public/intelweb/index.shtml (Jane's Defence and Security Intelligence and Analysis)
> http://jid.janes.com/public/jid/index.shtml (Jane's Intelligence Digest)
> http://jpr.janes.com/public/jpr/index.shtml (Jane's Police Digest)
> http://www.rand.org/ (the Rand Corporation)
> http://www.brookings.edu/ (the Brookings Institution)
> http://www.hudson.org/ (the Hudson Institute)
> http://www.cato.org/ (the Cato Institute)
> http://www.heritage.org/ (the Heritage Foundation)
> http://www.iwp.edu/ (the Institute of World Politics)
> http://www.eyespymag.com/ (*Eye Spy* magazine is a periodical, but of great interest with news and commentary)

Database Sources of Information

Here are a couple of nifty sources straightaway:

http://www.city-data.com/ (data on demographics, economy, and crime)

http://www.freebooter.com/ (mail drops, online privacy, identity and passport sources, diplomatic appointments and titles of nobility, etc.)

http://www.finaid.org/scholarships/maildropsearch.phtml or http://www.mbe.com/Pages/home.aspx (for more mail drops and mail boxes)

The investigator's *black book* of links to phone directory search tools, investigative and criminal justice organizations, government agencies, and other research sites: http://www.pacficnet.net/~blackbook/links.html.

Another database source is Internet Sleuth, with access to more than 1500 databases: http://www.isleuth.com.

LexisNexis is a subscription service with specialized databases and features. Lexis is a legal database, which includes statutes, regulations, case law, Shepard's Citations, and property records. MEDIS is a source of medical information, such as MEDLINE, *JAMA*, and Physician Data Query. LEGIS is a link to congressional bill tracking, vote reports, and campaign contributions. Nexis has information on news and business, including access to nearly 6000 magazines and periodicals, as well as biographies, company profiles, SEC reports, and other public records:

http://www.lexis-nexis.com

http://www.law.cornell.edu/uscode/ (Cornell University's U.S. Code lookup service)

Fact Checking Intellectual Property and Plagiarism

Intellectual property involves anything that is patented, copyrighted, or trademarked. Plagiarism involves using someone else's intellectual property (such as written material) without permission and citation (i.e., passing it off as your own when it is someone else's work or ideas). Information may be quoted, as long as it is cited, and if large amounts are reproduced, permission must be granted. Photographs and illustrations must also be cited and *used by permission*, although some material is so old or is not copyrighted as to enter the *public domain*. (For legal advice on this area, consult a competent legal counsel who is certified in *intellectual property* law.)

Other sources for fact checks and patent information are the following:

http://www.sunsite.unc.edu/patents/intropat.html (patent searches by class, subclass, patent number, patent titles and abstracts, etc.; also listed under *competitive intelligence*)

http://www.freepatentsonline.com/7669445.html (free patents online)

http://www.grammarly.com/?q=plagiarism&gclid=CLfPzpD7oakCFR DPKgodAH_ktw (grammar and plagiarism check software)

http://www.dustball.com/cs/plagiarism.checker/ (plagiarism check software)

http://www.articlechecker.com/ (plagiarism check software)

http://searchenginereports.net/articlecheck.aspx (plagiarism check software)

http://www.smallseotools.com/plagiarism-checker/ (plagiarism check software)

http://www.duplichecker.com/ (plagiarism check software)

http://www.academicplagiarism.com/ (plagiarism check software; membership)

http://www.plagiarismchecker.com/ (plagiarism check software)

https://www.writecheck.com/static/home.html?gclid=COD-6KuAoqk-CFQbCKgodYVHWsw (plagiarism check software)

http://turnitin.com/static/index.php (*TurnItIn* plagiarism check software; subscription software)

http://turnitinsafely.com/software_code_checker.html?gclid=CNa0hO-AoqkCFUW8KgodJHkyvQ (*TurnItIn* plagiarism check software; subscription software)(plagiarism check software)

http://www.reference.com (dictionary, thesaurus, translator, etc.)

Social Security Numbers and Vital Records

Social security numbers are the most common identifiers and have been used as military serial numbers. *Vital records* include birth, marriage, divorce, and death records. Some common and useful sources for this information include the following:

http://www.acronymfinder.com/Enumeration-Verification-System-(EVS).html (the Social Security Administration's guide for employers or Enumeration Verification System) (free)

http://www.infobases.com/ssdi/query01.htm (the Social Security Administration's death index; by searching by name, you can find SSN, DOB, date of death, last known address, and where payments were made)

http://www.veris-ssn.com (desktop software for verification of SSNs)

http://www.familytreemaker.com/00000825.html (family tree maker vital records)

http://www.medaccess.com/address/vital_toc.htm (medical records)

http://www.interment.net (international cemetery search site; subscription)

Driver's License and License Plate Information

http://www.docusearch.com/driver.html#plate (license plates, phones, SSNs, etc.)

http://registry.faa.gov/aircraftinquiry/ (FAA Aircraft Registration Database; searchable by name and current within last 4 years)

http://www.worldlicenceplates.com/hp.html (plate histories)

https://www.nicb.org// (National Insurance Crime Bureau; database to determine whether a vehicle has been declared an unrecovered, stolen, or salvage vehicle)

http://www.claim.org/index.htm (life insurance claim information)

Criminal History Checks and Court Records

http://mycase.in.gov/default.aspx (Indiana Public Records inquiry)

http://www.pacer.psc.uscourts.gov (PACER: public access to federal district, appellate, and bankruptcy court case and docket information by party and case index)

http://www.theinmatelocator.com/Home_Page.html (inmate locator)

http://www.inmatesplus.com/ (inmate locator)

http://www.theinmatelocator.com/Indiana.html (Indiana inmate locator)

http://www.bop.gov/ (federal inmate locator)

http://www.criminal-check.com/?hop=cawnat (criminal checks)

http://www.searchsystems.net (SearchSystems: largest public record database on the Internet, including criminal records, sex offender lists, civil court actions, vital records, corporate and professional licensing information, property records)

http://www.uscourts.gov/Home.aspx (automated information in U.S. federal courts)

http://www.icrimewatch.net/indiana.php (Indiana Sheriff's Association Sex and Violent Offender Registry)

http://www.nationalsexoffenderregistry.net (National Sex Offender Registry: lists sex offenders)

http://www.mostwanted.com (most wanted; private list)

http://www.fbi.gov/wanted/topten (FBI Ten Most Wanted)

http://www.usmarshals.gov/investigations/most_wanted/ (U.S. Marshal's 15 Most Wanted)

http://www.usdoj.gov/dea/fugitives/fuglist.htm (DEA's most wanted fugitives)

http://www.ustreas.gov/offices/enforcement/ofac/sdn/ (terrorist watch list)

Tracking Sources and Stolen Property

To track checks by bank routing numbers, use http://www.routingnumbers.org/.

To track packages, you can try typing in the air bill tracking number for Federal Express at http://www.fedex.com/us/track/index.html or use the tracking number for UPS at http://www.ups.com/tracking/tracking.html.

The ARC can provide airline ticket information for past and future domestic and international flights purchased by an individual (with an administrative subpoena that includes the individual's name and DOB; no dates of travel are needed). The company keeps records for a few years (https://www.arccorp.com/index.jsp).

The following site provides car rental security contact information for law enforcement, corporate security, and financial crime investigators: http://www.carrentalsecurity.com/.

SIRAS is a database that tracks the origin of products from the POS: http://www.siras.com/. SIRAS is the pioneer in POS electronic product registration, which encompasses patented business methodologies, including the creation of a unique *fingerprint*, for tracking products, validating return and warranty eligibility, and creating dynamic product data analytics. The secure online database is provided at no cost to authorized law enforcement professionals and helps in determining whether products recovered in their investigations may have been stolen or purchased with fraudulent tender. Today, SIRAS P.I. is used by more than 2000 law enforcement and government agencies nationwide and has aided in the arrest and successful prosecution of many criminals, including a multimillion dollar credit card fraud ring.

LeadsOnline is a database for law enforcement to check for stolen property that is pawned anywhere in the United States, including eBay listings: https://www.leadsonline.com/main/leads/login/ (Figure 11.1)

Figure 11.1 LeadsOnline logins.

Consumer Protection

Once again, most states regulate licensed professions and have regulatory and consumer protection law enforcement functions. There are also private consumer agencies. Here are some good sources:

http://www.fraud.org (daily reports on scams and rip-offs from the *National Fraud Information Center*)

http://ckfraud.org/ (the National Check Fraud Center, provides nation-wide, updated multisource information and intelligence to support local law enforcement, federal agencies, and financial and retail communities in the detection, investigation, and the prosecution of known check fraud and white collar crimes)

http://www.bbb.org (the *Better Business Bureau* takes consumer complaints and keeps tracks of consumer scams; you can search complaints by business name and get links to local BBB offices)

http://www.consumerworld.org (links and tags to consumer advocate sites)

http://www.netcheck.com (*Netcheck Commerce Bureau* database of company histories)

Credit Records

You may request your free credit report online, request your report by phone, or request your report through the mail. Free credit reports requested online are viewable immediately upon authentication of identity. Free credit reports requested by phone or mail will be processed within 15 days of receiving your request:

https://www.annualcreditreport.com/cra/index.jsp   (Annual Credit Report.com)

http://www.equifax.com (credit bureau reports [Equifax])

http://www.experian.com/ (credit bureau reports [Experian])

http://www.transunion.com/ (credit bureau reports ([TransUnion])

Checking credit reports is much more highly regulated and strict than before. (See section *Fair Credit Reporting Act* et al. in Appendix D) Basically, you can only check them if you have a legitimate business purpose and have the subject's written permission. Most of the sources that I checked with recently suggest merely having the subject fill out a request for their own credit report and submit it, requesting where to have it sent. They can get at least one free report each year. But one web page to be aware of is www.napbs.com (National Association of Professional Background Screeners: pre-employment screening and *Fair Credit Reporting Act* information).

Military and Genealogical Sources

If you are looking for someone who has ever served in the military, birth parents, or just a genealogy search, there are several good sources. You can search libraries and county offices, but you can start with a few of these sources:

> http://www.archives.gov/veterans/ (national archives military records)
> http://www.archives.gov/st-louis/ (National Personnel Records Center, Saint Louis, MO)
> http://www.military.com/benefits/resources/military-records/getting-records-of-military-personnel-or-others (Military.com)
> http://www.everton.com (genealogical data base)
> http://www.archives.com/ (genealogical data base)
> http://genealogy.org/NGS (genealogical data base)

Sources of Telephone Information: Names, Addresses, and Phone Numbers

To find an area code anywhere in the United States or Canada, try 555-1212. com at the following:

> http://www.555-1212.com/ACLOOKUP.HTML or http://www.computerhope.com/areacode.htm. For country calling codes, use http://www.countrycallingcodes.com/. Locate the Do Not Call List at https://www.donotcall.gov/.
> For an acronym and abbreviation database, try http://www.ucc.ie/info/net/acronyms/index.html.

More information on names, addresses, and phone numbers can be found in a variety of Internet databases. First, try doing a word search for the American Business Information (ABI) Yellow Pages. This lists names, addresses, phone numbers, and credit ratings for businesses in the United States and Canada. Other information includes annual reports and other SEC information and postal and bankruptcy information. Try using the name or *ABI* in a keyword search. Then try these databases:

> http://zip4.usps.com/zip4/ (USPS zip code locator by address, city, or company)
> http://www.bigbook.com (free)
> http://www.s12.bigyellow.com (free)
> http://www.switchboard.com (free)

http://www.yahoo.com/search/people (free) (search name, phone, or e-mail address)
http://www.whowhere.com (reverse phone search for a fee)
http://www.four11.com (reverse phone searches for a fee)

Internet Address Information

There seem to be a lot of databases out there for finding e-mail addresses for Internet users. Here are some of them:

http://www.vpm.com/emailbook (free)
http://www.iaf.net (free)
http://www.nova.edu/Inter-Links/netfind.html (free)
https://www.arin.net/index.html (American Registry for Internet Numbers)
http://www.archive.org/ (archived web pages)
http://www.iptools.com/ (search reverse by IP addresses to get name, phone, address, etc.)
http://www.dnsstuff.com/?ptype=free (IP information. Perform forensic analysis of name and e-mail servers and path analysis and authenticate and locate domains. Perform forensic analysis on a wide variety of domain and e-mail concerns—all in one comprehensive report. Monitor, track, and authenticate.)
http://www.networksolutions.com/whois/index.jsp (identify and locate ISPs or user name info for Internet)

Maps, Aerial and Satellite Photos, and Weather

Having a good source for maps, aerial and satellite photos, weather, and other imagery is a great tool to have available for investigators and intelligence officers. (See Chapter 10.) *MapQuest* is one source for maps, directions, and related information. I use this pretty often myself and find it to be very helpful. Sometimes, you can even get aerial and even street-view photos: http://www.mapquest.com.

MapsOnUs and *Map Blaster* are two similar map databases that I have found helpful. *Google Earth* is another great site that has maps, aerial and street-level photos, topographical features, etc.:

http://www.mapsonus.com/mapsonus/ (MapsOnUs)
http://images.google.com/images?q=Map+Blaster&hl=en&lr=&sa=N&tab=ii&oi=images (Map Blaster)
http://www.google.com/earth/index.html (Google Earth) or
http://www.google.com/intl/en/earth/download/thanks.html (Google Earth)

Professional Licenses

Most states regulate licensed professions. You may need to search each state's agency that licenses a profession. For example, the insurance industry is regulated in Indiana by the Indiana Department of Insurance. That agency keeps records on licensed agents within that state and on companies admitted to do (or prohibited from doing) business in Indiana. (Most states also have a law enforcement or investigative unit within such departments which keep records of violations.) Some states have a licensing agency for many professions, such as the Indiana Professional Licensing Agency, which regulates everything from acupuncturists to private investigators. Some professions have a self-regulating body. Here are some sources:

http://www.abanet.org (the American Bar Association—attorneys)
http://www.ama-assn.org (the American Medical Association)
http://www.medaccess.com/locator/hclocate.htm (board certification, hospital accreditation, HMOs, etc.)
http://www.medaccess.com/address/disc_bds.htm (physician disciplinary boards)
http://www.medaccess.com/address/lic_bds.htm (physician licensing boards)
https://secure.in.gov/apps/govboards/BoardDetails.aspx?BoardId=11123 (Indiana Boards and Commissions)
http://www.in.gov/pla/boards.htm (Indiana Professional Licensing Agency)
http://www.in.gov/idoi/ (Indiana Department of Insurance: company, agent, and bail bond licenses, financial examinations, investigations and enforcement records, etc.)
http://www.in.gov/dfi/ (Indiana Department of Financial Institutions)
http://www.in.gov/sos/ (Indiana Secretary of State: securities and auto dealers, corporations, investigations and enforcement records, etc.)
http://transition.fcc.gov/wcb/iatd/locator.html (Federal Communications Commission)

Education and Degree Checks

An investigator can check the university, college, or other educational institution for transcripts and degrees (usually with signed consent from the target) or there are database services that can help with this type of information. Here are some websites:

http://www.degreechk.com (Degree Check: educational verification and attendance)
http://www.studentclearinghouse.org (National Student Clearinghouse: educational verification and attendance)

Social Networks

http://www.facebook.com/places/ (Facebook)
https://foursquare.com/ (Foursquare)
http://gowalla.com/ (Gowalla)
http://www.scvngr.com/ (SCVNGR)

Background Investigations Online

Other background information (sometimes including credit reports and criminal histories) can be found from a variety of sources and information brokers:

http://www.spokeo.com/ (Spokeo)
http://www.integctr.com/Glossary.html (elements of a background investigation or BI)
http://www.state.in.us (access Indiana)
http://www.pdcny.com (public records in New York City)
http://www.locateplus.com (LocatePlus: database of people, property, motor vehicle records, court records, corporations, etc.)
http://www.theworknumber.com (verifies employment and income information)
http://www.softechinternational.com (Softech International: driver license and motor vehicle records)
http://www.infoam.com (names, addresses, phone numbers, social security numbers, financial abstracts, asset descriptions, bankruptcy records, lawsuits filed, etc.)
http://www.brbpub.com (database resources and links for background checks)
http://www.infocubic.net (pre-employment screening service)
http://www.irbsearch.com (database of information on people, addresses, phone numbers, assets, licenses, court documents, employers, etc.)
http://www.masterfiles.com (Master Files: phone numbers, unpublished numbers, reverse cell phone numbers, social security number verification, etc.)
http://www.usinterlink.com (database of addresses, phone numbers, social security numbers, assets, etc.)

Competitive Intelligence

Corporate spying or organizational investigation may involve acquiring trade secrets, a political opponent's weaknesses, or industrial espionage. Competitive intelligence involves gathering small pieces of the puzzle, putting them together to get the *big picture,* and gaining a tactical or strategic advantage or edge. This can be accomplished with spies or moles, dumpster diving or surveillance, or through good research from open sources in documents or on the Internet. Some sources of information for the web spook include the following:

http://www.sunsite.unc.edu/patents/intropat.html (patent searches by class, subclass, patent number, patent titles and abstracts, etc.; also listed under *fact checking intellectual property*)

http://www.sec.gov/edgarhp.htm (free Securities and Exchange Commission information on public companies)

http://www.edgar-online.com (a subscription service to access the SEC's EDGAR database; can create a *watch list* to monitor specified companies)

http://www.dnb.com/ (D&B credit reports on companies worldwide)

http://www.netvalue.com/netvalue/form.htm (a free report, based upon a search of words and phrases, on your competitors)

http://www.scip.org/ (news, events, case studies, software reviews, and other information from the Society of Competitive Intelligence Professionals)

http://smallbusiness2.dnb.com/14827054-1.html?tsalp=options&cm_mmc=Google-_-tsa_pd-_-GO000000111662737s_dun_AP-_-GO8 140706952&refcd=GO000000111662737s_dun_AP&tsacr=GO8 140706952&gclid=CNXqxaefzKkCFUPBKgodMWjaMg (Dun & Bradstreet background checks and security reports U.S. companies)

http://www.fuld.com (the Fuld & Company guide to data acquisition, analysis, and production of an intelligence product)

http://www.techstocks.com/investor (high-tech stock with graphs and chart patterns)

Internet Intelligence and Spyware

When consuming Internet-based intelligence, it is not only important to know something about hacking, viruses, and worms, but spyware, adware, POP mail packages. Hacking, of course, is unauthorized access and tampering, and viruses and worms are programmed theft and vandalism. POP spam will be discussed in a moment. Related to these are adware and spyware. *Adware* is software that displays unsolicited advertisements on your computer by a *pop-up* when searching for something else. *Spyware* is related but worse; it sends information from your computer to a third party without notice or permission. Both *adware* and *spyware* become installed on your computer covertly by either coaxing the user to click on a link that installs it or from freeware that installs it with the free software. *Cookies* are another matter but can be removed by using Internet options in your control panel.

It is worth mentioning at the outset a few things about *spam* (junk mail). This is a little difficult to grasp for those of us who have to ask our teenagers to explain high-tech things like *Facebook* and *Twitter*, but I once attended a training session that explained this as simply as possible. We all receive e-mail messages and, when we reply to ask them to stop sending it or remove us from their e-mail list, find that replies are undeliverable—the address does not exist. This occurs when the sender of spam uses *pop client e-mail* or a *third-party mail relay*. The best defense to this is to understand how this works.

The *pop client e-mail* may be easier but is more restricted (depending upon your ISP), so we will discuss this first. You may be able to do a *simple* reconfiguration of your pop e-mail client, for example, Outlook Express (from Internet Explorer) or Eudora.

For Outlook Express, (1) open your Outlook Express (in Internet Explorer), (2) click on "Tools" and "Accounts" to select your ISP account, and (3) click "Properties." A dialog box should appear with the heading "Mail Account Properties" and five options: (a) General, (b) Servers, (c) Connection, (d) Security, and (e) Advanced. You can leave the mail account line (the first line in the box) as is or name it whatever you choose (for the mail server connection). Under *User Information* (the next four lines in the box), do the following:

- Make the "Name" whatever (whoever) you want (e.g., "John" or JohnQuinceyAdams@JQA.com). This is the name that the receiver will see in the "FROM" field.
- You can leave "Organization" blank or make something up.
- For "E-mail address," you can use the same *address* that you used in the "Name" field.
- In the "Reply address," you can put a legitimate address in order to see the reply.

For Eudora, (1) open Eudora, (2) click on Tools, (3) Options, and (4) Getting Started and a dialog box should appear with the heading "Options" and five fields:

- Under "Real name" fill in whatever (whomever) you want (e.g., "John" or JohnQuinceyAdams@JQA.com).
- The "Return address" is (the same as the reply address in Outlook) a legitimate address in order to see the reply.

The original address is on a different dialog box and the server information is supplied by your ISP. Some ISPs, however, have restrictions, such as only allowing you to send outbound e-mail if you have been POP authenticated by the server. Additionally, the server may only accept outbound e-mail from its own domain. In each of these examples, you should receive an error message stating these restrictions.

A *third-party mail relay* is where a mail server processes e-mail where neither the sender nor the receiver is a local user. The mail server is a third party that is unrelated to the message transaction and the message should not even pass through the third party's server. Although rarely used today, in the past, network administrators have sometimes used third-party relays to legitimately debug mail connectivity and route around mail problems.

A third-party mail relay has also been used illegitimately by mail *hijackers* or *spammers* (junk e-mailers), when large volumes of e-mail messages are relayed through a server, to spread their unwanted messages over the Internet. These are sometimes referred to as *Spamhaus operations*. Relays can also be used illegitimately to send individual messages anonymously by concealing the sender's identity. To counter this prolific problem, network administrators have initiated filtering of network connections and instituted blockade measures. Hijackers and spammers have countered these counter-measures *laundering* their spam through third-party relays to evade spam filters. They access high-speed mail hosts to relay their messages through several servers in parallel. Spammers can conceal their identity from network administrators and evade having their connection traced and blocked. By concealing their identity, they can avoid complaints themselves and deflect them toward the hijacked hosts. This is often facilitated by the use of fake headers.

Mail relays are conducted using *telnet*, which is a program and a part of the TCP/IP protocol suite allowing remote access to a computer. Mail (SMTP) run on port 25 can be accessed using telnet to interact manually. Using UNIX, type the telnet hostname or IP address and <port> where the port number is optional. If it does not open automatically (e.g., you are using an older OS), select "Run" from the start menu and type in the telnet hostname or IP address <port>, for example, *telnet domainname.com 25*. (Not all servers allow telnet to use port 25 and are set up to deny relaying. You may need to search the Internet for a list of servers that are relay enabled.)

Mail servers usually reside on port 25, so telnet to port 25 of the host that is *relayable* using SMTP commands to communicate with the server. The RFC 821 (SMTP commands) shows what commands can be used and what they mean. Once connected, the screen should display something like this:

220 relay.com ESMTP Sendmail 8.87/8.8.7; Sat, 11 Sep 2012 23:45:00 -0500 (EST)

Note the message transfer agent (MTA) and its version number, then type *HELO somesite.com* to identify the sender SMTP to the receiver SMTP. (The first command must include the HELO command.) The *argument field* contains the host name of the sender SMTP, but you can use any domain name you want, as long as you can differentiate it when received. This value will appear in the "Received" header that the site generates, so the domain name selected is only seen when viewing the e-mail header.

Next, type "mail from: anyname@anyaddress.com" (make up a name and address or use someone's who you want to appear as if it is from). This is the address that will appear in the "From" field when it is received as e-mail.

Now, type "rcpt to: receivingperson@someaddress.com" (the e-mail address the system should send mail to) or to multiple addresses at once.

Then, type "DATA" and hit Enter and enter your e-mail message, including a subject header with a *space* after colon and separating the headers from the body with a blank line.

Finally, type a *period* at the start of a line and again hit Enter. If all of this works and the server return an acceptance message, the server apparently will relay from your IP address. To end the session with the telnet host, simply type "QUIT" and hit Enter.

To detect *forged* e-mail messages, IT managers look at the e-mail header to find the IP address that is unique to each PC (computer). Some hijackers or spammers use multiple third-party e-mail relays to try to cover their tracks. If this still sounds like *Greek* to you, ask your IT security manager to walk you through this or ask your teenager (they may have already done this). Remember, technology is ever evolving and so are hacks, cracks, countermeasures, and counter-countermeasures. Things change; be adaptable and stay as up to date as possible.

Net Spying and Web Surveillance

Monitoring chat rooms and inappropriate web surfing can be a surveillance concern to anyone from employers to parents. *Fingering* is the term used for monitoring e-mail accounts (usually for e-mail addresses or e-dresses ending in .org, .net, or .edu but usually not .com). Using a *finger command*, it is possible to find the target's login name, real name, location and phone number, login times, idle time, times mail was read, and other information. Plan files are text files that contain the information the person wants to include. On America Online, use the menu bar to select "Locate a Member Online" or Control F and type in the member's screen name. (This may be a "Friends List" or an IM screen.)

To monitor web surfing (where someone goes on the Internet), there are several useful web pages to help. These include the following:

http://www.cyberpatrol.com (monitor, filter, and blocker software)
http://www.cybersitter.com/ (monitors Internet activity and attempts to access blocked material; filters phrases and *bad sites* defined by the user)
http://www.netnanny.com (parental controls that shuts down systems when violated)

Intelligence Files and Analytical Investigative Methods

12

Intelligence Cycle

The intelligence cycle is used in the intelligence, military, and law enforcement communities to describe the cycle of intelligence activities, which denotes that each step is a continuous and ongoing process, rather than individual, terminal steps. The five steps in the cycle are (Figure 12.1)

1. Planning and direction
2. Collection
3. Processing
4. Analysis and production
5. Dissemination and feedback

Planning and Direction

Intelligence requirements are determined by a decision maker to meet organizational objectives, sometimes called *essential elements of intelligence* (EEI). All other data are referred to as other intelligence requirements (OIRs). Directing intelligence requirements involves the following: (1) determine intelligence requirements (EEIs and OIRs), (2) determine indicators, (3) determine specific items of information required, (4) select collection agencies, (5) issue orders and requests, and (6) follow-up.

Collection

In response to requirements (EEIs), the intelligence staff develops an intelligence collection plan to task available *sources and methods* and request intelligence from other agencies. Sources may include ELINT (electronic intelligence), SIGINT (signals intelligence), EMINT (emanations intelligence), IMINT (imagery intelligence), HUMINT (human intelligence), and OSINT (open-source or publicly available intelligence).

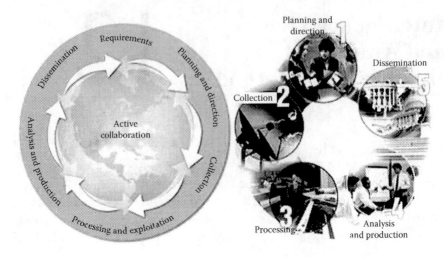

Figure 12.1 The intelligence cycle (FBI, left; CIA, right).

Processing

Once collection is accomplished and raw information is available, it is processed for exploitation. This involves the translation of raw materials contained in a foreign language source, evaluation of its relevance and reliability, and collation of the raw data in preparation for exploitation.

In combat intelligence, there are four methods commonly used to document tactical intelligence: (1) the *unit journal*, (2) the situation map, (3) the S2 workbook, and (4) intelligence files (see Figures 12.2 and 12.3). The S2 workbook is a temporary record for systematically recording information by subject groups for ready reference and used for the preparation of estimates, summaries, and reports. Another document, the intelligence summary (INTSUM), is a brief report of significant information developed or received by the unit or organization during a specified time period (see Figure 12.4). A situation report (SITREP) is prepared by the operations officer (see Figure 12.5). Other intelligence reports may include the supplemental intelligence report (SUPINTREP); the intelligence appraisal (sued at higher echelons to determine courses of action open to the opposition); the periodic intelligence report (PERINTREP), which is a summary of the intelligence situation covering longer periods than the INSUM; and other special reports, such as "shelling, motoring, and bombing reports" and "meaconing, intrusion, jamming, and interference (MIJI) feeder reports." (Meaconing is the interception and rebroadcast of navigation signals.)

DAILY STAFF JOURNAL OR DUTY OFFICER'S LOG (AR 220-345 & PM 101-5)				PAGE NO. 1		NO OF PAGES	
ORGANIZATION OR INSTALLATION 1st Battalion, 68th Inf S2 - S3			LOCATION Windmill Creek PA 514768	PERIOD COVERED			
				FROM		TO	
				HOUR 0001	DATE 18 Jul	HOUR 2400	DATE 18 Jul
ITEM NO	TIME		INCIDENTS, MESSAGES, ORDERS, ETC		ACTION TAKEN		INL
	IN	OUT					
3		0030	1st Bde: INTSUM for period 171800 - 172400 July submitted by RATT.		TF		JDC
			* * * * * * * * * *				
8	0520		Scout Plat: At checkpoint 5 continuing to move south. No enemy encountered.		MS		RLC
9	0540		1st Bde: Enemy mechanized battalion, reinforced by company of tanks moving north vic Highway 26. Head of column at REIDSBURG at 0525.		MSTF		RLC
10	0555		Co A: Encountered enemy roadblock at AB968512. No resistance.		MSTF		RLC
11		0620	1st Bde: Document. Document found at enemy road block (item 10) forwarded by messenger.		T F		RLC
TYPED NAME AND GRADE OF OFFICER OR OFFICIAL ON DUTY				SIGNATURE			

DA FORM 1594 NOV 62   PREVIOUS EDITION OF THIS FORM IS OBSOLETE.   * U S GOVERNMENT PRINTING OFFICE 1962 O—646754

Figure 12.2 Daily staff journal or duty officers log with S2 journal entries (DA Form 1594).

Analysis

Analysis integrates information by combining pieces of data with collateral information and patterns that can be interpreted to identify the significance and meanings of processed intelligence.

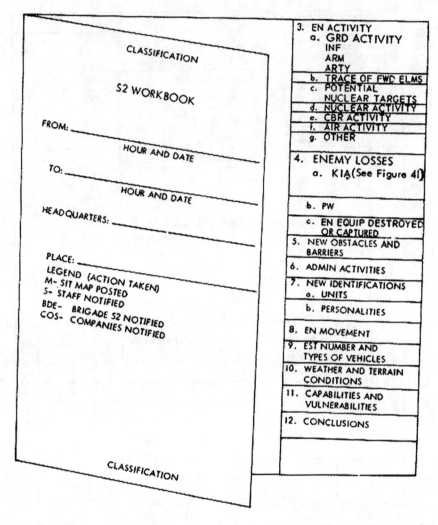

Figure 12.3 S2 workbook (a temporary record for systematically recording information by subject groups for ready reference and used for the preparation of estimates, summaries, and reports).

Dissemination and Feedback

Finished intelligence products are of little value if they do not meet the needs of the decision makers and intelligence consumers. Because the intelligence cycle is a closed loop, feedback is received from the decision maker or consumer and revised requirements (EEIs) are issued.

Because intelligence is confidential and of less value once its awareness is made known, it is important to restrict access to a *need to know* basis.

FORMAT OF AN INTELLIGENCE SUMMARY

1. Issuing unit
2. Time and date of issue
3. Summary of enemy activity for a period
    - Ground activity
    - Truce of forward elements
    - Potential targets for nuclear weapons
    - Nuclear, biological, chemical (NBC) activity
    - Air activity
    - Other (new tactics, jamming, counterintelligence. etc)
4. Personnel and equipment losses
    - Personnel (killed in action, wounded in action)
    - Prisoners of war
    - Equipment destroyed or captured
5. New obstacles and barriers
6. Administrative activities
7. New identification
    - Units
    - Personalities
8. Enemy movements
9. Estimated number and types of vehicles

Figure 12.4 Format for an INTSUM.

When distributing intelligence products, know the receiver and document this with an audit trail. Confirm the *need to know* and deny secondary distribution (the receiver should be aware that they are responsible for this information and for not redistributing it to undocumented and unauthorized sources). Intelligence may be restricted to consumers with a *need to*

ENEMY

Committed forces (overlay)

Forces committed against TF 2-80 are:
(1) Four mechanized platoons.
(2) Two medium tank platoons.
(3) Normal regimental artillery.
(4) Six 160mm mortars.
(5) Ten 122mm howitzers.
(6) Four 100mm artillery guns (SP).
(7) Two 140mm multiple rocket launchers.
(8) One 152mm gun (SP).
(9) Air and nuclear weapons.

Reinforcements (overlay)

Reinforcements presently capable of being employed in sector TF 2-80 now total: U/1 Medium Tank Plt vic BD4156, Mechanized Co of 281st Mechanized Regt vic BD4867, Mechanized Co of 282d Mechanized Regt vic BD4873, Mechanized Co of 281st Mechanized Regt vic AB4673, Mechanized Bn (-) of 281st Mechanized Regt vic AB4650, Mechanized Bn of 282d Mechanized Regt vic CD5060, U/I Tank Co vic DE5265.

Enemy Activity During Period 100600Z-101800z:

(1) Occupation of previously unoccupied positions vic BG3531, NT3633, OT3734, DT4239.
(2) Movement of combat units fwd vic ON4036.
(3) Dispersal of tanks to fwd units vic CG3136.
(4) Movement of assault boats into vic GO3338.
(5) Two 100mm AT guns (SP) vic OT3737, two 120mm AT guns (SP) vic ER3833.
(6) Six additional 122mm how vic DT3731.
(7) Increased OPFOR counterbattery fire in bde sector.
(8) Clearing lanes through minefield BC2937.
(9) Mechanized regt'l aid station vic CD3339.
(10) Increased OPFOR air activity vic FN2836, RB2437.
(11) Suspected jamming of VHF communications (intel net) at 100745Z and 101325Z.

Conclusions. OPFOR'S most probable courses of action:

(1) Continue defense now.
(2) Attack along our front within 8 hours.

Figure 12.5 Operation SITREP.

know and a *security clearance* of the appropriate level. It may be classified by its sensitivity and importance as

- CONFIDENTIAL (sensitive information of importance)
- SECRET (high sensitivity and importance)
- TOP SECRET (extremely high sensitivity and importance)

Intelligence Files

Despite what one hears in movies or from bar flies pretending to be a *secret agent*, intelligence files and those who have security clearances to access such information are classified as either CONFIDENTIAL, SECRET, or TOP

SECRET. Any additional designations are adjectives referring to the type of information accessed, such as CRYPTO and SCI (specially compartmented information). Terms such as EYES ONLY are used in other countries, such as Great Britain (MI5 and MI6 SIS).

Strategic intelligence supports long-range planning or policy. *Tactical intelligence* is for immediate operational use. *Reactive intelligence* refers to a response to a situation after the fact. *Proactive intelligence* refers to anticipation of needs and/or preemptive action before an incident.

Intelligence files were once literally paper files that were indexed by names and subjects, with file numbers. They were cross-referenced by primary categories and subcategories (primary, secondary, and tertiary). Source documents were indexed and filed (documenting the source of raw data or information). Source documents were rated for reliability, content, and classification. Folder logs and dissemination control forms were used to control information. Such manual systems can be of value in areas where technology is scarce but the need for intelligence files is great. Primarily, however, today, intelligence files are automated and computers are programmed to process massive amounts of stored data, information, and intelligence.

Intelligence Analysis

The analysis of intelligence can be conducted by two nearly identical processes, which were developed from scientific and engineering practices: *analytical investigation methods* (AIMs) and *visual investigative analysis* (VIA). Other methods of intelligence analysis are available, but AIM and VIA are commonly used by law enforcement, intelligence, and military analysts to present complex information with presentation media.

Analytical Investigative Methods

AIMs analyze large amounts of information using scientific concepts of investigation, data collection, and evaluation techniques, including the following:

- Construction of association matrices and link analysis
- Use of inductive and deductive logic from sources of information
- Flow charting and construction of charts for analysis
- The analytical process
- Development of inferences from analysis
- The delivery of clear and concise briefings and presentation media

AIMs, like VIA, emerged from using tools and techniques borrowed from science and engineering project management. Two such tools, critical path method (CPM) and program evaluation and review technique (PERT), are discussed further under section "Visual Investigative Analysis."

CPM is used for *scheduling, planning, and controlling* projects with deadlines. Users decide which path in a *network* will take the most time. This path then becomes a *critical path.*

PERT is a scientific management information system for *scheduling, planning, and controlling* complex research and development projects. It is oriented to events and uses a *network* to display graphically the sequence of events, dependent relationships, and estimated duration of times for all the activities.

A *network* is a series of interconnected and interrelated symbols that graphically displays the sequence of occurrences and dependent relationships. *Link network analysis* shows associations, while *time flow analysis* shows sequential events.

Visual Investigative Analysis

VIA was developed in the 1960s by the Los Angeles Police Department and named *VIA* by the California Department of Justice in the 1970s (Morris, 1982, p. iv). It was first used in trial support in Los Angeles in 1968 in the trial of Sirhan Sirhan for the murder of U.S. Senator (and former Attorney General) Robert F. Kennedy (Morris, 1982, p. 5).

VIA, or crime analysis charting if used in criminal cases, makes complex investigations more controllable and makes it easier for supervisors and managers to monitor the hour-by-hour use of resources to avoid duplication. It also helps trial attorneys to quickly understand complex cases and large amounts of information by providing a sort of roadmap of critical events and essential elements. It also helps judges and juries to understand cases by allowing them to see and hear the progress of the events presented. Such analysis saves time, often reducing trial time by half, and clearly states essential facts.

VIA developed from concepts borrowed from engineering, construction, and ship building that used techniques such as CPM and PERT. CPM is similar to PERT and is geared toward scheduling and controlling projects. PERT is geared toward facilitating control of research activity in scientific tasks. The two can be integrated into one system. VIA is such an *integration*, with modifications that are responsive to the law enforcement or intelligence functions. VIA is a network approach to displaying graphically the sequences of events and the relationships of each element of an incident (Morris, 1982, pp. 3–4).

VIA can be performed manually or by use of computer graphics and tools. While computers are more practical today, understanding the manual system can aid in practice or be used in more remote or primitive environments. To perform VIA manually, the analyst needs a few tools and supplies:

1. *Index cards*—3 × 5, using only one side, to tape or affix to the layout.
2. *Binders*—a case library for copies of all documentation supporting the VIA chart. Each binder is numbered and each page in each binder is numbered for quick reference (e.g., a document or information in Binder 2 and on page 25 would be noted on an index card as 2-25).
3. *Highlighter pens*—during the reading phase of the documentation, the analyst highlights items or information for transfer to the index cards. This can simply be in yellow highlight or various colors can be used to color-code specific aspects of information.
4. *Template*—symbols can be drawn using a template that includes circles, rectangles, arrows, triangles, and other symbols.
5. *Paper*—durable drafting paper can be used for the chart and tracing paper can be used for final drafts.
6. *Tape and pins*—pins can hold index cards on the drafting paper during layout and tape can be used to affix them when finalized. Here, the index cards are taped down after the lines, circles, arrows, and triangles are added and the chart takes the shape and appearance of a storyboard.
7. *Pens and pencils*—for compiling the index cards and drawing the chart. The final draft, of course, should be in ink.
8. *Copies of reports and documentation*—all materials for the case should be copied (never the originals) because they will be hole punched, page numbered, and highlighted.

The same process can be performed with a computer, using various computer-aided design (CAD) tools and programs (such as *Visio*®, IntelliVIEW®, and other commercially available programs). The important points of developing a VIA chart and library are as follows:

1. Determine the important elements and data in reports, documents, and other information from the case library:
   a. Does this information relate to the incident in question?
   b. Does this information provide a who, what, when, where, why, or how?
   c. Does this information build upon another known or suspected key element?
2. Summarize information into 50 words or less (for each element or key point):
   a. The index card's upper line might show *who* gave the data (W = Witness, I = Informant, V = Victim, O = Officer, etc., followed by the name).
   b. The bottom line might show *when*—day, date, time, and binder and page numbers.
3. Link the nexus between activities when dates, times, and other elemental details are unclear, ambiguous, or missing.

The VIA process should not be viewed as individual *steps*, but as a continuous process like the *intelligence cycle* itself. However, the *tasks* in the VIA process include the following:

- Confer with the client/consumer for *planning and direction* (trial attorney or intelligence consumer) on the EEIs.
- Collect source documents; *collection*.
- Develop the case library (documentation).
- Conduct first reading of source documents.
- Conduct second reading of source documents.
- Create index cards (*processing*) (Figure 12.6).
- Compare and edit materials.
- Conduct index card analysis (*analysis*).
  - Take the information from the reading and rereading of the source documents of the case library and write each activity on an individual index card.
  - Study the index cards to determine which event and card most likely starts the network and which one is the logical conclusion.
  - Arrange the remaining cards in a logical chain of activity (sequential, if possible).
    - Activity flow (sequential and logical)
    - Parallel activity (simultaneous)
    - Activity display—*nodes*

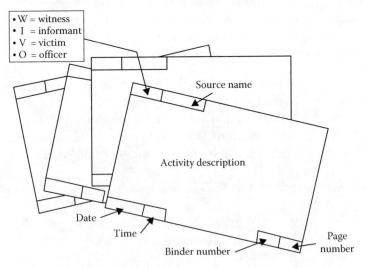

Figure 12.6 VIA index cards.

- Create chart (attaching information from index cards) (*analysis* and *production*).
  - Use Network Logic to show each nexus.
  - What activities precede the next one (logical sequence)?
  - What activities are concurrent with this one (simultaneous)?
  - What activities follow this one (continuing logical sequence)? (Morris, 1982, p. 16)
- Create *arrows* and *nodes* (arranged to show the logical sequence of activities and their relationship) and assign reference numbers (to source binders and pages from the case library) (*analysis* and *production*).
  - Use symbols to represent information in the network and on the chart.
  - Each *arrow* represents one activity (any portion of the case analysis that consumes time and/or resources and has a definable beginning and end).
  - A *circle* or *node*, between the arrows, denotes the start and stop of an activity. These *event nodes* consume no time or resources.
  - Every activity in a network must be preceded and succeeded by an event node (except the conclusion of the chart); there can only be one activity between every two nodes.
  - A *burst* (depicted by vertical sets of *event nodes*) is the initiation of two or more activities.
  - A *merge* depicts the completion of two or more activities.
  - The end of a VIA chart is signified by a *triangle* (the termination symbol) (Figure 12.7) (Morris, 1282, pp. 19–20, 22).
- Create activity and dummy lines (analysis and production).
  - An *activity arrow* (mentioned earlier) represents one activity.
  - A *dummy line* is represented by a *dotted arrow* and represents an activity that consumes no time.
    - It maintains network continuity and logic by indicating that, while a relationship exists between two activities, it does not warrant the strength of a solid line arrow.
    - The dotted dummy line completes a *straggler line* by attaching it to something—a continuing solid line (Figure 12.8) (Morris, 1982, pp. 20–22).
- Confer (again) with the client/consumer on the progress from the *planning and direction* phase (trial attorney or intelligence consumer).

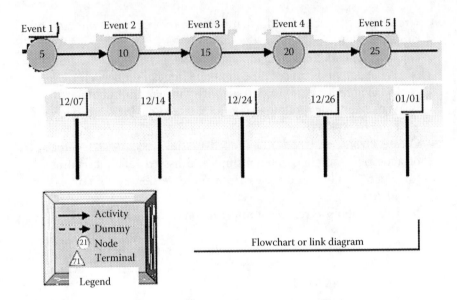

Figure 12.7 Flowchart or link diagram.

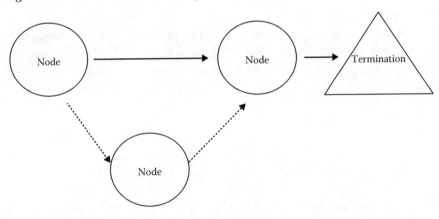

Figure 12.8 Nodes, activity lines, dummy lines, and termination.

- Finish drafting and finalizing (inking, if manually constructed) the chart.
  - Number each *node* or *circle* (in increments of five or more along the main line to allow for upgrades) for reference to points of interest.
  - No two nodes should have the same number except *fragnets* and *subnets* (Figure 12.9) (Morris, 1982, p. 22).
- Attach information from index cards (with tape, if manually constructed).
- Create a legend (of symbols), title, and credits (of who drafted the chart).

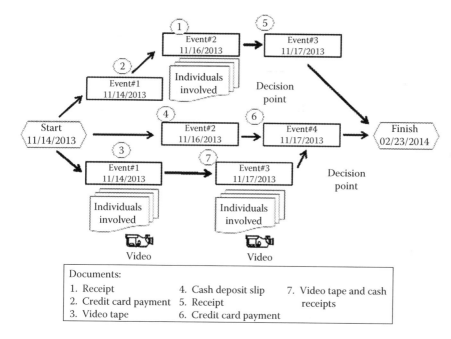

Figure 12.9 Network diagram.

- Develop *fragnets* and *subnets*, used to expand a complex chart.
  - *Fragnets* are an expansion that occurs as an appendage (for smaller amounts of information) on the face or surface of the original chart.
    - It is usually small (one to five activities) and always relates directly to one activity between two *nodes* on the original chart.
    - It is depicted by dotted lines, without arrow heads, attached to each end of the fragnet and to the nodes on the original chart.
    - Node numbering in the fragnet begins with the first node number to be fragneted on the original chart and ends with the next node number to the right (Morris, 1982, p. 23).
  - *Subnets* resemble a fragnet but are displayed on an independent chart and usually represent large amounts of information or numbers of activities.
    - It is usually represented as a separate chart of its own, often after the completion of the original (main) chart. (When created on a computer, it may be embedded and brought up, opened, or enlarged with a click.)
    - It follows the numbering of the original chart. (It begins with the first node number to be subnetted on the original chart and ends with the next node number to the right.) (Morris, 1982, p. 23).

- Conduct a final review with the client/consumer for *planning and direction* (trial attorney or intelligence consumer) (*dissemination* and *feedback*).

The use of computers can greatly simplify this process, especially the use of *fragnets* and *subnets*. The final draft of the chart can be copied using the trace paper or saved as a computer document, using overlays. Charts may then be present using presentation software, such as PowerPoint®.

Financial Information

Single-entry bookkeeping refers to the entry of information from all sources in one place without making an effort to balance the records. *Double-entry bookkeeping* refers to a system in which every transaction affects two or more accounts (with equal debits or credits) and is recorded in these accounts. Two or more adjustments must be made (never only one) and, in summary form, shows the results of many transactions and the force affecting the organization.

Fundamental Equation

Assets (items of value) = claims assets = *Liabilities* and *Capital*

$$A - L = C$$

Accounting Cycle

1. *Journalizing*—analyzing and recording transactions in a *journal*
2. *Posting*—copying the debits and credits of journal entries into the *ledger* accounts
3. *Preparing a trial balance*—summarizing the ledger accounts and testing the recording accuracy
4. Constructing a work sheet:
   a. Affecting the adjustments without making entries in the account
   b. Sorting the account balances into
      i. Balance sheet
      ii. Income statement accounts
   c. Determining the income or loss
5. *Preparing the statements*—rearranging the *work sheet* information into
   - A balance sheet
   - An income statement

6. *Adjusting the ledger accounts*—preparing *adjusting journal* entries from information in the *adjustments* columns of the *work sheet* and posting the entries in order to bring the account balances up to date

7. *Closing the temporary proprietorship accounts*—preparing and posting entries to close the *temporary proprietorship accounts* and transfer the net income or loss to the *capital account*

8. *Preparing a postclosing trial balance*—proving the accuracy of the adjusting and closing procedure (Figures 12.10 and 12.11)

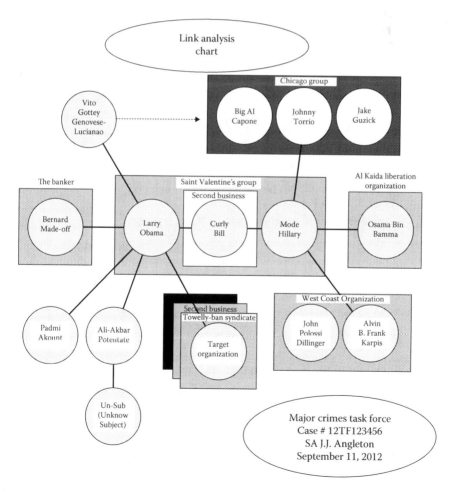

Figure 12.10 Example of a link analysis chart.

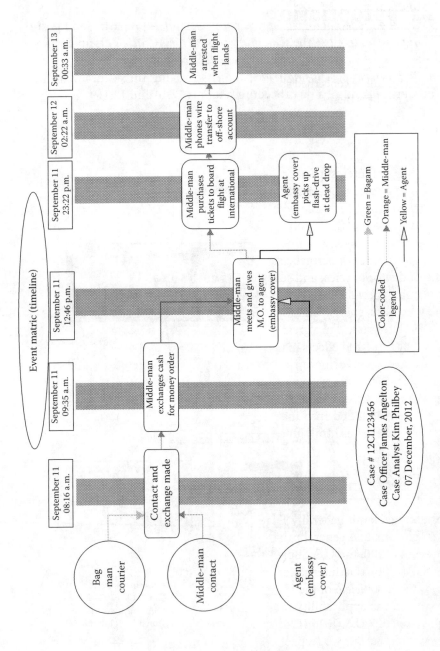

Figure 12.11 Timeline or event matrix.

Intelligence, Surveillance, and Misappropriation Law 13

We should all be concerned about the future because we will have to spend the rest of our lives there.

Charles F. Kettering
Inventor and Businessman

Technology of interest to national security is as diverse as it is rapidly emerging and ever evolving. *Metatechnology* is the application of *technologies* for problem-solving. Technology must be selected and adapted for each problem. *Nanotechnology* is the manipulation of matter on an atomic and molecular scale. Nanotechnology, defined by size, is broad and includes diverse fields of science such as microfabrication, molecular biology, organic chemistry, semiconductor physics, and surface science. Nanotechnology may be able to create many new materials and devices with applications, such as biomaterials, electronics, energy, and medicine.

Bill Gates said, "I'm a great believer that any tool that enhances communication has profound effects in terms of how people can learn from each other, and how they can achieve the kind of freedoms that they're interested in." He also said, "We always overestimate the change that will occur in the next two years and underestimate the change that will occur in the next ten. Don't let yourself be lulled into inaction" (http://www.brainyquote.com/quotes/authors/b/bill_gates.html; June 5, 2013).

Overview of International and Military Law

International law is generally a product of international *conventions*, international custom, and general principles of law recognized by civilized nations. As early as 1900, the U.S. Supreme Court ruled in *the Paquette Habana*, 175 U.S. 677 (1900), that international law is a part of U.S. law. Treaties are recognized under *Article 6* of the U.S. Constitution. The U.S. Supreme Court also recognized the applicability of the laws of war to military conduct in *In re Yamashita*, 327 U.S. 1, 16 (1945), in which the court said, "We do not make the laws of war but we respect them so far as they do not conflict with the commands of Congress or the Constitution."

The Supreme Court also recognized the international rule that a state has power and authority over criminal acts committed within its territory and the authority of the U.S. government to permit the trial of its military personnel when consistent with this rule and its treaty obligations. In *Wilson v. Girard*, 354 U.S. 524, 529 (1957), the court said, "A sovereign nation has exclusive jurisdiction to punish offenses against its laws committed within its borders...."

The legal status of military forces is determined by (1) a Status of Forces Agreement (SOFA), (2) a Military Assistance Advisory Agreement (for a MAAG), or (3) a Military Mission Agreement (for a mission). A *mission* was a designation given when established before WWII and a MAAG designation was assigned after WWII. The SOFA designation involved large numbers of equipment and civilian personnel and dependents usually accompany the forces.

A SOFA is an agreement between a host country and a foreign nation stationing forces in that country. SOFAs are often included, along with other types of military agreements, as part of a comprehensive security arrangement. A SOFA does not constitute a security arrangement; it establishes the rights and privileges of foreign personnel present in a host country in support of the larger security arrangement. SOFA grants to the United States the right to exercise authority over criminal acts committed within the territory of the host country by members of U.S. forces. (Other relevant legal issues are also involved in the SOFA.) Criminal offenses and war crimes are usually investigated by the USACIDC, the U.S. Air Force Office of Special Investigations (USAF OSI), and the Naval Criminal Investigation Service (NCIS). They are prosecuted by the respective branch Judge Advocate General (JAG) corps.

The *laws of war* are historically customary, rather than written, *laws*. Modern laws of war address declarations of war, acceptance of surrender, and the treatment of POWs. *Conventions*, such as the *Hague Conventions (of 1899, 1907, and 1954)* and the *Geneva Convention (of 1929 and 1949)*, are written conventions covering such issues as prohibitions on targets, illegal tricks and methods (such as pretending to surrender to facilitate an attack), prohibitions on weapons (i.e., those that are calculated to cause unnecessary suffering), humane treatment of noncombatants (including POWs), illegal means of interrogation, criminal violations of the law of war and criminal orders, and obligations to report violations of the laws war.

The *enemy population* is divided into two general classes: protected persons and unprotected persons. *Protected persons* include POWs, chaplains, medical personnel, and civilians who abstain from the fighting. The protection of noncombatant civilians exists whether the population is that of an enemy state, an ally state, or a state that does not have forces engaged in the conflict.

Unprotected persons include spies and guerillas or persons who commit hostile acts or engage in the fighting *without complying with the conditions of the law of war* for recognition as *legally organized resistance units*.

POWs are divided into two general categories: combatants and noncombatants. *Combatants* are participants in a war who are *lawfully entitled to carry on hostilities*:

1. Members of armed forces
2. Members of regular militia or volunteer units
3. Members of irregular partisan or guerilla units (who *comply with the conditions of the law of war* for recognition as *legally organized resistance units*)
4. Levee en masse (inhabitants of a nonoccupied territory who spontaneously take up arms to resist an invading force, without time to form regular units, upon the approach of the enemy; these people *must carry arms openly* and *respect the laws of war* in order to be recognized as POWs if captured)

Noncombatants who are protected as POWs when captured and those who accompany Armed Forces without being members of the Armed Forces include war correspondents (journalists), supply contractors, technical representatives, labor units, and welfare units.

The customary law of war and the *Geneva Convention of 1949* establish rules governing the treatment of noncombatants, POWs, sick and wounded, and other detained civilians. These rules are based upon the principle that they all receive the same humane treatment.

Some of the articles included in *the Hague Conventions* or *the Geneva Convention* related to spies are as follows:

Article 29—A person can only be considered a spy when, acting clandestinely or on false pretences [sic], he obtains or endeavours [sic] to obtain information in the zone of operations of a belligerent with the intention of communicating it to the hostile party.

Thus, soldiers not wearing a disguise who have penetrated into the zone of operations of the hostile army, for the purpose of obtaining information, are not considered spies. Similarly, the following are not considered spies: soldiers and civilians carrying out their mission openly, entrusted with the delivery of despatches [sic] intended either for their own army or for the enemy's army. To this class belong likewise persons sent in balloons for the purpose of carrying despatches [sic] and, generally, of maintaining communications between the different parts of an army or a territory.

The definition of a spy given in this article remains valid because the Geneva Convention contains no similar provision. However, a spy is also a protected person in so far as he conforms to the definition given in Article 4 of the Fourth Convention. Under Article 5 of the convention, the spy may nevertheless be deprived temporarily of certain rights, particularly the right of communication:

> *Article 30*—A spy taken in the act shall not be punished without previous trial.
>
> The Convention contains several provisions in this respect which extend the principle and make it precise. Thus Article 3 prohibits "the passing of sentences and the carrying out of executions without previous judgment pro- nounced by a regularly constituted court, affording all the judicial guarantees which are recognized as indispensable by civilized peoples."
>
> Article 3, although it applies only to armed conflicts not of an international character, contains rules of absolutely general application. The prohibition mentioned is, moreover, confirmed by Article 5 and Articles 64-76.
>
> [Paragraph 2 of Article 68 authorizes the Occupying Power under certain conditions to inflict the death penalty on protected persons found guilty of espionage.]
>
> *Article 31*—A spy who, after rejoining the army to which he belongs, is subse- quently captured by the enemy is treated as a prisoner of war, and incurs no responsibility for his previous acts of espionage.

Wiretap Surveillance

In *Katz v. United States* (1967), the U.S. Supreme Court established its "reasonable expectation of privacy" test. It overturned *Olmstead v. United States* and held that wiretaps were unconstitutional searches, because there was a reasonable expectation that the communication would be private. The government was then required to get a warrant to execute a wiretap. Ten years later, the Supreme Court held that a pen register is not a search because the "petitioner voluntarily conveyed numerical information to the telephone company" (*Smith v. Maryland*, 442 U.S. 735, 744 (1979)). Since the defendant had disclosed the dialed numbers to the TelCo so they could connect his call, he did not have a reasonable expectation of privacy in the numbers he dialed. The court did not distinguish between disclosing the numbers to a human operator and just the automatic equipment used by the TelCo. The *Smith* decision left pen registers outside the scope of con- stitutional protection. Any privacy protection would, therefore, have to be enacted as a privacy law statute. (This is criminal procedure, which is dif- ferent from the civil tort of invasion of privacy.)

The *Electronic Communications Privacy Act* (ECPA) was passed in 1986 and consisted of three main provisions or titles. Title III created the *Pen Register Act*, which included restrictions on private and law enforcement uses of pen registers. Private parties were generally restricted from using them unless they met one of the exceptions, which included an exception for the business providing the communication (usually the Telco) if it needed to do so to ensure the proper functioning of its business. Law enforcement agencies must get a court order from a judge to get a pen register approved for surveillance.

Under *18 U.S.C. § 3123(a)(1)*,

> the court shall enter an exparte order authorizing the installation and use of a **pen register or trap and trace device** anywhere within the United States, if the court finds that the *attorney* for the Government has *certified* to the court that the *information likely* to be obtained by such installation and use is relevant to an *ongoing criminal investigation* (emphasis added).

A government attorney must certify that information will *likely* be obtained in relation to an *ongoing criminal investigation*.

This is the lowest requirement for receiving a court order under the ECPA, because in *Smith v. Maryland*, the Supreme Court ruled that use of a pen register does not constitute a search. The court held that only the content of a conversation should receive constitutional protection under the right to privacy, because pen registers do not intercept conversation. The *Pen Register Act* did not include an exclusionary rule in the statute (although case law and civil remedies may still apply). Section 216 of the 2001 *USA PATRIOT Act* expanded the definition of a pen register to include devices or programs that provide an analogous function for Internet communications.

Surveillance, Satellites, and Civil Liberties

United States v. Jones, 615 F. 3d 544, affirmed (U.S. Supreme Court 2012)

The government obtained a search warrant permitting it to install a GPS tracking device on a vehicle registered to respondent Jones's wife. The warrant authorized installation in the District of Columbia and within 10 days, but agents installed the device on the 11th day and in Maryland. The government then tracked the vehicle's movements for 28 days. It subsequently secured an indictment of Jones and others on drug trafficking conspiracy charges. The district court suppressed the GPS data obtained while the vehicle was parked at Jones's residence but held the remaining data admissible because Jones had no reasonable expectation of privacy when the vehicle was on public streets. Jones was convicted. The DC Circuit reversed, concluding that admission of the evidence obtained by warrantless use of the GPS device violated the Fourth Amendment.

Held: The government's attachment of the GPS device to the vehicle, and its use of that device to monitor the vehicle's movements, constitutes a search under the Fourth Amendment.

a. The Fourth Amendment protects the "right of the people to be secure in their persons, houses, papers, and effects, against unreasonable searches and seizures." Here, the Government's physical intrusion on an "effect" for the purpose of obtaining information constitutes a "search." This type of encroachment on an area enumerated in the Amendment would have been considered a search within the meaning of the Amendment at the time it was adopted (pp. 3–4).

b. This conclusion is consistent with this Court's Fourth Amendment jurisprudence, which until the latter half of the 20th century was tied to common-law trespass. Later cases, which have deviated from that exclusively property-based approach, have applied the analysis of Justice Harlan's concurrence in *Katz v. United States*, 389 U.S. 347, which said that the Fourth Amendment protects a person's "reasonable expectation of privacy," *id.*, at 360. Here, the Court need not address the Government's contention that Jones had no "reasonable expectation of privacy," because Jones's Fourth Amendment rights do not rise or fall with the *Katz* formulation. At bottom, the Court must "assur[e] preservation of that degree of privacy against government that existed when the Fourth Amendment was adopted." *Kyllo v. United States*, 533 U.S. 27, 34. *Katz* did not repudiate the understanding that the Fourth Amendment embodies a particular concern for government trespass upon the areas it enumerates. The *Katz* reasonable-expectation-of-privacy test has been added to, but not substituted for, the common-law trespassory test. See *Alderman v. United States*, 394 U.S. 165, 176; *Soldal v. Cook County*, 506 U.S. 56, 64. *United States v. Knotts*, 460 U.S. 276, and *United States v. Karo*, 468 U.S. 705—post-*Katz* cases rejecting Fourth Amendment challenges to "beepers," electronic tracking devices representing another form of electronic monitoring—do not foreclose the conclusion that a search occurred here. *New York v. Class*, 475 U.S. 106, and *Oliver v. United States*, 466 U.S. 170, also do not support the Government's position (pp. 4–12).

c. The Government's alternative argument—that if the attachment and use of the device was a search, it was a reasonable one—is forfeited because it was not raised below (p. 12).

California v. Ciraola, 106 S.Ct. 1809, 1810 (1986)

The Santa Clara, California, police received an anonymous tip that the defendant was growing marijuana in his backyard. The investigating officers were unable to look into the backyard from the ground because it was shielded by a 6-foot tall outer fence and a 10-foot tall inner fence. Agents obtained the services of a private plane and had the pilot fly over the defendant's backyard at an altitude of 1000 feet. A fellow officer accompanied the agent on the flight; both were trained in the aerial identification of marijuana. Viewing the defendant's backyard with their naked eyes, the officers identified a garden of marijuana plants. The officers subsequently obtained a search warrant on the basis of an affidavit that described the anonymous tip and their observations. The police seized 73 marijuana plants, each 8–10 feet tall, from the defendant's backyard garden.

The defendant pleaded guilty to cultivating marijuana after the trial court denied his motion to suppress the evidence seized in the search. The California Court of Appeals reversed, holding that the aerial observation of the defendant's fenced-in backyard constituted a warrantless search violating the sanctity of the defendant's home. The California Supreme Court denied the state's petition for review. On certiorari to the U.S. Supreme Court, the court reversed state appeals court decision.

The court held that naked-eye aerial observations of areas within the curtilage do not constitute an unreasonable search under the Fourth Amendment.

U.S. v. Dunn, 480 U.S. 294, 107 S.Ct. 1134 (1987)

In 1980, the DEA discovered that Carpenter had purchased large quantities of chemical and equipment used in the manufacture of amphetamine and phenylacetone. DEA agents obtained warrants from a Texas state judge authorizing installation of tracking *beepers* in an electric hot plate stirrer, a drum of acetic anhydride, and a container holding phenylacetic acid (a precursor to phenylacetone). All of these had been ordered by Carpenter. Aerial photographs of the 198 acres ranch showed Carpenter's truck backed up to a barn behind the ranch house. The ranch was completely encircled by a perimeter fence. The property also contained several interior fences and was located about one-half mile from a public road. A fence encircled the residence and a nearby small greenhouse. Two barns were located approximately 50 yards from this fence. The front of the larger of the two barns was enclosed by a wooden fence and had an open overhang. Locked gates barred entry into the barn and netting material stretched from the ceiling to the top of the wooden gates.

Law enforcement officials made a warrantless entry onto respondent's ranch property. A DEA agent crossed over the perimeter fence and one interior fence. Standing approximately midway between the residence and the barns, the DEA agent smelled what he believed to be phenylacetic acid, the odor coming from the direction of the barns. He approached the smaller of the barns, crossing over a barbed wire fence and looking into the barn observed only empty boxes. He then proceeded to the larger barn, crossing another barbed wire fence as well as a wooden fence that enclosed the front portion of the barn. The officers walked under the barns overhang to the locked wooden gates and, shining a flashlight through the netting on top of the gates, peered into the barn. They observed illegal narcotics.

Later, a federal magistrate issued a warrant authorizing the search of the respondent's ranch. DEA agents and state law enforcement seized chemicals and equipment discovered in a closet in the ranch house. Carpenter and Dunn were convicted.

Procedure: The Court of Appeals reversed the conviction, concluding that the search warrant had been issued based on information obtained during the officers' unlawful warrantless entry onto respondent's ranch property, and therefore, all evidence seized pursuant to the warrant should have been suppressed. They held that "the barn in question was within the cartilage of the residence and was within protective ambit of the Fourth Amendment." On remand, the Court of Appeals reinstated the original opinion by asserting that "upon studied reflection, we now conclude and hold that the barn was inside the protected curtilage."

Holding: The U.S. Supreme Court held that this area was not within the *curtilage* of the home and is not granted Fourth Amendment protection.

Rule: The court held that there are four factors that need to be raised in order to resolve a question regarding cartilage:

1. The proximity of the area claimed to be the cartilage to the home
2. Whether the area is included within an enclosure surrounding the home
3. The nature of the uses to which the area is put
4. Steps taken by the resident to protect the area from observation by people passing by

The court further held that the record discloses that the barn was located 50 yards from the fence surrounding the house and 60 yards from the house itself. Also the barn did not lie within the area surrounding the house that was enclosed by a fence. Furthermore, the barn was not being used for intimate activities of the home. Lastly, the respondent did little to protect the barn area from observation by those standing in the *open fields*. The majority rejected the argument that the erection of fences on an open field, at least of the variety involved in those cases and in the present case, creates a constitutionally protected privacy interests. The term *open fields* may include an unoccupied or underdeveloped area outside of the curtilage. Finally, the court held that there is no constitutional difference between police observations conducted while in a public place and while standing in the open fields.

Dow Chemical Co. v. U.S., 106 S.Ct. 1819 (1986)

The Dow Chemical Company owned and operated a 2000 acre manufacturing facility in Midland, Michigan. The facility consisted of numerous enclosed buildings, with considerable outdoor manufacturing equipment and piping conduits located between the buildings. At all times, Dow maintained elaborate security measures to prohibit ground-level public viewing of its facility and to safeguard its industrial privacy.

In September of 1977, the Environmental Protection Agency (EPA) began an investigation of Dow's Midland facility, focused on whether emissions from two coal-burning power plants violated federal air quality standards. The EPA made one on-site inspection and then requested and received schematic diagrams of the power houses from Dow. Dow denied the EPA's request for a second inspection upon learning that as part of the inspection, the EPA would be taking photographs of Dow's layout and facility. The EPA responded by informing Dow that it would consider seeking a search warrant to gain entrance to the plant.

The EPA decided to obtain aerial photographs of Dow's facility and hired a private commercial aerial photography firm to take the photos at particular altitudes, locations, and directions. The private firm made at least six passes over the plant the next day at altitudes of 12,000, 3000, and 1200 feet. Approximately 75 color photographs of various parts of the Dow plant were taken.

The U.S. Supreme Court held that the aerial surveillance was not a search within the meaning of the Four Amendment. The decision upheld the Sixth Circuit's ruling that overruled the district court's ruling that the flyover was an illegal search because the EPA did not receive a search warrant or Dow's permission to do so.

United States Code

Title 18 U.S.C. § 2512(1)(a):
(a) sends through the mail, or sends or carries in interstate or foreign commerce, any electronic, mechanical, or other device, knowing or having reason to know that the design of such device renders it primarily useful for the purpose of the surreptitious interception of wire, oral, or electronic communications;

Indiana

The recording or acquiring of the contents of a telephonic or telegraphic communication by someone who is neither the sender nor the receiver is a felony and can be the basis for civil liability as well (*I.C. §35-33.5-1-5*).

Civil liability may require the payment of actual damages, $100 per day for each day of violation or $1000—whichever is greater—and punitive damages, court costs, and attorney fees (*I.C. §35-33.5-5-4*).

The Indiana Supreme Court held that the *Indiana Wiretap Act* requires the state to prove the eavesdropper acted with intent (*State v. Lombardo*, 738 N.E.2d 653 [Ind. 2000]).

The Indiana Court of Appeals held in 2007 that the interception and recording of calls made by prisoners from a jail did not violate the *Wiretap Act*, since recipients of calls were informed prior to accepting collect calls that the calls might be recorded or monitored and the recipients pressed zero, accepting the calls and indicating their consent (*Edwards v. State*, 862 N.E.2d 1254 [Ind. Ct. App. 2007]).

Ohio

It is not a crime to intercept a wire, oral, or electronic communication if the person recording is a party to the conversation, if one party has consented to taping, or if the conversation is not taped for the purpose of committing a criminal offense or tort (*Ohio Rev. Code Ann. § 2933.52*). Under the statute, consent is not required to tape a nonelectronic communication uttered by a person who does not have a reasonable expectation of privacy in that communication (*Ohio Rev. Code Ann. § 2933.51(b)*) defines *oral communication*.

The Ohio Supreme Court has held that prisoners do not have a reasonable expectation in their communications, for purposes of the wiretapping law (*State v. Robb*, 723 N.E.2d 1019 [Ohio 2000]).

Cordless telephone conversations purposely picked up by a neighbor's baby monitor were considered *oral communications* accompanied by a reasonable expectation of privacy (*Ohio v. Bidinost*, 644 N.E.2d 318 [Ohio 1994]).

Illegal interceptions are felonies and also carry potential civil liability for the greater of actual damages, $200 per day of violation or $10,000, along with punitive damages, attorney fees, and litigation expenses. There is a 2-year statute of limitations to bring a civil action (*Ohio Rev. Code Ann. § 2933.65*).

Ohio also has antivoyeurism law that prohibits surreptitiously invading a person's privacy for sexual purposes (*Ohio Rev. Code Ann. §2907.08*).

Michigan

Any person who willfully uses any device to overhear or record a conversation without the consent of *all parties* is guilty of illegal eavesdropping, whether or not they were present for the conversation. Illegal eavesdropping can be punished as a felony carrying a jail term of up to 2 years and a fine of up to $2000 (*Mich. Comp. Laws § 750.539c*).

In addition, any individual who divulges information he/she knows, or reasonably should know, was obtained through illegal eavesdropping is guilty of a felony punishable by imprisonment for up to 2 years and a fine of up to $2000 (*Mich. Comp. Laws § 750.539e*). Civil liability for actual and punitive damages also are sanctioned (*Mich. Comp. Laws § 750.539h*).

The eavesdropping statute has been interpreted by one court as applying only to situations in which a *third party* has intercepted a communication. This interpretation allows a participant in a conversation to record that conversation without the permission of other parties (*Sullivan v. Gray*, 324 N.W.2d 58 [Mich. Ct. App. 1982]).

The state supreme court stated in a July 1999 ruling that a participant in a conversation "may *not* unilaterally nullify other participants' expectations of privacy by secretly broadcasting the conversation" and that the overriding inquiry should be whether the parties "intended and reasonably expected that the conversation was private."

Therefore, it is likely that a recording party may not broadcast a recorded conversation without the consent of *all parties* (*Dickerson v. Raphael*, 601 N.W.2d 108 [Mich. 1999]).

It is a felony to observe, photograph, or eavesdrop on a person in a private place without the person's consent (*Mich. Comp. Laws § 750.539d*). A private place is a place where one may reasonably expect to be safe from intrusion or surveillance, but not a place where the public has access (*Mich. Comp. Laws § 750.539a*).

Additionally, the Court of Appeals of Michigan held in 2006 that neither the secretary to a school district superintendent who allegedly circulated a facsimile sent to the superintendent nor those who saw the facsimile were liable under the state eavesdropping statute, since the facsimile machine was not used to record or access the messages sent to the superintendent (*Vollmar v. Laura*, 2006 WL 1008995 [Mich. Ct. App. 2006] [Unreported]).

Illinois

In Illinois, an eavesdropping device cannot be used to record or overhear a conversation without the consent of all parties to the conversation (*720 Ill. Compiled Stat. Ann. 5/14-1, -2*). An eavesdropping device is defined as anything used to hear or record a conversation, even if the conversation is conducted in person.

In addition, it is illegal to disclose information one knows or should have known was obtained with an eavesdropping device. Violations of the eavesdropping law are punishable as felonies, with first offenses categorized as lesser felonies than subsequent offenses (*720 Ill. Compiled Stat. Ann. 5/14-4*). Civil liability for actual and punitive damages is authorized as well (*720 Ill. Compiled Stat. Ann. 5/14-6*). However, not disclosing the contents of the illegally obtained communication is an affirmative defense to the charge.

Standard radio scanners are not eavesdropping devices, according to a 1990 decision from an intermediate appellate court (*Illinois v. Wilson*, 554 N.E.2d 545 [Ill. App. Ct. 1990]). A camera is not an eavesdropping device (*Cassidy v. ABC*, 377 N.E. 2d 126 [Ill. App. Ct. 1978]).

It is also illegal for any person to "videotape, photograph, or film another person without that person's consent in a restroom, tanning bed or tanning salon, locker room, changing room or hotel bedroom," or in their residence without their consent (*720 Ill. Compiled Stat. Ann. 5/26-4(a)*).

The eavesdropping provisions do not prohibit private citizens from electronically recording the proceedings of any meeting subject to the Open Meetings Act.

Under Illinois law, when communications with individuals acting as agents or representatives of a company are taped in violation of the Illinois eavesdropping statute, claims under the eavesdropping statute belong to the company (*International Profit Associates, Inc., v. Paisola*, 461 F.Supp.2d 672 [N.D. Ill. 2006]).

Emerging Technology and Intelligence

Intelligence requirements in the future will depend upon how society and technology develops and what trends emerge. It is a symbiotic relationship—intelligence analyzes technology for future trends and future trends in technology influence how intelligence is gathered in the future.

Eric Schmidt, executive chairman of Google, and Jared Cohen, director of Google Ideas, write about the influence of future technology in their book, *The New Digital Age: Reshaping the Future of People, Nations, and Business*:

> And as adoption of these tools increases, so too will their speed and computing power. Moores Law, the rule of thumb in the technology industry, tells us that processor chips—the small circuit boards that form the backbone of every computing device—double in speed every eighteen months. That means a computer in 2025 will be sixty-four times faster than it is in 2013. Another predictive law, this one of *photonics* (regarding the transmission of information), tells us that the amount of data coming out of fiber-optic cables, the fastest form of connectivity, doubles roughly every nine months. Even if these laws have natural limits, the promise of *exponential* growth unleashes possibilities in graphics and virtual reality that will make the online experience as real as real life, or perhaps even better.

Schmidt and Cohen (2013, p. 5)

Photonics includes the generation, emission, transmission, modulation, signal processing, switching, amplification, and detection and sensing of light. Photonics emphasizes that photons are neither particles nor waves but have both particle and wave nature. It covers all technical applications of light over the whole spectrum, from ultraviolet, through the visible, to the near, mid, and far IR. The *exponential function* is used to model a relationship in which a constant change in the independent variable gives the same proportional change (i.e., percentage increase or decrease) in the dependent variable. The function is often written as exp(x), especially when it is impractical to write the independent variable as a superscript. The exponential function is widely used in physics, chemistry, engineering, mathematical biology, economics, and mathematics.

Steve Jobs said that

> Creativity is just connecting things. When you ask creative people how they did something, they feel a little guilty because they didn't really do it, they just saw something. It seemed obvious to them after a while. That's because they were able to connect experiences they've had and synthesize new things.

http://www.brainyquote.com/quotes/authors/s/steve_jobs.html
(June 5, 2013)

Schmidt and Cohen observe that current events influence technology and technology influences current events, saying "...just as we began to share ideas about the future, a string of highly visible world events occurred that exemplified the very concepts and problems we were debating." They illustrate this with several examples:

> The Chinese government launched sophisticated cyber attacks on Google and dozens of other American companies; Wikileaks burst onto the scene, making hundreds of thousands of classified digital records universally accessible; major earthquakes in Haiti and Japan devastated cities but generated innovative tech-driven responses; and the revolution of the Arab Spring shook the world with their speed, strength and contagious mobilization effects. Each turbulent development introduced new angles and possibilities about the future for us to consider.

Schmidt and Cohen (2013, pp. 10–11)

The importance of emerging technology in the national security arena cannot be overemphasized. Schmidt and Cohen write, "Some cyber-security experts peg the cost of the new 'cyber-industrial complex' somewhere between $80 billion and $150 billion annually." They opine that, "Countries with strong engineering sectors like the United States have the human capital to build their virtual weapons 'in-house,' but what of the states whose populations' technical potential is underdeveloped? ...China and the United States will be the largest suppliers but by no means the only ones; government agencies and private companies from all over the world will compete to offer products and services to acquisitive nations...." They go on to note, "A raid on the Egyptian state security building after the country's 2011 revolution produced explosive copies of contracts with private outlets, including an obscure British firm that sold online spyware to the Mubarak regime." (Schmidt & Cohen 2013, p. 110)

Strengths, Weaknesses, Opportunities, and Threats

Schmidt and Cohen write, "The unavoidable truth is that connectivity benefits terrorists and violent extremists too; as it spreads, so will the risks. Future terrorist activity will include physical and virtual aspects, from recruitment to implementation" (Schmidt & Cohen, 2013, p. 151). They also observe that

> This is the "big data" challenge that government bodies and other institutions around the world are facing: How can intelligence agencies, military divisions and law enforcement integrate all of their digital databases into a centralized structure so that the right dots can be connected without violating citizens' privacy? In the United States, for example, the FBI, State Department, CIA, and other government agencies all use different systems. We know computers can find patterns, anomalies and other relevant signifiers much more efficiently than human analysts can, yet bringing together disparate information systems (passport information, fingerprint scans, bank withdrawals, wiretaps, travel records) and building algorithms that can efficiently cross-reference them, eliminate redundancy and recognize red flags in the data is an incredibly difficult and time-consuming task.
>
> **Schmidt and Cohen (2013, p. 174)**

In mathematics and computer science, an *algorithm* is a step-by-step procedure for calculations, usually used for calculation, data processing, and automated reasoning.

Emerging technologies influence the tradecraft of every filed, including the intelligence community; Gen. Michael Hayden, former director of the CIA, stated

> Global security can be formed or threatened by heads of state whose wisdom, folly and obsessions shape global events. But often it is the security practitioners, those rarely in the headlines but whose craft and energy quietly break new ground, who keep us safe or put us in peril.

Innovation is the key to holding the tactical and strategic edge in a competitive world.

Misappropriation from Computers

Advantacare Health Partners, LP v. Access IV, 2004 WL 1837997 (N.D.Cal. 2004); sanctions for misappropriation.

The plaintiff brought an action against former employees for misappropriation of the plaintiff's computer files. The plaintiff performed a forensic analysis of the employees' former work computers and discovered that they had copied confidential files prior to leaving the company. These files included information such as the plaintiff's patient database, budget documents, employees' wages, referral statistics, marketing materials, and other items. Based on this evidence, the court granted the plaintiffs' request to make forensic copies of the defendants' current home and business computers. A computer forensic expert discovered that after the court issued the order, numerous computer searches for data deletion software were performed, and scrub software was used to delete more than 13,000 files from the defendant's home and office computers.

Based on these facts, the court ordered the defendants to permanently delete the remaining files and authorized the plaintiffs to reimage the defendants' hard drives to verify compliance. A forensic computer examiner reimaged the defendants' hard drives and found that thousands of the plaintiff's files remained on the drives. The plaintiff claimed that the actions of the defendant caused prejudice to the merits of its case and requested the court to enter a default judgment.

The court found that the defendants' actions, while culpable, did not warrant granting the sanction of default judgment. The court was not sure that the circumstances were *extraordinary* and determined that lesser sanctions would be as effective as a default judgment. The court granted evidence sanctions, instructing the trier of fact to presume that the defendants had copied all of the plaintiffs' computer files. The defendants were also ordered to pay monetary sanctions in the amount of $20,000 within 30 days.

Kalish v. Leapfrog Online, **Illinois Circuit Court of Cook County Case No. 03 L 11695 (Jason Kalish, an individual, *v.* Leapfrog Online Customer Acquisition, LLC, a Delaware limited liability company; David Husain, an individual; Scott Eskamp, an individual; and Jason Wadler, an individual); misappropriation of a trade secret.**

Plaintiff Jason Kalish sued Leapfrog Online after he left the company, claiming that the company owed him $781,632 in commissions and salary. A computer forensics firm was hired to inspect Jason Kalish's work computer and found a *zip* file of company data that had been e-mailed outside the company on Jason Kalish's last day of work. Leapfrog Online then sued Jason Kalish for misappropriation of a trade secret.

After several months, Jason Kalish admitted to e-mailing a *zip* file to his home computer but refused to allow inspection of that machine. Leapfrog Online sought a court order compelling an inspection of Jason Kalish's home computer, but Jason Kalish objected to the choice of the independent expert, since Leapfrog already used the firm in this case. The defendants' attorney, Peter Land of Babbitt & Melton, LLP, filed a Reply In Support of Motion to Compel, stating

> ...there is no reason not to select Forensicon. The company routinely works as a neutral third party examiner, is practiced at complying with protective orders, and fully understands the need to protect a producing party's privacy... There is no reason to suspect that Forensicon would disclose non-responsive materials to Defendants or anyone else... Plaintiff's true concern appears to be that Forensicon's experience with Mr. Jason Kalish's other deceptive computer conduct will result in a more thorough, effective search for responsive documents. This is a reason to select Forensicon, not reject it.

Cook County Circuit Court ordered the forensics firm to perform a forensic examination of Jason Kalish's home computer to establish whether the plaintiff left the company with Leapfrog Online property and the firm provided a report detailing their findings. Shortly thereafter, the parties agreed to dismiss all claims without any compensation to Jason Kalish or his counsel; plaintiff Jason Kalish paid Leapfrog Online a significant sum of money.

LeJeune v. Coin Acceptors, Inc., 2004 WL 1067795 (Md. 2004); employee's attempt to download employer's confidential documents shows misappropriation of trade secrets; doctrine of "inevitable disclosure" not applicable.

The plaintiff filed a motion for a temporary injunction to enjoin the defendant from using trade secrets that the plaintiff believed the defendant had misappropriated. The defendant claimed that any *trade secrets* that he had copied were coincidental. He claimed that he was attempting to copy personal photos that were in the "My Documents" folder of the hard drive and because he did not know how to separate files, he copied the whole "My Documents" folder.

The plaintiffs hired a computer forensic expert who was able to refute the defendant's statement by showing that not only had the defendant copied one of the plaintiff's files that was not in the "My Documents" folder, but the defendant had also attempted to erase the record of the file transfer.

The trial court ruled, and the appellate court affirmed, that this was a misappropriation of *trade secrets*. The trial court granted the plaintiff's motion for the preliminary injunction based on the *doctrine of inevitable disclosure*. However, the appellate court disagreed with this part of the ruling, vacated the injunction, and remanded the case for further proceedings.

The appellate court did not agree with the trial court's ruling on the issue of *inevitable disclosure* for the following reasons:

1. The doctrine permits an employer to enjoin the former employee without proof of the employee's actual or threatened use of trade

secrets based upon an inference (based upon circumstantial evidence) that the employee will use his or her knowledge of those trade secrets in the course of his new employment. The result is not merely an injunction against the use of trade secrets, but an injunction which restricts employment.

2. If "inevitable disclosure" was applied in this case, then the plaintiff would benefit from a noncompete agreement even though it never negotiated one with the defendant.

3. The adoption of the doctrine would permit the court to infer "inevitable disclosure" from the employee's mere exposure to trade secrets.

***Liebert Corporation v. Mazur*, 2005 WL 762954 (Ill. App. 2005); expert testimony shows misappropriation of trade secrets; doctrine of "inevitable disclosure."**

Liebert Corporation, a network protection equipment company, and Zonatherm, its exclusive sales representative, brought an action to enjoin a former employee of Zonatherm from using trade secrets in a competing business. The trial court denied the plaintiff's motion for a preliminary injunction on the basis that the plaintiff had not established that the price books, which had been established as trade secrets, were actually misappropriated. The trial court found that business cards and customer lists taken from the plaintiff were not trade secrets. In the case of the price books, the trial court found these to be trade secrets, but since the information was destroyed, there was no way of knowing whether it had been used by the defendant or if it had been disclosed to any other parties.

On appeal, the plaintiffs argued that the trial court abused its discretion when (1) it found the customer lists were not trade secrets, (2) it failed to decide whether the sales quotations were trade secrets, (3) it found the plaintiffs did not present a fair question on the likelihood of success on their trade secret misappropriation claims because the defendants no longer had the information, (4) it found no fair question that the defendants would inevitably use the trade secrets, and (5) it found that the plaintiffs' allegations of irreparable harm were speculative.

The court held that in order for something to be considered a trade secret (under Illinois statute), it must have two characteristics: (1) it must be sufficiently secret to give the plaintiff a competitive advantage, and (2) the plaintiff must take affirmative measures to keep others from acquiring the information.

The reviewing court found that although the price lists were secret, the plaintiff did not take affirmative steps to keep others from acquiring the customer lists. The court found the same in the case of the sales quotations. The plaintiff did not make its employees aware of the fact that the bids and sales quotations were confidential and did not require employees sign a confidentiality agreement.

The court agreed with the trial court that the price books were a trade secret. As to whether the plaintiff presented a fair question as to the likelihood of the success of its misappropriation claim, the court held that misappropriation can be found in one of three ways: (1) improper acquisition, (2) unauthorized disclosure, or (3) unauthorized use.

To determine whether there had been misappropriation, the court examined the testimony of both the defendant and plaintiff's computer forensics expert. The expert was hired by the plaintiffs to examine the hard drive of the defendant's laptop computer. The expert created an image of the laptop's hard drive, performed extensive searches for the plaintiff's files, and compared files he found on the laptop's hard drive with those he had been provided with by the plaintiffs. The expert testified that he had found files, which contained the plaintiff's price books on the defendant's hard drive, and that these files had been compressed on the defendant's hard drive and then put into a folder containing the plaintiff's price book documents. The files were then transferred into a CD burning folder on the defendant's laptop.

According to the expert, most users are not aware of the CD burning file folder. He testified that the fact that the folder of compressed files from the defendant's hard drive went into the CD burning folder 3 minutes after the additional price book files were added to it made it more likely than not that the defendant had successfully burned the CD. He also testified that on the same day the files went into the CD burning folder, the defendant began a *mass wave of deletion*. The expert found that the defendant had purged his application log, which would have established when the CD burning program was used, and how many CDs were successfully burned.

In the defendant's testimony, he provided two explanations for his downloading and deletions of the plaintiff's files onto and off of his laptop. First, he said that he wanted to preserve a record for his outstanding commissions. The court found that this would explain his need for the price quotations, but not for the price books. Second, he explained that he was trying to create a *closeout* document for his team and that he wasn't sure that his colleagues would know which price quotes he had used for which bids.

The court was not persuaded by this explanation because (1) if the defendant could get this information, then his team members, with the same access, could as well, and (2) the defendant never handed off the information to his team. The defendant said that the reason for his deletion was that the files were no longer needed. The court did not believe this because the defendant had testified that his efforts to burn a CD were unsuccessful, but he had also testified that the files were necessary for his team.

The reviewing court found that the plaintiffs had presented a fair question on misappropriation against the defendant. The next part of the inquiry was to determine whether preliminary injunctive relief was an appropriate remedy. In this case, the plaintiff used the theory of *inevitable disclosure*.

Using the theory of inevitable disclosure, the plaintiff may prove trade secret misappropriation by showing that the defendant's new employment will inevitably lead him to rely on the plaintiff's trade secrets.

The trial court found no fair question on inevitable disclosure based on the defendant's testimony that he had destroyed his copies of the plaintiff's price books and he, therefore, could not disclose the plaintiff's pricing structure. The reviewing court examined the expert's testimony, which stated that it was likely that the defendant had successfully created a CD with the price books and noted that the only evidence to refute this was the defendant's questionable testimony. The court found it even more suspicious that evidence that would definitively show whether the defendant had successfully burned a CD was not available because the defendant had purged the application log on his hard drive a day after attempting to burn the CD.

The court said that since the defendant had erased the crucial piece of evidence, the court presumed that the application log would have shown that the defendant had successfully created the CD in question. Based on this, the court rejected the trial court's finding on inevitable use.

The court affirmed the trial court's finding that Zonatherm's customer list was not a trade secret. Although the trial court abused its discretion in failing to consider the bids and sales quotation records, the court found that the plaintiff failed to make a fair showing that the information was a trade secret. The court also found that the trial court abused its discretion when it found that the plaintiffs did not show a likelihood of success on their trade secret misappropriation claim against Mazur or irreparable harm concerning the price books.

The court remanded the case and directed the trial court to grant the plaintiffs a preliminary injunction against the defendant Mazur, reasonable in scope and duration, to prevent any actual or threatened misappropriation of the price books.

SKF USA, Inc., v. Bjerkness, 2010 U.S. Dist. LEXIS 80776 (N.D. Ill. August 9, 2010); plaintiff award for the misappropriation of trade secrets.

The Northern District of Illinois ordered compensatory and exemplary damage awards totaling more than $80,000 for the misappropriation of trade secrets contained within the thousands of computer files the defendants stole from their former employer.

Defendant Dale Bjerkness left his employment at plaintiff SKF USA, Inc., in 2008 to start a competing company, Equipment Reliability Services, Inc. (ERSI). Three additional SKF employees followed Bjerkness to ERSI in the subsequent 2 months.

Before leaving SKF, each of the four copied thousands of computer files from SKF computers onto external hard drives, flash drives, and CDs. These files contained important SKF data, including price quotes, customer databases, reports, and training materials.

Counsel for SKF notified the defendants of its belief that the defendants were in violation of secrecy agreements they had signed as employees at SKF, which prohibited use or disclosure of SKF trade secrets and confidential business information. When SKF's counsel requested that the devices used to copy SKF files be returned, the defendants turned over several such devices to their lawyer. Forensic analysis showed, however, that two devices that had been connected to both SKF and ERSI computers had not been produced.

SKF filed suit, arguing unfair competition, breach of secrecy agreements, and a violation of the Illinois Trade Secrets Act. The Northern District of Illinois issued a preliminary injunction requiring the defendants to destroy all information obtained from SKF, fearing that the defendants still had trade secret information in their possession. The court ordered a third-party computer expert to inspect ERSI computers to confirm compliance with the injunction.

On the trade secret claim, the court held that the information taken from SKF was confidential information that provided SKF a competitive advantage. The information was protected by reasonable measures to maintain confidentiality, including password protection and the secrecy agreements the defendants had signed.

In determining damages, the court reasoned that the "Defendants' theft of thousands of computer files is circumstantial evidence that they intended to use SKF's trade secrets" to divert SKF customers to their new business at ERSI. However, the court found that SKF failed to prove causality because the defendants had not specifically informed their customers that they were using SKF trade secrets in their new business. Instead, the court found that the defendants were liable for *unjust enrichment* under the Illinois Trade Secrets Act. The court ordered damages equal to the profits the defendants had earned using SKF trade secrets. It also issued an exemplary damage award of $40,000 for willful and malicious misappropriation of trade secrets, reasoning that the defendants had admitted to taking confidential information without authorization and had been less than forthcoming in returning that data when requested.

Computer Forensics
Searches, Evidence, and Notice

14

Both Carl Sagan and Stephen Hawking, two of the most brilliant men of our time, longed to understand the universe and what is in it. Stephen Hawking said, "Intelligence is the ability to adapt to change." He also said, "I think computer viruses should count as life. I think it says something about human nature that the only form of life we have created so far is purely destructive. We've created life in our own image" (http://www.brainyquote.com/quotes/authors/s/stephen_hawking.html, retrieved June 5, 2013).

Searching Computers

***United States v. Arnold*, 523F.3d941 (9th Cir. 2008); reasonable suspicion not required for searching laptops or other digital devices at the borders.**

In this case, the U.S. Court of Appeals for the Ninth Circuit held that the Fourth Amendment to the U.S. Constitution does not require government agents to have reasonable suspicion before searching laptops or other digital devices at the border, including international airports.

***Ranta v. Ranta*, 2004 WL 504588 (Conn. Super. 2004); party ordered to stop using laptop and turn it over to the court.**

In a divorce proceeding, the judge ordered the plaintiff "to stop using, accessing, turning on, powering, copying, deleting, removing or uninstalling any programs, files and or folders, or booting up her laptop computer." The court order required the plaintiff to turn in her laptop to the court clerk's office and to produce all floppy disks, CDs, and other similar storage devices. The cost of hiring a computer forensics expert would be split equally between the parties, and the forensics expert would be required to sign a confidentiality agreement. If the parties could not agree on a computer forensics expert, the court would make the selection from a list comprised of two recommendations by each party. The defendant was also ordered to purchase a replacement laptop for the plaintiff.

***In re: Search of 3817 W. West End*, 321 F. Supp. 2d 953 (N.D. Ill. 2004); court orders government to submit search protocol prior to examining seized computer.**

This case involved the seizure of a computer and electronic storage media. The government sought relief from the court's order, which instructed the government to submit a search protocol before it forensically examined the seized items. The original order outlined the search protocol to ensure that irrelevant or privileged data were not examined. The government objected to the court's order, arguing that courts could not regulate the manner in which a computer was searched once probable cause was established. The government compared the search of a computer hard drive to the search of a file cabinet concerning papers and urged that just as the court could not regulate the manner in which a file cabinet was searched, it could not regulate the search of computer files.

The court found the government's argument unpersuasive and distinguished between the analogies based on the existence of tools allowing the search of computer information to be more targeted than a search of hard copy documents. The court held that these tools afforded the government the ability to limit its search by date range, key words, specific files, and specific software programs. Thus, the court held the search protocol was necessary in order to meet the particularity requirement of a constitutional search warrant.

ADHI Parasakthi Charitable v. Township of W. Pikeland, 2009 WL 1047894 (E.D. Pa. 2010); plaintiff ordered by court to allow forensic investigative analysis of computers.

The plaintiff sought a variance from the town zoning board's zoning regulations in order to build a religious temple on a parcel of land within the township. In an appeal from the defendant's decision, the district court ordered the plaintiff to allow the defendant's computer expert to inspect the plaintiff's computers for responsive e-mails not produced in the first round of discovery.

During discovery, the defendant made several interrogatories and document requests that it felt would demonstrate that the plaintiff had insufficiently answered. After the court ordered the plaintiff's compliance with the discovery requests, the plaintiff produced 2600 pages of responsive documents. This production, however, contained only three e-mails.

Believing there must be more e-mails related to the planned development, the defendant again sought a court order to enforce the document requests. The plaintiff argued that if any additional responsive e-mails had existed, they had since been deleted in the ordinary course of business and could not be produced. The defendant responded that mere deletion does not mean the e-mails were lost forever. Some e-mails, the defendant argued, could be recovered by a forensic collection.

Agreeing with the defendant, the court ordered the plaintiff to allow the defendant's computer expert to forensically examine its computer systems for any responsive documents. The court reasoned that the plaintiff had not argued the e-mails never existed and that the defendant was entitled to fully discover any relevant information that may still exist on the computers.

Supreme Court Established Search Protocol

During the discovery phase of a martial dispute, the New York Supreme Court established guidelines for a search protocol to assist the forensic examination of the defendant-husband's work computer.

Plaintiff-wife Sarah Schreiber moved for an order compelling the production of her husband's office computer, claiming that it contained valuable information about his income and financial assets not previously disclosed to her. The defendant responded that he had fully disclosed his financial matters and that a forensic examination of his work computer would be a groundless fishing expedition.

After noting that parties in a marital dispute are entitled to full disclosure of financial assets, the supreme court of New York expressed concern that unfettered access to the defendant's computer could reveal privileged and irrelevant documents. The court denied the plaintiff's motion to compel production of the computer, reasoning that she was not entitled to unrestricted access. The court emphasized that the plaintiff would be permitted to renew her motion if she provided a search protocol that would adequately protect the defendant's privileged and confidential information.

The court then indicated several areas that a search protocol must adder: (1) A discovery referee must be appointed to supervise discovery, (2) a forensic computer expert must be hired and he or she must sign a confidentiality agreement governing nondisclosure of the contents of the computer hard drive, and (3) the computer expert should (a) examine a mirror image of the computer hard drive, (b) look for evidence of wiping utilities that could be used to delete files, and (c) recover all files and fragments available on the drive.

The plaintiff must then establish a set of keywords and a relevant time period for which to search. The plaintiff should narrowly tailor the keywords and time period to the immediate discovery needs. The computer expert would search the recovered files, exporting the relevant documents to CD or DVD for delivery to the defendant's counsel, who would examine the files for privilege.

Finally, the defendant's counsel was instructed to deliver nonprivileged documents, as well as a privilege log, to the plaintiff's counsel within 20 days. Costs of the forensic analysis would be borne by the plaintiff, and the cloned hard drive would be returned to and destroyed by the defendant's counsel at the termination of the litigation.

The court stressed that the discovery should be limited to produce only relevant documents and to protect any privilege.

Super Film of Am., Inc., v. UCB Films, Inc., 219 F.R.D. 649 (D. Kan. 2004); party cannot shift electronic discovery obligations unless an undue burden exists.

In an action for breach of contract, the defendant filed a motion to compel the plaintiff to produce electronic versions of documents including e-mails, databases, and spreadsheets. In its response to the motion to compel, the plaintiff stated that it attempted to provide electronic copies of the documents requested within its *knowledge* or *expertise*. The plaintiff argued that it did not have the expertise to recover any further electronic documents and the court's order requiring such production would be unduly burdensome. As an alternative to a court order compelling production, the plaintiff proposed to make its computers available to the defendant's technicians to inspect and make copies of any responsive electronic files or documents.

The court held that the plaintiff's contention that it did not have the expertise to retrieve such electronic data to be inadequate. The court said that it "cannot relieve a party of its discovery obligations based simply on that party's unsupported assertion that such obligations are unduly burdensome. The party opposing electronic discovery on the grounds of undue burden must provide sufficient detail and explanation about the nature of the burden in terms of time, money and procedure which would be required to produce the requested documents." The court agreed with the defendant that allowing the plaintiff to satisfy its electronic discovery obligations by simply turning over its two computers to the defendant for inspection would unfairly shift the burden and expense of discovery.

YCA, LLC v. Berry, 2004 WL 1093385 (N.D. Ill. 2004); inconsistent testimony justifies delayed disclosure of computer forensic expert.

In a case involving an alleged breach of a restrictive covenant, the defendant moved to strike the testimony of a computer expert who recovered deleted documents from the defendant's computer. The defendant argued that allowing the expert's testimony would be unfairly prejudicial because the plaintiff failed to disclose the computer expert by the required discovery deadline. The plaintiff asserted the delay was justified as it was a result of the defendant's own deposition testimony.

During a deposition, the defendant stated that an e-mail exchange regarding documents at issue took place on outside e-mail accounts (Yahoo and AOL), making a search of his computer unnecessary. However, in a subsequent affidavit, the defendant acknowledged creating a document that theoretically could exist on his computer and not just on his outside e-mail accounts.

The court found the inconsistent testimonies of the defendant were a sufficient excuse for the delay. In doing so, the court stated that if the defendant "wanting to avoid 'unfair surprise' concerning his legal strategy, perhaps he should have followed the spirit of the discovery rules and informed [defendant] that [plaintiff's] computer might contain relevant documents." The defendant's motion was denied and the computer expert's testimony and the recovered documents were admitted.

Zakre v. Norddeutsche Landesbank, 2004 WL 764895 (S.D. N.Y. 2004); index of documents on a CD-ROM is not required when contents of the disk are searchable.

The defendant provided the plaintiff with two CD-ROM disks and the plaintiff filed a motion to compel further discovery. The defendant had already reviewed the disks to ensure that none of the defendant's privileged information was on the disks. But the defendant did not review the disks to identify the files that were responsive to the plaintiff's request.

The court held that as long as the disks were searchable, the defendant did not have to provide the plaintiff with an index of the documents or have to search the disks themselves for files that were responsive to the plaintiff's requests. The defendant did not have to provide further discovery with respect to the CD-ROM disks that it had already turned over to the plaintiff.

Capricorn Power Co. v. Siemens Westinghouse Power Corp., 220 F.R.D 429 (W.D.Pa. 2004); preservation order denied without proof of destruction or degradation of evidence.

In this case, both parties requested a preservation order for documents to be used as evidence. Finding no definitive test outlining when to grant a preservation order, the district court formulated the following factors to consider: (1) the level of concern for the continuing existence and integrity of the evidence, (2) the possibility of irreparable harm to the party requesting the preservation order in the absence of a preservation order, and (3) the ability to maintain and preserve the evidence in question.

The defendant's motion was denied based on the fact that it could not show the likelihood that the material sought to preserve was actually in danger of being destroyed. The plaintiff's motion was denied because it would have been better filed as a motion to compel and did not even allege the possible destruction or degradation of the evidence, which it sought to preserve.

The court discussed the third prong of electronic evidence, saying that evidence stored on a floppy disk or on a hard drive may not be hard to store, but that information contained within the hard drive may be difficult to store because of the possibility of degradation or deletion when new information is added and old information is deleted. The court went on to say that timing of a preservation order could be critical in those cases where preservation is difficult, especially in cases where the person in possession of the hard drive is unaware that the information on the hard drive is evidence that needs to be preserved.

Heriot v. Byrne, 2009 U.S. Dist. LEXIS 22552 (N.D. Ill. 2009); error in ESI production allows plaintiff to "claw back" documents.

On cross motions to compel ESI production of documents related to a copyright infringement suit, the district court examined the application of *Federal Rule of Evidence 502* in finding that the plaintiff's disclosure was inadvertent and did not cause a waiver of the attorney–client privilege.

The plaintiff alleged that the defendant's made-for-TV documentary infringed its copyrights and unjustly enriched the defendant. In response to the defendant's motion to compel ESI production, the plaintiff hired a vendor to electronically scan and provide optical character recognition for documents in its production. Due to the vendor's error, 196 documents containing attorney–client communications were produced to the defendant. Within 24 hours of discovering the mistake, the plaintiff notified the defendant and the defendant sealed the documents for its motion to the court.

The defendant argued that the plaintiff should not be permitted to *claw back* the documents in its ESI production. The parties disputed whether the newly amended *Federal Rule of Evidence 502* applied and whether it would supersede the test formulated in the Seventh Circuit decision *Judson Atkinson Candies, Inc., v. Latini-Hohberger Dhimantec*, 529 F.3d 371, 387-88 (7th Cir. 2008).

The court concluded that it must first determine whether the documents in question were privileged and then apply *FRE 502*. The *Judson* factors could, however, be used in the *FRE 502* analysis.

Here, the court examined the documents in question and found that the majority were protected by the attorney–client privilege. The court then applied *FRE 502*, finding that, even though a large percentage of the privileged documents were produced, the disclosure was inadvertent because the plaintiff used reasonable procedures to review the documents and the disclosure would not have occurred but for the vendor's error. The plaintiff's notice to the defendant was also reasonably prompt. Because the plaintiff had satisfied *FRE 502*, the court found that the disclosure did not waive the attorney–client privilege. Reasoning that it would be unfair to punish the plaintiff for a disclosure it neither caused nor anticipated, the court allowed the plaintiff to *claw back* the documents.

United States v. Segal, 2004 WL 635065 (N.D. Ill. 2004); government ordered not to review defendant's privileged electronic documents.

The government seized 200 boxes of the defendant's documents and a significant amount of the defendant's electronic information, including several personal computers and backup tapes of the defendant's payroll, fax, and accounting servers. The defendant moved for a return of all privileged information that was seized and to bar the government from using this information for any purpose. The motion was initially granted, but the court subsequently granted the government's motion to reconsider.

The court also ordered the defendant to create a privilege log. The defendant gave the court a privilege log containing 13,000 privileged communications. The defendants claimed that the government had reviewed privileged communications because it failed to use proper screening techniques. The defendant stated that the government could have screened the communications and separated out the privileged information by using commercial software or a third party. The defendant also pointed out that the government did not follow Department of Justice guidelines for searching seized materials.

The court stated that for the defendant's due process to have been violated, the government's violation of the defendant's attorney–client privilege must "shock the court's conscience." The court laid out a three-part test to determine whether something *shocks* its conscience: (1) The government must have knowledge of the attorney–client privilege, (2) the government must make a deliberate intrusion into that relationship, and (3) there must be actual and substantial prejudice.

The court held that although the government's actions should not be condoned, they did not rise to a level that shocked the court, did not violate the defendant's due process rights, and did not warrant the suppression of evidence that the plaintiff was seeking. The court did, however, order the government not to review documents from the privilege log or to present any of the documents from the privilege log without a court determination that those documents were not privileged.

Portis v. City of Chicago, 2004 WL 1535854 (N.D. Ill. 2004); plaintiffs' electronic database discoverable as a "fact work product."

The plaintiffs filed a class action suit against the City of Chicago for detaining people for hours after the completion of administrative processes associated with noncustodial ordinance violations. The plaintiffs had created a database that organized the names and other information for individuals who would be considered as part of the class for purposes of the suit. The defendant filed a motion to compel access to this database, stating that it had a real need for the information and that it could not obtain the information in the database without undue hardship. Since the plaintiffs created the database in anticipation of litigation, the issue before the court was whether the database was *fact work product* or *opinion work product*.

The court reasoned that since the information in the database was so extensive, it did not contain any specific insight into the plaintiffs' legal strategy. Based on this, the court held that the database was *fact work product* and that sharing the database with the defendant would not seriously prejudice the plaintiffs. The court granted the defendant's motion to compel and held that the defendants would have to split the costs of the creation of the database with the plaintiff.

Notice

Campbell v. General Dynamics Government Systems Corp., 321 F.Supp.2d 142 (Mass. 2004); e-mail insufficient notification of mandatory arbitration for employee disputes.

The plaintiff brought an action against his former employer alleging that he was wrongfully terminated due to his medical condition. The employer had the case removed to federal court and motioned to stay all federal court proceedings and compel arbitration pursuant to the defendant's dispute resolution policy (DRP).

The case turned on the issue of whether the defendant's e-mail to its employees was sufficient notice that the employee would be giving up his right to use the federal judicial forum. The defendant offered an e-mail tracking log that showed that the plaintiff had opened the e-mail in question. The defendant offered this as evidence that the plaintiff had notice of the DRP. The plaintiff asserted that he had not read the e-mail and was not aware of the DRP.

The court examined the e-mail and noted that the DRP was vaguely outlined in the bottom paragraph and that to get more specific information on the DRP, an employee would have had to click on the two links at the bottom of the message. The court noted that the defendant did nothing to verify that its employees had read or understood the e-mail and suggested that the defendant could have made its employees verify that they had read and understood the e-mail with a signature in the form of an electronic reply or an actual written signature. The court also said that the defendant could have had mandatory meetings with a sign in sheet where the DRP would be explained. The court ruled that the plaintiff did not have knowledge of the DRP and the defendant could not deprive him of his right to a federal judicial forum.

As previously stated, you should always seek competent legal counsel before relying on case law or statutes that evolve and change. A proper contemporary search of current case law and statutes should always be conducted before relying upon any source. The cases and statutes provided are current at the time this work was compiled and can serve as a starting point in researching any changes in the law.

Computer Forensics
Discovery and Spoliation

15

Discovery Issues

In Re: A&M Florida Properties II, LLC, 2010 Bankr. LEXIS 1217 (S.D.N.Y. Bankr. Ct. April 7, 2010); monetary sanctions for failure to produce requested e-mails in a timely manner.

During the discovery phase of a suit alleging the breach of a purchase and sale contract, the Bankruptcy Court for the Southern District of New York ordered monetary sanctions against the plaintiff and its counsel for their failure to timely produce requested e-mails that remained hidden due to a misunderstanding of the plaintiff's e-mail retention procedures.

Plaintiff GFI Acquisition sued American Federated Title Corporation for the alleged breach of their $41 million agreement for the sale of four properties. GFI alleged that American Federated failed to disclose certain lock-out features contained in loans GFI promised to assume upon the sale. At issue were several e-mails that American Federated had sent GFI that would allegedly demonstrate GFI's knowledge of the loan terms.

When GFI's initial search did not produce the relevant e-mails, American Federated requested a more extensive search. GFI subsequently produced an additional 346 documents, but did not find the e-mails. The parties hired a joint computer forensic expert to search GFI's e-mail system, but this search also failed to produce the e-mails that American Federated was sure GFI had in its possession.

After the initial forensic search, GFI's counsel discovered that GFI's e-mail system allowed its users to archive e-mail. A second search of the archived e-mails discovered nearly 10,000 relevant e-mails previously undisclosed to American Federated. The joint computer expert produced a small portion of the new e-mails to American Federated and the rest to GFI for privilege review. However, due to further misunderstandings, GFI's counsel failed to review the e-mails for more than 2 months. American Federated eventually received a full production, including the e-mails that it had expected in the initial production.

American Federated filed a motion for sanctions, arguing that GFI had obstructed its discovery with unnecessary delays and costs. The court found both dismissal of GFI's action and an adverse inference instruction too harsh, noting that there was no evidence that GFI or its counsel had acted in bad faith. Instead, monetary sanctions were warranted. The court reasoned that the initial production would have disclosed all relevant e-mail if GFI's counsel had made a diligent effort to learn about and search all of GFI's e-mail system, including the archived mails. Because counsel's failure to investigate the e-mail system caused the need for additional motions and forensic searches, the court ordered GFI and its counsel to reimburse American Federated for both its motion costs and its half of the forensic searches.

CE Design Ltd. v. Cy's Crabhouse North, Inc., 2010 U. S. Dist. LEXIS 59000 (N.D. Ill. June 11, 2010); court orders supplemental expert report on new hard drive evidence.

This case involved an alleged violation of the *Telephone Consumer Protection Act* (TCPA) due to the use of an automated fax advertisement service. Plaintiff CE Design sued under the TCPA after receiving an unsolicited fax advertisement for Cy's Crabhouse via a third-party company, Business to Business Solutions (B2B). The Northern District of Illinois ordered the defendant's computer expert to issue a supplemental report after the plaintiff disclosed a previously unproduced hard drive.

During discovery, Cy's Crabhouse requested all documents in CE Design's possession relating to other TCPA suits involving B2B. At issue was a list of fax numbers utilized by B2B to send advertisements. B2B's sole employee, Caroline Abraham, first asserted that she could not provide the requested fax numbers because they had been maintained by B2B's parent company and she had lost any relevant data in a hard drive crash 2 years before. Counsel for Cy's Crabhouse later learned, however, that Abraham had produced the requested information to CE Design's counsel pursuant to a show cause order in a separate case involving B2B. Abraham had provided CE Design with backup tape data burned to a DVD, as well as the crashed hard drive. Cy's Crabhouse later received a copy of the DVD but had not been granted access to the hard drive.

Cy's Crabhouse moved to dismiss as sanction for CE Design's discovery violations, including the failure to produce the requested hard drive. Shortly after the motion was filed against it, CE Design produced the missing hard drive.

The court found the failure to disclose the hard drive to be *somewhat more substantial* than the other alleged discovery violations. The court did not, however, find any prejudice to Cy's Crabhouse because the hard drive had eventually been produced. Finding dismissal to be too severe a sanction, the court ordered Cy's Crabhouse to submit a supplemental report from its computer expert based upon a forensic analysis of the hard drive. The court noted that it would assess the costs of the computer expert's new report against CE Design if the hard drive data required material changes to the expert's opinion in the case.

***Custodian of Records v. State of Wisconsin (In Re: Doe)*, 680 N.W.2d 792 (Wis., 2004); subpoena ordering backup tapes for all government servers quashed for being overly broad.**

In a suit involving the criminal investigation of state legislators, the trial court issued a subpoena ordering the Legislative Technology Service Bureau (LTSB) to produce backup tapes for all 54 government computer servers, or alternatively, to extract all documents for certain named individuals. The order defined documents to include all digital computer information or data maintained by the LTSB, including, but not limited to, all e-mail, electronic calendars, recycle bin files, temporary Internet files, and image files.

On appeal, the Wisconsin supreme court quashed the subpoena as being unreasonable because it was overly broad. The court held the subpoena was overly broad because it compelled production of computer data from an entire branch of government, rather than requesting specific topics, document types, or time periods. The court also held that because the documents that the plaintiffs sought were computer records, "a key word search would not have been too difficult to incorporate into the subpoena."

***Andrew Corp. v. Cassinelli*, 2009 U.S. Dist. LEXIS 22105 (N.D. Ill. 2009); noncompliance with employment agreement causes competitor to cover costs.**

During an employment dispute in which an employer alleged a breach of a confidentiality agreement, the Northern District of Illinois found the defendant's forensic analysis insufficient for its failure to report a list of responsive files.

After the employee resigned from the plaintiff corporation and joined a competitor company, the plaintiff filed suit for breach of an employment agreement, under which the employee was prohibited from soliciting or servicing the plaintiff's customers or sharing confidential information with new employers. The employee claimed that he had complied with the agreement and had maintained a record of all communications with the plaintiff's customers, whom he referred to other associates at the competitor company.

The court ordered limited discovery to determine if the employee and competitor had complied with the employment agreement. The competitor hired forensic experts to create a forensic image of the employee's computer, which was then supplied to the plaintiff. In this forensic image, the plaintiff found seven e-mails containing its confidential information.

The experts conducted a search of the competitor's e-mail server and some of office computers, using 26 keywords from the e-mails discovered on the employee's computer. The competitor asserted that the forensic experts had permanently deleted all 813 responsive documents discovered in its search.

The court found the competitor's assertion insufficient evidence to show compliance with the employment agreement. Because the list of 26 keywords was developed only by the competitor company and was not comprehensive, the court was not confident that the forensic analysis had recovered all responsive files. In addition, the forensics experts should have provided a report of all responsive files, their locations, and whether they had been deleted. The court ordered a *special master* to oversee compliance with the agreement and ordered the competitor to pay all associated costs and attorneys' fees.

Arista Records, Inc. v. Sakfield Holding Co., 314 F. Supp 2d. 27. (D.D.C., 2004); general jurisdiction over defendant established by computer forensic evidence.

The plaintiff record company brought suit against the defendant website for allowing people to download the record company's music. The defendant claimed that the District Court for the District of Columbia did not have jurisdiction over it. The court stated that there was enough evidence to show specific jurisdiction because the case was based on the declaration of a man who lived in the District of Columbia who said that he had downloaded music files from the defendant's website.

During jurisdictional discovery, the plaintiff's computer expert was able to uncover evidence that the defendant had deleted a log that listed all of the people who had downloaded music from its website. From the information that he was able to recover, the expert determined that 241 of the people who had downloaded music from the defendant's website were in fact from the District of Columbia.

The court found these contacts with people in the District of Columbia to be sufficient to establish the continuous and systematic contacts, which are necessary to establish general jurisdiction over the defendant.

Hollingsworth v. Time Warner, 812 N.E.2d 976 (Ohio App. 1. Dist. 2004); inadvertent disclosure of e-mail waives attorney–client privilege.

The plaintiff filed an employment discrimination suit seeking unemployment benefits, because she felt that she was wrongfully discharged. The plaintiff had been granted intermittent leave from her position under the Family Medical Leave Act (FMLA) because of her chronic sinusitis. While the plaintiff was on one of these leaves, her supervisor called her physician to ask about the plaintiff's absences. The plaintiff immediately filed a complaint with the Department of Labor (DOL). A DOL investigator concluded that, with the exception of the plaintiff's supervisor contacting the plaintiff's physician, the defendant appeared to be in full compliance with the FMLA with regard to the plaintiff's employment.

Following her complaint, the plaintiff's attorney sent a letter to the defendant expressing his concern over how the plaintiff was being treated after her FMLA-protected absences and her complaint to the DOL. Soon after this, the defendant found an error that it was able to attribute to the plaintiff and discharged her for it.

At trial, the court granted the defendant's motion for summary judgment and the plaintiff appealed. In her appeal, the plaintiff cited two errors on the part of the trial court:

1. The error in granting summary judgment; the plaintiff showed that there was an issue of material fact as to whether she was discharged based on discriminatory intent or for poor work performance.
2. The trial court's granting of a motion for a protective order filed by the defendant. At a hearing before the Unemployment Compensation Review Commission, the defendants had produced an e-mail from the plaintiff's supervisor to the defendant's attorney. During discovery, the plaintiff asked for production of all documents electronic and otherwise concerning her discharge, her FMLA-protected absences, and her DOL complaint.

After receiving only the e-mail that was produced at the unemployment hearing, the plaintiff made a second request for the production of the documents she had requested. At this point, Time Warner sought a protective order to get the e-mail message back and to stop the plaintiff from using the message or referring to it.

The trial court granted the defendant's motion for a protective order. The appellate court reversed, reasoning that attorney–client communications are privileged, but where any of these communications are voluntarily divulged to a third party, they are no longer privileged, and the plaintiff should have access to all other documentation related to the same subject.

Invision Media Communications, Inc. v. Federal Ins. Co., 2004 WL 396037 (S.D.N.Y. 2004); sanctions imposed against party failing to reasonably produce e-mails upon discovery request.
In an action for breach of an insurance contract, the defendant moved for sanctions against the plaintiff for discovery misconduct. The allegations of misconduct against the plaintiff included making false statements regarding the location and existence of its documents, failing to timely disclose requested documents, and destroying evidence relevant to the pending case.

Among the documents requested by the defendant were "all e-mail communications sent or received by the plaintiffs during August 2001, September 2001, and October 2001." In response to the request for e-mail communications, the plaintiff contended that the e-mails could not be produced because all e-mails were archived on servers for 2 weeks only. The court found this statement to be false, as demonstrated by the plaintiff's eventual disclosure of the e-mail.

The court held that "a reasonable inquiry by the plaintiff's counsel prior to responding to [defendant's] document request... would have alerted counsel that the plaintiff possessed e-mail that fell within the scope of [defendant's] document request." The court imposed sanctions against the plaintiff in the form of costs and attorney's fees incurred by the defendant in pretrial discovery.

In Re: Lernout & Hauspie Sec. Litigation, 222 F.R.D. 29 (Mass. 2004); party who voluntarily discloses e-mail message cannot claim attorney–client privilege when refusing to turn over other e-mails regarding the same subject.

Investors who held equity in the software firm Lernout & Hauspie brought a class action suit for securities fraud against the software firm as well as its accounting firm, KPMG. One of the issues in dispute was whether e-mails sent from an audit partner at KPMG to his legal counsel were protected by attorney–client privilege. The accounting firm had received anonymous calls from a sales rep that worked for Lernout & Hauspie, but the sales rep did not identify the firm he worked for to the audit partner. The sales rep asked a partner in the audit department about certain sales procedures that the software firm had been engaging in and whether they were illegal. The partner at the accounting firm told him that the procedures were indeed illegal. The sales rep gave the partner clues as to who his employer was.

In response to the conversations that the partner had with the client company's sales rep, the partner contacted the accounting firm's legal counsel via e-mail to seek advice. There were 15 e-mails that discussed the situation. In discovery, one of the e-mails was accidentally released by KPMG to the class plaintiffs. The class plaintiffs requested the rest of the e-mails during discovery, but KPMG claimed that they were protected by attorney–client privilege.

The court ruled that the *accidental* disclosure of the first e-mail acted as a waiver of the attorney–client privilege with respect to that e-mail and all others relating to the same subject.

In Re: Lowe's Companies, 134 S.W.3d 876 (Tex. App. 2004); order compelling production of database during deposition overbroad.

In a personal injury case, the defendant appealed a court order compelling the production of a database, which was used to compile information on accidents and injuries that occurred in the defendant's stores. The order instructed that, during an upcoming deposition, the defendant needed to bring either (a) the database and application necessary to search, sort, and print data from it, or (b) computer access to the database that would enable searching, sorting, and printing data as requested by the plaintiff's counsel.

The defendant challenged the order on the ground that it was overbroad and that complete access to the database would provide plaintiff with privileged and irrelevant information. The defendant also alleged that the manner in which it gathered information concerning accidents in its stores was a trade secret.

The appellate court sided with the defendant, stating that discovery should be limited to matters that are relevant to the case and that "requests for information that are not reasonably tailored as to time, place, or subject matter amount to impermissible 'fishing expeditions.'" Ruling that the discovery order was overbroad, the appellate court issued a writ of mandamus vacating the portion of the order that required production of the defendant's database.

Merck Eprova AG v. Gnosis SPA, 2010 U.S. Dist. LEXIS 38867 (S.D.N.Y. April 20, 2010); court grants plaintiff's motion for sanctions due to discovery deficiencies.

On the plaintiff's motion for sanctions due to discovery deficiencies, the Southern District of New York imposed a $25,000 fine on a litigant whose failure to properly install a litigation hold and conduct appropriate searches for relevant e-mail represented a diligence that fell "well below the minimum standard that a reasonably prudent person would use."

What began as a false labeling allegation under the *Lanham Act* became a discovery dispute when defendant Gnosis' initial production amounted to only 107 pages. Believing relevant documents and e-mail had been withheld, the plaintiff identified several deficiencies and requested further discovery from the defendant. After 2 months and several additional requests, the defendant had produced an additional 6200 pages but had not disclosed the allegedly missing documents.

During an evidentiary hearing, the defendant admitted that the defendant had not installed a written litigation hold and had not stopped the automatic deletion of all e-mails that were more than 15 days old. The company had performed only a cursory document search and argued that it had failed to produce the requested documents because of its poor understanding of the search tool provided in its e-mail client.

Relying on the analysis in *Pension Committee of University of Montreal Pension Plan v. Banc of America Securities*, the court found that the defendant's failure to issue a written litigation hold amounted to gross negligence. The court noted that the defendant's first search for relevant e-mail had been insufficient and could have easily been improved to produce the wealth of documents that were later discovered. Additionally, the defendant's decision to withhold documents it believed to be *insufficiently important* displayed *an unacceptable disrespect for the judicial process.*

The court granted the plaintiff's motion for sanctions by awarding costs and imposing a $25,000 fine on the defendant to prevent future discovery misconduct and to install a *modicum of respect for the judicial process.*

In Re: Merrill Lynch & Co., Inc. Research Reports Sec. Litigation, 2004 WL 305601 (S.D.N.Y 2004); party moves to lift discovery stay to protect deleted data.

The plaintiff motioned the court pursuant to the *Securities Exchange Act of 1934* for an order lifting the automatic stay of discovery during the pendency of a motion to dismiss. The plaintiff's essential claim was that discovery was necessary to preserve and restore e-mails that the defendant had deleted. The court said,

> *The Private Securities Litigation Reform Act* mandates that all discovery... shall be stayed during the pendency of a motion to dismiss. This provision is balanced by one imposing a contemporaneous duty on parties to preserve all relevant evidence as if they were the subject of a continuing request for production of documents.

However, the court referred to the fact that the "defendants avow that they are aware of their obligations and have taken and are continuing to take all necessary steps to preserve all potentially relevant electronic evidence." The court concluded that an order lifting the mandatory stay of discovery was not warranted because there was no *imminent risk*, which established that deleted data would be overwritten and thus rendered irretrievable.

Northern Crossarm v. Chemical Specialties, Inc., 2004 WL 635606 (W.D. Wis. 2004); party must specify the format for production of e-documents.

During discovery proceedings, the plaintiff requested copies of the defendant's e-mails. The defendant produced copies of the e-mails that the plaintiff had requested, but did so in hard copy. When the plaintiff received the hard copies of the e-mails, which totaled 65,000 pages, the plaintiff then stated that it wanted the e-mails in electronic format. The defendant claimed that electronic reproduction would be too time consuming and expensive. When the plaintiff originally requested the material under *rule 34(a)* of the F.R.D, it did not specify what format it wanted the documents in.

The court held that the defendant was compelled only to provide the documents in the form that the defendant used them in during the normal course of business. A mimicking of this form, such as paper copies of electronic communications, would also be acceptable. But if the plaintiff had requested the documents in a specific format, then the defendants would have had to either comply with the request, compromise with the plaintiff, or seek shelter from the court.

In this case, since the plaintiff did not initially seek a specific format for the production of the documents, the court did not require the defendants to reproduce the information electronically.

People v. Dominguez, 2004 WL 1068809 (Cal. Ct. App. 2004); no distinction between computer files found on inactive or active memory.

In a criminal case, the defendant appealed his conviction involving the possession of child pornography. Among the defendant's arguments was the contention that the evidence supporting his conviction was insufficient because it was discovered on the inactive memory of his computer and was only retrieved by the use of special programs that the defendant did not possess.

The court found the fact that the files were on the inactive memory of the computer to be of no consequence. During trial, the jury was instructed that there are two types of possession: (1) actual (the person has possession of an object if he knowingly exercised direct physical control over that object) or (2) constructive (a person has possession if he knowingly exercised control over an object or has the right to control that object). The court reasoned that the evidence found on the inactive memory was "the result of searches conducted by appellant that resulted in child pornography being intentionally and knowingly downloaded to the active memory of his computer."

The court held that the defendant "was in actual possession of those images at the time they first appeared on his machine" and that the evidence was sufficient to support his conviction on the child pornography–related charges.

Baptiste v. Cushman & Wakefield, Inc., 2004 WL 330235 (S.D.N.Y. 2004); attorney–client privilege of e-mail containing legal advice.

In an employment discrimination lawsuit, the court addressed the issue of whether the contents of an e-mail were protected by attorney–client privilege. The plaintiff contended (1) that the e-mail was not protected by the attorney–client privilege because it was not labeled as being privileged and (2) that the e-mail was not privileged because it did not refer to legal advice.

The court said, "the attorney–client privilege affords confidentiality to communications among clients and their attorneys, for the purpose of seeking and rendering an opinion on law or legal services, or assistance in some legal proceeding, so long as the communications were intended to be, and were in fact, kept confidential." The court held that the e-mail sent to an employee of the defendant was clearly conveying information and advice. The advice referred to what the defendant's outside counsel anticipated would occur and how the defendant should conduct itself during pending legal matters. The court ordered that the original e-mail be returned to the defendant and that the plaintiff receive a redacted version not containing privileged information.

Comrie v. Ipsco, Inc., 2009 WL 4403364 (N.D. Ill. 2009); defendant's failure to support assertion waives attorney–client privilege.

On the plaintiff's motion to compel production of ESI, the Northern District ruled that the defendant's failure to support its assertion that an e-mail was inadvertently produced waived the attorney–client privilege.

During the discovery phase of a suit under the Employee Retirement Income Security Act (ERISA), the defendant produced more than 5500 documents, including a relevant e-mail sent from its general counsel to its outside counsel. The plaintiff's counsel read the e-mail and questioned the general counsel about its meaning during a deposition. The defense claimed the e-mail was protected by the attorney–client privilege and should be returned pursuant to the parties' protective order. The plaintiff complied but filed a motion to compel, arguing that (1) the e-mail did not fall under the privilege; (2) even if the e-mail were privileged, the privilege had been waived; and (3) the e-mail fell within the fiduciary exception to the privilege.

After finding that the e-mail was protected by the attorney–client privilege, the court applied *FRE 502(b)* on waiver, as interpreted in *Heriot v. Byrne*, 2009 U.S. Dist. LEXIS 22552 (N.D.Ill.2009). Whether a disclosure was inadvertent and whether the holder of the privilege took reasonable steps to prevent disclosure are dependent on a number of considerations, including the number of documents and how they were reviewed prior to production.

Here, the defendant asserted that the e-mail was inadvertently produced but had not presented any evidence informing the court of its efforts to review and control the disclosure of documents. The failure to meet this burden constituted waiver of the attorney–client privilege. The court also held that the e-mail fell within the fiduciary exception and granted the plaintiff's motion to compel production of the e-mail.

Schreiber v. Schreiber, 2010 N.Y. Misc. LEXIS 6058 (N.Y. Sup. Ct. June 25, 2010); NY.

During the discovery phase of a martial dispute, the New York Supreme Court established guidelines for a search protocol to assist the forensic examination of the defendant-husband's work computer. The court denied the plaintiff's motion to compel production of her husband's work computer, reasoning that she was not entitled to unrestricted access. The court emphasized that the plaintiff would be permitted to renew her motion if she provided a search protocol that would adequately protect the defendant's privileged and confidential information.

Spoliation

Allstate Insurance Co. v. St. Anthony's Spine & Joint Institute, 2010 U.S. Dist. LEXIS 11475 (N.D. Ill. 2010); failure to maintain electronic records suggests negligent spoliation.

In a case brought by an insurance company alleging fraud in insurance claims, the defendant's failure to maintain electronic patient records was enough to defeat his motion for summary judgment on a charge of negligent spoliation.

The insurance company alleged that the defendant chiropractor had billed patients for unnecessary testing and for higher levels of service than were rendered. The insurance company suspected that the fraudulent activity began in 2000 when the defendant began use of a special x-ray technique believed to be unnecessary for chiropractic patients.

At issue were electronically stored x-rays and patient studies created in 2000 and 2001, which the defendant claimed he could not produce because the computer hard drives containing the data had crashed. The insurance company's expert testified that the defendant had a professional and ethical responsibility to maintain the patient records.

The court found that the expert's testimony created a disputed material fact sufficient to defeat the defendant's motion for summary judgment on the claim of negligent spoliation. The defendant's inability to produce the records suggested negligent spoliation of evidence that he was under a duty to maintain.

Genworth Fin. Wealth Mgmt., Inc. v. McMullan, **2010 U.S. Dist. LEXIS 53145 (D.Conn. 2010); defendants ordered to pay imaging costs due to willful spoliation.**

The plaintiff, Genworth Financial Wealth Management, filed suit against a group of former employees under the CFAA and the Connecticut Uniform Trade Secrets Act, alleging that the employees stole the company's client information database as part of a plan to set up a competing business. On the plaintiff's motion to compel, the district court ordered the defendant employees to submit their personal computers to a neutral computer expert for mirror imaging and to pay 80% of the cost due to their intentional spoliation.

The plaintiff alleged that the employees had used its customer list to solicit hundreds of its clients and to interfere with other business relationships. The defendants argued that they had collected the client information through permissible means and did not have the client database. One month before filing suit, the plaintiff notified the defendants of their duty to preserve electronic evidence. During discovery, however, the plaintiff determined one of the employees had recently discarded the computer on which he had allegedly downloaded the client database.

On the plaintiff's motion to compel, the court found the defendants' argument of *independent collection* unconvincing, reasoning that the client data were very detailed and unlikely to be created from memory or mere Internet searches. Noting that a mirror image of the relevant computer equipment was the only way for the plaintiff to obtain the electronic evidence to which it was entitled, the court ordered the defendants to submit their computers to a neutral expert and to pay 80% of the associated cost.

The court rejected the defendants' argument that they could not afford to pay a neutral computer expert and agreed with the plaintiff that sanctions may be warranted. The timing of the defendants' disposal of a relevant computer suggested consciousness of wrongdoing and intentional spoliation. The court agreed that the defendants may be subject to discovery sanctions if they did not fully comply with the order. It was unreasonable, the court said, to make the plaintiff seek a court order to obtain the electronic evidence to which it was already entitled.

Grochocinski v. Schlossberg, **402 B.R. 825, 2009 U.S. Dist. LEXIS 19523 (N.D. Ill. 2009); bankruptcy court affirms bad faith spoliation of electronic evidence.**

On an appeal from the bankruptcy court, the district court affirmed an order of sanctions for bad faith spoliation of electronic evidence. During a bankruptcy proceeding, the debtor's trustee filed a complaint to recover two allegedly fraudulent transfers of real estate made to the appellants. The trustee then filed a motion to compel the production of electronic data related to the transfers.

A computer forensics expert was hired to mirror and analyze the appellants' hard drives. The expert discovered that one appellant had installed a disk-cleaning program and had used it to destroy at least 16,000 files. Another program was then installed to verify that the data had been deleted and new operating systems were installed on two of the hard drives.

On the trustee's motion for sanctions, the bankruptcy court found that the deletion amounted to spoliation. The court issued an adverse inference instruction and required the appellant to pay costs for counsel and the computer expert.

On appeal, the appellant argued that the bankruptcy court had failed to make a finding that he acted in bad faith. The district court, reviewing for an abuse of discretion, deferred to the bankruptcy court's finding that the appellant had acted with reckless disregard for his discovery obligations and affirmed the sanctions. Such a disregard was sufficient to establish bad faith and the imposition of sanctions were reasonable under the circumstances.

Grubb v. University of Illinois, 2010 U.S. Dist. LEXIS 78485 (N.D. Ill. August 4, 2010); motion for sanctions for spoliation unsuccessful.

A university's motion for sanctions for spoliation of evidence was unsuccessful when it failed to show the spoliating party's bad faith.

Plaintiff John Grubb, a professor at the UIC (University of Illinois, College of Dentistry), was terminated, but just before he left, the information technology department contacted him to remove UIC software from Grubb's laptop computer. Grubb asked the employee to return in a few days so that he might supervise the work, fearing unauthorized access of unrelated confidential information on the laptop. When Grubb returned from lunch that day, he discovered that the employee had accessed his laptop and removed the UIC software without him being present.

Grubb subsequently contacted the American Board of Orthodontics (ABO), which had issued him the laptop, and informed the board of his concern that confidential patient information had been accessed. Approximately 1 month later, a lawyer for ABO informed Grubb that he should stop using the laptop so that any digital evidence concerning the incident would not be lost. When Grubb discussed the matter with an ABO computer specialist, however, he was told that any data concerning the incident were likely lost due to his consistent use of the laptop in the interim month.

Four months later, ABO issued Grubb a new laptop. Grubb claimed that he received a new laptop because he needed a faster machine with more memory. ABO's computer technician initially made a mirror image of the hard drive from Grubb's old laptop but later wiped both the hard drive and the mirror image.

Grubb eventually filed suit against UIC for unauthorized access of a computer system under the *CFAA*. UIC moved for sanctions due to spoliation of evidence, arguing that the wiping of Grubb's laptop hard drive had made it impossible to determine what actions the UIC employee had performed on Grubb's laptop.

After determining that the appropriate standard of proof for a sanctions motion is *preponderance of the evidence,* the district court held that UIC could not show that Grubb had acted in bad faith, but had merely returned the laptop to its owner and not knowing at that time that ABO would delete all of the evidence contained on its hard drive. Additionally, ABO's computer specialist told Grubb that any digital evidence of the incident that had once existed was likely lost due to Grubb's continued use of the laptop. The court said that this opinion made it unlikely that any useable data were available when Grubb returned the laptop to ABO. The court denied UIC's motion for sanctions, reasoning that the preponderance of the evidence showed that no useable data were lost and that Grubb had not acted in bad faith.

Krumwiede v. Brighton Associates, U.S. District Court for the Northern District of Illinois Case No. 05 C 3003: Charles A. Krumwiede, an individual *v.* Brighton Associates, LLC, and Ismaeil C. Reyes, an individual; willful (deliberate) and bad faith spoliation of evidence.

What began as an employee's claims for breach of an employment agreement and back pay resulted in a counterclaim alleging tortuous interference, breach of noncompete and confidentiality duties, and violation of the Illinois Trade Secrets Act.

Brighton Associates claimed that Krumwiede went to work for a competitor and misappropriated a business opportunity with a potential client. Brighton sought to recover the laptop computer that Krumwiede used when he worked for Brighton in order to determine whether Brighton's data were improperly used. Krumwiede refused to produce the laptop despite Brighton's preservation letter demanding that Krumwiede immediately cease using the laptop and that any changes to the contents of the laptop would be regarded as deliberate spoliation of evidence.

After a motion to compel was filed by Brighton, the court ordered that a neutral third-party computer forensics firm be allowed to inspect the computer. The firm (1) created a forensic copy of the hard drive, (2) issued a report identifying numerous instances of files accessed and deleted, (3) identified connections of external devices suggesting the transfer of files to other computers, (4) discovered instances of defragmentation, and (5) tracked activity of ZIP files with suspicious filenames that were deleted and overwritten.

Krumwiede attempted to suggest that Brighton's counsel compromised the neutrality of the consulting firm by coaching the firm's employees and meddling in the expert's report.

The court held that neither counsel's contact nor prior dealings with the firm compromised the neutrality of the investigation and report, as evidenced by the consistency of the initial and final versions of the expert reports. The court also held that Krumwiede's actions amounted to *willful and bad faith spoliation of evidence* and warranted a default judgment in favor of Brighton.

In deciding between default and lesser sanctions, the court considered prejudice to Brighton, prejudice to the judicial system, deterrence, and punishment. Krumwiede's conduct showed blatant contempt for the court and a fundamental disregard for the judicial process that could only be adequately sanctioned with a default judgment. In addition, Brighton was entitled to an award of costs and fees relating to its motion for sanctions, including fees paid to Brighton's attorneys and the consulting firm.

MasterCard, Inc. v. Moulton, 2004 WL 1393992 (S.D.N.Y. 2004); spoliation sanctions for negligent destruction of e-mail.

In an action to assert a copyright infringement claim, the plaintiff sought spoliation sanctions against the defendant because the defendant had negligently destroyed an e-mail that was pertinent to the litigation. The defendant and an employee of the defendant both testified that the server automatically destroyed the e-mail that was over 21 days old and that neither of them had tried to print out or save the e-mail. The defendant could not comply with the discovery instructions because he could not produce those e-mails that were over 21 days old.

The plaintiff sought a sanction of a conclusive determination on the issues of *confusion by the public* and *dilution and tarnishment of the marks*. In the alternative, the plaintiff requested that the trier of fact be permitted to infer such conclusions from the destruction of the e-mails.

The court granted the sanction in the form of a jury instruction that would allow the jury to infer that the defendant's negligent destruction of the e-mail destroyed evidence of *confusion by the public* and *dilution and tarnishment of the marks*.

Pension Committee v. Banc of America Securities, 2010 WL 184312 (S.D.N.Y. Jan. 15, 2010); negligent conduct.

A party is negligent if it fails to meet its obligation to participate meaningfully and fairly in the discovery process. A party may be negligent even if it acted with good intentions. The following conduct will likely be deemed negligent:

- Failure to obtain records from all employees (presumably relevant)
- Failure to take all appropriate measures to preserve evidence
- Failure to assess the accuracy and validity of selected search terms

When evidence is lost as a result of negligent conduct, the court will issue an adverse inference instruction only if the innocent party can prove that the lost evidence was relevant to its claims or defenses and that the loss prejudiced its case. The innocent party need not provide overwhelming evidence of such relevance or prejudice. The court may also shift the costs of production to or issue monetary fines against the spoliating party.

A party is *grossly negligent* if it fails to exercise even the most basic discovery obligations. The following conduct will likely be deemed grossly negligent:

- Failure to issue a written litigation hold to prevent the destruction of e-mail or backup tapes
- Failure to identify all key players
- Failure to collect records from all key players
- Failure to cease deletion of and/or collect from a former employee (when his or her files remain in the party's possession, custody, or control)
- Failure to preserve backup tapes (when they are the sole source of records or when they relate to the key players) and such records are not available from a readily accessible source

When evidence is lost as a result of *grossly negligent conduct*, the court may issue either a mandatory presumption or a permitted presumption of relevance and prejudice. A *mandatory presumption* instructs the jury to presume that lost evidence would have been relevant to the innocent party's claims or defenses and that the loss was prejudicial to its case. Such a presumption is rebuttable: the spoliating party may submit evidence to show that the lost evidence was not relevant to the innocent party's claims or defenses. A *permitted presumption*, also known as a *spoliation charge*, is an instruction to the jury that it *may*, but need not, presume that the lost evidence was relevant and favorable to the innocent party. The presumption is also subject to the spoliating party's rebuttal.

Most courts group willful, wanton, and reckless conduct into a single category characterized by *intentional conduct*. A willful, wanton, or reckless party acts with either the purpose to destroy evidence or a conscious indifference to a high likelihood that evidence could be destroyed. The following conduct will likely be deemed willful, wanton, or reckless:

- Intentional destruction or deletion of evidence
- Intentional tampering with or falsification of evidence

When evidence is lost as a result of intentional conduct, the harshest sanctions may be applied, up to and including default judgment or dismissal. Courts often, however, impose lesser sanctions, such as fines, adverse instructions, or the preclusion of evidence offered by the spoliating party. An adverse instruction imposed as a sanction for intentional spoliation will likely instruct the jury that certain facts detrimental to the spoliating party are to be accepted as true, and the spoliating party will not be offered an opportunity to rebut the instruction.

Rambus, Inc. v. Infineon Techs. AG, 222 F.R.D. 280 (D. Va., 2004); document retention policy must be suspended when a party reasonably anticipates litigation.

In a patent infringement action, the defendant filed a motion to compel production of various documents including those related to the plaintiff's document retention policy. The defendant alleged that the plaintiff implemented a _document retention policy_, which provided for the destruction of documents that would have been harmful in litigation.

The plaintiff provided evidence of the defendant's _shred day_ where employees shredded about two million documents as part of the defendant's document retention policy. The plaintiff argued that its motive was not to destroy potentially discoverable information and that the plaintiff was legitimately trying to reduce search and review costs.

The court held that when a party is aware of pending litigation or should reasonably anticipate pending litigation, it has a duty to suspend the destruction of documents that may be relevant to anticipated litigation. The firm must also suspend any routine document purging system that might be in effect. Failure to do so constitutes spoliation. The court said that "even if a party's intentional destruction of documents was not in bad faith, it would be guilty of spoliation if it reasonably anticipated litigation when it did so." Here, the court granted the defendant's motion and ordered the plaintiff to produce documents relating to its document retention policy.

University Sports Publications Co. v. Playmakers Media Co., 2010 U.S. Dist. LEXIS 70361 (S.D.N.Y. July 14, 2010); defendant's bad faith spoliation leads to adverse inference jury instruction.

On a claim for unauthorized access of a computer system under the _CFAA_, the district court issued an adverse inference instruction due to the defendant's bad faith spoliation of evidence.

Plaintiff USP filed suit against several of its former employees who had quit to join the codefendant Playmakers Media Company. USP alleged that one of its former employees (Pitta) had obtained unauthorized access to its customer and sales database, which was password protected and maintained by an offsite third-party vendor. Forensic analysis showed that Pitta had obtained an exact copy of a spreadsheet from the database.

At issue in the case was the method by which Pitta obtained the database information. If Pitta had accessed the database sometime after his departure from USP, his copying of the file would constitute an unauthorized access supporting the claim under the CFAA. If, however, Pitta had received the spreadsheet from an employee of the third-party vendor, he would not have committed an unauthorized access and could not be liable under the CFAA.

No direct evidence supported a conclusion on this dispositive issue. USP had requested that Playmakers produce the laptop Pitta used during his time at Playmakers, believing that an examination would provide evidence of Pitta's unauthorized access. Forensic analysis of the laptop Playmakers provided during discovery showed that Pitta had not used that laptop. The relevant laptop remained missing.

On the defendant's motion for summary judgment, the court examined whether the evidence could support USP's claim under the CFAA. The fact that Pitta had obtained a direct copy of the spreadsheet alone could not provide enough evidence to show his unauthorized access of USP's database. Pitta's intentional bad faith spoliation of the laptop evidence, however, justified an adverse inference that the laptop had contained evidence supporting the claim. The jury could reasonably infer that Pitta had destroyed the laptop because it would provide evidence of his unauthorized access. Because the adverse inference provided support for the CFAA claim, the court denied the defendant's motion for summary judgment.

Ethics, Standards of Conduct, and Sanctions

***Attorney Grievance Commission of Maryland v. Potter*, 844 A.2d 367 (Md. 2004); attorney violates rules of professional conduct by deleting files from former employer's computer.**

The court heard a petition for disciplinary action against the defendant, an attorney, alleging violations of the Maryland Rules of Professional Conduct. The defendant worked for a law firm that paid him a base salary plus a percentage of the fees generated by cases he worked on. Before leaving the firm, the defendant took paper files pertaining to two clients believing the clients would have him continue to represent them. The defendant also deleted, without permission, all files relating to matters involving the two clients from the firm's computer.

The court held that this was a crime under Maryland criminal law because the defendant exceeded his authorized access to a computer with the intent to destroy data stored on the computer. The defendant was authorized to use the law firm's computers to generate and store documents relating to client matters, but was not authorized to delete client files without the consent of his employer. The court held that the defendant violated the rules of professional conduct because his actions reflected adversely on his honesty, trustworthiness, and fitness as a lawyer. The defendant received a 90-day suspension from the practice of law.

***United States v. Phillip Morris*, 327 F. Supp 2d 21, (D.D.C 2004); sanctions for violating order preventing destruction of e-mail.**

The court had initially ordered the defendants to retain all relevant documentation to the proceedings, as well as all e-mails. After the order, the defendant continued to destroy all e-mails over 60 days old monthly on a system-wide basis. The defendant became aware that its lack of retention was not in compliance with either the court order or the defendant's own document retention policy. The defendant did not notify the court for 4 months after it initially realized that some of the documents, which were relevant to the proceedings, had been destroyed.

Particularly troubling to the court was the fact that the 11 employees of the defendant, who were identified as not having followed the defendant's documentation retention policy, were employees who held some of the highest positions with the most responsibility in the company.

The court imposed two sanctions upon the defendant: (1) the defendant was precluded from calling as a witness any individual who failed to comply with the defendant's own internal document retention program, and (2) the defendant was required to pay a monetary fine (in the amount of $2,500,000.00) to the court registry. The court also stipulated that the defendant would have to reimburse the United States for the costs associated with depositions on e-mail destruction issues (which totaled $5027.48).

Jones v. Bremen High School District 228, 2010 U.S. Dist. LEXIS 51312 (N.D. Ill. 2010); sanctions for failure to issue litigation hold.

In a race discrimination case, the defendant high school was sanctioned for its failure to issue a litigation hold after receiving notice of the plaintiff's filing with the EEOC. The defendant did not install a litigation hold but instructed several key players to maintain their own e-mail relevant to the dispute. The key players did not have the assistance of counsel and each was able to permanently delete e-mail at his own discretion. A proper litigation hold was not installed for over a year and potentially relevant e-mails were lost during this time.

The court found that the defendant had breached its duty to preserve evidence. The defendant had not shown that installing a litigation hold would have been a burden and the incomplete production had harmed the plaintiff. Because the loss of evidence did not appear to be deliberate, the court found an adverse inference instruction inappropriate. Instead, the defendant was precluded from arguing that the absence of e-mail containing discriminatory statements demonstrated that no such statements were made.

QZO, Inc. v. Moyer, 594 S.E. 2d 541 (S.C. App. 2004); default judgment for destroying computer evidence.

The plaintiff suspected that the defendant, a former officer at the plaintiff's corporation, had plans to compete. The plaintiff was granted a TRO, which required the defendant to turn over his work laptop computer to the plaintiff. The defendant took 7 days to turn over his computer and, when he did so, a computer forensic expert determined that the hard drive had been reformatted the day before. The reformatting destroyed any possible evidence that would have shown the defendant's plan to compete. The court held that the defendant had willfully destroyed evidence related to the case and violated the TRO. Based on this, the court assigned liability to the defendant.

The appellate court affirmed the judgment denying the defendant's argument that there was insufficient evidence to support the sanctions the plaintiff was seeking.

Appendix A: Electronic Surveillance Law*

Wire and Electronic Communications Intercept and Interception of Oral Communications (18 U.S.C. 2510–2521)

The Wiretap Act
(18 U.S.C. 2511) United States Code Annotated
Title 18. Crimes and Criminal Procedure
PART I—Crimes
Chapter 119: Wire and Electronic Communications Interception and
Interception of Oral Communications

§ 2510. Definitions

As used in this chapter—

(1) "wire communication" means any aural transfer made in whole or in part through the use of facilities for the transmission of communications by the aid of wire, cable, or other like connection between the point of origin and the point of reception (including the use of such connection in a switching station) furnished or operated by any person engaged in providing or operating such facilities for the transmission of interstate or foreign communications or communications affecting interstate or foreign commerce;

(2) "oral communication" means any oral communication uttered by a person exhibiting an expectation that such communication is not subject to interception under circumstances justifying such expectation, but such term does not include any electronic communication;

(3) "State" means any State of the United States, the District of Columbia, the Commonwealth of Puerto Rico, and any territory or possession of the United States;

---

* *Note*: Statutes and case laws change constantly. Do not rely upon any source of law as being current without conducting legal research or consulting competent legal counsel. Statutes and case law included here are current at the time of research but should be researched for current and up-to-date law before relying upon them. Always seek competent legal counsel on any legal questions.

(4) "intercept" means the aural or other acquisition of the contents of any wire, electronic, or oral communication through the use of any electronic, mechanical, or other device;

(5) "electronic, mechanical, or other device" means any device or apparatus which can be used to intercept a wire, oral, or electronic communication other than—

    (a)   any telephone or telegraph instrument, equipment or facility, or any component thereof, (i) furnished to the subscriber or user by a provider of wire or electronic communication service in the ordinary course of its business and being used by the subscriber or user in the ordinary course of its business or furnished by such subscriber or user for connection to the facilities of such service and used in the ordinary course of its business; or (ii) being used by a provider of wire or electronic communication service in the ordinary course of its business, or by an investigative or law enforcement officer in the ordinary course of his duties;

    (b)   a hearing aid or similar device being used to correct subnormal hearing to not better than normal;

(6) "person" means any employee, or agent of the United States or any State or political subdivision thereof, and any individual, partnership, association, joint stock company, trust, or corporation;

(7) "investigative or law enforcement officer" means any officer of the United States or of a State or political subdivision thereof, who is empowered by law to conduct investigations of or to make arrests for offenses enumerated in this chapter, and any attorney authorized by law to prosecute or participate in the prosecution of such offenses;

(8) "contents", when used with respect to any wire, oral, or electronic communication, includes any information concerning the substance, purport, or meaning of that communication;

(9) "judge of competent jurisdiction" means—

    (a)   a judge of a United States district court or a United States court of appeals; and

    (b)   a judge of any court of general criminal jurisdiction of a State who is authorized by a statute of that State to enter orders authorizing interceptions of wire, oral, or electronic communications;

(10) "communication common carrier" has the meaning given that term in section 3 of the Communications Act of 1934;

(11) "aggrieved person" means a person who was a party to any intercepted wire, oral, or electronic communication or a person against whom the interception was directed;

(12) "electronic communication" means any transfer of signs, signals, writing, images, sounds, data, or intelligence of any nature transmitted in whole or in part by a wire, radio, electromagnetic, photo electronic or photo optical system that affects interstate or foreign commerce, but does not include—

   (A)   any wire or oral communication;
   (B)   any communication made through a tone-only paging device;
   (C)   any communication from a tracking device (as defined in section 3117 of this title); or
   (D)   electronic funds transfer information stored by a financial institution in a communications system used for the electronic storage and transfer of funds;

(13) "user" means any person or entity who—

   (A)   uses an electronic communication service; and
   (B)   is duly authorized by the provider of such service to engage in such use;

(14) "electronic communications system" means any wire, radio, electromagnetic, photo optical or photo electronic facilities for the transmission of wire or electronic communications, and any computer facilities or related electronic equipment for the electronic storage of such communications;

(15) "electronic communication service" means any service which provides to users thereof the ability to send or receive wire or electronic communications;

(16) "readily accessible to the general public" means, with respect to a radio communication, that such communication is not—

   (A)   scrambled or encrypted;
   (B)   transmitted using modulation techniques whose essential parameters have been withheld from the public with the intention of preserving the privacy of such communication;
   (C)   carried on a subcarrier or other signal subsidiary to a radio transmission;
   (D)   transmitted over a communication system provided by a common carrier, unless the communication is a tone only paging system communication; or
   (E)   transmitted on frequencies allocated under part 25, subpart D, E, or F of part 74, or part 94 of the Rules of the Federal Communications Commission, unless, in the case of a communication transmitted on a frequency allocated under part 74 that is not exclusively allocated to broadcast auxiliary services, the communication is a two-way voice communication by radio;

(17) "electronic storage" means—
- (A) any temporary, intermediate storage of a wire or electronic communication incidental to the electronic transmission thereof; and
- (B) any storage of such communication by an electronic communication service for purposes of backup protection of such communication;

(18) "aural transfer" means a transfer containing the human voice at any point between and including the point of origin and the point of reception;

(19) "foreign intelligence information," for purposes of section 2517 (6) of this title, means—
- (A) information, whether or not concerning a United States person, that relates to the ability of the United States to protect against—
  - (i) actual or potential attack or other grave hostile acts of a foreign power or an agent of a foreign power;
  - (ii) sabotage or international terrorism by a foreign power or an agent of a foreign power; or
  - (iii) clandestine intelligence activities by an intelligence service or network of a foreign power or by an agent of a foreign power; or
- (B) information, whether or not concerning a United States person, with respect to a foreign power or foreign territory that relates to—
  - (i) the national defense or the security of the United States; or
  - (ii) the conduct of the foreign affairs of the United States;

(20) "protected computer" has the meaning set forth in section 1030; and

(21) "computer trespasser"—
- (A) means a person who accesses a protected computer without authorization and thus has no reasonable expectation of privacy in any communication transmitted to, through, or from the protected computer; and
- (B) does not include a person known by the owner or operator of the protected computer to have an existing contractual relationship with the owner or operator of the protected computer for access to all or part of the protected computer.

§ 2511. Interception and Disclosure of Wire, Oral, or Electronic Communications Prohibited

(1) Except as otherwise specifically provided in this chapter any person who—
- (a) intentionally intercepts, endeavors to intercept, or procures any other person to intercept or endeavor to intercept, any wire, oral, or electronic communication;

(b)   intentionally uses, endeavors to use, or procures any other person to use or endeavor to use any electronic, mechanical, or other device to intercept any oral communication when—

   (i)   such device is affixed to, or otherwise transmits a signal through, a wire, cable, or other like connection used in wire communication; or

   (ii)   such device transmits communications by radio, or interferes with the transmission of such communication; or

   (iii) such person knows, or has reason to know, that such device or any component thereof has been sent through the mail or transported in interstate or foreign commerce; or

   (iv)   such use or endeavor to use (A) takes place on the premises of any business or other commercial establishment the operations of which affect interstate or foreign commerce; or (B) obtains or is for the purpose of obtaining information relating to the operations of any business or other commercial establishment the operations of which affect interstate or foreign commerce; or

   (v)   such person acts in the District of Columbia, the Commonwealth of Puerto Rico, or any territory or possession of the United States;

(c)   intentionally discloses, or endeavors to disclose, to any other person the contents of any wire, oral, or electronic communication, knowing or having reason to know that the information was obtained through the interception of a wire, oral, or electronic communication in violation of this subsection;

(d)   intentionally uses, or endeavors to use, the contents of any wire, oral, or electronic communication, knowing or having reason to know that the information was obtained through the interception of a wire, oral, or electronic communication in violation of this subsection; or

(e)   (i) intentionally discloses, or endeavors to disclose, to any other person the contents of any wire, oral, or electronic communication, intercepted by means authorized by sections 2511(2)(a)(ii), 2511(2)(b)-(c), 2511(2)(e), 2516, and 2518 of this chapter, (ii) knowing or having reason to know that the information was obtained through the interception of such a communication in connection with a criminal investigation, (iii) having obtained or received the information in connection with a criminal investigation, and (iv) with intent to improperly obstruct, impede, or interfere with a duly authorized criminal investigation, shall be punished as provided in subsection (4) or shall be subject to suit as provided in subsection (5).

(2)(a)   (i) It shall not be unlawful under this chapter for an operator
               of a switchboard, or an officer, employee, or agent of a pro-
               vider of wire or electronic communication service, whose
               facilities are used in the transmission of a wire or electronic
               communication, to intercept, disclose, or use that commu-
               nication in the normal course of his employment while
               engaged in any activity which is a necessary incident to the
               rendition of his service or to the protection of the rights or
               property of the provider of that service, except that a pro-
               vider of wire communication service to the public shall not
               utilize service observing or random monitoring except for
               mechanical or service quality control checks.

          (ii) Notwithstanding any other law, providers of wire or elec-
               tronic communication service, their officers, employees,
               and agents, landlords, custodians, or other persons, are
               authorized to provide information, facilities, or technical
               assistance to persons authorized by law to intercept wire,
               oral, or electronic communications or to conduct elec-
               tronic surveillance, as defined in section 101 of the Foreign
               Intelligence Surveillance Act of 1978, if such provider, its
               officers, employees, or agents, landlord, custodian, or other
               specified person, has been provided with—

               (A) a court order directing such assistance signed by the
                    authorizing judge, or

               (B) a certification in writing by a person specified in sec-
                    tion 2518 (7) of this title or the Attorney General of
                    the United States that no warrant or court order is
                    required by law, that all statutory requirements have
                    been met, and that the specified assistance is required,
                    setting forth the period of time during which the
                    provision of the information, facilities, or technical
                    assistance is authorized and specifying the informa-
                    tion, facilities, or technical assistance required. No
                    provider of wire or electronic communication ser-
                    vice, officer, employee, or agent thereof, or landlord,
                    custodian, or other specified person shall disclose
                    the existence of any interception or surveillance or
                    the device used to accomplish the interception or
                    surveillance with respect to which the person has
                    been furnished a court order or certification under
                    this chapter, except as may otherwise be required by
                    legal process and then only after prior notification to
                    the Attorney General or to the principal prosecuting

attorney of a State or any political subdivision of a State, as may be appropriate. Any such disclosure, shall render such person liable for the civil damages provided for in section 2520. No cause of action shall lie in any court against any provider of wire or electronic communication service, its officers, employees, or agents, landlord, custodian, or other specified person for providing information, facilities, or assistance in accordance with the terms of a court order, statutory authorization, or certification under this chapter.

(b) It shall not be unlawful under this chapter for an officer, employee, or agent of the Federal Communications Commission, in the normal course of his employment and in discharge of the monitoring responsibilities exercised by the Commission in the enforcement of chapter 5 of title 47 of the United States Code, to intercept a wire or electronic communication, or oral communication transmitted by radio, or to disclose or use the information thereby obtained.

(c) It shall not be unlawful under this chapter for a person acting under color of law to intercept a wire, oral, or electronic communication, where such person is a party to the communication or one of the parties to the communication has given prior consent to such interception.

(d) It shall not be unlawful under this chapter for a person not acting under color of law to intercept a wire, oral, or electronic communication where such person is a party to the communication or where one of the parties to the communication has given prior consent to such interception unless such communication is intercepted for the purpose of committing any criminal or tortious act in violation of the Constitution or laws of the United States or of any State.

(e) Notwithstanding any other provision of this title or section 705 or 706 of the Communications Act of 1934, it shall not be unlawful for an officer, employee, or agent of the United States in the normal course of his official duty to conduct electronic surveillance, as defined in section 101 of the Foreign Intelligence Surveillance Act of 1978, as authorized by that Act.

(f) Nothing contained in this chapter or chapter 121 or 206 of this title, or section 705 of the Communications Act of 1934, shall be deemed to affect the acquisition by the United States Government of foreign intelligence information from international or foreign communications, or foreign intelligence activities conducted in accordance with otherwise applicable federal law involving a foreign electronic communications system, utilizing a means other than electronic surveillance as defined in section 101 of the Foreign Intelligence Surveillance Act of 1978, and procedures in this chapter or chapter 121 and the Foreign Intelligence Surveillance Act of 1978 shall be the exclusive means by which electronic surveillance, as defined in section 101 of such Act, and the interception of domestic wire, oral, and electronic communications may be conducted.

(g)   It shall not be unlawful under this chapter or chapter 121 of this title for any person—

    (i)   to intercept or access an electronic communication made through an electronic communication system that is configured so that such electronic communication is readily accessible to the general public;

    (ii)   to intercept any radio communication which is transmitted—

        (I)   by any station for the use of the general public, or that relates to ships, aircraft, vehicles, or persons in distress;

        (II)   by any governmental, law enforcement, civil defense, private land mobile, or public safety communications system, including police and fire, readily accessible to the general public;

        (III)   by a station operating on an authorized frequency within the bands allocated to the amateur, citizens band, or general mobile radio services; or

        (IV)   by any marine or aeronautical communications system;

    (iii)   to engage in any conduct which—

        (I)   is prohibited by section 633 of the Communications Act of 1934; or

        (II)   is excepted from the application of section 705(a) of the Communications Act of 1934 by section 705(b) of that Act;

    (iv)   to intercept any wire or electronic communication the transmission of which is causing harmful interference to any lawfully operating station or consumer electronic equipment, to the extent necessary to identify the source of such interference; or

    (v)   for other users of the same frequency to intercept any radio communication made through a system that utilizes frequencies monitored by individuals engaged in the provision or the use of such system, if such communication is not scrambled or encrypted.

(h)   It shall not be unlawful under this chapter—

> (i)   to use a pen register or a trap and trace device (as those terms are defined for the purposes of chapter 206 (relating to pen registers and trap and trace devices) of this title); or
>
> (ii)   for a provider of electronic communication service to record the fact that a wire or electronic communication was initiated or completed in order to protect such provider, another provider furnishing service toward the completion of the wire or electronic communication, or a user of that service, from fraudulent, unlawful or abusive use of such service.

(i)   It shall not be unlawful under this chapter for a person acting under color of law to intercept the wire or electronic communications of a computer trespasser transmitted to, through, or from the protected computer, if—

> (I)   the owner or operator of the protected computer authorizes the interception of the computer trespasser's communications on the protected computer;
>
> (II)   the person acting under color of law is lawfully engaged in an investigation;
>
> (III)   the person acting under color of law has reasonable grounds to believe that the contents of the computer trespasser's communications will be relevant to the investigation; and
>
> (IV)   such interception does not acquire communications other than those transmitted to or from the computer trespasser.

(3)(a)   Except as provided in paragraph (b) of this subsection, a person or entity providing an electronic communication service to the public shall not intentionally divulge the contents of any communication (other than one to such person or entity, or an agent thereof) while in transmission on that service to any person or entity other than an addressee or intended recipient of such communication or an agent of such addressee or intended recipient.

(b)   A person or entity providing electronic communication service to the public may divulge the contents of any such communication—

> (i)   as otherwise authorized in section 2511 (2)(a) or 2517 of this title;
>
> (ii)   with the lawful consent of the originator or any addressee or intended recipient of such communication;
>
> (iii)   to a person employed or authorized, or whose facilities are used, to forward such communication to its destination; or
>
> (iv)   which were inadvertently obtained by the service provider and which appear to pertain to the commission of a crime, if such divulgence is made to a law enforcement agency.

(4)(a) Except as provided in paragraph (b) of this subsection or in subsec-
       tion (5), whoever violates subsection (1) of this section shall be fined
       under this title or imprisoned not more than five years, or both.
  (b) Conduct otherwise an offense under this subsection that consists
       of or relates to the interception of a satellite transmission that is
       not encrypted or scrambled and that is transmitted—
    (i) to a broadcasting station for purposes of retransmission to
         the general public; or
   (ii) as an audio subcarrier intended for redistribution to facili-
         ties open to the public, but not including data transmissions
         or telephone calls, is not an offense under this subsection
         unless the conduct is for the purposes of direct or indirect
         commercial advantage or private financial gain.
  [(c) Redesignated (b)]
(5)(a) (i) If the communication is—
   (A) a private satellite video communication that is not scrambled
        or encrypted and the conduct in violation of this chapter is
        the private viewing of that communication and is not for a
        tortious or illegal purpose or for purposes of direct or indi-
        rect commercial advantage or private commercial gain; or
   (B) a radio communication that is transmitted on frequen-
        cies allocated under subpart D of part 74 of the rules of
        the Federal Communications Commission that is not
        scrambled or encrypted and the conduct in violation of
        this chapter is not for a tortious or illegal purpose or for
        purposes of direct or indirect commercial advantage or
        private commercial gain, then the person who engages
        in such conduct shall be subject to suit by the Federal
        Government in a court of competent jurisdiction.
   (ii) In an action under this subsection—
   (A) if the violation of this chapter is a first offense for the
        person under paragraph (a) of subsection (4) and such
        person has not been found liable in a civil action under
        section 2520 of this title, the Federal Government shall
        be entitled to appropriate injunctive relief; and
   (B) if the violation of this chapter is a second or subsequent
        offense under paragraph (a) of subsection (4) or such
        person has been found liable in any prior civil action
        under section 2520, the person shall be subject to a man-
        datory $500 civil fine.
  (b) The court may use any means within its authority to enforce an
       injunction issued under paragraph (ii)(A), and shall impose a civil
       fine of not less than $500 for each violation of such an injunction.

§ 2512. Manufacture, Distribution, Possession, and Advertising of Wire, Oral, or Electronic Communication Intercepting Devices Prohibited

(1) Except as otherwise specifically provided in this chapter, any person who intentionally—

(a) sends through the mail, or sends or carries in interstate or foreign commerce, any electronic, mechanical, or other device, knowing or having reason to know that the design of such device renders it primarily useful for the purpose of the surreptitious interception of wire, oral, or electronic communications;

(b) manufactures, assembles, possesses, or sells any electronic, mechanical, or other device, knowing or having reason to know that the design of such device renders it primarily useful for the purpose of the surreptitious interception of wire, oral, or electronic communications, and that such device or any component thereof has been or will be sent through the mail or transported in interstate or foreign commerce; or

(c) places in any newspaper, magazine, handbill, or other publication or disseminates by electronic means any advertisement of—

(i) any electronic, mechanical, or other device knowing the content of the advertisement and knowing or having reason to know that the design of such device renders it primarily useful for the purpose of the surreptitious interception of wire, oral, or electronic communications; or

(ii) any other electronic, mechanical, or other device, where such advertisement promotes the use of such device for the purpose of the surreptitious interception of wire, oral, or electronic communications, knowing the content of the advertisement and knowing or having reason to know that such advertisement will be sent through the mail or transported in interstate or foreign commerce, shall be fined under this title or imprisoned not more than five years, or both.

(2) It shall not be unlawful under this section for—

(a) a provider of wire or electronic communication service or an officer, agent, or employee of, or a person under contract with, such a provider, in the normal course of the business of providing that wire or electronic communication service, or

(b) an officer, agent, or employee of, or a person under contract with, the United States, a State, or a political subdivision thereof, in the normal course of the activities of the

United States, a State, or a political subdivision thereof, to send through the mail, send or carry in interstate or foreign commerce, or manufacture, assemble, possess, or sell any electronic, mechanical, or other device knowing or having reason to know that the design of such device renders it primarily useful for the purpose of the surreptitious interception of wire, oral, or electronic communications.

(3) It shall not be unlawful under this section to advertise for sale a device described in subsection (1) of this section if the advertisement is mailed, sent, or carried in interstate or foreign commerce solely to a domestic provider of wire or electronic communication service or to an agency of the United States, a State, or a political subdivision thereof which is duly authorized to use such device.

§ 2513. Confiscation of Wire, Oral, or Electronic Communication Intercepting Devices

Any electronic, mechanical, or other device used, sent, carried, manufactured, assembled, possessed, sold, or advertised in violation of section 2511 or section 2512 of this chapter may be seized and forfeited to the United States. All provisions of law relating to

(1) the seizure, summary and judicial forfeiture, and condemnation of vessels, vehicles, merchandise, and baggage for violations of the customs laws contained in title 19 of the United States Code,

(2) the disposition of such vessels, vehicles, merchandise, and baggage or the proceeds from the sale thereof,

(3) the remission or mitigation of such forfeiture,

(4) the compromise of claims, and

(5) the award of compensation to informers in respect of such forfeitures,

shall apply to seizures and forfeitures incurred, or alleged to have been incurred, under the provisions of this section, insofar as applicable and not inconsistent with the provisions of this section; except that such duties as are imposed upon the collector of customs or any other person with respect to the seizure and forfeiture of vessels, vehicles, merchandise, and baggage under the provisions of the customs laws contained in title 19 of the United States Code shall be performed with respect to seizure and forfeiture of electronic, mechanical, or other intercepting devices under this section by such officers, agents, or other persons as may be authorized or designated for that purpose by the Attorney General.

§ 2515. Prohibition of Use as Evidence of Intercepted Wire or Oral Communications

Whenever any wire or oral communication has been intercepted, no part of the contents of such communication and no evidence derived therefrom may be received in evidence in any trial, hearing, or other proceeding in or before any court, grand jury, department, officer, agency, regulatory body, legislative committee, or other authority of the United States, a State, or a political subdivision thereof if the disclosure of that information would be in violation of this chapter.

§ 2516. Authorization for Interception of Wire, Oral, or Electronic Communications

(1) The Attorney General, Deputy Attorney General, Associate Attorney General, or any Assistant Attorney General, any acting Assistant Attorney General, or any Deputy Assistant Attorney General or acting Deputy Assistant Attorney General in the Criminal Division specially designated by the Attorney General, may authorize an application to a Federal judge of competent jurisdiction for, and such judge may grant in conformity with section 2518 of this chapter an order authorizing or approving the interception of wire or oral communications by the Federal Bureau of Investigation, or a Federal agency having responsibility for the investigation of the offense as to which the application is made, when such interception may provide or has provided evidence of—

    (a)   any offense punishable by death or by imprisonment for more than one year under sections 2274 through 2277 of title 42 of the United States Code (relating to the enforcement of the Atomic Energy Act of 1954), section 2284 of title 42 of the United States Code (relating to sabotage of nuclear facilities or fuel), or under the following chapters of this title: chapter 37 (relating to espionage), chapter 55 (relating to kidnapping), chapter 90 (relating to protection of trade secrets), chapter 105 (relating to sabotage), chapter 115 (relating to treason), chapter 102 (relating to riots), chapter 65 (relating to malicious mischief), chapter 111 (relating to destruction of vessels), or chapter 81 (relating to piracy);

    (b)   a violation of section 186 or section 501 (c) of title 29, United States Code (dealing with restrictions on payments and loans to labor organizations), or any offense which involves murder, kidnapping, robbery, or extortion, and which is punishable under this title;

(c)   any offense which is punishable under the following sections of
      this title: section 201 (bribery of public officials and witnesses),
      section 215 (relating to bribery of bank officials), section 224
      (bribery in sporting contests), subsection (d), (e), (f), (g), (h),
      or (i) of section 844 (unlawful use of explosives), section 1032
      (relating to concealment of assets), section 1084 (transmission
      of wagering information), section 751 (relating to escape), sec-
      tion 1014 (relating to loans and credit applications generally;
      renewals and discounts), sections 1503, 1512, and 1513 (influ-
      encing or injuring an officer, juror, or witness generally), sec-
      tion 1510 (obstruction of criminal investigations), section 1511
      (obstruction of State or local law enforcement), section 1591
      (sex trafficking of children by force, fraud, or coercion), section
      1751 (Presidential and Presidential staff assassination, kidnap-
      ping, and assault), section 1951 (interference with commerce by
      threats or violence), section 1952 (interstate and foreign travel
      or transportation in aid of racketeering enterprises), section
      1958 (relating to use of interstate commerce facilities in the
      commission of murder for hire), section 1959 (relating to vio-
      lent crimes in aid of racketeering activity), section 1954 (offer,
      acceptance, or solicitation to influence operations of employee
      benefit plan), section 1955 (prohibition of business enterprises of
      gambling), section 1956 (laundering of monetary instruments),
      section 1957 (relating to engaging in monetary transactions in
      property derived from specified unlawful activity), section 659
      (theft from interstate shipment), section 664 (embezzlement
      from pension and welfare funds), section 1343 (fraud by wire,
      radio, or television), section 1344 (relating to bank fraud), sec-
      tions 2251 and 2252 (sexual exploitation of children), section
      2251A (selling or buying of children), section 2252A (relating
      to material constituting or containing child pornography), sec-
      tion 1466A (relating to child obscenity), section 2260 (produc-
      tion of sexually explicit depictions of a minor for importation
      into the United States), sections 2421, 2422, 2423, and 2425
      (relating to transportation for illegal sexual activity and related
      crimes), sections 2312, 2313, 2314, and 2315 (interstate trans-
      portation of stolen property), section 2321 (relating to traffick-
      ing in certain motor vehicles or motor vehicle parts), section
      1203 (relating to hostage taking), section 1029 (relating to fraud
      and related activity in connection with access devices), section
      3146 (relating to penalty for failure to appear), section 3521(b)(3)
      (relating to witness relocation and assistance), section 32 (relat-
      ing to destruction of aircraft or aircraft facilities), section 38

(relating to aircraft parts fraud), section 1963 (violations with respect to racketeer influenced and corrupt organizations), section 115 (relating to threatening or retaliating against a Federal official), section 1341 (relating to mail fraud), a felony violation of section 1030 (relating to computer fraud and abuse), section 351 (violations with respect to congressional, Cabinet, or Supreme Court assassinations, kidnapping, and assault), section 831 (relating to prohibited transactions involving nuclear materials), section 33 (relating to destruction of motor vehicles or motor vehicle facilities), section 175 (relating to biological weapons), section 1992 (relating to wrecking trains), a felony violation of section 1028 (relating to production of false identification documentation), section 1425 (relating to the procurement of citizenship or nationalization unlawfully), section 1426 (relating to the reproduction of naturalization or citizenship papers), section 1427 (relating to the sale of naturalization or citizenship papers), section 1541 (relating to passport issuance without authority), section 1542 (relating to false statements in passport applications), section 1543 (relating to forgery or false use of passports), section 1544 (relating to misuse of passports), or section 1546 (relating to fraud and misuse of visas, permits, and other documents);

(d) any offense involving counterfeiting punishable under section 471, 472, or 473 of this title;

(e) any offense involving fraud connected with a case under title 11 or the manufacture, importation, receiving, concealment, buying, selling, or otherwise dealing in narcotic drugs, marihuana, or other dangerous drugs, punishable under any law of the United States;

(f) any offense including extortionate credit transactions under sections 892, 893, or 894 of this title;

(g) a violation of section 5322 of title 31, United States Code (dealing with the reporting of currency transactions);

(h) any felony violation of sections 2511 and 2512 (relating to interception and disclosure of certain communications and to certain intercepting devices) of this title;

(i) any felony violation of chapter 71 (relating to obscenity) of this title;

(j) any violation of section 60123(b) (relating to destruction of a natural gas pipeline) or section 46502 (relating to aircraft piracy) of title 49;

(k) any criminal violation of section 2778 of title 22 (relating to the Arms Export Control Act);

(l)   the location of any fugitive from justice from an offense described in this section;

(m) a violation of section 274, 277, or 278 of the Immigration and Nationality Act (8 U.S.C. 1324, 1327, or 1328) (relating to the smuggling of aliens);

(n)   any felony violation of sections 922 and 924 of title 18, United States Code (relating to firearms);

(o)   any violation of section 5861 of the Internal Revenue Code of 1986 (relating to firearms);

(p)   a felony violation of section 1028 (relating to production of false identification documents), section 1542 (relating to false statements in passport applications), section 1546 (relating to fraud and misuse of visas, permits, and other documents) of this title or a violation of section 274, 277, or 278 of the Immigration and Nationality Act (relating to the smuggling of aliens);

(q)   any criminal violation of section 229 (relating to chemical weapons); or sections 2332, 2332a, 2332b, 2332d, 2332f, 2339A, 2339B, or 2339C of this title (relating to terrorism); or

(r)   any conspiracy to commit any offense described in any subparagraph of this paragraph.

(2) The principal prosecuting attorney of any State, or the principal prosecuting attorney of any political subdivision thereof, if such attorney is authorized by a statute of that State to make application to a State court judge of competent jurisdiction for an order authorizing or approving the interception of wire, oral, or electronic communications, may apply to such judge for, and such judge may grant in conformity with section 2518 of this chapter and with the applicable State statute an order authorizing, or approving the interception of wire, oral, or electronic communications by investigative or law enforcement officers having responsibility for the investigation of the offense as to which the application is made, when such interception may provide or has provided evidence of the commission of the offense of murder, kidnapping, gambling, robbery, bribery, extortion, or dealing in narcotic drugs, marihuana or other dangerous drugs, or other crime dangerous to life, limb, or property, and punishable by imprisonment for more than one year, designated in any applicable State statute authorizing such interception, or any conspiracy to commit any of the foregoing offenses.

(3) Any attorney for the Government (as such term is defined for the purposes of the Federal Rules of Criminal Procedure) may authorize an application to a Federal judge of competent jurisdiction for, and such judge may grant, in conformity with section 2518 of this

title, an order authorizing or approving the interception of electronic communications by an investigative or law enforcement officer having responsibility for the investigation of the offense as to which the application is made, when such interception may provide or has provided evidence of any Federal felony.

§ 2517. Authorization for Disclosure and Use of Intercepted Wire, Oral, or Electronic Communications

(1) Any investigative or law enforcement officer who, by any means authorized by this chapter, has obtained knowledge of the contents of any wire, oral, or electronic communication, or evidence derived there from, may disclose such contents to another investigative or law enforcement officer to the extent that such disclosure is appropriate to the proper performance of the official duties of the officer making or receiving the disclosure.

(2) Any investigative or law enforcement officer who, by any means authorized by this chapter, has obtained knowledge of the contents of any wire, oral, or electronic communication or evidence derived there from may use such contents to the extent such use is appropriate to the proper performance of his official duties.

(3) Any person who has received, by any means authorized by this chapter, any information concerning a wire, oral, or electronic communication, or evidence derived there from intercepted in accordance with the provisions of this chapter may disclose the contents of that communication or such derivative evidence while giving testimony under oath or affirmation in any proceeding held under the authority of the United States or of any State or political subdivision thereof.

(4) No otherwise privileged wire, oral, or electronic communication intercepted in accordance with, or in violation of, the provisions of this chapter shall lose its privileged character.

(5) When an investigative or law enforcement officer, while engaged in intercepting wire, oral, or electronic communications in the manner authorized herein, intercepts wire, oral, or electronic communications relating to offenses other than those specified in the order of authorization or approval, the contents thereof, and evidence derived there from, may be disclosed or used as provided in subsections (1) and (2) of this section. Such contents and any evidence derived there from may be used under subsection (3) of this section when authorized or approved by a judge of competent jurisdiction where such judge finds on subsequent application that the contents were otherwise intercepted in accordance with the provisions of this chapter. Such application shall be made as soon as practicable.

(6) Any investigative or law enforcement officer, or attorney for the Government, who by any means authorized by this chapter, has obtained knowledge of the contents of any wire, oral, or electronic communication, or evidence derived there from, may disclose such contents to any other Federal law enforcement, intelligence, protective, immigration, national defense, or national security official to the extent that such contents include foreign intelligence or counterintelligence (as defined in section 3 of the National Security Act of 1947 (50 U.S.C. 401a)), or foreign intelligence information (as defined in subsection (19) of section 2510 of this title), to assist the official who is to receive that information in the performance of his official duties. Any Federal official who receives information pursuant to this provision may use that information only as necessary in the conduct of that person's official duties subject to any limitations on the unauthorized disclosure of such information.

(7) Any investigative or law enforcement officer, or other Federal official in carrying out official duties as such Federal official, who by any means authorized by this chapter, has obtained knowledge of the contents of any wire, oral, or electronic communication, or evidence derived there from, may disclose such contents or derivative evidence to a foreign investigative or law enforcement officer to the extent that such disclosure is appropriate to the proper performance of the official duties of the officer making or receiving the disclosure, and foreign investigative or law enforcement officers may use or disclose such contents or derivative evidence to the extent such use or disclosure is appropriate to the proper performance of their official duties.

(8) Any investigative or law enforcement officer, or other Federal official in carrying out official duties as such Federal official, who by any means authorized by this chapter, has obtained knowledge of the contents of any wire, oral, or electronic communication, or evidence derived there from, may disclose such contents or derivative evidence to any appropriate Federal, State, local, or foreign government official to the extent that such contents or derivative evidence reveals a threat of actual or potential attack or other grave hostile acts of a foreign power or an agent of a foreign power, domestic or international sabotage, domestic or international terrorism, or clandestine intelligence gathering activities by an intelligence service or network of a foreign power or by an agent of a foreign power, within the United States or elsewhere, for the purpose of preventing or responding to such a threat. Any official who receives information pursuant to this provision may use that information only as necessary in the conduct of that person's official duties subject to any limitations on the unauthorized disclosure of such information, and any State, local, or foreign

official who receives information pursuant to this provision may use that information only consistent with such guidelines as the Attorney General and Director of Central Intelligence shall jointly issue.

§ 2518. Procedure for Interception of Wire, Oral, or Electronic Communications

(1) Each application for an order authorizing or approving the interception of a wire, oral, or electronic communication under this chapter shall be made in writing upon oath or affirmation to a judge of competent jurisdiction and shall state the applicant's authority to make such application. Each application shall include the following information:

   (a)   the identity of the investigative or law enforcement officer making the application, and the officer authorizing the application;

   (b)   a full and complete statement of the facts and circumstances relied upon by the applicant, to justify his belief that an order should be issued, including (i) details as to the particular offense that has been, is being, or is about to be committed, (ii) except as provided in subsection (11), a particular description of the nature and location of the facilities from which or the place where the communication is to be intercepted, (iii) a particular description of the type of communications sought to be intercepted, (iv) the identity of the person, if known, committing the offense and whose communications are to be intercepted;

   (c)   a full and complete statement as to whether or not other investigative procedures have been tried and failed or why they reasonably appear to be unlikely to succeed if tried or to be too dangerous;

   (d)   a statement of the period of time for which the interception is required to be maintained. If the nature of the investigation is such that the authorization for interception should not automatically terminate when the described type of communication has been first obtained, a particular description of facts establishing probable cause to believe that additional communications of the same type will occur thereafter;

   (e)   a full and complete statement of the facts concerning all previous applications known to the individual authorizing and making the application, made to any judge for authorization to intercept, or for approval of interceptions of, wire, oral, or electronic communications involving any of the same persons, facilities or places specified in the application, and the action taken by the judge on each such application; and

(f) where the application is for the extension of an order, a statement setting forth the results thus far obtained from the interception, or a reasonable explanation of the failure to obtain such results.

(2) The judge may require the applicant to furnish additional testimony or documentary evidence in support of the application.

(3) Upon such application the judge may enter an ex parte order, as requested or as modified, authorizing or approving interception of wire, oral, or electronic communications within the territorial jurisdiction of the court in which the judge is sitting (and outside that jurisdiction but within the United States in the case of a mobile interception device authorized by a Federal court within such jurisdiction), if the judge determines on the basis of the facts submitted by the applicant that—

(a) there is probable cause for belief that an individual is committing, has committed, or is about to commit a particular offense enumerated in section 2516 of this chapter;

(b) there is probable cause for belief that particular communications concerning that offense will be obtained through such interception;

(c) normal investigative procedures have been tried and have failed or reasonably appear to be unlikely to succeed if tried or to be too dangerous;

(d) except as provided in subsection (11), there is probable cause for belief that the facilities from which, or the place where, the wire, oral, or electronic communications are to be intercepted are being used, or are about to be used, in connection with the commission of such offense, or are leased to, listed in the name of, or commonly used by such person.

(4) Each order authorizing or approving the interception of any wire, oral, or electronic communication under this chapter shall specify—

(a) the identity of the person, if known, whose communications are to be intercepted;

(b) the nature and location of the communications facilities as to which, or the place where, authority to intercept is granted;

(c) a particular description of the type of communication sought to be intercepted, and a statement of the particular offense to which it relates;

(d) the identity of the agency authorized to intercept the communications, and of the person authorizing the application; and

(e) the period of time during which such interception is authorized, including a statement as to whether or not the interception shall automatically terminate when the described communication has been first obtained.

An order authorizing the interception of a wire, oral, or electronic communication under this chapter shall, upon request of the applicant, direct that a provider of wire or electronic communication service, landlord, custodian or other person shall furnish the applicant forthwith all information, facilities, and technical assistance necessary to accomplish the interception unobtrusively and with a minimum of interference with the services that such service provider, landlord, custodian, or person is according the person whose communications are to be intercepted. Any provider of wire or electronic communication service, landlord, custodian or other person furnishing such facilities or technical assistance shall be compensated therefore by the applicant for reasonable expenses incurred in providing such facilities or assistance. Pursuant to section 2522 of this chapter, an order may also be issued to enforce the assistance capability and capacity requirements under the Communications Assistance for Law Enforcement Act.

(5) No order entered under this section may authorize or approve the interception of any wire, oral, or electronic communication for any period longer than is necessary to achieve the objective of the authorization, nor in any event longer than thirty days. Such thirty-day period begins on the earlier of the day on which the investigative or law enforcement officer first begins to conduct an interception under the order or ten days after the order is entered. Extensions of an order may be granted, but only upon application for an extension made in accordance with subsection (1) of this section and the court making the findings required by subsection (3) of this section. The period of extension shall be no longer than the authorizing judge deems necessary to achieve the purposes for which it was granted and in no event for longer than thirty days. Every order and extension thereof shall contain a provision that the authorization to intercept shall be executed as soon as practicable, shall be conducted in such a way as to minimize the interception of communications not otherwise subject to interception under this chapter, and must terminate upon attainment of the authorized objective, or in any event in thirty days. In the event the intercepted communication is in a code or foreign language, and an expert in that foreign language or code is not reasonably available during the interception period, minimization may be accomplished as soon as practicable after such interception. An interception under this chapter may be conducted in whole or in part by Government personnel, or by an individual operating under a contract with the Government, acting under the supervision of an investigative or law enforcement officer authorized to conduct the interception.

(6) Whenever an order authorizing interception is entered pursuant to this chapter, the order may require reports to be made to the judge who issued the order showing what progress has been made toward achievement of the authorized objective and the need for continued interception. Such reports shall be made at such intervals as the judge may require.

(7) Notwithstanding any other provision of this chapter, any investigative or law enforcement officer, specially designated by the Attorney General, the Deputy Attorney General, the Associate Attorney General, or by the principal prosecuting attorney of any State or subdivision thereof acting pursuant to a statute of that State, who reasonably determines that—

    (a) an emergency situation exists that involves—

        (i) immediate danger of death or serious physical injury to any person,

        (ii) conspiratorial activities threatening the national security interest, or

        (iii) conspiratorial activities characteristic of organized crime, that requires a wire, oral, or electronic communication to be intercepted before an order authorizing such interception can, with due diligence, be obtained, and

    (b) there are grounds upon which an order could be entered under this chapter to authorize such interception, may intercept such wire, oral, or electronic communication if an application for an order approving the interception is made in accordance with this section within forty-eight hours after the interception has occurred, or begins to occur. In the absence of an order, such interception shall immediately terminate when the communication sought is obtained or when the application for the order is denied, whichever is earlier. In the event such application for approval is denied, or in any other case where the interception is terminated without an order having been issued, the contents of any wire, oral, or electronic communication intercepted shall be treated as having been obtained in violation of this chapter, and an inventory shall be served as provided for in subsection (d) of this section on the person named in the application.

(8) (a) The contents of any wire, oral, or electronic communication intercepted by any means authorized by this chapter shall, if possible, be recorded on tape or wire or other comparable device. The recording of the contents of any wire, oral, or electronic communication under this subsection shall be done in such a way as will protect the recording from editing or other alterations. Immediately upon the expiration of the period of the order, or extensions thereof, such recordings shall be made available to

the judge issuing such order and sealed under his directions. Custody of the recordings shall be wherever the judge orders. They shall not be destroyed except upon an order of the issuing or denying judge and in any event shall be kept for ten years. Duplicate recordings may be made for use or disclosure pursuant to the provisions of subsections (1) and (2) of section 2517 of this chapter for investigations. The presence of the seal provided for by this subsection, or a satisfactory explanation for the absence thereof, shall be a prerequisite for the use or disclosure of the contents of any wire, oral, or electronic communication or evidence derived there from under subsection (3) of section 2517.

(b) Applications made and orders granted under this chapter shall be sealed by the judge. Custody of the applications and orders shall be wherever the judge directs. Such applications and orders shall be disclosed only upon a showing of good cause before a judge of competent jurisdiction and shall not be destroyed except on order of the issuing or denying judge, and in any event shall be kept for ten years.

(c) Any violation of the provisions of this subsection may be punished as contempt of the issuing or denying judge.

(d) Within a reasonable time but not later than ninety days after the filing of an application for an order of approval under section 2518(7)(b) which is denied or the termination of the period of an order or extensions thereof, the issuing or denying judge shall cause to be served, on the persons named in the order or the application, and such other parties to intercepted communications as the judge may determine in his discretion that is in the interest of justice, an inventory which shall include notice of—

(1) the fact of the entry of the order or the application;

(2) the date of the entry and the period of authorized, approved or disapproved interception, or the denial of the application; and

(3) the fact that during the period wire, oral, or electronic communications were or were not intercepted.

The judge, upon the filing of a motion, may in his discretion make available to such person or his counsel for inspection such portions of the intercepted communications, applications and orders as the judge determines to be in the interest of justice. On an ex parte showing of good cause to a judge of competent jurisdiction the serving of the inventory required by this subsection may be postponed.

(9) The contents of any wire, oral, or electronic communication intercepted pursuant to this chapter or evidence derived there from shall not be received in evidence or otherwise disclosed

in any trial, hearing, or other proceeding in a Federal or State court unless each party, not less than ten days before the trial, hearing, or proceeding, has been furnished with a copy of the court order, and accompanying application, under which the interception was authorized or approved. This ten-day period may be waived by the judge if he finds that it was not possible to furnish the party with the above information ten days before the trial, hearing, or proceeding and that the party will not be prejudiced by the delay in receiving such information.

(10)(a) Any aggrieved person in any trial, hearing, or proceeding in or before any court, department, officer, agency, regulatory body, or other authority of the United States, a State, or a political subdivision thereof, may move to suppress the contents of any wire or oral communication intercepted pursuant to this chapter, or evidence derived there from, on the grounds that—

(i) the communication was unlawfully intercepted;

(ii) the order of authorization or approval under which it was intercepted is insufficient on its face; or

(iii) the interception was not made in conformity with the order of authorization or approval.

Such motion shall be made before the trial, hearing, or proceeding unless there was no opportunity to make such motion or the person was not aware of the grounds of the motion. If the motion is granted, the contents of the intercepted wire or oral communication, or evidence derived there from, shall be treated as having been obtained in violation of this chapter. The judge, upon the filing of such motion by the aggrieved person, may in his discretion make available to the aggrieved person or his counsel for inspection such portions of the intercepted communication or evidence derived there from as the judge determines to be in the interests of justice.

(b) In addition to any other right to appeal, the United States shall have the right to appeal from an order granting a motion to suppress made under paragraph (a) of this subsection, or the denial of an application for order of approval, if the United States attorney shall certify to the judge or other official granting such motion or denying such application that the appeal is not taken for purposes of delay. Such appeal shall be taken within thirty days after the date the order was entered and shall be diligently prosecuted.

(c) The remedies and sanctions described in this chapter with respect to the interception of electronic communications are the only judicial remedies and sanctions for nonconstitutional violations of this chapter involving such communications.

(11) The requirements of subsections (1)(b)(ii) and (3)(d) of this section relating to the specification of the facilities from which, or the place where, the communication is to be intercepted do not apply if—

    (a)   in the case of an application with respect to the interception of an oral communication—

        (i)   the application is by a Federal investigative or law enforcement officer and is approved by the Attorney General, the Deputy Attorney General, the Associate Attorney General, an Assistant Attorney General, or an acting Assistant Attorney General;

        (ii)   the application contains a full and complete statement as to why such specification is not practical and identifies the person committing the offense and whose communications are to be intercepted; and

        (iii)   the judge finds that such specification is not practical; and

    (b)   in the case of an application with respect to a wire or electronic communication—

        (i)   the application is by a Federal investigative or law enforcement officer and is approved by the Attorney General, the Deputy Attorney General, the Associate Attorney General, an Assistant Attorney General, or an acting Assistant Attorney General;

        (ii)   the application identifies the person believed to be committing the offense and whose communications are to be intercepted and the applicant makes a showing that there is probable cause to believe that the person's actions could have the effect of thwarting interception from a specified facility;

        (iii)   the judge finds that such showing has been adequately made; and

        (iv)   the order authorizing or approving the interception is limited to interception only for such time as it is reasonable to presume that the person identified in the application is or was reasonably proximate to the instrument through which such communication will be or was transmitted.

(12) An interception of a communication under an order with respect to which the requirements of subsections (1)(b)(ii) and (3)(d) of this section do not apply by reason of subsection (11)(a) shall not begin until the place where the communication is to be intercepted is ascertained by the person implementing the interception order. A provider of wire or electronic communications service that has received an order as provided for in subsection (11)(b) may move the court to modify or quash the

order on the ground that its assistance with respect to the interception cannot be performed in a timely or reasonable fashion. The court, upon notice to the government, shall decide such a motion expeditiously.

§ 2519. Reports Concerning Intercepted Wire, Oral, or Electronic Communications

(1) Within thirty days after the expiration of an order (or each extension thereof) entered under section 2518, or the denial of an order approving an interception, the issuing or denying judge shall report to the Administrative Office of the U.S. Courts—

   (a)   the fact that an order or extension was applied for;

   (b)   the kind of order or extension applied for (including whether or not the order was an order with respect to which the requirements of sections 2518(1)(b)(ii) and 2518(3)(d) of this title did not apply by reason of section 2518(11) of this title);

   (c)   the fact that the order or extension was granted as applied for, was modified, or was denied;

   (d)   the period of interceptions authorized by the order, and the number and duration of any extensions of the order;

   (e)   the offense specified in the order or application, or extension of an order;

   (f)   the identity of the applying investigative or law enforcement officer and agency making the application and the person authorizing the application; and

   (g)   the nature of the facilities from which or the place where communications were to be intercepted.

(2) In January of each year, the Attorney General, an Assistant Attorney General specially designated by the Attorney General, or the principal prosecuting attorney of a State, or the principal prosecuting attorney for any political subdivision of a State, shall report to the Administrative Office of the U.S. Courts—

   (a)   the information required by paragraphs (a) through (g) of subsection (1) of this section with respect to each application for an order or extension made during the preceding calendar year;

   (b)   a general description of the interceptions made under such order or extension, including (i) the approximate nature and frequency of incriminating communications intercepted, (ii) the approximate nature and frequency of other communications intercepted, (iii) the approximate number of persons whose communications were intercepted, (iv) the number of orders in which encryption was encountered and whether such encryption prevented law enforcement from obtaining the plain text of communications intercepted pursuant to such order, and (v) the approximate nature, amount, and cost of the manpower and other resources used in the interceptions;

(c)   the number of arrests resulting from interceptions made under such order or extension, and the offenses for which arrests were made;

(d)   the number of trials resulting from such interceptions;

(e)   the number of motions to suppress made with respect to such interceptions, and the number granted or denied;

(f)   the number of convictions resulting from such interceptions and the offenses for which the convictions were obtained and a general assessment of the importance of the interceptions; and

(g)   the information required by paragraphs (b) through (f) of this subsection with respect to orders or extensions obtained in a preceding calendar year.

(3) In April of each year the Director of the Administrative Office of the United States Courts shall transmit to the Congress a full and complete report concerning the number of applications for orders authorizing or approving the interception of wire, oral, or electronic communications pursuant to this chapter and the number of orders and extensions granted or denied pursuant to this chapter during the preceding calendar year. Such report shall include a summary and analysis of the data required to be filed with the Administrative Office by subsections (1) and (2) of this section. The Director of the Administrative Office of the United States Courts is authorized to issue binding regulations dealing with the content and form of the reports required to be filed by subsections (1) and (2) of this section.

§ 2520. Recovery of Civil Damages Authorized

(a) *In general*—Except as provided in section 2511(2)(a)(ii), any person whose wire, oral, or electronic communication is intercepted, disclosed, or intentionally used in violation of this chapter may in a civil action recover from the person or entity, other than the United States, which engaged in that violation such relief as may be appropriate.

(b) *Relief*—In an action under this section, appropriate relief includes—

(1)   such preliminary and other equitable or declaratory relief as may be appropriate;

(2)   damages under subsection (c) and punitive damages in appropriate cases; and

(3)   a reasonable attorney's fee and other litigation costs reasonably incurred.

(c) *Computation of damages—*
  (1) In an action under this section, if the conduct in violation of this chapter is the private viewing of a private satellite video communication that is not scrambled or encrypted or if the communication is a radio communication that is transmitted on frequencies allocated under subpart D of part 74 of the rules of the Federal Communications Commission that is not scrambled or encrypted and the conduct is not for a tortious or illegal purpose or for purposes of direct or indirect commercial advantage or private commercial gain, then the court shall assess damages as follows:
    (A) If the person who engaged in that conduct has not previously been enjoined under section 2511(5) and has not been found liable in a prior civil action under this section, the court shall assess the greater of the sum of actual damages suffered by the plaintiff, or statutory damages of not less than $50 and not more than $500.
    (B) If, on one prior occasion, the person who engaged in that conduct has been enjoined under section 2511(5) or has been found liable in a civil action under this section, the court shall assess the greater of the sum of actual damages suffered by the plaintiff, or statutory damages of not less than $100 and not more than $1000.
  (2) In any other action under this section, the court may assess as damages whichever is the greater of—
    (A) the sum of the actual damages suffered by the plaintiff and any profits made by the violator as a result of the violation; or
    (B) statutory damages of whichever is the greater of $100 a day for each day of violation or $10,000.
(d) *Defense—*A good faith reliance on—
  (1) a court warrant or order, a grand jury subpoena, a legislative authorization, or a statutory authorization;
  (2) a request of an investigative or law enforcement officer under section 2518(7) of this title; or
  (3) a good faith determination that section 2511(3) or 2511(2)(i) of this title permitted the conduct complained of; is a complete defense against any civil or criminal action brought under this chapter or any other law.
(e) *Limitation—*A civil action under this section may not be commenced later than two years after the date upon which the claimant first has a reasonable opportunity to discover the violation.
(f) *Administrative discipline—*If a court or appropriate department or agency determines that the United States or any of its departments or

agencies has violated any provision of this chapter, and the court or appropriate department or agency finds that the circumstances surrounding the violation raise serious questions about whether or not an officer or employee of the United States acted willfully or intentionally with respect to the violation, the department or agency shall, upon receipt of a true and correct copy of the decision and findings of the court or appropriate department or agency promptly initiate a proceeding to determine whether disciplinary action against the officer or employee is warranted. If the head of the department or agency involved determines that disciplinary action is not warranted, he or she shall notify the Inspector General with jurisdiction over the department or agency concerned and shall provide the Inspector General with the reasons for such determination.

(g) *Improper disclosure is violation*—Any willful disclosure or use by an investigative or law enforcement officer or governmental entity of information beyond the extent permitted by section 2517 is a violation of this chapter for purposes of section 2520(a).

§ 2521. Injunction against Illegal Interception

Whenever it shall appear that any person is engaged or is about to engage in any act which constitutes or will constitute a felony violation of this chapter, the Attorney General may initiate a civil action in a district court of the United States to enjoin such violation. The court shall proceed as soon as practicable to the hearing and determination of such an action, and may, at any time before final determination, enter such a restraining order or prohibition, or take such other action, as is warranted to prevent a continuing and substantial injury to the United States or to any person or class of persons for whose protection the action is brought. A proceeding under this section is governed by the Federal Rules of Civil Procedure, except that, if an indictment has been returned against the respondent, discovery is governed by the Federal Rules of Criminal Procedure.

§ 2522. Enforcement of the Communications Assistance for Law Enforcement Act

(a) *Enforcement by court issuing surveillance order*—If a court authorizing an interception under this chapter, a State statute, or the Foreign Intelligence Surveillance Act of 1978 (50 U.S.C. 1801 et seq.) or authorizing use of a pen register or a trap and trace device under chapter 206 or a State statute finds that a telecommunications carrier has failed to comply with the requirements of the Communications Assistance for Law Enforcement Act, the court may, in accordance with section 108 of such Act, direct that the carrier comply forthwith and may direct that a provider of support services to the carrier or the manufacturer of the carrier's transmission or switching equipment furnish forthwith modifications necessary for the carrier to comply.

(b) *Enforcement upon application by Attorney General*—The Attorney General may, in a civil action in the appropriate United States district court, obtain an order, in accordance with section 108 of the Communications Assistance for Law Enforcement Act, directing that a telecommunications carrier, a manufacturer of telecommunications transmission or switching equipment, or a provider of telecommunications support services comply with such Act.

(c) *Civil penalty*—

(1) *In general*—A court issuing an order under this section against a telecommunications carrier, a manufacturer of telecommunications transmission or switching equipment, or a provider of telecommunications support services may impose a civil penalty of up to $10,000 per day for each day in violation after the issuance of the order or after such future date as the court may specify.

(2) *Considerations*—In determining whether to impose a civil penalty and in determining its amount, the court shall take into account—

(A) the nature, circumstances, and extent of the violation;

(B) the violator's ability to pay, the violator's good faith efforts to comply in a timely manner, any effect on the violator's ability to continue to do business, the degree of culpability, and the length of any delay in undertaking efforts to comply; and

(C) such other matters as justice may require.

(d) *Definitions*—As used in this section, the terms defined in section 102 of the Communications Assistance for Law Enforcement Act have the meanings provided, respectively, in such section.

Stored Wire and Electronic Communications and Transactional Records Access (18 U.S.C. §§ 2701–2712)

Stored Wire and Electronic Communications
and
Transactional Records Access
(18 U.S.C. 2702, 2707, and 2708)
18 U.S.C. 2702
Disclosure of Contents

§ 2702. Disclosure of Contents

(a) Prohibitions—Except as provided in subsection (b)—

    (1) a person or entity providing an electronic communication service to the public shall not knowingly divulge to any person or entity the contents of a communication while in electronic storage by that service; and

    (2) a person or entity providing remote computing service to the public shall not knowingly divulge to any person or entity the contents of any communication which is carried or maintained on that service—

        (A) on behalf of, and received by means of electronic transmission from (or created by means of computer processing of communications received by means of electronic transmission from), a subscriber or customer of such service; and

        (B) solely for the purpose of providing storage or computer processing services to such subscriber or customer, if the provider is not authorized to access the contents of any such communications for purposes of providing any services other than storage or computer processing; and

    (3) a provider of remote computing service or electronic communication service to the public shall not knowingly divulge a record or other information pertaining to a subscriber to or customer of such service (not including the contents of communications covered by paragraph (1) or (2)) to any governmental entity.

(b) Exceptions—A person or entity may divulge the contents of a communication—

    (1) to an addressee or intended recipient of such communication or an agent of such addressee or intended recipient;

    (2) as otherwise authorized in section 2517, 2511(2)(a), or 2703 of this title;

    (3) with the lawful consent of the originator or an addressee or intended recipient of such communication, or the subscriber in the case of remote computing service;

    (4) to a person employed or authorized or whose facilities are used to forward such communication to its destination;

    (5) as may be necessarily incident to the rendition of the service or to the protection of the rights or property of the provider of that service; or

    (6) to a law enforcement agency—

        (A) if the contents—

            (i) were inadvertently obtained by the service provider; and

            (ii) appear to pertain to the commission of a crime; or

(B) if required by section 227 of the Crime Control Act of 1990
       [42 U.S.C.A S 13032].

(C) if the provider reasonably believes that an emergency involving
       immediate danger of death or serious physical injury to any per-
       son requires disclosure of the information without delay.

(c) Exceptions for disclosure of customer records. A provider described
     in subsection (a) may divulge a record or other information pertaining
     to a subscriber to or customer of such service (not including the con-
     tents of communications covered by subsection (a)(1) or (a)(2))—

   (1) as otherwise authorized in section 2703;

   (2) with the lawful consent of the customer or subscriber;

   (3) as may be necessarily incident to the rendition of the service or to the
        protection of the rights or property of the provider of that service;

   (4) to a governmental entity, if the provider reasonably believes that an
        emergency involving immediate danger of death or serious physi-
        cal injury to any person justifies disclosure of the information; or

   (5) to any person other than a governmental entity.

§ 2703 (c) Authorization to Release (AT&T)
18 U.S.C. 2707

§ 2707. Civil Action

(a) *Cause of Action*—Except as provided in section 2703 (e), any provider of
     electronic communication service, subscriber, or other person aggrieved
     by any violation of this chapter in which the conduct constituting the
     violation is engaged in with a knowing or intentional state of mind may,
     in a civil action, recover from the person or entity, other than the United
     States, which engaged in that violation such relief as may be appropriate.

(b) *Relief*—In a civil action under this section, appropriate relief includes—

   (1) such preliminary and other equitable or declaratory relief as may
        be appropriate;

   (2) damages under subsection (c); and

   (3) a reasonable attorney's fee and other litigation costs reasonably
        incurred.

(c) *Damages*—The court may assess as damages in a civil action under
     this section the sum of the actual damages suffered by the plaintiff
     and any profits made by the violator as a result of the violation, but in
     no case shall a person entitled to recover receive less than the sum of
     $1,000. If the violation is willful or intentional, the court may assess
     punitive damages. In the case of a successful action to enforce liabil-
     ity under this section, the court may assess the costs of the action,
     together with reasonable attorney fees determined by the court.

(d) *Administrative Discipline*—If a court or appropriate department or agency determines that the United States or any of its departments or agencies has violated any provision of this chapter, and the court or appropriate department or agency finds that the circumstances surrounding the violation raise serious questions about whether or not an officer or employee of the United States acted willfully or intentionally with respect to the violation, the department or agency shall, upon receipt of a true and correct copy of the decision and findings of the court or appropriate department or agency promptly initiate a proceeding to determine whether disciplinary action against the officer or employee is warranted. If the head of the department or agency involved determines that disciplinary action is not warranted, he or she shall notify the Inspector General with jurisdiction over the department or agency concerned and shall provide the Inspector General with the reasons for such determination.

(e) *Defense*—A good faith reliance on—

   (1) a court warrant or order, a grand jury subpoena, a legislative authorization, or a statutory authorization (including a request of a governmental entity under section 2703 (f) of this title);

   (2) a request of an investigative or law enforcement officer under section 2518 (7) of this title; or

   (3) a good faith determination that section 2511 (3) of this title permitted the conduct complained of; is a complete defense to any civil or criminal action brought under this chapter or any other law.

(f) *Limitation*—A civil action under this section may not be commenced later than two years after the date upon which the claimant first discovered or had a reasonable opportunity to discover the violation.

(g) *Improper Disclosure*—Any willful disclosure of a "record", as that term is defined in section 552a (a) of title 5, United States Code, obtained by an investigative or law enforcement officer, or a governmental entity, pursuant to section 2703 of this title, or from a device installed pursuant to section 3123 or 3125 of this title, that is not a disclosure made in the proper performance of the official functions of the officer or governmental entity making the disclosure, is a violation of this chapter. This provision shall not apply to information previously lawfully disclosed (prior to the commencement of any civil or administrative proceeding under this chapter) to the public by a Federal, State, or local governmental entity or by the plaintiff in a civil action under this chapter.

§ 2708. Exclusivity of Remedies

The remedies and sanctions described in this chapter are the only judicial remedies and sanctions for nonconstitutional violations of this chapter.

Last modified: April 13, 2006

The Pen Register and Trap and Trace Act (18 U.S.C. §§ 3121–3127)

18 U.S.C. § 3121. General Prohibition on Pen Register and Trap and Trace Device Use; Exception

(a) *In General.* Except as provided in this section, no person may install or use a pen register or a trap and trace device without first obtaining a court order under *section* 3123 of this title or under the *Foreign Intelligence Surveillance Act of 1978* (50 U.S.C. 1801 et seq.).

(b) *Exception.* The prohibition of subsection (a) does not apply with respect to the use of a pen register or a trap and trace device by a provider of electronic or wire communication service

   (1) relating to the operation, maintenance, and testing of a wire or electronic communication service or to the protection of the rights or property of such provider, or to the protection of users of that service from abuse of service or unlawful use of service; or

   (2) to record the fact that a wire or electronic communication was initiated or completed in order to protect such provider, another provider furnishing service toward the completion of the wire communication, or a user of that service, from fraudulent, unlawful or abusive use of service; or

   (3) where the consent of the user of that service has been obtained.

(c) *Limitation.* A government agency authorized to install and use a pen register or trap and trace device under this chapter or under State law shall use technology reasonably available to it that restricts the recording or decoding of electronic or other impulses to the dialing, routing, addressing, and signaling information utilized in the processing and transmitting of wire or electronic communications so as not to include the contents of any wire or electronic communications.

(d) *Penalty.* Whoever knowingly violates subsection (a) shall be fined under this title or imprisoned not more than 1 year, or both.

18 U.S.C. § 3122. Application for an Order for a Pen Register or a Trap and Trace Device

(a) *Application.*

    (1) An attorney for the Government may make application for an order or an extension of an order under section 3123 of this title authorizing or approving the installation and use of a pen register or a trap and trace device under this chapter, in writing under oath or equivalent affirmation, to a court of competent jurisdiction.

    (2) Unless prohibited by State law, a State investigative or law enforcement officer may make application for an order or an extension of an order under section 3123 of this title authorizing or approving the installation and use of a pen register or a trap and trace device under this chapter, in writing under oath or equivalent affirmation, to a court of competent jurisdiction of such State.

(b) *Contents of Application.* An application under subsection (a) of this section shall include—

    (1) the identity of the attorney for the Government or the State law enforcement or investigative officer making the application and the identity of the law enforcement agency conducting the investigation; and

    (2) a certification by the applicant that the information likely to be obtained is relevant to an ongoing criminal investigation being conducted by that agency.

§ 3123. Issuance of an Order for a Pen Register or a Trap and Trace Device

(a) *In General.*

    (1) *Attorney for the Government*—Upon an application made under section 3122 (a)(1), the court shall enter an *ex parte* order authorizing the installation and use of a pen register or trap and trace device anywhere within the United States, if the court finds that the attorney for the Government has certified to the court that the information likely to be obtained by such installation and use is relevant to an ongoing criminal investigation. The order, upon service of that order, shall apply to any person or entity providing wire or electronic communication service in the United States whose assistance may facilitate the execution of the order. Whenever such an order is served on any person or entity not specifically named in the order, upon request of such person or entity, the attorney for the Government or law enforcement

or investigative officer that is serving the order shall provide written or electronic certification that the order applies to the person or entity being served.

(2) *State Investigative or Law Enforcement Officer*—Upon an application made under section 3122 (a)(2), the court shall enter an *ex parte* order authorizing the installation and use of a pen register or trap and trace device within the jurisdiction of the court, if the court finds that the State law enforcement or investigative officer has certified to the court that the information likely to be obtained by such installation and use is relevant to an ongoing criminal investigation.

(3) (A) Where the law enforcement agency implementing an *ex parte* order under this subsection seeks to do so by installing and using its own pen register or trap and trace device on a packet-switched data network of a provider of electronic communication service to the public, the agency shall ensure that a record will be maintained which will identify—

  (i) any officer or officers who installed the device and any officer or officers who accessed the device to obtain information from the network;

  (ii) the date and time the device was installed, the date and time the device was uninstalled, and the date, time, and duration of each time the device is accessed to obtain information;

  (iii) the configuration of the device at the time of its installation and any subsequent modification thereof; and

  (iv) any information which has been collected by the device. To the extent that the pen register or trap and trace device can be set automatically to record this information electronically, the record shall be maintained electronically throughout the installation and use of such device.

 (B) The record maintained under subparagraph (A) shall be provided *ex parte* and under seal to the court which entered the *ex parte* order authorizing the installation and use of the device within 30 days after termination of the order (including any extensions thereof).

(b) *Contents of Order.* An order issued under this section—

 (1) shall specify—

  (A) the identity, if known, of the person to whom is leased or in whose name is listed the telephone line or other facility to which the pen register or trap and trace device is to be attached or applied;

  (B) the identity, if known, of the person who is the subject of the criminal investigation;

(C) the attributes of the communications to which the order applies, including the number or other identifier and, if known, the location of the telephone line or other facility to which the pen register or trap and trace device is to be attached or applied, and, in the case of an order authorizing installation and use of a trap and trace device under subsection (a)(2), the geographic limits of the order; and

(D) a statement of the offense to which the information likely to be obtained by the pen register or trap and trace device relates; and

(2) shall direct, upon the request of the applicant, the furnishing of information, facilities, and technical assistance necessary to accomplish the installation of the pen register or trap and trace device under section 3124 of this title.

(c) *Time Period and Extensions—*

(1) An order issued under this section shall authorize the installation and use of a pen register or a trap and trace device for a period not to exceed 60 days.

(2) Extensions of such an order may be granted, but only upon an application for an order under section 3122 of this title and upon the judicial finding required by subsection (a) of this section. The period of extension shall be for a period not to exceed 60 days.

(d) *Nondisclosure of Existence of Pen Register or a Trap and Trace Device.* An order authorizing or approving the installation and use of a pen register or a trap and trace device shall direct that—

(1) the order be sealed until otherwise ordered by the court; and

(2) the person owning or leasing the line or other facility to which the pen register or a trap and trace device is attached or applied, or who is obligated by the order to provide assistance to the applicant, not disclose the existence of the pen register or trap and trace device or the existence of the investigation to the listed subscriber, or to any other person, unless or until otherwise ordered by the court.

§ 3124. Assistance in Installation and Use of a Pen Register or a Trap and Trace Device

(a) *Pen Registers.* Upon the request of an attorney for the Government or an officer of a law enforcement agency authorized to install and use a pen register under this chapter, a provider of wire or electronic communication service, landlord, custodian, or other person shall furnish such investigative or law enforcement officer forthwith all information, facilities, and technical assistance necessary to accomplish the installation of the pen register unobtrusively and with a minimum of interference with the services that the person so ordered by the court accords the party with respect to whom the installation and use is to take place, if such assistance is directed by a court order as provided in section 3123 (b)(2) of this title.

(b) *Trap and Trace Device.* Upon the request of an attorney for the Government or an officer of a law enforcement agency authorized to receive the results of a trap and trace device under this chapter, a provider of a wire or electronic communication service, landlord, custodian, or other person shall install such device forthwith on the appropriate line or other facility and shall furnish such investigative or law enforcement officer all additional information, facilities and technical assistance including installation and operation of the device unobtrusively and with a minimum of interference with the services that the person so ordered by the court accords the party with respect to whom the installation and use is to take place, if such installation and assistance is directed by a court order as provided in section 3123 (b)(2) of this title. Unless otherwise ordered by the court, the results of the trap and trace device shall be furnished, pursuant to section 3123 (b) or section 3125 of this title, to the officer of a law enforcement agency, designated in the court order, at reasonable intervals during regular business hours for the duration of the order.

(c) *Compensation.* A provider of a wire or electronic communication service, landlord, custodian, or other person who furnishes facilities or technical assistance pursuant to this section shall be reasonably compensated for such reasonable expenses incurred in providing such facilities and assistance.

(d) *No Cause of Action against a Provider Disclosing Information Under This Chapter.* No cause of action shall lie in any court against any provider of a wire or electronic communication service, its officers, employees, agents, or other specified persons for providing information, facilities, or assistance in accordance with a court order under this chapter or request pursuant to section 3125 of this title.

(e) *Defense.* A good faith reliance on a court order under this chapter, a request pursuant to section 3125 of this title, a legislative authorization, or a statutory authorization is a complete defense against any civil or criminal action brought under this chapter or any other law.

(f) *Communications Assistance Enforcement Orders.* Pursuant to section 2522, an order may be issued to enforce the assistance capability and capacity requirements under the Communications Assistance for Law Enforcement Act.

§ 3125. Emergency Pen Register and Trap and Trace Device Installation

(a) Notwithstanding any other provision of this chapter, any investigative or law enforcement officer, specially designated by the Attorney General, the Deputy Attorney General, the Associate Attorney General, any Assistant Attorney General, any acting Assistant Attorney General, or any Deputy Assistant Attorney General, or by the principal prosecuting attorney of any State or subdivision thereof acting pursuant to a statute of that State, who reasonably determines that—

   (1) an emergency situation exists that involves—

      (A) immediate danger of death or serious bodily injury to any person;

      (B) conspiratorial activities characteristic of organized crime;

      (C) an immediate threat to a national security interest; or

      (D) an ongoing attack on a protected computer (as defined in section 1030) that constitutes a crime punishable by a term of imprisonment greater than 1 year; that requires the installation and use of a pen register or a trap and trace device before an order authorizing such installation and use can, with due diligence, be obtained, and

   (2) there are grounds upon which an order could be entered under this chapter to authorize such installation and use; may have installed and use a pen register or trap and trace device if, within 48 hours after the installation has occurred, or begins to occur, an order approving the installation or use is issued in accordance with section 3123 of this title.

(b) In the absence of an authorizing order, such use shall immediately terminate when the information sought is obtained, when the application for the order is denied or when 48 hours have lapsed since the installation of the pen register or trap and trace device, whichever is earlier.

(c) The knowing installation or use by any investigative or law enforcement officer of a pen register or trap and trace device pursuant to subsection (a) without application for the authorizing order within 48 hours of the installation shall constitute a violation of this chapter.

(d) A provider of a wire or electronic service, landlord, custodian, or other person who furnished facilities or technical assistance pursuant to this section shall be reasonably compensated for such reasonable expenses incurred in providing such facilities and assistance.

§ 3126. Reports Concerning Pen Registers and Trap and Trace Devices

The Attorney General shall annually report to Congress on the number of pen register orders and orders for trap and trace devices applied for by law enforcement agencies of the Department of Justice, which report shall include information concerning—

(1) the period of interceptions authorized by the order, and the number and duration of any extensions of the order;
(2) the offense specified in the order or application, or extension of an order;
(3) the number of investigations involved;
(4) the number and nature of the facilities affected; and
(5) the identity, including district, of the applying investigative or law enforcement agency making the application and the person authorizing the order.

§ 3127. Definitions for Chapter

As used in this chapter—

(1) the terms "wire communication," "electronic communication," "electronic communication service," and "contents" have the meanings set forth for such terms in section 2510 of this title;
(2) the term "court of competent jurisdiction" means—
    (A) any district court of the United States (including a magistrate judge of such a court) or any U.S. court of appeals that—
        (i) has jurisdiction over the offense being investigated;
        (ii) is in or for a district in which the provider of a wire or electronic communication service is located;
        (iii) is in or for a district in which a landlord, custodian, or other person subject to subsections (a) or (b) of section 3124 of this title is located; or
        (iv) is acting on a request for foreign assistance pursuant to section 3512 of this title; or
    (B) a court of general criminal jurisdiction of a State authorized by the law of that State to enter orders authorizing the use of a pen register or a trap and trace device;
(3) the term "pen register" means a device or process which records or decodes dialing, routing, addressing, or signaling information transmitted by an instrument or facility from which a wire or electronic communication is transmitted, provided, however, that such

information shall not include the contents of any communication, but such term does not include any device or process used by a provider or customer of a wire or electronic communication service for billing, or recording as an incident to billing, for communications services provided by such provider or any device or process used by a provider or customer of a wire communication service for cost accounting or other like purposes in the ordinary course of its business;

(4) the term "trap and trace device" means a device or process which captures the incoming electronic or other impulses which identify the originating number or other dialing, routing, addressing, and signaling information reasonably likely to identify the source of a wire or electronic communication, provided, however, that such information shall not include the contents of any communication;

(5) the term "attorney for the Government" has the meaning given such term for the purposes of the Federal Rules of Criminal Procedure; and

(6) the term "State" means a State, the District of Columbia, Puerto Rico, and any other possession or territory of the United States.

Communications Assistance Law Enforcement Act of 1994 (47 U.S.C. 1001–1021)

Communications Assistance for Law Enforcement Act of 1994
Pub. L. No. 103-414, 108 Stat. 4279
One Hundred Third Congress
of the
United States of America
at the Second Session

An Act

To amend title 18, United States Code, to make clear a telecommunications carrier's duty to cooperate in the interception of communications for law enforcement purposes, and for other purposes.

Be it enacted by the Senate and House of Representatives of the United States of America in Congress assembled

Title I: Interception of Digital and Other Communications

§ 101. Short Title

This title may be cited as the "Communications Assistance for Law Enforcement Act".

§ 102. Definitions

For purposes of this title—

(1) The terms defined in section 2510 of title 18, United States Code, have, respectively, the meanings stated in that section.

(2) The term "call-identifying information" means dialing or signaling information that identifies the origin, direction, destination, or termination of each communication generated or received by a subscriber by means of any equipment, facility, or service of a telecommunications carrier.

(3) The term "Commission" means the Federal Communications Commission.

(4) The term "electronic messaging services" means software-based services that enable the sharing of data, images, sound, writing, or other information among computing devices controlled by the senders or recipients of the messages.

(5) The term "government" means the government of the United States and any agency or instrumentality thereof, the District of Columbia, any commonwealth, territory, or possession of the United States, and any State or political subdivision thereof authorized by law to conduct electronic surveillance.

(6) The term "information services"—
   (A) means the offering of a capability for generating, acquiring, storing, transforming, processing, retrieving, utilizing, or making available information via telecommunications; and
   (B) includes—
      (i) a service that permits a customer to retrieve stored information from, or file information for storage in, information storage facilities;
      (ii) electronic publishing; and
      (iii) electronic messaging services; but
   (C) does not include any capability for a telecommunications carrier's internal management, control, or operation of its telecommunications network.

(7) The term "telecommunications support services" means a product, software, or service used by a telecommunications carrier for the internal signaling or switching functions of its telecommunications network.

(8) The term "telecommunications carrier"—
   (A) means a person or entity engaged in the transmission or switching of wire or electronic communications as a common carrier for hire; and

(B) includes—
 (i) a person or entity engaged in providing commercial mobile
      service (as defined in section 332(d) of the Communications
      Act of 1934 (47 U.S.C. 332(d)); or
 (ii) a person or entity engaged in providing wire or electronic
       communication switching or transmission service to the
       extent that the Commission finds that such service is a
       replacement for a substantial portion of the local telephone
       exchange service and that it is in the public interest to deem
       such a person or entity to be a telecommunications carrier
       for purposes of this title; but
(C) does not include—
 (i) persons or entities insofar as they are engaged in providing
      information services; and
 (ii) any class or category of telecommunications carriers that
       the Commission exempts by rule after consultation with
       the Attorney General.

§ 103. Assistance Capability Requirements

(a) Capability Requirements—Except as provided in subsections (b), (c),
     and (d) of this section and sections 108(a) and 109(b) and (d), a tele-
     communications carrier shall ensure that its equipment, facilities,
     or services that provide a customer or subscriber with the ability to
     originate, terminate, or direct communications are capable of—
 (1) expeditiously isolating and enabling the government, pursuant
      to a court order or other lawful authorization, to intercept, to the
      exclusion of any other communications, all wire and electronic
      communications carried by the carrier within a service area to
      or from equipment, facilities, or services of a subscriber of such
      carrier concurrently with their transmission to or from the sub-
      scriber's equipment, facility, or service, or at such later time as
      may be acceptable to the government;
 (2) expeditiously isolating and enabling the government, pursuant to a
      court order or other lawful authorization, to access call-identifying
      information that is reasonably available to the carrier—
   (A) before, during, or immediately after the transmission of a
        wire or electronic communication (or at such later time as
        may be acceptable to the government); and
   (B) in a manner that allows it to be associated with the com-
        munication to which it pertains, except that, with regard
        to information acquired solely pursuant to the author-
        ity for pen registers and trap and trace devices (as defined

in section 3127 of title 18, United States Code), such call-identifying information shall not include any information that may disclose the physical location of the subscriber (except to the extent that the location may be determined from the telephone number);

(3) delivering intercepted communications and call-identifying information to the government, pursuant to a court order or other lawful authorization, in a format such that they may be transmitted by means of equipment, facilities, or services procured by the government to a location other than the premises of the carrier; and

(4) facilitating authorized communications interceptions and access to call-identifying information unobtrusively and with a minimum of interference with any subscriber's telecommunications service and in a manner that protects—

   (A) the privacy and security of communications and call-identifying information not authorized to be intercepted; and

   (B) information regarding the government's interception of communications and access to call-identifying information.

(b) Limitations—

   (1) Design of Features and Systems Configurations—This title does not authorize any law enforcement agency or officer—

      (A) to require any specific design of equipment, facilities, services, features, or system configurations to be adopted by any provider of a wire or electronic communication service, any manufacturer of telecommunications equipment, or any provider of telecommunications support services; or

      (B) to prohibit the adoption of any equipment, facility, service, or feature by any provider of a wire or electronic communication service, any manufacturer of telecommunications equipment, or any provider of telecommunications support services.

   (2) Information Services; Private Networks and Interconnection Services and Facilities—The requirements of subsection (a) do not apply to—

      (A) information services; or

      (B) equipment, facilities, or services that support the transport or switching of communications for private networks or for the sole purpose of interconnecting telecommunications carriers.

   (3) Encryption—A telecommunications carrier shall not be responsible for decrypting, or ensuring the government's ability to decrypt, any communication encrypted by a subscriber or customer, unless the encryption was provided by the carrier and the carrier possesses the information necessary to decrypt the communication.

(c) Emergency or Exigent Circumstances—In emergency or exigent circumstances (including those described in sections 2518 (7) or (11)(b) and 3125 of title 18, United States Code, and section 1805(e) of title 50 of such Code), a carrier at its discretion may comply with subsection (a) (3) by allowing monitoring at its premises if that is the only means of accomplishing the interception or access.

(d) Mobile Service Assistance Requirements—A telecommunications carrier that is a provider of commercial mobile service (as defined in section 332(d) of the Communications Act of 1934) offering a feature or service that allows subscribers to redirect, hand off, or assign their wire or electronic communications to another service area or another service provider or to utilize facilities in another service area or of another service provider shall ensure that, when the carrier that had been providing assistance for the interception of wire or electronic communications or access to call-identifying information pursuant to a court order or lawful authorization no longer has access to the content of such communications or call-identifying information within the service area in which interception has been occurring as a result of the subscriber's use of such a feature or service, information is made available to the government (before, during, or immediately after the transfer of such communications) identifying the provider of a wire or electronic communication service that has acquired access to the communications.

§ 104. Notices of Capacity Requirements

(a) Notices of Maximum and Actual Capacity Requirements—

(1) In General—Not later than 1 year after the date of enactment of this title, after consulting with State and local law enforcement agencies, telecommunications carriers, providers of telecommunications support services, and manufacturers of telecommunications equipment, and after notice and comment, the Attorney General shall publish in the Federal Register and provide to appropriate telecommunications industry associations and standard-setting organizations—

(A) notice of the actual number of communication interceptions, pen registers, and trap and trace devices, representing a portion of the maximum capacity set forth under subparagraph (B), that the Attorney General estimates that government agencies authorized to conduct electronic surveillance may conduct and use simultaneously by the date that is 4 years after the date of enactment of this title; and

(B) notice of the maximum capacity required to accommodate all of the communication interceptions, pen registers, and trap and trace devices that the Attorney General estimates that government agencies authorized to conduct electronic surveillance may conduct and use simultaneously after the date that is 4 years after the date of enactment of this title.

(2) Basis of Notices—The notices issued under paragraph (1)—

    (A) may be based upon the type of equipment, type of service, number of subscribers, type or size or carrier, nature of service area, or any other measure; and

    (B) shall identify, to the maximum extent practicable, the capacity required at specific geographic locations.

(b) Compliance with Capacity Notices—

  (1) Initial Capacity—Within 3 years after the publication by the Attorney General of a notice of capacity requirements or within 4 years after the date of enactment of this title, whichever is longer, a telecommunications carrier shall, subject to subsection (e), ensure that its systems are capable of—

    (A) accommodating simultaneously the number of interceptions, pen registers, and trap and trace devices set forth in the notice under subsection (a)(1)(A); and

    (B) expanding to the maximum capacity set forth in the notice under subsection (a)(1)(B).

  (2) Expansion to Maximum Capacity—After the date described in paragraph (1), a telecommunications carrier shall, subject to subsection (e), ensure that it can accommodate expeditiously any increase in the actual number of communication interceptions, pen registers, and trap and trace devices that authorized agencies may seek to conduct and use, up to the maximum capacity requirement set forth in the notice under subsection (a)(1)(B).

(c) Notices of Increased Maximum Capacity Requirements—

  (1) Notice—The Attorney General shall periodically publish in the Federal Register, after notice and comment, notice of any necessary increases in the maximum capacity requirement set forth in the notice under subsection (a)(1)(B).

  (2) Compliance—Within 3 years after notice of increased maximum capacity requirements is published under paragraph (1), or within such longer time period as the Attorney General may specify, a telecommunications carrier shall, subject to subsection (e), ensure that its systems are capable of expanding to the increased maximum capacity set forth in the notice.

(d) Carrier Statement—Within 180 days after the publication by the Attorney General of a notice of capacity requirements pursuant to subsection (a) or (c), a telecommunications carrier shall submit to the Attorney General a statement identifying any of its systems or services that do not have the capacity to accommodate simultaneously the number of interceptions, pen registers, and trap and trace devices set forth in the notice under such subsection.

(e) Reimbursement Required for Compliance—The Attorney General shall review the statements submitted under subsection (d) and may, subject to the availability of appropriations, agree to reimburse a telecommunications carrier for costs directly associated with modifications to attain such capacity requirement that are determined to be reasonable in accordance with section 109(e). Until the Attorney General agrees to reimburse such carrier for such modification, such carrier shall be considered to be in compliance with the capacity notices under subsection (a) or (c).

§ 105. Systems Security and Integrity

A telecommunications carrier shall ensure that any interception of communications or access to call-identifying information effected within its switching premises can be activated only in accordance with a court order or other lawful authorization and with the affirmative intervention of an individual officer or employee of the carrier acting in accordance with regulations prescribed by the Commission.

§ 106. Cooperation of Equipment Manufacturers and Providers of Telecommunications Support Services

(a) Consultation—A telecommunications carrier shall consult, as necessary, in a timely fashion with manufacturers of its telecommunications transmission and switching equipment and its providers of telecommunications support services for the purpose of ensuring that current and planned equipment, facilities, and services comply with the capability requirements of section 103 and the capacity requirements identified by the Attorney General under section 104.

(b) Cooperation—Subject to sections 104(e), 108(a), and 109 (b) and (d), a manufacturer of telecommunications transmission or switching equipment and a provider of telecommunications support services shall, on a reasonably timely basis and at a reasonable charge, make available to the telecommunications carriers using its equipment, facilities, or services such features or modifications as are necessary to permit such carriers to comply with the capability requirements of section 103 and the capacity requirements identified by the Attorney General under section 104.

§ 107. Technical Requirements and Standards; Extension of Compliance Date

(a) Safe Harbor—

    (1) Consultation—To ensure the efficient and industry-wide implementation of the assistance capability requirements under section 103, the Attorney General, in coordination with other Federal, State, and local law enforcement agencies, shall consult with appropriate associations and standard-setting organizations of the telecommunications industry, with representatives of users of telecommunications equipment, facilities, and services, and with State utility commissions.

    (2) Compliance Under Accepted Standards—A telecommunications carrier shall be found to be in compliance with the assistance capability requirements under section 103, and a manufacturer of telecommunications transmission or switching equipment or a provider of telecommunications support services shall be found to be in compliance with section 106, if the carrier, manufacturer, or support service provider is in compliance with publicly available technical requirements or standards adopted by an industry association or standard-setting organization, or by the Commission under subsection (b), to meet the requirements of section 103.

    (3) Absence of Standards—The absence of technical requirements or standards for implementing the assistance capability requirements of section 103 shall not—

        (A) preclude a telecommunications carrier, manufacturer, or telecommunications support services provider from deploying a technology or service; or

        (B) relieve a carrier, manufacturer, or telecommunications support services provider of the obligations imposed by section 103 or 106, as applicable.

(b) Commission Authority—If industry associations or standard-setting organizations fail to issue technical requirements or standards or if a Government agency or any other person believes that such requirements or standards are deficient, the agency or person may petition the Commission to establish, by rule, technical requirements or standards that—

    (1) meet the assistance capability requirements of section 103 by cost-effective methods;

    (2) protect the privacy and security of communications not authorized to be intercepted;

    (3) minimize the cost of such compliance on residential ratepayers;

(4) serve the policy of the United States to encourage the provision of new technologies and services to the public; and

(5) provide a reasonable time and conditions for compliance with and the transition to any new standard, including defining the obligations of telecommunications carriers under section 103 during any transition period.

(c) Extension of Compliance Date for Equipment, Facilities, and Services—

(1) Petition—A telecommunications carrier proposing to install or deploy, or having installed or deployed, any equipment, facility, or service prior to the effective date of section 103 may petition the Commission for 1 or more extensions of the deadline for complying with the assistance capability requirements under section 103.

(2) Grounds for Extension—The Commission may, after consultation with the Attorney General, grant an extension under this subsection, if the Commission determines that compliance with the assistance capability requirements under section 103 is not reasonably achievable through application of technology available within the compliance period.

(3) Length of Extension—An extension under this subsection shall extend for no longer than the earlier of—

(A) the date determined by the Commission as necessary for the carrier to comply with the assistance capability requirements under section 103; or

(B) the date that is 2 years after the date on which the extension is granted.

(4) Applicability of Extension—An extension under this subsection shall apply to only that part of the carrier's business on which the new equipment, facility, or service is used.

§ 108. Enforcement Orders

(a) Grounds for Issuance—A court shall issue an order enforcing this title under section 2522 of title 18, United States Code, only if the court finds that—

(1) alternative technologies or capabilities or the facilities of another carrier are not reasonably available to law enforcement for implementing the interception of communications or access to call-identifying information; and

(2) compliance with the requirements of this title is reasonably achievable through the application of available technology to the equipment, facility, or service at issue or would have been reasonably achievable if timely action had been taken.

(b) Time for Compliance—Upon issuing an order enforcing this title, the court shall specify a reasonable time and conditions for complying with its order, considering the good faith efforts to comply in a timely manner, any effect on the carrier's, manufacturer's, or service provider's ability to continue to do business, the degree of culpability or delay in undertaking efforts to comply, and such other matters as justice may require.

(c) Limitations—An order enforcing this title may not—

　(1) require a telecommunications carrier to meet the Government's demand for interception of communications and acquisition of call-identifying information to any extent in excess of the capacity for which the Attorney General has agreed to reimburse such carrier;

　(2) require any telecommunications carrier to comply with assistance capability requirement of section 103 if the Commission has determined (pursuant to section 109(b)(1)) that compliance is not reasonably achievable, unless the Attorney General has agreed (pursuant to section 109(b)(2)) to pay the costs described in section 109(b)(2)(A); or

　(3) require a telecommunications carrier to modify, for the purpose of complying with the assistance capability requirements of section 103, any equipment, facility, or service deployed on or before January 1, 1995, unless—

　　(A) the Attorney General has agreed to pay the telecommunications carrier for all reasonable costs directly associated with modifications necessary to bring the equipment, facility, or service into compliance with those requirements; or

　　(B) the equipment, facility, or service has been replaced or significantly upgraded or otherwise undergoes major modification.

§ 109. Payment of Costs of Telecommunications Carriers to Comply with Capability Requirements

(a) Equipment, Facilities, and Services Deployed on or Before January 1, 1995—The Attorney General may, subject to the availability of appropriations, agree to pay telecommunications carriers for all reasonable costs directly associated with the modifications performed by carriers in connection with equipment, facilities, and services installed or deployed on or before January 1, 1995, to establish the capabilities necessary to comply with section 103.

(b) Equipment, Facilities, and Services Deployed after January 1, 1995—

　(1) Determinations of Reasonably Achievable—The Commission, on petition from a telecommunications carrier or any other interested person, and after notice to the Attorney General, shall determine whether compliance with the assistance capability requirements

of section 103 is reasonably achievable with respect to any equipment, facility, or service installed or deployed after January 1, 1995. The Commission shall make such determination within 1 year after the date such petition is filed. In making such determination, the Commission shall determine whether compliance would impose significant difficulty or expense on the carrier or on the users of the carrier's systems and shall consider the following factors:

(A) The effect on public safety and national security.

(B) The effect on rates for basic residential telephone service.

(C) The need to protect the privacy and security of communications not authorized to be intercepted.

(D) The need to achieve the capability assistance requirements of section 103 by cost-effective methods.

(E) The effect on the nature and cost of the equipment, facility, or service at issue.

(F) The effect on the operation of the equipment, facility, or service at issue.

(G) The policy of the United States to encourage the provision of new technologies and services to the public.

(H) The financial resources of the telecommunications carrier.

(I) The effect on competition in the provision of telecommunications services.

(J) The extent to which the design and development of the equipment, facility, or service was initiated before January 1, 1995.

(K) Such other factors as the Commission determines are appropriate.

(2) Compensation—If compliance with the assistance capability requirements of section 103 is not reasonably achievable with respect to equipment, facilities, or services deployed after January 1, 1995—

(A) the Attorney General, on application of a telecommunications carrier, may agree, subject to the availability of appropriations, to pay the telecommunications carrier for the additional reasonable costs of making compliance with such assistance capability requirements reasonably achievable; and

(B) if the Attorney General does not agree to pay such costs, the telecommunications carrier shall be deemed to be in compliance with such capability requirements.

(c) Allocation of Funds for Payment—The Attorney General shall allocate funds appropriated to carry out this title in accordance with law enforcement priorities determined by the Attorney General.

(d) Failure to Make Payment with Respect to Equipment, Facilities, and Services Deployed on or Before January 1, 1995—If a carrier has requested payment in accordance with procedures promulgated pursuant to subsection (e), and the Attorney General has not agreed to pay the telecommunications carrier for all reasonable costs directly associated with modifications necessary to bring any equipment, facility, or service deployed on or before January 1, 1995, into compliance with the assistance capability requirements of section 103, such equipment, facility, or service shall be considered to be in compliance with the assistance capability requirements of section 103 until the equipment, facility, or service is replaced or significantly upgraded or otherwise undergoes major modification.

(e) Cost Control Regulations—

   (1) In General—The Attorney General shall, after notice and comment, establish regulations necessary to effectuate timely and cost-efficient payment to telecommunications carriers under this title, under chapters 119 and 121 of title 18, United States Code, and under the Foreign Intelligence Surveillance Act of 1978 (50 U.S.C. 1801 et seq.).

   (2) Contents of Regulations—The Attorney General, after consultation with the Commission, shall prescribe regulations for purposes of determining reasonable costs under this title. Such regulations shall seek to minimize the cost to the Federal Government and shall—

      (A) permit recovery from the Federal Government of—

         (i) the direct costs of developing the modifications described in subsection (a), of providing the capabilities requested under subsection (b)(2), or of providing the capacities requested under section 104(e), but only to the extent that such costs have not been recovered from any other governmental or non-governmental entity;

        (ii) the costs of training personnel in the use of such capabilities or capacities; and

        (iii) the direct costs of deploying or installing such capabilities or capacities;

      (B) in the case of any modification that may be used for any purpose other than lawfully-authorized electronic surveillance by a law enforcement agency of a government, permit recovery of only the incremental cost of making the modification suitable for such law enforcement purposes; and

      (C) maintain the confidentiality of trade secrets.

   (3) Submission of Claims—Such regulations shall require any telecommunications carrier that the Attorney General has agreed to pay for modifications pursuant to this section and that has installed or deployed such modification to submit to the Attorney General a claim for payment that contains or is accompanied by such information as the Attorney General may require.

§ 110. Authorization of Appropriations

There are authorized to be appropriated to carry out this title a total of $500,000,000 for fiscal years 1995, 1996, 1997, and 1998. Such sums are authorized to remain available until expended.

§ 111. Effective Date

(a) In General—Except as provided in subsection (b), this title shall take effect on the date of enactment of this Act.

(b) Assistance Capability and Systems Security and Integrity Requirements—Sections 103 and 105 of this title shall take effect on the date that is 4 years after the date of enactment of this Act.

§ 112. Reports

(a) Reports by the Attorney General—

    (1) In General—On or before November 30, 1995, and on or before November 30 of each year thereafter, the Attorney General shall submit to Congress and make available to the public a report on the amounts paid during the preceding fiscal year to telecommunications carriers under sections 104(e) and 109.

    (2) Contents—A report under paragraph (1) shall include—

        (A) a detailed accounting of the amounts paid to each carrier and the equipment, facility, or service for which the amounts were paid; and

        (B) projections of the amounts expected to be paid in the current fiscal year, the carriers to which payment is expected to be made, and the equipment, facilities, or services for which payment is expected to be made.

(b) Reports by the Comptroller General—

    (1) Payments for Modifications—On or before April 1, 1996, and every 2 years thereafter, the Comptroller General of the United States, after consultation with the Attorney General and the telecommunications industry, shall submit to the Congress a report—

        (A) describing the type of equipment, facilities, and services that have been brought into compliance under this title; and

        (B) reflecting its analysis of the reasonableness and cost-effectiveness of the payments made by the Attorney General to telecommunications carriers for modifications necessary to ensure compliance with this title.

    (2) Compliance Cost Estimates—A report under paragraph (1) shall include the findings and conclusions of the Comptroller General on the costs to be incurred by telecommunications carriers to comply with the assistance capability requirements of section

103 after the effective date of such section 103, including projections of the amounts expected to be incurred and a description of the equipment, facilities, or services for which they are expected to be incurred.

Title II: Amendments to Title 18, United States Code

§ 201. Court Enforcement of Communications Assistance for Law Enforcement Act

(a) Court Orders under Chapter 119: Chapter 119 of title 18, United States Code, is amended by inserting after section 2521 the following new section:

"§ 2522. Enforcement of the Communications Assistance for Law Enforcement Act

"(a) Enforcement by Court Issuing Surveillance Order—If a court authorizing an interception under this chapter, a State statute, or the Foreign Intelligence Surveillance Act of 1978 (50 U.S.C. 1801 et seq.) or authorizing use of a pen register or a trap and trace device under chapter 206 or a State statute finds that a telecommunications carrier has failed to comply with the requirements of the Communications Assistance for Law Enforcement Act, the court may, in accordance with section 108 of such Act, direct that the carrier comply forthwith and may direct that a provider of support services to the carrier or the manufacturer of the carrier's transmission or switching equipment furnish forthwith modifications necessary for the carrier to comply.

"(b) Enforcement upon Application by Attorney General—The Attorney General may, in a civil action in the appropriate United States district court, obtain an order, in accordance with section 108 of the Communications Assistance for Law Enforcement Act, directing that a telecommunications carrier, a manufacturer of telecommunications transmission or switching equipment, or a provider of telecommunications support services comply with such Act.

"(c) Civil Penalty—

"(1) In General—A court issuing an order under this section against a telecommunications carrier, a manufacturer of telecommunications transmission or switching equipment, or a provider of telecommunications support services may impose a civil penalty of up to $10,000 per day for each day in violation after the issuance of the order or after such future date as the court may specify.

"(2) Considerations—In determining whether to impose a civil penalty and in determining its amount, the court shall take into account—

    "(A) the nature, circumstances, and extent of the violation;

    "(B) the violator's ability to pay, the violator's good faith efforts to comply in a timely manner, any effect on the violator's ability to continue to do business, the degree of culpability, and the length of any delay in undertaking efforts to comply; and

    "(C) such other matters as justice may require.

"(d) Definitions—As used in this section, the terms defined in section 102 of the Communications Assistance for Law Enforcement Act have the meanings provided, respectively, in such section."

(e) Conforming Amendments—

    (1) Section 2518(4) of title 18, United States Code, is amended by adding at the end the following new sentence: "Pursuant to section 2522 of this chapter, an order may also be issued to enforce the assistance capability and capacity requirements under the Communications Assistance for Law Enforcement Act."

    (2) Section 3124 of such title is amended by adding at the end the following new subsection:

"(f) Communications Assistance Enforcement Orders—Pursuant to section 2522, an order may be issued to enforce the assistance capability and capacity requirements under the Communications Assistance for Law Enforcement Act."

    (1) The table of sections at the beginning of chapter 119 of title 18, United States Code, is amended by inserting after the item pertaining to section 2521 the following new item:

"2522. Enforcement of the Communications Assistance for Law Enforcement Act."

§ 202. Cordless Telephones

(a) Definitions—Section 2510 of title 18, United States Code, is amended—

    (1) in paragraph (1), by striking ", but such term does not include" and all that follows through "base unit"; and

    (2) in paragraph (12), by striking subparagraph (A) and redesignating subparagraphs (B), (C), and (D) as subparagraphs (A), (B), and (C), respectively.

(b) Penalty—Section 2511 of title 18, United States Code, is amended—
   (1) in subsection (4)(b)(i) by inserting "a cordless telephone com-
        munication that is transmitted between the cordless telephone
        handset and the base unit," after "cellular telephone communica-
        tion,"; and
   (2) in subsection (4)(b)(ii) by inserting "a cordless telephone com-
        munication that is transmitted between the cordless tele-
        phone handset and the base unit," after "cellular telephone
        communication,".

§ 203. Radio-Based Data Communications

Section 2510(16) of title 18, United States Code, is amended—

   (1) by striking "or" at the end of subparagraph (D);
   (2) by inserting "or" at the end of subparagraph (E); and
   (3) by inserting after subparagraph (E) the following new subparagraph:
        "(F) an electronic communication;"

§ 204. Penalties for Monitoring Radio Communications That Are Transmitted Using Modulation Techniques with Nonpublic Parameters

Section 2511(4)(b) of title 18, United States Code, is amended by striking "or
encrypted, then" and inserting ", encrypted, or transmitted using modulation
techniques the essential parameters of which have been withheld from the public with the intention of preserving the privacy of such communication, then".

§ 205. Technical Correction

Section 2511(2)(a)(i) of title 18, United States Code, is amended by striking
"used in the transmission of a wire communication" and inserting "used in
the transmission of a wire or electronic communication".

§ 206. Fraudulent Alteration of Commercial Mobile Radio Instruments

(a) Offense—Section 1029(a) of title 18, United States Code, is
     amended—
   (1) by striking "or" at the end of paragraph (3); and
   (2) by inserting after paragraph (4) the following new paragraphs:
   "(5) knowingly and with intent to defraud uses, produces, traffics
         in, has control or custody of, or possesses a telecommunications
         instrument that has been modified or altered to obtain unau-
         thorized use of telecommunications services; or

"(6) knowingly and with intent to defraud uses, produces, traffics in, has control or custody of, or possesses—

"(A) a scanning receiver; or

"(B) hardware or software used for altering or modifying telecommunications instruments to obtain unauthorized access to telecommunications services,"

(b) Penalty—Section 1029(c)(2) of title 18, United States Code, is amended by striking "(a)(1) or (a)(4)" and inserting "(a) (1), (4), (5), or (6)".

(c) Definitions–Section 1029(e) of title 18, United States Code, is amended—

(1) in paragraph (1) by inserting "electronic serial number, mobile identification number, personal identification number, or other telecommunications service, equipment, or instrument identifier," after "account number,";

(2) by striking "and" at the end of paragraph (5);

(3) by striking the period at the end of paragraph (6) and inserting "; and"; and

(4) by adding at the end the following new paragraph:

"(7) the term 'scanning receiver' means a device or apparatus that can be used to intercept a wire or electronic communication in violation of chapter 119."

§ 207. Transactional Data

(a) Disclosure of Records—Section 2703 of title 18, United States Code, is amended—

(1) in subsection (c)(1)—

(A) in subparagraph (B)—

(i) by striking clause (i); and

(ii) by redesignating clauses (ii), (iii), and (iv) as clauses (i), (ii), and (iii), respectively; and

(B) by adding at the end the following new subparagraph:

"(C) A provider of electronic communication service or remote computing service shall disclose to a governmental entity the name, address, telephone toll billing records, telephone number or other subscriber number or identity, and length of service of a subscriber to or customer of such service and the types of services the subscriber or customer utilized, when the governmental entity uses an administrative subpoena authorized by a Federal or State statute or a Federal or State grand jury or trial subpoena or any means available under subparagraph (B)."; and

(2) by amending the first sentence of subsection (d) to read as follows: "A court order for disclosure under subsection (b) or (c) may
be issued by any court that is a court of competent jurisdiction
described in section 3126(2)(A) and shall issue only if the governmental entity offers specific and articulable facts showing that there
are reasonable grounds to believe that the contents of a wire or electronic communication, or the records or other information sought,
are relevant and material to an ongoing criminal investigation."

(b) Pen Registers and Trap and Trace Devices—Section 3121 of title 18,
United States Code, is amended—
  (1) by redesignating subsection (c) as subsection (d); and
  (2) by inserting after subsection (b) the following new subsection:

"(c) Limitation—A government agency authorized to install and use a pen
register under this chapter or under State law shall use technology
reasonably available to it that restricts the recording or decoding of
electronic or other impulses to the dialing and signaling information
utilized in call processing."

§ 208. Authorization for Acting Deputy Attorneys General in the Criminal Division to Approve Certain Court Applications

Section 2516(1) of title 18, United States Code, is amended by inserting "or acting
Deputy Assistant Attorney General" after "Deputy Assistant Attorney General".

Title III: Amendments to the Communications Act of 1934

§ 301. Compliance Cost Recovery

Title II of the Communications Act of 1934 is amended by inserting after
section 228 (47 U.S.C. 228) the following new section:

"§ 229. Communications Assistance for Law Enforcement Act Compliance

"(a) In General—The Commission shall prescribe such rules as are
necessary to implement the requirements of the Communications
Assistance for Law Enforcement Act.

"(b) Systems Security and Integrity—The rules prescribed pursuant to
subsection (a) shall include rules to implement section 105 of the
Communications Assistance for Law Enforcement Act that require
common carriers—
  "(1) to establish appropriate policies and procedures for the supervision and control of its officers and employees—
    "(A) to require appropriate authorization to activate inter-
ception of communications or access to call-identifying
information; and

"(B) to prevent any such interception or access without such authorization;

"(2) to maintain secure and accurate records of any interception or access with or without such authorization; and

"(3) to submit to the Commission the policies and procedures adopted to comply with the requirements established under paragraphs (1) and (2).

"(c) Commission Review of Compliance—The Commission shall review the policies and procedures submitted under subsection (b)(3) and shall order a common carrier to modify any such policy or procedure that the Commission determines does not comply with Commission regulations. The Commission shall conduct such investigations as may be necessary to insure compliance by common carriers with the requirements of the regulations prescribed under this section.

"(d) Penalties—For purposes of this Act, a violation by an officer or employee of any policy or procedure adopted by a common carrier pursuant to subsection (b), or of a rule prescribed by the Commission pursuant to subsection (a), shall be considered to be a violation by the carrier of a rule prescribed by the Commission pursuant to this Act.

"(e) Cost Recovery for Communications Assistance for Law Enforcement Act Compliance—

"(1) Petitions Authorized—A common carrier may petition the Commission to adjust charges, practices, classifications, and regulations to recover costs expended for making modifications to equipment, facilities, or services pursuant to the requirements of section 103 of the Communications Assistance for Law Enforcement Act.

"(2) Commission Authority—The Commission may grant, with or without modification, a petition under paragraph (1) if the Commission determines that such costs are reasonable and that permitting recovery is consistent with the public interest. The Commission may, consistent with maintaining just and reasonable charges, practices, classifications, and regulations in connection with the provision of interstate or foreign communication by wire or radio by a common carrier, allow carriers to adjust such charges, practices, classifications, and regulations in order to carry out the purposes of this Act.

"(3) Joint Board—The Commission shall convene a Federal-State joint board to recommend appropriate changes to part 36 of the Commission's rules with respect to recovery of costs pursuant to charges, practices, classifications, and regulations under the jurisdiction of the Commission."

§ 302. Recovery of Cost of Commission Proceedings

The schedule of application fees in section 8(g) of the Communications Act of 1934 (47 U.S.C. 158(g)) is amended by inserting under item 1 of the matter pertaining to common carrier services the following additional subitem:

"(d) Proceeding under section 109(b) of the Communications Assistance for Law Enforcement Act—5,000."

§ 303. Clerical and Technical Amendments

(a) Amendments *to* the Communications Act of 1934—The Communications Act of 1934 is amended—

  (1) in section 4(f)(3), by striking "overtime exceeds beyond" and inserting "overtime extends beyond";

  (2) in section 5, by redesignating subsection (f) as subsection (e);

  (3) in section 8(d)(2), by striking "payment of a" and inserting "payment of an";

  (4) in the schedule contained in section 8(g), in item 7.f. under the heading "Equipment Approval Services/Experimental Radio" by striking "Additional Charge" and inserting "Additional Application Fee";

  (5) in section 9(f)(1), by inserting before the second sentence the following:
    "(A) Installment Payments—";

  (6) in the schedule contained in section 9(g), in the item pertaining to interactive video data services under the private radio bureau, insert "95" after "47 C.F.R. Part";

  (7) in section 220(a)—
    (A) by inserting "(1)" after "(a)"; and
    (B) by adding at the end the following new paragraph:
      "(i) The Commission shall, by rule, prescribe a uniform system of accounts for use by telephone companies. Such uniform system shall require that each common carrier shall maintain a system of accounting methods, procedures, and techniques (including accounts and supporting records and memoranda) which shall ensure a proper allocation of all costs to and among telecommunications services, facilities, and products (and to and among classes of such services, facilities, and products) which are developed, manufactured, or offered by such common carrier.";

  (8) in section 220(b), by striking "classes" and inserting "classes";

  (9) in section 223(b)(3), by striking "defendant restrict access" and inserting "defendant restricted access";

(10) in section 226(d), by striking paragraph (2) and redesignating paragraphs (3) and (4) as paragraphs (2) and (3), respectively;

(11) in section 227(b)(2)(C), by striking "paragraphs" and inserting "paragraph";

(12) in section 227(e)(2), by striking "national database" and inserting "national database";

(13) in section 228(c), by redesignating the second paragraph (2) and paragraphs (3) through (6) as paragraphs (3) through (7), respectively;

(14) in section 228(c)(6)(D), by striking "conservation" and inserting "conversation";

(15) in section 308(c), by striking "May 24, 1921" and inserting "May 27, 1921";

(16) in section 309(c)(2)(F), by striking "section 325(b)" and inserting "section 325(c)";

(17) in section 309(i)(4)(A), by striking "Communications Technical Amendments Act of 1982" and inserting "Communications Amendments Act of 1982";

(18) in section 331, by amending the heading of such section to read as follows:
"Very High Frequency Stations and AM Radio Stations";

(19) in section 358, by striking "(a)";

(20) in part III of title III—

(A) by inserting before section 381 the following heading:
"Vessels Transporting More Than Six Passengers for Hire Required to Be Equipped with Radio Telephone";

(B) by inserting before section 382 the following heading:
"Vessels Excepted from Radio Telephone Requirement";

(C) by inserting before section 383 the following heading:
"Exemptions by Commission";

(D) by inserting before section 384 the following heading:
"Authority of Commission; Operations, Installations, and Additional Equipment";

(E) by inserting before section 385 the following heading:
"Inspections"; and

(F) by inserting before section 386 the following heading:
"Forfeitures";

(21) in section 410(c), by striking ", as referred to in sections 202(b) and 205(f) of the Interstate Commerce Act,";

(22) in section 613(b)(2), by inserting a comma after "pole" and after "line";

(23) in section 624(d)(2)(A), by inserting "of" after "viewing";

(24) in section 634(h)(1), by striking "section 602(6)(A)" and inserting "section 602(7)(A)";

(25) in section 705(d)(6), by striking "subsection (d)" and inserting
"subsection (e)";

(26) in section 705(e)(3)(A), by striking "paragraph (4) of subsection
(d)" and inserting "paragraph (4) of this subsection";

(27) in section 705, by redesignating subsections (f) and (g) (as added
by Public Law 100-667) as subsections (g) and (h); and

(28) in section 705(h) (as so redesignated), by striking "subsection
(f)" and inserting "subsection (g)."

(b) Amendments to the Communications Satellite Act of 1962—The
Communications Satellite Act of 1962 is amended—

(1) in section 303(a)—

(A) by striking "section 27(d)" and inserting "section 327(d)";

(B) by striking "sec. 29-911(d)" and inserting "sec. 29-327(d)";

(C) by striking "section 36" and inserting "section 336"; and

(D) by striking "sec. 29-916d" and inserting "section 29-336(d)";

(2) in section 304(d), by striking "paragraphs (1), (2), (3), (4), and (5)
of section 310(a)" and inserting "subsection (a) and paragraphs
(1) through (4) of subsection (b) of section 310"; and

(3) in section 304(e)—

(A) by striking "section 45(b)" and inserting "section 345(b)"; and

(B) by striking "sec. 29-920(b)" and inserting "sec. 29-345(b)"; and

(4) in sections 502(b) and 503(a)(1), by striking "the Communications
Satellite Corporation" and inserting "the communications satellite corporation established pursuant to title III of this Act."

(c) Amendment to the Children's Television Act of 1990—Section
103(a) of the Children's Television Act of 1990 (47 U.S.C.
303b(a)) is amended by striking "noncommerical" and inserting
"noncommercial".

(d) Amendments to the Telecommunications Authorization Act of
1992—Section 205(1) of the Telecommunications Authorization Act
of 1992 is amended—

(1) by inserting an open parenthesis before "other than"; and

(2) by inserting a comma after "stations)".

(e) Conforming Amendment—Section 1253 of the Omnibus Budget
Reconciliation Act of 1981 is repealed.

(f) Stylistic Consistency—The Communications Act of 1934 and the
Communications Satellite Act of 1962 are amended so that the
section designation and section heading of each section of such

Acts shall be in the form and typeface of the section designation and heading of this section.

§ 304. Elimination of Expired and Outdated Provisions

(a) Amendments to the Communications Act of 1934—The Communications Act of 1934 is amended—

    (1) in section 7(b), by striking "or twelve months after the date of the enactment of this section, if later" both places it appears;

    (2) in section 212, by striking "After sixty days from the enactment of this Act it shall" and inserting "It shall";

    (3) in section 213, by striking subsection (g) and redesignating subsection (h) as subsection (g);

    (4) in section 214, by striking "section 221 or 222" and inserting "section 221";

    (5) in section 220(b), by striking ", as soon as practicable,";

    (6) by striking section 222;

    (7) in section 224(b)(2), by striking "Within 180 days from the date of enactment of this section the Commission" and inserting "The Commission";

    (8) in 226(e), by striking "within 9 months after the date of enactment of this section,";

    (9) in section 309(i)(4)(A), by striking "The commission, not later than 180 days after the date of the enactment of the Communications Technical Amendments Act of 1982, shall," and inserting "The Commission shall,";

    (10) by striking section 328;

    (11) in section 413, by striking ", within 60 days after the taking effect of this Act,";

    (12) in section 624(d)(2)(B)—

        (A) by striking out "(A)";

        (B) by inserting "of" after "restrict the viewing"; and

        (C) by striking subparagraph (B);

    (13) by striking sections 702 and 703;

    (14) in section 704—

        (A) by striking subsections (b) and (d); and

        (B) by redesignating subsection (c) as subsection (b);

    (15) in section 705(g) (as redesignated by section 304(25)), by striking "within 6 months after the date of enactment of the Satellite

Home Viewer Act of 1988, the Federal Communications Commission" and inserting "The Commission";

(16) in section 710(f)—

(A) by striking the first and second sentences; and

(B) in the third sentence, by striking "Thereafter, the Commission" and inserting "The Commission";

(17) in section 712(a), by striking ", within 120 days after the effective date of the Satellite Home Viewer Act of 1988,"; and

(18) by striking section 713.

(b) Amendments to the Communications Satellite Act of 1962—The Communications Satellite Act of 1962 is amended—

(1) in section 201(a)(1), by striking "as expeditiously as possible,";

(2) by striking sections 301 and 302 and inserting the following:

"§ 301. Creation of Corporation

"There is authorized to be created a communications satellite corporation for profit which will not be an agency or establishment of the United States Government.

"§ 302. Applicable Laws

"The corporation shall be subject to the provisions of this Act and, to the extent consistent with this Act, to the District of Columbia Business Corporation Act. The right to repeal, alter, or amend this Act at any time is expressly reserved.";

(3) in section 304(a), by striking "at a price not in excess of $100 for each share and";

(4) in section 404—

(A) by striking subsections (a)–(c); and

(B) by redesignating subsection (b) as section 404;

(5) in section 503—

(A) by striking paragraph (2) of subsection (a); and

(B) by redesignating paragraph (3) of subsection (a) as paragraph (2) of such subsection;

(C) by striking subsection (b);

(D) in subsection (g)—

(i) by striking "subsection (c)(3)" and inserting "subsection (b)(3)"; and

(ii) by striking the last sentence; and

(E) by redesignating subsections (c)–(h) as subsections (b)–(g), respectively;

(5) by striking sections 505–507; and

(6) by redesignating section 508 as section 505.

Approved October 25, 1994

Foreign Intelligence Surveillance Act (50 U.S.C. 1861)

§ 1861. Access to Certain Business Records for Foreign Intelligence and International Terrorism Investigations

(a) *Application for Order; Conduct of Investigation Generally*

    (1) Subject to paragraph (3), the Director of the Federal Bureau of Investigation or a designee of the Director (whose rank shall be no lower than Assistant Special Agent in Charge) may make an application for an order requiring the production of any tangible things (including books, records, papers, documents, and other items) for an investigation to obtain foreign intelligence information not concerning a United States person or to protect against international terrorism or clandestine intelligence activities, provided that such investigation of a United States person is not conducted solely upon the basis of activities protected by the first amendment to the Constitution.

    (2) An investigation conducted under this section shall—

        (A) be conducted under guidelines approved by the Attorney General under Executive Order 12333 (or a successor order); and

        (B) not be conducted of a United States person solely upon the basis of activities protected by the first amendment to the Constitution of the United States.

    (3) In the case of an application for an order requiring the production of library circulation records, library patron lists, book sales records, book customer lists, firearms sales records, tax return records, educational records, or medical records containing information that would identify a person, the Director of the Federal Bureau of Investigation may delegate the authority to make such application to either the Deputy Director of the Federal Bureau of Investigation or the Executive Assistant Director for National Security (or any successor position). The Deputy Director or the Executive Assistant Director may not further delegate such authority.

(b) *Recipient and Contents of Application*
Each application under this section—
(1) shall be made to—
   (A) a judge of the court established by section 1803 (a) of this title; or
   (B) a United States Magistrate Judge under chapter 43 of title 28, who is publicly designated by the Chief Justice of the United States to have the power to hear applications and grant orders for the production of tangible things under this section on behalf of a judge of that court; and
(2) shall include—
   (A) a statement of facts showing that there are reasonable grounds to believe that the tangible things sought are relevant to an authorized investigation (other than a threat assessment) conducted in accordance with subsection (a)(2) to obtain foreign intelligence information not concerning a United States person or to protect against international terrorism or clandestine intelligence activities, such things being presumptively relevant to an authorized investigation if the applicant shows in the statement of the facts that they pertain to—
      (i) a foreign power or an agent of a foreign power;
      (ii) the activities of a suspected agent of a foreign power who is the subject of such authorized investigation; or
      (iii) an individual in contact with, or known to, a suspected agent of a foreign power who is the subject of such authorized investigation; and
   (B) an enumeration of the minimization procedures adopted by the Attorney General under subsection (g) that are applicable to the retention and dissemination by the Federal Bureau of Investigation of any tangible things to be made available to the Federal Bureau of Investigation based on the order requested in such application.
(c) *Ex Parte Judicial Order of Approval*
(1) Upon an application made pursuant to this section, if the judge finds that the application meets the requirements of subsections (a) and (b), the judge shall enter an ex parte order as requested, or as modified, approving the release of tangible things. Such order shall direct that minimization procedures adopted pursuant to subsection (g) be followed.

(2) An order under this subsection—

    (A) shall describe the tangible things that are ordered to be produced with sufficient particularity to permit them to be fairly identified;

    (B) shall include the date on which the tangible things must be provided, which shall allow a reasonable period of time within which the tangible things can be assembled and made available;

    (C) shall provide clear and conspicuous notice of the principles and procedures described in subsection (d);

    (D) may only require the production of a tangible thing if such thing can be obtained with a subpoena duces tecum issued by a court of the United States in aid of a grand jury investigation or with any other order issued by a court of the United States directing the production of records or tangible things; and

    (E) shall not disclose that such order is issued for purposes of an investigation described in subsection (a).

(d) *Nondisclosure*

    (1) No person shall disclose to any other person that the Federal Bureau of Investigation has sought or obtained tangible things pursuant to an order under this section, other than to—

        (A) those persons to whom disclosure is necessary to comply with such order;

        (B) an attorney to obtain legal advice or assistance with respect to the production of things in response to the order; or

        (C) other persons as permitted by the Director of the Federal Bureau of Investigation or the designee of the Director.

    (2)

        (A) A person to whom disclosure is made pursuant to paragraph (1) shall be subject to the nondisclosure requirements applicable to a person to whom an order is directed under this section in the same manner as such person.

        (B) Any person who discloses to a person described in subparagraph (A), (B), or (C) of paragraph (1) that the Federal Bureau of Investigation has sought or obtained tangible things pursuant to an order under this section shall notify such person of the nondisclosure requirements of this subsection.

    (C)   At the request of the Director of the Federal Bureau of Investigation or the designee of the Director, any person making or intending to make a disclosure under subparagraph (A) or (C) of paragraph (1) shall identify to the Director or such designee the person to whom such disclosure will be made or to whom such disclosure was made prior to the request.

(e) *Liability for Good Faith Disclosure; Waiver*

A person who, in good faith, produces tangible things under an order pursuant to this section shall not be liable to any other person for such production. Such production shall not be deemed to constitute a waiver of any privilege in any other proceeding or context.

(f) *Judicial Review of FISA Orders*

  (1) In this subsection—

    (A) the term "production order" means an order to produce any tangible thing under this section; and

    (B) the term "nondisclosure order" means an order imposed under subsection (d).

  (2)

    (A)

       (i) A person receiving a production order may challenge the legality of that order by filing a petition with the pool established by section 1803 (e)(1) of this title. Not less than 1 year after the date of the issuance of the production order, the recipient of a production order may challenge the nondisclosure order imposed in connection with such production order by filing a petition to modify or set aside such nondisclosure order, consistent with the requirements of subparagraph (C), with the pool established by section 1803 (e)(1) of this title.

      (ii) The presiding judge shall immediately assign a petition under clause (i) to 1 of the judges serving in the pool established by section 1803 (e)(1) of this title. Not later than 72 hours after the assignment of such petition, the assigned judge shall conduct an initial review of the petition. If the assigned judge determines that the petition is frivolous, the assigned judge shall immediately deny the petition and affirm the production order or nondisclosure order. If the assigned judge determines the petition is not frivolous, the assigned judge shall promptly consider the petition in accordance with the procedures established under section 1803 (e)(2) of this title.

       (iii) The assigned judge shall promptly provide a written statement for the record of the reasons for any determination under this subsection. Upon the request of the Government, any order setting aside a nondisclosure order shall be stayed pending review pursuant to paragraph (3).

  (B) A judge considering a petition to modify or set aside a production order may grant such petition only if the judge finds that such order does not meet the requirements of this section or is otherwise unlawful. If the judge does not modify or set aside the production order, the judge shall immediately affirm such order, and order the recipient to comply therewith.

  (C)

       (i) A judge considering a petition to modify or set aside a nondisclosure order may grant such petition only if the judge finds that there is no reason to believe that disclosure may endanger the national security of the United States, interfere with a criminal, counterterrorism, or counterintelligence investigation, interfere with diplomatic relations, or endanger the life or physical safety of any person.

      (ii) If, upon filing of such a petition, the Attorney General, Deputy Attorney General, an Assistant Attorney General, or the Director of the Federal Bureau of Investigation certifies that disclosure may endanger the national security of the United States or interfere with diplomatic relations, such certification shall be treated as conclusive, unless the judge finds that the certification was made in bad faith.

      (iii) If the judge denies a petition to modify or set aside a nondisclosure order, the recipient of such order shall be precluded for a period of 1 year from filing another such petition with respect to such nondisclosure order.

  (D) Any production or nondisclosure order not explicitly modified or set aside consistent with this subsection shall remain in full effect.

 (3) A petition for review of a decision under paragraph (2) to affirm, modify, or set aside an order by the Government or any person receiving such order shall be made to the court of review established under section 1803 (b) of this title, which shall have jurisdiction to consider such petitions. The court of review shall provide for the record a written statement of the reasons for its decision and, on petition by the Government or any person receiving such order for writ of certiorari, the record shall be transmitted under seal to the Supreme Court of the United States, which shall have jurisdiction to review such decision.

(4) Judicial proceedings under this subsection shall be concluded as expeditiously as possible. The record of proceedings, including petitions filed, orders granted, and statements of reasons for decision, shall be maintained under security measures established by the Chief Justice of the United States, in consultation with the Attorney General and the Director of National Intelligence.

(5) All petitions under this subsection shall be filed under seal. In any proceedings under this subsection, the court shall, upon request of the Government, review ex parte and in camera any Government submission, or portions thereof, which may include classified information.

(g) *Minimization Procedures*

(1) *In General*

Not later than 180 days after March 9, 2006, the Attorney General shall adopt specific minimization procedures governing the retention and dissemination by the Federal Bureau of Investigation of any tangible things, or information therein, received by the Federal Bureau of Investigation in response to an order under this subchapter.

(2) *Defined*

In this section, the term "minimization procedures" means—

(A) specific procedures that are reasonably designed in light of the purpose and technique of an order for the production of tangible things, to minimize the retention, and prohibit the dissemination, of nonpublicly available information concerning unconsenting United States persons consistent with the need of the United States to obtain, produce, and disseminate foreign intelligence information;

(B) procedures that require that nonpublicly available information, which is not foreign intelligence information, as defined in section 1801 (e)(1) of this title, shall not be disseminated in a manner that identifies any United States person, without such person's consent, unless such person's identity is necessary to understand foreign intelligence information or assess its importance; and

(C) notwithstanding subparagraphs (A) and (B), procedures that allow for the retention and dissemination of information that is evidence of a crime which has been, is being, or is about to be committed and that is to be retained or disseminated for law enforcement purposes.

(h) *Use of Information*

Information acquired from tangible things received by the Federal Bureau of Investigation in response to an order under this subchapter concerning any United States person may be used and disclosed by Federal officers and employees without the consent of the United States person only in accordance with the minimization procedures adopted pursuant to subsection (g). No otherwise privileged information acquired from tangible things received by the Federal Bureau of Investigation in accordance with the provisions of this subchapter shall lose its privileged character. No information acquired from tangible things received by the Federal Bureau of Investigation in response to an order under this subchapter may be used or disclosed by Federal officers or employees except for lawful purposes.

Appendix B: Computer Crime and Privacy Laws*

USA Patriot Act

Because the USA Patriot Act is comprised of more than 100 pages and affects sections of different statutes (some of which are included in separate Appendices here), only the Table of Contents for the act will be included as a ready reference to looking up the appropriate provision of the act.

USA Patriot Act

AN ACT

To deter and punish terrorist acts in the United States and around the world, to enhance law enforcement investigatory tools, and for other purposes.

Be it enacted by the Senate and House of Representatives of the United States of America in Congress assembled,

§ 1. Short Title and Table of Contents

(a) *Short Title*—This Act may be cited as the "Uniting and Strengthening America by Providing Appropriate Tools Required to Intercept and Obstruct Terrorism (USA Patriot Act) Act of 2001."

(b) *Table of Contents*—The table of contents for this Act is as follows:
Sec. 1. Short title and table of contents.
Sec. 2. Construction; severability.

Title I: Enhancing Domestic Security against Terrorism

Sec. 101. Counterterrorism fund.
Sec. 102. Sense of Congress condemning discrimination against Arab and Muslim Americans.

---

* *Note*: Statutes and case laws change constantly. Do not rely upon any source of law as being current without conducting legal research or consulting competent legal counsel. Statutes and case law included here are current at the time of research but should be researched for current and up-to-date law before relying upon them. Always seek competent legal counsel on any legal questions.

Sec. 103. Increased funding for the technical support center at the Federal Bureau of Investigation.

Sec. 104. Requests for military assistance to enforce prohibition in certain emergencies.

Sec. 105. Expansion of National Electronic Crime Task Force Initiative.

Sec. 106. Presidential authority.

Title II: Enhanced Surveillance Procedures

Sec. 201. Authority to intercept wire, oral, and electronic communications relating to terrorism.

Sec. 202. Authority to intercept wire, oral, and electronic communications relating to computer fraud and abuse offenses.

Sec. 203. Authority to share criminal investigative information.

Sec. 204. Clarification of intelligence exceptions from limitations on interception and disclosure of wire, oral, and electronic communications.

Sec. 205. Employment of translators by the Federal Bureau of Investigation.

Sec. 206. Roving surveillance authority under the Foreign Intelligence Surveillance Act of 1978.

Sec. 207. Duration of FISA surveillance of non-United States persons who are agents of a foreign power.

Sec. 208. Designation of judges.

Sec. 209. Seizure of voice-mail messages pursuant to warrants.

Sec. 210. Scope of subpoenas for records of electronic communications.

Sec. 211. Clarification of scope.

Sec. 212. Emergency disclosure of electronic communications to protect life and limb.

Sec. 213. Authority for delaying notice of the execution of a warrant.

Sec. 214. Pen register and trap and trace authority under FISA.

Sec. 215. Access to records and other items under the Foreign Intelligence Surveillance Act.

Sec. 216. Modification of authorities relating to use of pen registers and trap and trace devices.

Sec. 217. Interception of computer trespasser communications.

Sec. 218. Foreign intelligence information.

Sec. 219. Single-jurisdiction search warrants for terrorism.

Sec. 220. Nationwide service of search warrants for electronic evidence.

Sec. 221. Trade sanctions.

Sec. 222. Assistance to law enforcement agencies.

Sec. 223. Civil liability for certain unauthorized disclosures.

Sec. 224. Sunset.

Sec. 225. Immunity for compliance with FISA wiretap.

Title III: International Money Laundering Abatement and Anti-Terrorist Financing Act of 2001

Subtitle A: International Counter Money Laundering and Related Measures

Subtitle B: Bank Secrecy Act Amendments and Related Improvements

Sec. 354. Anti-money laundering strategy.

Sec. 355. Authorization to include suspicions of illegal activity in written employment references.

Sec. 356. Reporting of suspicious activities by securities brokers and dealers; investment company study.

Sec. 357. Special report on administration of bank secrecy provisions.

Sec. 358. Bank secrecy provisions and activities of United States intelligence agencies to fight international terrorism.

Sec. 359. Reporting of suspicious activities by underground banking systems.

Sec. 360. Use of authority of United States Executive Directors.

Sec. 361. Financial crimes enforcement network.

Sec. 362. Establishment of highly secure network.

Sec. 363. Increase in civil and criminal penalties for money laundering.

Sec. 364. Uniform protection authority for Federal Reserve facilities.

Sec. 365. Reports relating to coins and currency received in nonfinancial trade or business.

Sec. 366. Efficient use of currency transaction report system.

Subtitle C: Currency Crimes and Protection

Sec. 371. Bulk cash smuggling into or out of the United States.

Sec. 372. Forfeiture in currency reporting cases.

Sec. 373. Illegal money transmitting businesses.

Sec. 374. Counterfeiting domestic currency and obligations.

Sec. 375. Counterfeiting foreign currency and obligations.

Sec. 376. Laundering the proceeds of terrorism.

Sec. 377. Extraterritorial jurisdiction.

Title IV: Protecting the Border

Subtitle A: Protecting the Northern Border

Sec. 401. Ensuring adequate personnel on the northern border.

Sec. 402. Northern border personnel.

Sec. 403. Access by the Department of State and the INS to certain identifying information in the criminal history records of visa applicants and applicants for admission to the United States.

Sec. 404. Limited authority to pay overtime.

Sec. 405. Report on the integrated automated fingerprint identification system for ports of entry and overseas consular posts.

Subtitle B: Enhanced Immigration Provisions

Sec. 411. Definitions relating to terrorism.

Sec. 412. Mandatory detention of suspected terrorists; habeas corpus; judicial review.

Subtitle B: Amendments to the Victims of Crime Act of 1984

Sec. 621. Crime victims fund.
Sec. 622. Crime victim compensation.
Sec. 623. Crime victim assistance.
Sec. 624. Victims of terrorism.

Title VII: Increased Information Sharing for Critical Infrastructure Protection

Sec. 711. Expansion of regional information sharing system to facilitate Federal-State-local law enforcement response related to terrorist attacks.

Title VIII: Strengthening the Criminal Laws against Terrorism

Sec. 801. Terrorist attacks and other acts of violence against mass transportation systems.
Sec. 802. Definition of domestic terrorism.
Sec. 803. Prohibition against harboring terrorists.
Sec. 804. Jurisdiction over crimes committed at U.S. facilities abroad.
Sec. 805. Material support for terrorism.
Sec. 806. Assets of terrorist organizations.
Sec. 807. Technical clarification relating to provision of material support to terrorism.
Sec. 808. Definition of Federal crime of terrorism.
Sec. 809. No statute of limitation for certain terrorism offenses.
Sec. 810. Alternate maximum penalties for terrorism offenses.
Sec. 811. Penalties for terrorist conspiracies.
Sec. 812. Post-release supervision of terrorists.
Sec. 813. Inclusion of acts of terrorism as racketeering activity.
Sec. 814. Deterrence and prevention of cyberterrorism.
Sec. 815. Additional defense to civil actions relating to preserving records in response to Government requests.
Sec. 816. Development and support of cybersecurity forensic capabilities.
Sec. 817. Expansion of the biological weapons statute.

Title IX: Improved Intelligence

Sec. 901. Responsibilities of Director of Central Intelligence regarding foreign intelligence collected under Foreign Intelligence Surveillance Act of 1978.
Sec. 902. Inclusion of international terrorist activities within scope of foreign intelligence under National Security Act of 1947.

Sec. 903. Sense of Congress on the establishment and maintenance of intelligence relationships to acquire information on terrorists and terrorist organizations.

Sec. 904. Temporary authority to defer submittal to Congress of reports on intelligence and intelligence-related matters.

Sec. 905. Disclosure to Director of Central Intelligence of foreign intelligence-related information with respect to criminal investigations.

Sec. 906. Foreign terrorist asset tracking center.

Sec. 907. National Virtual Translation Center.

Sec. 908. Training of government officials regarding identification and use of foreign intelligence.

Title X: Miscellaneous

Sec. 1001. Review of the department of justice.

Sec. 1002. Sense of congress.

Sec. 1003. Definition of "electronic surveillance."

Sec. 1004. Venue in money laundering cases.

Sec. 1005. First responders assistance act.

Sec. 1006. Inadmissibility of aliens engaged in money laundering.

Sec. 1007. Authorization of funds for DEA police training in south and central Asia.

Sec. 1008. Feasibility study on use of biometric identifier scanning system with access to the FBI integrated automated fingerprint identification system at overseas consular posts and points of entry to the United States.

Sec. 1009. Study of access.

Sec. 1010. Temporary authority to contract with local and State governments for performance of security functions at United States military installations.

Sec. 1011. Crimes against charitable Americans.

Sec. 1012. Limitation on issuance of hazmat licenses.

Sec. 1013. Expressing the sense of the senate concerning the provision of funding for bioterrorism preparedness and response.

Sec. 1014. Grant program for State and local domestic preparedness support.

Sec. 1015. Expansion and reauthorization of the crime identification technology act for antiterrorism grants to States and localities.

Sec. 1016. Critical infrastructures protection.

Computer Fraud and Abuse Act (18 U.S.C. 1030)

§ 1030. Fraud and Related Activity in Connection with Computers

(a) Whoever

   (1) having knowingly accessed a computer without authorization or exceeding authorized access, and by means of such conduct having obtained information that has been determined by the United States Government pursuant to an Executive order or statute to require protection against unauthorized disclosure for reasons of national defense or foreign relations, or any restricted data, as defined in paragraph y. of section 11 of the Atomic Energy Act of 1954, with reason to believe that such information so obtained could be used to the injury of the United States, or to the advantage of any foreign nation willfully communicates, delivers, transmits, or causes to be communicated, delivered, or transmitted, or attempts to communicate, deliver, transmit or cause to be communicated, delivered, or transmitted the same to any person not entitled to receive it, or willfully retains the same and fails to deliver it to the officer or employee of the United States entitled to receive it;

   (2) intentionally accesses a computer without authorization or exceeds authorized access, and thereby obtains

      (A) information contained in a financial record of a financial institution, or of a card issuer as defined in section 1602 (n) of title 15, or contained in a file of a consumer reporting agency on a consumer, as such terms are defined in the Fair Credit Reporting Act (15 U.S.C. 1681 et seq.);

      (B) information from any department or agency of the United States; or

      (C) information from any protected computer;

   (3) intentionally, without authorization to access any nonpublic computer of a department or agency of the United States, accesses such a computer of that department or agency that is exclusively for the use of the Government of the United States or, in the case of a computer not exclusively for such use, is used by or for the Government of the United States and such conduct affects that use by or for the Government of the United States;

   (4) knowingly and with intent to defraud, accesses a protected computer without authorization, or exceeds authorized access, and by means of such conduct furthers the intended fraud and obtains anything of value, unless the object of the fraud and the

thing obtained consists only of the use of the computer and the value of such use is not more than $5000 in any 1-year period;

(5)

(A) knowingly causes the transmission of a program, information, code, or command, and as a result of such conduct, intentionally causes damage without authorization, to a protected computer;

(B) intentionally accesses a protected computer without authorization, and as a result of such conduct, recklessly causes damage; or

(C) intentionally accesses a protected computer without authorization, and as a result of such conduct, causes damage and loss.

(6) knowingly and with intent to defraud traffics (as defined in section 1029) in any password or similar information through which a computer may be accessed without authorization, if—

(A) such trafficking affects interstate or foreign commerce; or

(B) such computer is used by or for the Government of the United States;

(7) with intent to extort from any person any money or other thing of value, transmits in interstate or foreign commerce any communication containing any—

(A) threat to cause damage to a protected computer;

(B) threat to obtain information from a protected computer without authorization or in excess of authorization or to impair the confidentiality of information obtained from a protected computer without authorization or by exceeding authorized access; or

(C) demand or request for money or other thing of value in relation to damage to a protected computer, where such damage was caused to facilitate the extortion; shall be punished as provided in subsection (c) of this section.

(b) Whoever conspires to commit or attempts to commit an offense under subsection (a) of this section shall be punished as provided in subsection (c) of this section.

(c) The punishment for an offense under subsection (a) or (b) of this section is—

(1)

(A) a fine under this title or imprisonment for not more than ten years, or both, in the case of an offense under subsection (a) (1) of this section which does not occur after a conviction for another offense under this section, or an attempt to commit an offense punishable under this subparagraph; and

(B) a fine under this title or imprisonment for not more than twenty years, or both, in the case of an offense under subsection (a) (1) of this section which occurs after a conviction for another offense under this section, or an attempt to commit an offense punishable under this subparagraph;

(2)

(A) except as provided in subparagraph (B), a fine under this title or imprisonment for not more than one year, or both, in the case of an offense under subsection (a)(2), (a)(3), or (a)(6) of this section which does not occur after a conviction for another offense under this section, or an attempt to commit an offense punishable under this subparagraph;

(B) a fine under this title or imprisonment for not more than 5 years, or both, in the case of an offense under subsection (a)(2), or an attempt to commit an offense punishable under this subparagraph, if—

 (i) the offense was committed for purposes of commercial advantage or private financial gain;

 (ii) the offense was committed in furtherance of any criminal or tortious act in violation of the Constitution or laws of the United States or of any State; or

 (iii) the value of the information obtained exceeds $5,000; and

(C) a fine under this title or imprisonment for not more than ten years, or both, in the case of an offense under subsection (a)(2), (a)(3) or (a)(6) of this section which occurs after a conviction for another offense under this section, or an attempt to commit an offense punishable under this subparagraph;

(3)

(A) a fine under this title or imprisonment for not more than five years, or both, in the case of an offense under subsection (a)(4) or (a)(7) of this section which does not occur after a conviction for another offense under this section, or an attempt to commit an offense punishable under this subparagraph; and

(B) a fine under this title or imprisonment for not more than ten years, or both, in the case of an offense under subsection (a)(4), or (a)(7) of this section which occurs after a conviction for another offense under this section, or an attempt to commit an offense punishable under this subparagraph;

(4)

(A) except as provided in subparagraphs (E) and (F), a fine under this title, imprisonment for not more than 5 years, or both, in the case of—

(i) an offense under subsection (a)(5)(B), which does not occur after a conviction for another offense under this section, if the offense caused (or, in the case of an attempted offense, would, if completed, have caused)—

(I) loss to 1 or more persons during any 1-year period (and, for purposes of an investigation, prosecution, or other proceeding brought by the United States only, loss resulting from a related course of conduct affecting 1 or more other protected computers) aggregating at least $5,000 in value;

(II) the modification or impairment, or potential modification or impairment, of the medical examination, diagnosis, treatment, or care of 1 or more individuals;

(III) physical injury to any person;

(IV) a threat to public health or safety;

(V) damage affecting a computer used by or for an entity of the United States Government in furtherance of the administration of justice, national defense, or national security; or

(VI) damage affecting 10 or more protected computers during any 1-year period; or

(ii) an attempt to commit an offense punishable under this subparagraph;

(B) except as provided in subparagraphs (E) and (F), a fine under this title, imprisonment for not more than 10 years, or both, in the case of—

(i) an offense under subsection (a)(5)(A), which does not occur after a conviction for another offense under this section, if the offense caused (or, in the case of an attempted offense, would, if completed, have caused) a harm provided in subclauses (I) through (VI) of subparagraph (A)(i); or

(ii) an attempt to commit an offense punishable under this subparagraph;

(C)   except as provided in subparagraphs (E) and (F), a fine under this title, imprisonment for not more than 20 years, or both, in the case of—

   (i)   an offense or an attempt to commit an offense under subparagraphs (A) or (B) of subsection (a)(5) that occurs after a conviction for another offense under this section; or

   (ii) an attempt to commit an offense punishable under this subparagraph;

(D)   a fine under this title, imprisonment for not more than 10 years, or both, in the case of—

   (i)   an offense or an attempt to commit an offense under subsection (a)(5)(C) that occurs after a conviction for another offense under this section; or

   (ii) an attempt to commit an offense punishable under this subparagraph;

(E)   if the offender attempts to cause or knowingly or recklessly causes serious bodily injury from conduct in violation of subsection (a)(5)(A), a fine under this title, imprisonment for not more than 20 years, or both;

(F)   if the offender attempts to cause or knowingly or recklessly causes death from conduct in violation of subsection (a)(5) (A), a fine under this title, imprisonment for any term of years or for life, or both; or

(G)   a fine under this title, imprisonment for not more than 1 year, or both, for—

   (i)   any other offense under subsection (a)(5); or

   (ii) an attempt to commit an offense punishable under this subparagraph.

(d)

(1)   The United States Secret Service shall, in addition to any other agency having such authority, have the authority to investigate offenses under this section.

(2)   The Federal Bureau of Investigation shall have primary authority to investigate offenses under subsection (a)(1) for any cases involving espionage, foreign counterintelligence, information protected against unauthorized disclosure for reasons of national defense or foreign relations, or Restricted Data (as that term is defined in section 11y of the Atomic Energy Act of 1954 (42 U.S.C. 2014 (y)), except for offenses affecting the duties of the U.S. Secret Service pursuant to section 3056 (a) of this title.

(3)   Such authority shall be exercised in accordance with an agreement which shall be entered into by the Secretary of the Treasury and the Attorney General.

(e) As used in this section—

(1) the term "computer" means an electronic, magnetic, optical, electrochemical, or other high speed data processing device performing logical, arithmetic, or storage functions, and includes any data storage facility or communications facility directly related to or operating in conjunction with such device, but such term does not include an automated typewriter or typesetter, a portable hand held calculator, or other similar device;

(2) the term "protected computer" means a computer

(A) exclusively for the use of a financial institution or the United States Government, or, in the case of a computer not exclusively for such use, used by or for a financial institution or the United States Government and the conduct constituting the offense affects that use by or for the financial institution or the Government; or

(B) which is used in or affecting interstate or foreign commerce or communication, including a computer located outside the United States that is used in a manner that affects interstate or foreign commerce or communication of the United States;

(3) the term "State" includes the District of Columbia, the Commonwealth of Puerto Rico, and any other commonwealth, possession or territory of the United States;

(4) the term "financial institution" means—

(A) an institution, with deposits insured by the Federal Deposit Insurance Corporation;

(B) the Federal Reserve or a member of the Federal Reserve including any Federal Reserve Bank;

(C) a credit union with accounts insured by the National Credit Union Administration;

(D) a member of the Federal home loan bank system and any home loan bank;

(E) any institution of the Farm Credit System under the Farm Credit Act of 1971;

(F) a broker-dealer registered with the Securities and Exchange Commission pursuant to section 15 of the Securities Exchange Act of 1934;

(G) the Securities Investor Protection Corporation;

(H) a branch or agency of a foreign bank (as such terms are defined in paragraphs (1) and (3) of section 1(b) of the International Banking Act of 1978); and

(I) an organization operating under section 25 or section 25(a) of the Federal Reserve Act;

(5) the term "financial record" means information derived from any record held by a financial institution pertaining to a customer's relationship with the financial institution;

(6) the term "exceeds authorized access" means to access a computer with authorization and to use such access to obtain or alter information in the computer that the accesser is not entitled so to obtain or alter;

(7) the term "department of the United States" means the legislative or judicial branch of the Government or one of the executive departments enumerated in section 101 of title 5;

(8) the term "damage" means any impairment to the integrity or availability of data, a program, a system, or information;

(9) the term "government entity" includes the Government of the United States, any State or political subdivision of the United States, any foreign country, and any state, province, municipality, or other political subdivision of a foreign country;

(10) the term "conviction" shall include a conviction under the law of any State for a crime punishable by imprisonment for more than 1 year, an element of which is unauthorized access, or exceeding authorized access, to a computer;

(11) the term "loss" means any reasonable cost to any victim, including the cost of responding to an offense, conducting a damage assessment, and restoring the data, program, system, or information to its condition prior to the offense, and any revenue lost, cost incurred, or other consequential damages incurred because of interruption of service; and

(12) the term "person" means any individual, firm, corporation, educational institution, financial institution, governmental entity, or legal or other entity.

(f) This section does not prohibit any lawfully authorized investigative, protective, or intelligence activity of a law enforcement agency of the United States, a State, or a political subdivision of a State, or of an intelligence agency of the United States.

(g) Any person who suffers damage or loss by reason of a violation of this section may maintain a civil action against the violator to obtain compensatory damages and injunctive relief or other equitable relief. A civil action for a violation of this section may be brought only if the conduct involves 1 of the factors set forth in subclauses (I), (II), (III), (IV), or (V) of subsection (c)(4)(A)(i). Damages for a violation involving only conduct described in subsection (c)(4)(A)(i)(I) are limited to economic damages. No action may be brought under this subsection unless such action is begun within 2 years of the date of the act complained of or the date of the discovery of the damage. No action may be brought under this subsection for the negligent design or manufacture of computer hardware, computer software, or firmware.

(h) The Attorney General and the Secretary of the Treasury shall report to the Congress annually, during the first 3 years following the date of the enactment of this subsection, concerning investigations and prosecutions under subsection (a)(5).

(i)

  (1) The court, in imposing sentence on any person convicted of a violation of this section, or convicted of conspiracy to violate this section, shall order, in addition to any other sentence imposed and irrespective of any provision of State law, that such person forfeit to the United States

  (A) such person's interest in any personal property that was used or intended to be used to commit or to facilitate the commission of such violation; and

  (B) any property, real or personal, constituting or derived from, any proceeds that such person obtained, directly or indirectly, as a result of such violation.

  (2) The criminal forfeiture of property under this subsection, any seizure and disposition thereof, and any judicial proceeding in relation thereto, shall be governed by the provisions of section 413 of the Comprehensive Drug Abuse Prevention and Control Act of 1970 (21 U.S.C. 853), except subsection (d) of that section.

(j) For purposes of subsection (i), the following shall be subject to forfeiture to the United States and no property right shall exist in them:

  (1) Any personal property used or intended to be used to commit or to facilitate the commission of any violation of this section, or a conspiracy to violate this section.

  (2) Any property, real or personal, which constitutes or is derived from proceeds traceable to any violation of this section, or a conspiracy to violate this section.

Children's Online Privacy Act (15 U.S.C. §§ 6501–6506)

Chapter 91: Children's Online Privacy Protection

- § 6501. Definitions
- § 6502. Regulation of Unfair and Deceptive Acts and Practices in Connection with Collection and Use of Personal Information from and about Children on the Internet

- § 6503. Safe Harbors
- § 6504. Actions by States
- § 6505. Administration and Applicability
- § 6506. Review

§ 6501. *Definitions*

In this chapter:

(1) *Child*
   The term "child" means an individual under the age of 13.
(2) *Operator*
   The term "operator"—
   (A) means any person who operates a website located on the Internet or an online service and who collects or maintains personal information from or about the users of or visitors to such website or online service, or on whose behalf such information is collected or maintained, where such website or online service is operated for commercial purposes, including any person offering products or services for sale through that website or online service, involving commerce—
      (i)   among the several States or with 1 or more foreign nations;
      (ii) in any territory of the United States or in the District of Columbia, or between any such territory and—
         (I) another such territory; or
         (II) any State or foreign nation; or
      (iii) between the District of Columbia and any State, territory, or foreign nation; but
   (B) does not include any nonprofit entity that would otherwise be exempt from coverage under section 45 of this title.
(3) *Commission*
   The term "Commission" means the Federal Trade Commission.
(4) *Disclosure*
   The term "disclosure" means, with respect to personal information—
   (A) the release of personal information collected from a child in identifiable form by an operator for any purpose, except where such information is provided to a person other than the operator who provides support for the internal operations of the website and does not disclose or use that information for any other purpose; and
   (B) making personal information collected from a child by a website or online service directed to children or with actual knowledge that such information was collected from a child, publicly

available in identifiable form, by any means including by a
public posting, through the Internet, or through—
  (i)   a home page of a website;
  (ii) a pen pal service;
  (iii) an electronic mail service;
  (iv) a message board; or
  (v)   a chat room.
(5) *Federal agency*
   The term "Federal agency" means an agency, as that term is defined
   in section 551 (1) of title 5.
(6) *Internet*
   The term "Internet" means collectively the myriad of computer and
   telecommunications facilities, including equipment and operating software, which comprise the interconnected world-wide network of networks that employ the Transmission Control Protocol/
   Internet Protocol, or any predecessor or successor protocols to such
   protocol, to communicate information of all kinds by wire or radio.
(7) *Parent*
   The term "parent" includes a legal guardian.
(8) *Personal information*
   The term "personal information" means individually identifiable
   information about an individual collected online, including—
   (A) a first and last name;
   (B) a home or other physical address including street name and
       name of a city or town;
   (C) an e-mail address;
   (D) a telephone number;
   (E) a Social Security number;
   (F) any other identifier that the Commission determines per-
       mits the physical or online contacting of a specific indivi-
       dual; or
   (G) information concerning the child or the parents of that child
       that the website collects online from the child and combines
       with an identifier described in this paragraph.
(9) *Verifiable parental consent*
   The term "verifiable parental consent" means any reasonable effort
   (taking into consideration available technology), including a request
   for authorization for future collection, use, and disclosure described
   in the notice, to ensure that a parent of a child receives notice of the
   operator's personal information collection, use, and disclosure practices, and authorizes the collection, use, and disclosure, as applicable,
   of personal information and the subsequent use of that information
   before that information is collected from that child.

(10) *Website or online service directed to children*
    (A) *In general*

        The term "website or online service directed to children" means—

        (i)   a commercial website or online service that is targeted to children; or

        (ii) that portion of a commercial website or online service that is targeted to children.

    (B) *Limitation*

        A commercial website or online service, or a portion of a commercial website or online service, shall not be deemed directed to children solely for referring or linking to a commercial website or online service directed to children by using information location tools, including a directory, index, reference, pointer, or hypertext link.

(11) *Person*

The term "person" means any individual, partnership, corporation, trust, estate, cooperative, association, or other entity.

(12) *Online contact information*

The term "online contact information" means an e-mail address or another substantially similar identifier that permits direct contact with a person online.

§ 6502. Regulation of Unfair and Deceptive Acts and Practices in Connection with Collection and Use of Personal Information from and about Children on the Internet

  (a) *Acts prohibited*

    (1) *In general*

        It is unlawful for an operator of a website or online service directed to children, or any operator that has actual knowledge that it is collecting personal information from a child, to collect personal information from a child in a manner that violates the regulations prescribed under subsection (b) of this section.

    (2) *Disclosure to parent protected*

        Notwithstanding paragraph (1), neither an operator of such a website or online service nor the operator's agent shall be held to be liable under any Federal or State law for any disclosure made in good faith and following reasonable procedures in responding to a request for disclosure of personal information under subsection (b)(1)(B)(iii) of this section to the parent of a child.

(b) *Regulations*

  (1) *In general*

      Not later than 1 year after October 21, 1998, the Commission shall promulgate under section 553 of title 5 regulations that—

      (A) require the operator of any website or online service directed to children that collects personal information from children or the operator of a website or online service that has actual knowledge that it is collecting personal information from a child—

          (i) to provide notice on the website of what information is collected from children by the operator, how the operator uses such information, and the operator's disclosure practices for such information; and

          (ii) to obtain verifiable parental consent for the collection, use, or disclosure of personal information from children;

      (B) require the operator to provide, upon request of a parent under this subparagraph whose child has provided personal information to that website or online service, upon proper identification of that parent, to such parent—

          (i) a description of the specific types of personal information collected from the child by that operator;

          (ii) the opportunity at any time to refuse to permit the operator's further use or maintenance in retrievable form, or future online collection, of personal information from that child; and

          (iii) notwithstanding any other provision of law, a means that is reasonable under the circumstances for the parent to obtain any personal information collected from that child;

      (C) prohibit conditioning a child's participation in a game, the offering of a prize, or another activity on the child disclosing more personal information than is reasonably necessary to participate in such activity; and

      (D) require the operator of such a website or online service to establish and maintain reasonable procedures to protect the confidentiality, security, and integrity of personal information collected from children.

  (2) *When consent not required*

      The regulations shall provide that verifiable parental consent under paragraph (1)(A)(ii) is not required in the case of—

      (A) online contact information collected from a child that is used only to respond directly on a one-time basis to a specific request from the child and is not used to recontact the child and is not maintained in retrievable form by the operator;

(B) a request for the name or online contact information of a parent or child that is used for the sole purpose of obtaining parental consent or providing notice under this section and where such information is not maintained in retrievable form by the operator if parental consent is not obtained after a reasonable time;

(C) online contact information collected from a child that is used only to respond more than once directly to a specific request from the child and is not used to recontact the child beyond the scope of that request—

    (1) if, before any additional response after the initial response to the child, the operator uses reasonable efforts to provide a parent notice of the online contact information collected from the child, the purposes for which it is to be used, and an opportunity for the parent to request that the operator make no further use of the information and that it not be maintained in retrievable form; or

    (2) without notice to the parent in such circumstances as the Commission may determine are appropriate, taking into consideration the benefits to the child of access to information and services, and risks to the security and privacy of the child, in regulations promulgated under this subsection;

(D) the name of the child and online contact information (to the extent reasonably necessary to protect the safety of a child participant on the site)—

    (1) used only for the purpose of protecting such safety;

    (2) not used to recontact the child or for any other purpose; and

    (3) not disclosed on the site, if the operator uses reasonable efforts to provide a parent notice of the name and online contact information collected from the child, the purposes for which it is to be used, and an opportunity for the parent to request that the operator make no further use of the information and that it not be maintained in retrievable form; or

(E) the collection, use, or dissemination of such information by the operator of such a website or online service necessary—

    (1) to protect the security or integrity of its website;

    (2) to take precautions against liability;

      (iii) to respond to judicial process; or

      (iv) to the extent permitted under other provisions of law, to provide information to law enforcement agencies or for an investigation on a matter related to public safety.

(3) *Termination of service*

The regulations shall permit the operator of a website or an online service to terminate service provided to a child whose parent has refused, under the regulations prescribed under paragraph (1) (B)(ii), to permit the operator's further use or maintenance in retrievable form, or future online collection, of personal information from that child.

(c) *Enforcement*

Subject to sections 6503 and 6505 of this title, a violation of a regulation prescribed under subsection (a) of this section shall be treated as a violation of a rule defining an unfair or deceptive act or practice prescribed under section 57a (a)(1)(B) of this title.

(d) *Inconsistent State law*

No State or local government may impose any liability for commercial activities or actions by operators in interstate or foreign commerce in connection with an activity or action described in this chapter that is inconsistent with the treatment of those activities or actions under this section.

§ 6503. Safe Harbors

(a) *Guidelines*

An operator may satisfy the requirements of regulations issued under section 6502 (b) of this title by following a set of self-regulatory guidelines, issued by representatives of the marketing or online industries, or by other persons, approved under subsection (b) of this section.

(b) *Incentives*

(1) *Self-regulatory incentives*

In prescribing regulations under section 6502 of this title, the Commission shall provide incentives for self-regulation by operators to implement the protections afforded children under the regulatory requirements described in subsection (b) of that section.

(2) *Deemed compliance*

Such incentives shall include provisions for ensuring that a person will be deemed to be in compliance with the requirements of the regulations under section 6502 of this title if that person complies with guidelines that, after notice and comment, are approved by the Commission upon making a determination that the guidelines meet the requirements of the regulations issued under section 6502 of this title.

(3) *Expedited response to requests*
The Commission shall act upon requests for safe harbor treatment within 180 days of the filing of the request, and shall set forth in writing its conclusions with regard to such requests.

(c) *Appeals*
Final action by the Commission on a request for approval of guidelines, or the failure to act within 180 days on a request for approval of guidelines, submitted under subsection (b) of this section may be appealed to a district court of the United States of appropriate jurisdiction as provided for in section 706 of title 5.

§ 6504. Actions by States

(a) *In general*
   (1) *Civil actions*
   In any case in which the attorney general of a State has reason to believe that an interest of the residents of that State has been or is threatened or adversely affected by the engagement of any person in a practice that violates any regulation of the Commission prescribed under section 6502 (b) of this title, the State, as parens patriae, may bring a civil action on behalf of the residents of the State in a district court of the United States of appropriate jurisdiction to—
   (A) enjoin that practice;
   (B) enforce compliance with the regulation;
   (C) obtain damage, restitution, or other compensation on behalf of residents of the State; or
   (D) obtain such other relief as the court may consider to be appropriate.
   (2) *Notice*
   (A) *In general*
      Before filing an action under paragraph (1), the attorney general of the State involved shall provide to the Commission—
      (i) written notice of that action; and
      (ii) a copy of the complaint for that action.
   (B) *Exemption*
      (i) *In general:* Subparagraph (A) shall not apply with respect to the filing of an action by an attorney general of a State under this subsection, if the attorney general determines that it is not feasible to provide the notice described in that subparagraph before the filing of the action.

      (ii) *Notification:* In an action described in clause (i), the attorney general of a State shall provide notice and a copy of the complaint to the Commission at the same time as the attorney general files the action.

(b) *Intervention*

  (1) *In general*

On receiving notice under subsection (a)(2) of this section, the Commission shall have the right to intervene in the action that is the subject of the notice.

  (2) *Effect of intervention*

If the Commission intervenes in an action under subsection (a) of this section, it shall have the right—

    (A) to be heard with respect to any matter that arises in that action; and

    (B) to *file* a petition for appeal.

  (3) *Amicus curiae*

Upon application to the court, a person whose self-regulatory guidelines have been approved by the Commission and are relied upon as a defense by any defendant to a proceeding under this section may file amicus curiae in that proceeding.

(c) *Construction*

For purposes of bringing any civil action under subsection (a) of this section, nothing in this chapter shall be construed to prevent an attorney general of a State from exercising the powers conferred on the attorney general by the laws of that State to—

  (1) conduct investigations;

  (2) administer oaths or affirmations; or

  (3) compel the attendance of witnesses or the production of documentary and other evidence.

(d) *Actions by Commission*

In any case in which an action is instituted by or on behalf of the Commission for violation of any regulation prescribed under section 6502 of this title, no State may, during the pendency of that action, institute an action under subsection (a) of this section against any defendant named in the complaint in that action for violation of that regulation.

(e) *Venue; service of process*

  (1) *Venue*

Any action brought under subsection (a) of this section may be brought in the district court of the United States that meets applicable requirements relating to venue under section 1391 of title 28.

(2) *Service of process*
In an action brought under subsection (a) of this section, process
may be served in any district in which the defendant—
(A) is an inhabitant; or
(B) may be found.

§ 6505. *Administration and Applicability*

(a) *In general*
Except as otherwise provided, this chapter shall be enforced by the
Commission under the Federal Trade Commission Act (15 U.S.C. 41
et seq.).

(b) *Provisions*
Compliance with the requirements imposed under this chapter shall
be enforced under—
(1) section 8 of the Federal Deposit Insurance Act (12 U.S.C. 1818),
in the case of—
(A) national banks, and Federal branches and Federal agencies of
foreign banks, by the Office of the Comptroller of the Currency;
(B) member banks of the Federal Reserve System (other than
national banks), branches and agencies of foreign banks (other
than Federal branches, Federal agencies, and insured State
branches of foreign banks), commercial lending companies
owned or controlled by foreign banks, and organizations operating under section 25 or 25(a) of the Federal Reserve Act (12
U.S.C. 601 et seq. and 611 et seq.), by the Board; and
(C) banks insured by the Federal Deposit Insurance Corporation
(other than members of the Federal Reserve System) and
insured State branches of foreign banks, by the Board of
Directors of the Federal Deposit Insurance Corporation;
(2) section 8 of the Federal Deposit Insurance Act (12 U.S.C. 1818),
by the Director of the Office of Thrift Supervision, in the case of
a savings association the deposits of which are insured by the
Federal Deposit Insurance Corporation;
(3) the Federal Credit Union Act (12 U.S.C. 1751 et seq.) by the
National Credit Union Administration Board with respect to any
Federal credit union;
(4) part A of subtitle VII of title 49 by the Secretary of Transportation
with respect to any air carrier or foreign air carrier subject to that part;
(5) the Packers and Stockyards Act, 1921 (7 U.S.C. 181 et. seq.)
(except as provided in section 406 of that Act (7 U.S.C. 226, 227)),
by the Secretary of Agriculture with respect to any activities subject to that Act; and

(6) the Farm Credit Act of 1971 (12 U.S.C. 2001 et seq.) by the Farm Credit Administration with respect to any Federal land bank, Federal land bank association, Federal intermediate credit bank, or production credit association.

(c) *Exercise of certain powers*

For the purpose of the exercise by any agency referred to in subsection (a) of this section of its powers under any Act referred to in that subsection, a violation of any requirement imposed under this chapter shall be deemed to be a violation of a requirement imposed under that Act. In addition to its powers under any provision of law specifically referred to in subsection (a) of this section, each of the agencies referred to in that subsection may exercise, for the purpose of enforcing compliance with any requirement imposed under this chapter, any other authority conferred on it by law.

(d) *Actions by Commission*

The Commission shall prevent any person from violating a rule of the Commission under section 6502 of this title in the same manner, by the same means, and with the same jurisdiction, powers, and duties as though all applicable terms and provisions of the Federal Trade Commission Act (15 U.S.C. 41 et seq.) were incorporated into and made a part of this chapter. Any entity that violates such rule shall be subject to the penalties and entitled to the privileges and immunities provided in the Federal Trade Commission Act in the same manner, by the same means, and with the same jurisdiction, power, and duties as though all applicable terms and provisions of the Federal Trade Commission Act were incorporated into and made a part of this chapter.

(e) *Effect on other laws*

Nothing contained in this chapter shall be construed to limit the authority of the Commission under any other provisions of law.

§ 6506. Review

Not later than 5 years after the effective date of the regulations initially issued under section 6502 of this title, the Commission shall

(1) review the implementation of this chapter, including the effect of the implementation of this chapter on practices relating to the collection and disclosure of information relating to children, children's ability to obtain access to information of their choice online, and on the availability of websites directed to children; and

(2) prepare and submit to Congress a report on the results of the review under paragraph (1).

Appendix C: Government Data Privacy Laws*

E-Government Act (44 U.S.C. § 101)

Chapter 1: Homeland Security Organization

- § 101. Definitions
- § 102. Construction; Severability
- § 103. Use of Appropriated Funds

  Subchapter I: Department of Homeland Security (§§ 111–115)

  Subchapter II: Information Analysis and Infrastructure Protection (§§ 121–165)

  Subchapter III: Science and Technology in Support of Homeland Security (§§ 181–195c)

  Subchapter IV: Directorate of Border and Transportation Security (§§ 201–298)

  Subchapter V: National Emergency Management (§§ 311–321n)

  Subchapter VI: Treatment of Charitable Trusts for Members of the Armed Forces of the United States and Other Governmental Organizations (§ 331)

  Subchapter VII: Management (§§ 341–347)

  Subchapter VIII: Coordination with Non-Federal Entities; Inspector General; United States Secret Service; Coast Guard; General Provisions (§§ 361–488i)

  Subchapter IX: National Homeland Security Council (§§ 491–496)

  Subchapter X: Construction (§§ 511–513)

  Subchapter XI: Department of Justice Divisions (§§ 521–533)

  Subchapter XII: Transition (§§ 541–557)

---

* *Note*: Statutes and case laws change constantly. Do not rely upon any source of law as being current without conducting legal research or consulting competent legal counsel. Statutes and case law included here are current at the time of research but should be researched for current and up-to-date law before relying upon them. Always seek competent legal counsel on any legal questions.

§ 101. Definitions

In this chapter, the following definitions apply:

(1) Each of the terms "American homeland" and "homeland" means the United States.

(2) The term "appropriate congressional committee" means any committee of the House of Representatives or the Senate having legislative or oversight jurisdiction under the Rules of the House of Representatives or the Senate, respectively, over the matter concerned.

(3) The term "assets" includes contracts, facilities, property, records, unobligated or unexpended balances of appropriations, and other funds or resources (other than personnel).

(4) The term "critical infrastructure" has the meaning given that term in section 5195c (e) of title 42.

(5) The term "Department" means the Department of Homeland Security.

(6) The term "emergency response providers" includes Federal, State, and local governmental and nongovernmental emergency public safety, fire, law enforcement, emergency response, emergency medical (including hospital emergency facilities), and related personnel, agencies, and authorities.

(7) The term "executive agency" means an executive agency and a military department, as defined, respectively, in sections 105 and 102 of title 5.

(8) The term "functions" includes authorities, powers, rights, privileges, immunities, programs, projects, activities, duties, and responsibilities.

(9) The term "intelligence component of the Department" means any element or entity of the Department that collects, gathers, processes, analyzes, produces, or disseminates intelligence information within the scope of the information sharing environment, including homeland security information, terrorism information, and weapons of mass destruction information, or national intelligence, as defined under section 401a (5) of title 50, except—

(A) the United States Secret Service; and

(B) the Coast Guard, when operating under the direct authority of the Secretary of Defense or Secretary of the Navy pursuant to section 3 of title 14, except that nothing in this paragraph shall affect or diminish the authority and responsibilities of the Commandant of the Coast Guard to command or control the Coast Guard as an armed force or the authority of the Director of National Intelligence with respect to the Coast Guard as an element of the intelligence community (as defined under section 401a (4) of title 50).

(10) The term "key resources" means publicly or privately controlled resources essential to the minimal operations of the economy and government.

(11) The term "local government" means—

(A) a county, municipality, city, town, township, local public authority, school district, special district, intrastate district, council of governments (regardless of whether the council of governments is incorporated as a nonprofit corporation under State law), regional or interstate government entity, or agency or instrumentality of a local government;

(B) an Indian tribe or authorized tribal organization, or in Alaska a Native village or Alaska Regional Native Corporation; and

(C) a rural community, unincorporated town or village, or other public entity.

(12) The term "major disaster" has the meaning given in section 5122 (2) of title 42.

(13) The term "personnel" means officers and employees.

(14) The term "Secretary" means the Secretary of Homeland Security.

(15) The term "State" means any State of the United States, the District of Columbia, the Commonwealth of Puerto Rico, the Virgin Islands, Guam, American Samoa, the Commonwealth of the Northern Mariana Islands, and any possession of the United States.

(16) The term "terrorism" means any activity that—

(A) involves an act that—

(i) is dangerous to human life or potentially destructive of critical infrastructure or key resources; and

(ii) is a violation of the criminal laws of the United States or of any State or other subdivision of the United States; and

(B) appears to be intended—

(i) to intimidate or coerce a civilian population;

(ii) to influence the policy of a government by intimidation or coercion; or

(iii) to affect the conduct of a government by mass destruction, assassination, or kidnapping.

(17)

(A) The term "United States", when used in a geographic sense, means any State of the United States, the District of Columbia, the Commonwealth of Puerto Rico, the Virgin Islands, Guam, American Samoa, the Commonwealth of the Northern Mariana

Islands, any possession of the United States, and any waters within the jurisdiction of the United States.

(B) Nothing in this paragraph or any other provision of this chapter shall be construed to modify the definition of "United States" for the purposes of the Immigration and Nationality Act [8 U.S.C. 1101 et seq.] or any other immigration or nationality law.

(18) The term "voluntary preparedness standards" means a common set of criteria for preparedness, disaster management, emergency management, and business continuity programs, such as the American National Standards Institute's National Fire Protection Association Standard on Disaster/Emergency Management and Business Continuity Programs (ANSI/NFPA 1600).

Federal Information Security Management Act (44 U.S.C. § 3541)

Subchapter III: Information Security

- § 3541. Purposes
- § 3542. Definitions
- § 3543. Authority and functions of the director
- § 3544. Federal agency responsibilities
- § 3545. Annual independent evaluation
- § 3546. Federal information security incident center
- § 3547. National security systems
- § 3548. Authorization of appropriations
- § 3549. Effect on existing law

§ 3541. Purposes

The purposes of this subchapter are to

(1) provide a comprehensive framework for ensuring the effectiveness of information security controls over information resources that support Federal operations and assets;

(2) recognize the highly networked nature of the current Federal computing environment and provide effective government wide management and oversight of the related information security risks, including coordination of information security efforts throughout the civilian, national security, and law enforcement communities;

(3) provide for development and maintenance of minimum controls required to protect Federal information and information systems;

(4) provide a mechanism for improved oversight of Federal agency information security programs;

(5) acknowledge that commercially developed information security products offer advanced, dynamic, robust, and effective information security solutions, reflecting market solutions for the protection of critical information infrastructures important to the national defense and economic security of the nation that are designed, built, and operated by the private sector; and

(6) recognize that the selection of specific technical hardware and software information security solutions should be left to individual agencies from among commercially developed products.

§ 3542. Definitions

(a) *In General*—Except as provided under subsection (b), the definitions under section 3502 shall apply to this subchapter.

(b) *Additional Definitions*—As used in this subchapter:

(1) The term "information security" means protecting information and information systems from unauthorized access, use, disclosure, disruption, modification, or destruction in order to provide

(A) integrity, which means guarding against improper information modification or destruction, and includes ensuring information nonrepudiation and authenticity;

(B) confidentiality, which means preserving authorized restrictions on access and disclosure, including means for protecting personal privacy and proprietary information; and

(C) availability, which means ensuring timely and reliable access to and use of information.

(2)

(A) The term "national security system" means any information system (including any telecommunications system) used or operated by an agency or by a contractor of an agency, or other organization on behalf of an agency

(i) the function, operation, or use of which

(I) involves intelligence activities;

(II) involves cryptologic activities related to national security;

(III) involves command and control of military forces;

(IV) involves equipment that is an integral part of a weapon or weapons system; or

(V) subject to subparagraph (B), is critical to the direct fulfillment of military or intelligence missions; or

(ii) is protected at all times by procedures established for information that have been specifically authorized under criteria established by an Executive order or an

Act of Congress to be kept classified in the interest of national defense or foreign policy.

    (B) Subparagraph (A)(i)(V) does not include a system that is to be used for routine administrative and business applications (including payroll, finance, logistics, and personnel management applications).

  (3) The term "information technology" has the meaning given that term in section 11101 of title 40.

§ 3543. Authority and Functions of the Director

(a) *In General*—The Director shall oversee agency information security policies and practices, including

  (1) developing and overseeing the implementation of policies, principles, standards, and guidelines on information security, including through ensuring timely agency adoption of and compliance with standards promulgated under section 11331 of title 40;

  (2) requiring agencies, consistent with the standards promulgated under such section 11331 and the requirements of this subchapter, to identify and provide information security protections commensurate with the risk and magnitude of the harm resulting from the unauthorized access, use, disclosure, disruption, modification, or destruction of—

    (A) information collected or maintained by or on behalf of an agency; or

    (B) information systems used or operated by an agency or by a contractor of an agency or other organization on behalf of an agency;

  (3) coordinating the development of standards and guidelines under section 20 of the National Institute of Standards and Technology Act (15 U.S.C. 278g–3) with agencies and offices operating or exercising control of national security systems (including the National Security Agency) to assure, to the maximum extent feasible, that such standards and guidelines are complementary with standards and guidelines developed for national security systems;

  (4) overseeing agency compliance with the requirements of this subchapter, including through any authorized action under section 11303 of title 40, to enforce accountability for compliance with such requirements;

  (5) reviewing at least annually, and approving or disapproving, agency information security programs required under section 3544 (b);

  (6) coordinating information security policies and procedures with related information resources management policies and procedures;

(7) overseeing the operation of the Federal information security incident center required under section 3546; and

(8) reporting to Congress no later than March 1 of each year on agency compliance with the requirements of this subchapter, including—

(A) a summary of the findings of evaluations required by section 3545;

(B) an assessment of the development, promulgation, and adoption of, and compliance with, standards developed under section 20 of the National Institute of Standards and Technology Act (15 U.S.C. 278g–3) and promulgated under section 11331 of title 40;

(C) significant deficiencies in agency information security practices;

(D) planned remedial action to address such deficiencies; and

(E) a summary of, and the views of the Director on, the report prepared by the National Institute of Standards and Technology under section 20(d)(10) of the National Institute of Standards and Technology Act (15 U.S.C. 278g–3).

(b) *National Security Systems*—Except for the authorities described in paragraphs (4) and (8) of subsection (a), the authorities of the Director under this section shall not apply to national security systems.

(c) *Department of Defense and Central Intelligence Agency Systems.*

(1) The authorities of the Director described in paragraphs (1) and (2) of subsection (a) shall be delegated to the Secretary of Defense in the case of systems described in paragraph (2) and to the Director of Central Intelligence in the case of systems described in paragraph (3).

(2) The systems described in this paragraph are systems that are operated by the Department of Defense, a contractor of the Department of Defense, or another entity on behalf of the Department of Defense that processes any information the unauthorized access, use, disclosure, disruption, modification, or destruction of which would have a debilitating impact on the mission of the Department of Defense.

(3) The systems described in this paragraph are systems that are operated by the Central Intelligence Agency, a contractor of the Central Intelligence Agency, or another entity on behalf of the Central Intelligence Agency that processes any information the unauthorized access, use, disclosure, disruption, modification, or destruction of which would have a debilitating impact on the mission of the Central Intelligence Agency.

§ 3544. *Federal Agency Responsibilities*

(a) *In General*—The head of each agency shall
- (1) be responsible for
  - (A) providing information security protections commensurate with the risk and magnitude of the harm resulting from unauthorized access, use, disclosure, disruption, modification, or destruction of—
    - (i) information collected or maintained by or on behalf of the agency; and
    - (ii) information systems used or operated by an agency or by a contractor of an agency or other organization on behalf of an agency;
  - (B) complying with the requirements of this subchapter and related policies, procedures, standards, and guidelines, including—
    - (i) information security standards promulgated under section 11331 of title 40; and
    - (ii) information security standards and guidelines for national security systems issued in accordance with law and as directed by the President; and
  - (C) ensuring that information security management processes are integrated with agency strategic and operational planning processes;
- (2) ensure that senior agency officials provide information security for the information and information systems that support the operations and assets under their control, including through
  - (A) assessing the risk and magnitude of the harm that could result from the unauthorized access, use, disclosure, disruption, modification, or destruction of such information or information systems;
  - (B) determining the levels of information security appropriate to protect such information and information systems in accordance with standards promulgated under section 11331 of title 40, for information security classifications and related requirements;
  - (C) implementing policies and procedures to cost-effectively reduce risks to an acceptable level; and
  - (D) periodically testing and evaluating information security controls and techniques to ensure that they are effectively implemented;
- (3) delegate to the agency Chief Information Officer established under section 3506 (or comparable official in an agency not

covered by such section) the authority to ensure compliance with the requirements imposed on the agency under this subchapter, including

    (A) designating a senior agency information security officer who shall—

        (i) carry out the Chief Information Officer's responsibilities under this section;

        (ii) possess professional qualifications, including training and experience, required to administer the functions described under this section;

        (iii) have information security duties as that official's primary duty; and

        (iv) head an office with the mission and resources to assist in ensuring agency compliance with this section;

    (B) developing and maintaining an agency-wide information security program as required by subsection (b);

    (C) developing and maintaining information security policies, procedures, and control techniques to address all applicable requirements, including those issued under section 3543 of this title, and section 11331 of title 40;

    (D) training and overseeing personnel with significant responsibilities for information security with respect to such responsibilities; and

    (E) assisting senior agency officials concerning their responsibilities under paragraph (2);

  (4) ensure that the agency has trained personnel sufficient to assist the agency in complying with the requirements of this subchapter and related policies, procedures, standards, and guidelines; and

  (5) ensure that the agency Chief Information Officer, in coordination with other senior agency officials, reports annually to the agency head on the effectiveness of the agency information security program, including progress of remedial actions.

(b) *Agency Program*—Each agency shall develop, document, and implement an agency-wide information security program, approved by the Director under section 3543 (a)(5), to provide information security for the information and information systems that support the operations and assets of the agency, including those provided or managed by another agency, contractor, or other source, that includes—

  (1) periodic assessments of the risk and magnitude of the harm that could result from the unauthorized access, use, disclosure, disruption, modification, or destruction of information and information systems that support the operations and assets of the agency;

(2) policies and procedures that
   (A) are based on the risk assessments required by paragraph (1);
   (B) cost-effectively reduce information security risks to an acceptable level;
   (C) ensure that information security is addressed throughout the life cycle of each agency information system; and
   (D) ensure compliance with—
      (i) the requirements of this subchapter;
      (ii) policies and procedures as may be prescribed by the Director, and information security standards promulgated under section 11331 of title 40;
      (iii) minimally acceptable system configuration requirements, as determined by the agency; and
      (iv) any other applicable requirements, including standards and guidelines for national security systems issued in accordance with law and as directed by the President;
(3) subordinate plans for providing adequate information security for networks, facilities, and systems or groups of information systems, as appropriate;
(4) security awareness training to inform personnel, including contractors and other users of information systems that support the operations and assets of the agency, of
   (A) information security risks associated with their activities; and
   (B) their responsibilities in complying with agency policies and procedures designed to reduce these risks;
(5) periodic testing and evaluation of the effectiveness of information security policies, procedures, and practices, to be performed with a frequency depending on risk, but no less than annually, of which such testing—
   (A) shall include testing of management, operational, and technical controls of every information system identified in the inventory required under section 3505 (c); and
   (B) may include testing relied on in an evaluation under section 3545;
(6) a process for planning, implementing, evaluating, and documenting remedial action to address any deficiencies in the information security policies, procedures, and practices of the agency;
(7) procedures for detecting, reporting, and responding to security incidents, consistent with standards and guidelines issued pursuant to section 3546 (b), including—
   (A) mitigating risks associated with such incidents before substantial damage is done;

    (B) notifying and consulting with the Federal information security incident center referred to in section 3546; and

    (C) notifying and consulting with, as appropriate—

       (i) law enforcement agencies and relevant Offices of Inspector General;

       (ii) an office designated by the President for any incident involving a national security system; and

       (iii) any other agency or office, in accordance with law or as directed by the President; and

  (8) plans and procedures to ensure continuity of operations for information systems that support the operations and assets of the agency.

(c) *Agency Reporting*—Each agency shall—

  (1) report annually to the Director, the Committees on Government Reform and Science of the House of Representatives, the Committees on Governmental Affairs and Commerce, Science, and Transportation of the Senate, the appropriate authorization and appropriations committees of Congress, and the Comptroller General on the adequacy and effectiveness of information security policies, procedures, and practices, and compliance with the requirements of this subchapter, including compliance with each requirement of subsection (b);

  (2) address the adequacy and effectiveness of information security policies, procedures, and practices in plans and reports relating to—

  (A) annual agency budgets;

  (B) information resources management under subchapter 1 of this chapter;

  (C) information technology management under subtitle III of title 40;

  (D) program performance under sections 1105 and 1115–1119 of title 31, and sections 2801 and 2805 of title 39;

  (E) financial management under chapter 9 of title 31, and the Chief Financial Officers Act of 1990 (31 U.S.C. 501 note; Public Law 101–576) (and the amendments made by that Act);

  (F) financial management systems under the Federal Financial Management Improvement Act (31 U.S.C. 3512 note); and

  (G) internal accounting and administrative controls under section 3512 of title 31, (known as the "Federal Managers Financial Integrity Act"); and

    (3) report any significant deficiency in a policy, procedure, or practice identified under paragraph (1) or (2)

        (A) as a material weakness in reporting under section 3512 of title 31; and

        (B) if relating to financial management systems, as an instance of a lack of substantial compliance under the Federal Financial Management Improvement Act (31 U.S.C. 3512 note).

(d) *Performance Plan—*

    (1) In addition to the requirements of subsection (c), each agency, in consultation with the Director, shall include as part of the performance plan required under section 1115 of title 31 a description of—

        (A) the time periods, and

        (B) the resources, including budget, staffing, and training, that are necessary to implement the program required under subsection (b).

    (2) The description under paragraph (1) shall be based on the risk assessments required under subsection (b)(2)(1).

(e) *Public Notice and Comment—*Each agency shall provide the public with timely notice and opportunities for comment on proposed information security policies and procedures to the extent that such policies and procedures affect communication with the public.

§ 3545. Annual Independent Evaluation

(a) *In General.*

    (1) Each year each agency shall have performed an independent evaluation of the information security program and practices of that agency to determine the effectiveness of such program and practices.

    (2) Each evaluation under this section shall include—

        (A) testing of the effectiveness of information security policies, procedures, and practices of a representative subset of the agency's information systems;

        (B) an assessment (made on the basis of the results of the testing) of compliance with

           (i) the requirements of this subchapter; and

          (ii) related information security policies, procedures, standards, and guidelines; and

        (C) separate presentations, as appropriate, regarding information security relating to national security systems.

(b) *Independent Auditor*—Subject to subsection (c)
   (1) for each agency with an Inspector General appointed under the Inspector General Act of 1978 or any other law, the annual evaluation required by this section shall be performed by the Inspector General or by an independent external auditor, as determined by the Inspector General of the agency; and
   (2) for each agency to which paragraph (1) does not apply, the head of the agency shall engage an independent external auditor to perform the evaluation.
(c) *National Security Systems*—For each agency operating or exercising control of a national security system, that portion of the evaluation required by this section directly relating to a national security system shall be performed—
   (1) only by an entity designated by the agency head; and
   (2) in such a manner as to ensure appropriate protection for information associated with any information security vulnerability in such system commensurate with the risk and in accordance with all applicable laws.
(d) *Existing Evaluations*—The evaluation required by this section may be based in whole or in part on an audit, evaluation, or report relating to programs or practices of the applicable agency.
(e) *Agency Reporting.*
   (1) Each year, not later than such date established by the Director, the head of each agency shall submit to the Director the results of the evaluation required under this section.
   (2) To the extent an evaluation required under this section directly relates to a national security system, the evaluation results submitted to the Director shall contain only a summary and assessment of that portion of the evaluation directly relating to a national security system.
(f) *Protection of Information*—Agencies and evaluators shall take appropriate steps to ensure the protection of information which, if disclosed, may adversely affect information security. Such protections shall be commensurate with the risk and comply with all applicable laws and regulations.
(g) *OMB Reports to Congress.*
   (1) The Director shall summarize the results of the evaluations conducted under this section in the report to Congress required under section 3543 (a)(8).
   (2) The Director's report to Congress under this subsection shall summarize information regarding information security relating to national security systems in such a manner as

to ensure appropriate protection for information associated with any information security vulnerability in such system commensurate with the risk and in accordance with all applicable laws.

(3) Evaluations and any other descriptions of information systems under the authority and control of the Director of Central Intelligence or of National Foreign Intelligence Programs systems under the authority and control of the Secretary of Defense shall be made available to Congress only through the appropriate oversight committees of Congress, in accordance with applicable laws.

(h) *Comptroller General*—The Comptroller General shall periodically evaluate and report to Congress on

(1) the adequacy and effectiveness of agency information security policies and practices; and

(2) implementation of the requirements of this subchapter.

§ 3546. *Federal Information Security Incident Center*

(a) *In General*—The Director shall ensure the operation of a central Federal information security incident center to—

(1) provide timely technical assistance to operators of agency information systems regarding security incidents, including guidance on detecting and handling information security incidents;

(2) compile and analyze information about incidents that threaten information security;

(3) inform operators of agency information systems about current and potential information security threats, and vulnerabilities; and

(4) consult with the National Institute of Standards and Technology, agencies or offices operating or exercising control of national security systems (including the National Security Agency), and such other agencies or offices in accordance with law and as directed by the President regarding information security incidents and related matters.

(b) *National Security Systems*—Each agency operating or exercising control of a national security system shall share information about information security incidents, threats, and vulnerabilities with the Federal information security incident center to the extent consistent with standards and guidelines for national security systems, issued in accordance with law and as directed by the President.

§ 3547. National Security Systems

The head of each agency operating or exercising control of a national security system shall be responsible for ensuring that the agency—

(1) provides information security protections commensurate with the risk and magnitude of the harm resulting from the unauthorized access, use, disclosure, disruption, modification, or destruction of the information contained in such system;

(2) implements information security policies and practices as required by standards and guidelines for national security systems, issued in accordance with law and as directed by the President; and

(3) complies with the requirements of this subchapter.

§ 3548. Authorization of Appropriations

There are authorized to be appropriated to carry out the provisions of this subchapter such sums as may be necessary for each of fiscal years 2003 through 2007.

§ 3549. Effect on Existing Law

Nothing in this subchapter, section 11331 of title 40, or section 20 of the National Standards [1] and Technology Act (15 U.S.C. 278g–3) may be construed as affecting the authority of the President, the Office of Management and Budget or the Director thereof, the National Institute of Standards and Technology, or the head of any agency, with respect to the authorized use or disclosure of information, including with regard to the protection of personal privacy under section 552a of title 5, the disclosure of information under section 552 of title 5, the management and disposition of records under chapters 29, 31, or 33 of title 44, the management of information resources under subchapter I of chapter 35 of this title, or the disclosure of information to the Congress or the Comptroller General of the United States. While this subchapter is in effect, subchapter II of this chapter shall not apply.

Appendix D: Consumer and Credit Data Privacy Laws[*]

Freedom of Information Act (FOIA) (5 U.S.C. § 552)

The Freedom of Information Act
5 U.S.C. § 552
FOIA Update Vol. XVII, No. 4 (1996)
As Amended By
Public Law No. 104-231, 110 Stat. 3048

Below is the full text of the Freedom of Information Act in a form showing all amendments to the statute made by the "Electronic Freedom of Information Act Amendments of 1996." All newly enacted provisions are in boldface type.

§ 552. Public Information; Agency Rules, Opinions, Orders, Records, and Proceedings

(a) Each agency shall make available to the public information as follows:

    (1) Each agency shall separately state and currently publish in the Federal Register for the guidance of the public—

        (A) descriptions of its central and field organization and the established places at which, the employees (and in the case of a uniformed service, the members) from whom, and the methods whereby, the public may obtain information, make submittals or requests, or obtain decisions;

        (B) statements of the general course and method by which its functions are channeled and determined, including the nature and requirements of all formal and informal procedures available;

[*] *Note*: Statutes and case laws change constantly. Do not rely upon any source of law as being current without conducting legal research or consulting competent legal counsel. Statutes and case law included here are current at the time of research but should be researched for current and up-to-date law before relying upon them. Always seek competent legal counsel on any legal questions.

(C) rules of procedure, descriptions of forms available or the places at which forms may be obtained, and instructions as to the scope and contents of all papers, reports, or examinations;

(D) substantive rules of general applicability adopted as authorized by law, and statements of general policy or interpretations of general applicability formulated and adopted by the agency; and

(E) each amendment, revision, or repeal of the foregoing.

Except to the extent that a person has actual and timely notice of the terms thereof, a person may not in any manner be required to resort to, or be adversely affected by, a matter required to be published in the Federal Register and not so published. For the purpose of this paragraph, matter reasonably available to the class of persons affected thereby is deemed published in the Federal Register when incorporated by reference therein with the approval of the Director of the Federal Register.

(2) Each agency, in accordance with published rules, shall make available for public inspection and copying—

(A) final opinions, including concurring and dissenting opinions, as well as orders, made in the adjudication of cases;

(B) those statements of policy and interpretations which have been adopted by the agency and are not published in the Federal Register; and

(C) administrative staff manuals and instructions to staff that affect a member of the public;

(D) copies of all records, regardless of form or format, which have been released to any person under paragraph (3) and which, because of the nature of their subject matter, the agency determines have become or are likely to become the subject of subsequent requests for substantially the same records; and

(E) a general index of the records referred to under subparagraph (D); unless the materials are promptly published and copies offered for sale. **For records created on or after November 1, 1996, within one year after such date, each agency shall make such records available, including by computer telecommunications or, if computer telecommunications means have not been established by the agency, by other electronic means.** To the extent required to prevent a clearly unwarranted invasion of personal privacy, an agency may delete identifying details when it makes available or publishes an opinion, statement of policy, interpretation, or staff

~~manual or instruction,~~ **staff manual, instruction, or copies of records referred to in subparagraph (D).** However, in each case the justification for the deletion shall be explained fully in writing, **and the extent of such deletion shall be indicated on the portion of the record which is made available or published, unless including that indication would harm an interest protected by the exemption in subsection (b) under which the deletion is made. If technically feasible, the extent of the deletion shall be indicated at the place in the record where the deletion was made.** Each agency shall also maintain and make available for public inspection and copying current indexes providing identifying information for the public as to any matter issued, adopted, or promulgated after July 4, 1967, and required by this paragraph to be made available or published. Each agency shall promptly publish, quarterly or more frequently, and distribute (by sale or otherwise) copies of each index or supplements thereto unless it determines by order published in the Federal Register that the publication would be unnecessary and impracticable, in which case the agency shall nonetheless provide copies of an index on request at a cost not to exceed the direct cost of duplication. **Each agency shall make the index referred to in subparagraph (E) available by computer telecommunications by December 31, 1999.** A final order, opinion, statement of policy, interpretation, or staff manual or instruction that affects a member of the public may be relied on, used, or cited as precedent by an agency against a party other than an agency only if—

(i)   it has been indexed and either made available or published as provided by this paragraph; or

(ii) the party has actual and timely notice of the terms thereof.

(3)

(A) Except with respect to the records made available under paragraphs (1) and (2) of this subsection, each agency, upon request for records which ~~(A)~~ **(i)** reasonably describes such records and ~~(B)~~ **(ii)** is made in accordance with published rules stating the time, place, fees (if any), and procedures to be followed, shall make the records promptly available to any person.

(B) **In making any record available to a person under this paragraph, an agency shall provide the record in any form or format requested by the person if the record is readily reproducible by the agency in that form or format.**

Each agency shall make reasonable efforts to maintain its records in forms or formats that are reproducible for purposes of this section.

(C) In responding under this paragraph to a request for records, an agency shall make reasonable efforts to search for the records in electronic form or format, except when such efforts would significantly interfere with the operation of the agency's automated information system.

(D) For purposes of this paragraph, the term "search" means to review, manually or by automated means, agency records for the purpose of locating those records which are responsive to a request.

(4)

  (A)

    (i) In order to carry out the provisions of this section, each agency shall promulgate regulations, pursuant to notice and receipt of public comment, specifying the schedule of fees applicable to the processing of requests under this section and establishing procedures and guidelines for determining when such fees should be waived or reduced. Such schedule shall conform to the guidelines which shall be promulgated, pursuant to notice and receipt of public comment, by the Director of the Office of Management and Budget and which shall provide for a uniform schedule of fees for all agencies.

    (ii) Such agency regulations shall provide that—

      (I) fees shall be limited to reasonable standard charges for document search, duplication, and review, when records are requested for commercial use;

      (II) fees shall be limited to reasonable standard charges for document duplication when records are not sought for commercial use and the request is made by an educational or noncommercial scientific institution, whose purpose is scholarly or scientific research; or a representative of the news media; and

      (III) for any request not described in (I) or (II), fees shall be limited to reasonable standard charges for document search and duplication.

    (iii) Documents shall be furnished without any charge or at a charge reduced below the fees established under clause (ii) if disclosure of the information is in the public interest because it is likely to contribute significantly to public understanding of the operations or activities of the government and is not primarily in the commercial interest of the requester.

(iv) Fee schedules shall provide for the recovery of only the direct costs of search, duplication, or review. Review costs shall include only the direct costs incurred during the initial examination of a document for the purposes of determining whether the documents must be disclosed under this section and for the purposes of withholding any portions exempt from disclosure under this section. Review costs may not include any costs incurred in resolving issues of law or policy that may be raised in the course of processing a request under this section. No fee may be charged by any agency under this section—

(I) if the costs of routine collection and processing of the fee are likely to equal or exceed the amount of the fee; or

(II) for any request described in clause (ii)(II) or (III) of this subparagraph for the first two hours of search time or for the first one hundred pages of duplication.

(v) No agency may require advance payment of any fee unless the requester has previously failed to pay fees in a timely fashion, or the agency has determined that the fee will exceed $250.

(vi) Nothing in this subparagraph shall supersede fees chargeable under a statute specifically providing for setting the level of fees for particular types of records.

(vii) In any action by a requester regarding the waiver of fees under this section, the court shall determine the matter de novo, provided that the court's review of the matter shall be limited to the record before the agency.

(B) On complaint, the district court of the United States in the district in which the complainant resides, or has his principal place of business, or in which the agency records are situated, or in the District of Columbia, has jurisdiction to enjoin the agency from withholding agency records and to order the production of any agency records improperly withheld from the complainant. In such a case the court shall determine the matter de novo, and may examine the contents of such agency records in camera to determine whether such records or any part thereof shall be withheld under any of the exemptions set forth in subsection (b) of this section, and the burden is on the agency to sustain its action. **In addition to any other matters to which a court accords substantial weight, a court shall accord substantial weight to an affidavit of an agency concerning the agency's determination as to technical feasibility under paragraph (2)(C) and subsection (b) and reproducibility under paragraph (3)(B).**

(C) Notwithstanding any other provision of law, the defendant shall serve an answer or otherwise plead to any complaint made under this subsection within thirty days after service upon the defendant of the pleading in which such complaint is made, unless the court otherwise directs for good cause shown.

[~~(D) Except as to cases the court considers of greater importance, proceedings before the district court, as authorized by this subsection, and appeals there from, take precedence on the docket over all cases and shall be assigned for hearing and trial or for argument at the earliest practicable date and expedited in every way.~~ Repealed by Pub. L. 98-620, Title IV, 402(2), Nov. 8, 1984, 98 Stat. 3335, 3357.]

(E) The court may assess against the United States reasonable attorney fees and other litigation costs reasonably incurred in any case under this section in which the complainant has substantially prevailed.

(F) Whenever the court orders the production of any agency records improperly withheld from the complainant and assesses against the United States reasonable attorney fees and other litigation costs, and the court additionally issues a written finding that the circumstances surrounding the withholding raise questions whether agency personnel acted arbitrarily or capriciously with respect to the withholding, the Special Counsel shall promptly initiate a proceeding to determine whether disciplinary action is warranted against the officer or employee who was primarily responsible for the withholding. The Special Counsel, after investigation and consideration of the evidence submitted, shall submit his findings and recommendations to the administrative authority of the agency concerned and shall send copies of the findings and recommendations to the officer or employee or his representative. The administrative authority shall take the corrective action that the Special Counsel recommends.

(G) In the event of noncompliance with the order of the court, the district court may punish for contempt the responsible employee, and in the case of a uniformed service, the responsible member.

(5) Each agency having more than one member shall maintain and make available for public inspection a record of the final votes of each member in every agency proceeding.

(6)

(A) Each agency, upon any request for records made under paragraph (1), (2), or (3) of this subsection, shall—

(i) determine within ~~ten days~~ **twenty days** (excepting Saturdays, Sundays, and legal public holidays) after the receipt of any such request whether to comply with such request and shall immediately notify the person making such request of such determination and the reasons therefore, and of the right of such person to appeal to the head of the agency any adverse determination; and

(ii) make a determination with respect to any appeal within twenty days (excepting Saturdays, Sundays, and legal public holidays) after the receipt of such appeal. If on appeal the denial of the request for records is in whole or in part upheld, the agency shall notify the person making such request of the provisions for judicial review of that determination under paragraph (4) of this subsection.

~~(B) In unusual circumstances as specified in this subparagraph, the time limits prescribed in either clause (i) or clause (ii) of subparagraph (A) may be extended by written notice to the person making such request setting forth the reasons for such extension and the date on which a determination is expected to be dispatched. No such notice shall specify a date that would result in an extension for more than ten working days. As used in this subparagraph, "unusual circumstances" means, but only to the extent reasonably necessary to the proper processing of the particular request—~~

~~(i) the need to search for and collect the requested records from field facilities or other establishments that are separate from the office processing the request;~~

~~(ii) the need to search for, collect, and appropriately examine a voluminous amount of separate and distinct records which are demanded in a single request; or~~

~~(iii) the need for consultation, which shall be conducted with all practicable speed, with another agency having a substantial interest in the determination of the request or among two or more components of the agency having substantial subject matter interest therein.~~

(B)

(i) In unusual circumstances as specified in this subparagraph, the time limits prescribed in either clause (i) or clause (ii) of subparagraph (A) may be extended by written notice to the person making such request setting forth the unusual circumstances for such extension and the date on which a determination is expected to be dispatched. No such notice shall specify a date that would result in an extension for more than ten working days, except as provided in clause (ii) of this subparagraph.

(ii) With respect to a request for which a written notice under clause (i) extends the time limits prescribed under clause (i) of subparagraph (A), the agency shall notify the person making the request if the request cannot be processed within the time limit specified in that clause and shall provide the person an opportunity to limit the scope of the request so that it may be processed within that time limit or an opportunity to arrange with the agency an alternative time frame for processing the request or a modified request. Refusal by the person to reasonably modify the request or arrange such an alternative time frame shall be considered as a factor in determining whether exceptional circumstances exist for purposes of subparagraph (C).

(iii) As used in this subparagraph, "unusual circumstances" means, but only to the extent reasonably necessary to the proper processing of the particular requests—

    (I) the need to search for and collect the requested records from field facilities or other establishments that are separate from the office processing the request;

    (II) the need to search for, collect, and appropriately examine a voluminous amount of separate and distinct records which are demanded in a single request; or

    (III) the need for consultation, which shall be conducted with all practicable speed, with another agency having a substantial interest in the determination of the request or among two or more components of the agency having substantial subject matter interest therein.

(iv) Each agency may promulgate regulations, pursuant to notice and receipt of public comment, providing for the aggregation of certain requests by the same requestor, or by a group of requestors acting in concert, if the agency reasonably believes that such requests actually constitute a single request, which would otherwise satisfy the unusual circumstances specified in this subparagraph, and the requests involve clearly related matters. Multiple requests involving unrelated matters shall not be aggregated.

(C)

(i) Any person making a request to any agency for records under paragraph (1), (2), or (3) of this subsection shall be deemed to have exhausted his administrative remedies with respect to such request if the agency fails to comply with the applicable time limit provisions of this paragraph. If the Government can show exceptional circumstances exist and that the agency is exercising due diligence in responding to the request, the court may retain jurisdiction and allow the agency additional time to complete its review of the records. Upon any determination by an agency to comply with a request for records, the records shall be made promptly available to such person making such request. Any notification of denial of any request for records under this subsection shall set forth the names and titles or positions of each person responsible for the denial of such request.

(ii) For purposes of this subparagraph, the term "exceptional circumstances" does not include a delay that results from a predictable agency workload of requests under this section, unless the agency demonstrates reasonable progress in reducing its backlog of pending requests.

(iii) Refusal by a person to reasonably modify the scope of a request or arrange an alternative time frame for processing the request (or a modified request) under clause (ii) after being given an opportunity to do so by the agency to whom the person made the request shall be considered as a factor in determining whether exceptional circumstances exist for purposes of this subparagraph.

(D)

  (i) Each agency may promulgate regulations, pursuant to notice and receipt of public comment, providing for multitrack processing of requests for records based on the amount of work or time (or both) involved in processing requests.

  (ii) Regulations under this subparagraph may provide a person making a request that does not qualify for the fastest multitrack processing an opportunity to limit the scope of the request in order to qualify for faster processing.

  (iii) This subparagraph shall not be considered to affect the requirement under subparagraph (C) to exercise due diligence.

(E)

  (i) Each agency shall promulgate regulations, pursuant to notice and receipt of public comment, providing for expedited processing of requests for records—

    (I) in cases in which the person requesting the records demonstrates a compelling need; and

    (II) in other cases determined by the agency.

  (ii) Notwithstanding clause (i), regulations under this subparagraph must ensure—

    (I) that a determination of whether to provide expedited processing shall be made, and notice of the determination shall be provided to the person making the request, within 10 days after the date of the request; and

    (II) expeditious consideration of administrative appeals of such determinations of whether to provide expedited processing.

  (iii) An agency shall process as soon as practicable any request for records to which the agency has granted expedited processing under this subparagraph. Agency action to deny or affirm denial of a request for expedited processing pursuant to this subparagraph, and failure by an agency to respond in a timely manner to such a request shall be subject to judicial review under paragraph (4), except that the judicial review shall be based on the record before the agency at the time of the determination.

  (iv) A district court of the United States shall not have jurisdiction to review an agency denial of expedited processing of a request for records after the agency has provided a complete response to the request.

(v) For purposes of this subparagraph, the term "compelling need" means—

    (I)   that a failure to obtain requested records on an expedited basis under this paragraph could reasonably be expected to pose an imminent threat to the life or physical safety of an individual; or

    (II) with respect to a request made by a person primarily engaged in disseminating information, urgency to inform the public concerning actual or alleged Federal Government activity.

(vi) A demonstration of a compelling need by a person making a request for expedited processing shall be made by a statement certified by such person to be true and correct to the best of such person's knowledge and belief.

(F) In denying a request for records, in whole or in part, an agency shall make a reasonable effort to estimate the volume of any requested matter the provision of which is denied, and shall provide any such estimate to the person making the request, unless providing such estimate would harm an interest protected by the exemption in subsection (b) pursuant to which the denial is made.

(b) This section does not apply to matters that are—

(1) (A) specifically authorized under criteria established by an Executive order to be kept secret in the interest of national defense or foreign policy and (B) are in fact properly classified pursuant to such Executive order;

(2) related solely to the internal personnel rules and practices of an agency;

(3) specifically exempted from disclosure by statute (other than section 552b of this title), provided that such statute (A) requires that the matters be withheld from the public in such a manner as to leave no discretion on the issue, or (B) establishes particular criteria for withholding or refers to particular types of matters to be withheld;

(4) trade secrets and commercial or financial information obtained from a person and privileged or confidential;

(5) inter-agency or intra-agency memorandums or letters which would not be available by law to a party other than an agency in litigation with the agency;

(6) personnel and medical files and similar files the disclosure of which would constitute a clearly unwarranted invasion of personal privacy;

(7) records or information compiled for law enforcement purposes, but only to the extent that the production of such law enforcement records or information (A) could reasonably be expected to interfere with enforcement proceedings, (B) would deprive a person of a right to a fair trial or an impartial adjudication, (C) could reasonably be expected to constitute an unwarranted invasion of personal privacy, (D) could reasonably be expected to disclose the identity of a confidential source, including a State, local, or foreign agency or authority or any private institution which furnished information on a confidential basis, and, in the case of a record or information compiled by a criminal law enforcement authority in the course of a criminal investigation or by an agency conducting a lawful national security intelligence investigation, information furnished by a confidential source, (E) would disclose techniques and procedures for law enforcement investigations or prosecutions, or would disclose guidelines for law enforcement investigations or prosecutions if such disclosure could reasonably be expected to risk circumvention of the law, or (F) could reasonably be expected to endanger the life or physical safety of any individual;

(8) contained in or related to examination, operating, or condition reports prepared by, on behalf of, or for the use of an agency responsible for the regulation or supervision of financial institutions; or

(9) geological and geophysical information and data, including maps, concerning wells.

Any reasonably segregable portion of a record shall be provided to any person requesting such record after deletion of the portions which are exempt under this subsection. **The amount of information deleted shall be indicated on the released portion of the record, unless including that indication would harm an interest protected by the exemption in this subsection under which the deletion is made. If technically feasible, the amount of the information deleted shall be indicated at the place in the record where such deletion is made.**

(c)

(1) Whenever a request is made which involves access to records described in subsection (b)(7)(A) and—

(A) the investigation or proceeding involves a possible violation of criminal law; and

    (B) there is reason to believe that (i) the subject of the investigation or proceeding is not aware of its pendency, and (ii) disclosure of the existence of the records could reasonably be expected to interfere with enforcement proceedings, the agency may, during only such time as that circumstance continues, treat the records as not subject to the requirements of this section.

  (2) Whenever informant records maintained by a criminal law enforcement agency under an informant's name or personal identifier are requested by a third party according to the informant's name or personal identifier, the agency may treat the records as not subject to the requirements of this section unless the informant's status as an informant has been officially confirmed.

  (3) Whenever a request is made which involves access to records maintained by the Federal Bureau of Investigation pertaining to foreign intelligence or counterintelligence, or international terrorism, and the existence of the records is classified information as provided in subsection (b)(1), the Bureau may, as long as the existence of the records remains classified information, treat the records as not subject to the requirements of this section.

(d) This section does not authorize the withholding of information or limit the availability of records to the public, except as specifically stated in this section. This section is not authority to withhold information from Congress.

(e) On or before March 1 of each calendar year, each agency shall submit a report covering the preceding calendar year to the Speaker of the House of Representatives and President of the Senate for referral to the appropriate committees of the Congress. The report shall include—

  (1) the number of determinations made by such agency not to comply with requests for records made to such agency under subsection (a) and the reasons for each such determination;

  (2) the number of appeals made by persons under subsection (a)(6), the result of such appeals, and the reason for the action upon each appeal that results in a denial of information;

  (3) the names and titles or positions of each person responsible for the denial of records requested under this section, and the number of instances of participation for each;

  (4) the results of each proceeding conducted pursuant to subsection (a)(4)(F), including a report of the disciplinary action taken against the officer or employee who was primarily responsible for

~~improperly withholding records or an explanation of why disciplinary action was not taken;~~

~~(5) a copy of every rule made by such agency regarding this section;~~

~~(6) a copy of the fee schedule and the total amount of fees collected by the agency for making records available under this section; and~~

~~(7) such other information as indicates efforts to administer fully this section.~~

~~The Attorney General shall submit an annual report on or before March 1 of each calendar year which shall include for the prior calendar year a listing of the number of cases arising under this section, the exemption involved in each case, the disposition of such case, and the cost, fees, and penalties assessed under subsections (a)(4)(E), (F), and (G). Such report shall also include a description of the efforts undertaken by the Department of Justice to encourage agency compliance with this section.~~

(e)

(1) On or before February 1 of each year, each agency shall submit to the Attorney General of the United States a report which shall cover the preceding fiscal year and which shall include—

(A) the number of determinations made by the agency not to comply with requests for records made to such agency under subsection (a) and the reasons for each such determination;

(B)

   (i) the number of appeals made by persons under subsection (a)(6), the result of such appeals, and the reason for the action upon each appeal that results in a denial of information; and

   (ii) a complete list of all statutes that the agency relies upon to authorize the agency to withhold information under subsection (b)(3), a description of whether a court has upheld the decision of the agency to withhold information under each such statute, and a concise description of the scope of any information withheld;

(C) the number of requests for records pending before the agency as of September 30 of the preceding year, and the median number of days that such requests had been pending before the agency as of that date;

(D) the number of requests for records received by the agency and the number of requests which the agency processed;

(E) the median number of days taken by the agency to process different types of requests;

(F) the total amount of fees collected by the agency for processing requests; and

(G) the number of full-time staff of the agency devoted to processing requests for records under this section, and the total amount expended by the agency for processing such requests.

(2) Each agency shall make each such report available to the public including by computer telecommunications, or if computer telecommunications means have not been established by the agency, by other electronic means.

(3) The Attorney General of the United States shall make each report which has been made available by electronic means available at a single electronic access point. The Attorney General of the United States shall notify the Chairman and ranking minority member of the Committee on Government Reform and Oversight of the House of Representatives and the Chairman and ranking minority member of the Committees on Governmental Affairs and the Judiciary of the Senate, no later than April 1 of the year in which each such report is issued, that such reports are available by electronic means.

(4) The Attorney General of the United States, in consultation with the Director of the Office of Management and Budget, shall develop reporting and performance guidelines in connection with reports required by this subsection by October 1, 1997, and may establish additional requirements for such reports as the Attorney General determines may be useful.

(5) The Attorney General of the United States shall submit an annual report on or before April 1 of each calendar year which shall include for the prior calendar year a listing of the number of cases arising under this section, the exemption involved in each case, the disposition of such case, and the cost, fees, and penalties assessed under subparagraphs (E), (F), and (G) of subsection (a)(4). Such report shall also include a description of the efforts undertaken by the Department of Justice to encourage agency compliance with this section.

(f) For purposes of this section, the term "agency" as defined in section 551(1) of this title includes any Executive department, military department, Government corporation, Government controlled corporation, or other establishment in the executive branch of the Government (including the Executive Office of the President), or any independent regulatory agency.

   (f) For purposes of this section, the term—
      (1) "agency" as defined in section 551(1) of this title includes any executive department, military department, Government corporation, Government controlled corporation, or other establishment in the executive branch of the Government (including the Executive Office of the President), or any independent regulatory agency; and
      (2) "record" and any other term used in this section in reference to information includes any information that would be an agency record subject to the requirements of this section when maintained by an agency in any format, including an electronic format.
   (g) The head of each agency shall prepare and make publicly available upon request, reference material or a guide for requesting records or information from the agency, subject to the exemptions in subsection (b), including—
      (1) an index of all major information systems of the agency;
      (2) a description of major information and record locator systems maintained by the agency; and
      (3) a handbook for obtaining various types and categories of public information from the agency pursuant to chapter 35 of title 44, and under this section.

* * * * *

§ 12. Effective Date [Not to be Codified]

   (a) Except as provided in subsection (b), this Act shall take effect 180 days after the date of the enactment of this Act [March 31, 1997].
   (b) Sections 7 and 8 shall take effect one year after the date of the enactment of this Act [October 2, 1997].

Below is the full text of the statement issued by President Clinton upon signing the 1996 FOIA amendments into law on October 2, 1996:

I am pleased to sign into law today H.R. 3802, the "Electronic Freedom of Information Act Amendments of 1996."

    This bill represents the culmination of several years of leadership by Senator Patrick Leahy to bring this important law up to date. Enacted in

1966, the Freedom of Information Act (FOIA) was the first law to establish an effective legal right of access to government information, underscoring the crucial need in a democracy for open access to government information by citizens. In the last 30 years, citizens, scholars, and reporters have used FOIA to obtain vital and valuable government information.

Since 1966, the world has changed a great deal. Records are no longer principally maintained in paper format. Now, they are maintained in a variety of technologies, including CD ROM and computer tapes and diskettes, making it easier to put more information on-line.

My Administration has launched numerous initiatives to bring more government information to the public. We have established World Wide Web pages, which identify and link information resources throughout the Federal Government. An enormous range of documents and data, including the Federal budget, is now available on-line or in electronic format, making government more accessible than ever. And in the last year, we have declassified unprecedented amounts of national security material, including information on nuclear testing.

The legislation I sign today brings FOIA into the information and electronic age by clarifying that it applies to records maintained in electronic format. This law also broadens public access to government information by placing more material on-line and expanding the role of the agency reading room. As the Government actively disseminates more information, I hope that there will be less need to use FOIA to obtain government information.

This legislation not only affirms the importance, but also the challenge of maintaining openness in government. In a period of government downsizing, the numbers of requests continue to rise. In addition, growing numbers of requests are for information that must be reviewed for declassification, or in which there is a proprietary interest or a privacy concern. The result in many agencies is huge backlogs of requests.

In this Act, the Congress recognized that with today's limited resources, it is frequently difficult to respond to a FOIA request within the 10 days formerly required in the law. This legislation extends the legal response period to 20 days.

More importantly, it recognizes that many FOIA requests are so broad and complex that they cannot possibly be completed even within this longer period, and the time spent processing them only delays other requests. Accordingly, H.R. 3802 establishes procedures for an agency to discuss with requesters ways of tailoring large requests to improve responsiveness. This approach explicitly recognizes that FOIA works best when agencies and requesters work together.

Our country was founded on democratic principles of openness and accountability, and for 30 years, FOIA has supported these principles. Today, the "Electronic Freedom of Information Act Amendments of 1996" reforges an important link between the United States Government and the American people.

Privacy Act of 1974 (5 U.S.C. § 552a: As Amended)

§ 552a. Records Maintained on Individuals

(a) Definitions

For purposes of this section—

(1) the term "agency" means agency as defined in section 552(f) of this title;

(2) the term "individual" means a citizen of the United States or an alien lawfully admitted for permanent residence;

(3) the term "maintain" includes maintain, collect, use, or disseminate;

(4) the term "record" means any item, collection, or grouping of information about an individual that is maintained by an agency, including, but not limited to, his education, financial transactions, medical history, and criminal or employment history and that contains his name, or the identifying number, symbol, or other identifying particular assigned to the individual, such as a finger or voice print or a photograph;

(5) the term "system of records" means a group of any records under the control of any agency from which information is retrieved by the name of the individual or by some identifying number, symbol, or other identifying particular assigned to the individual;

(6) the term "statistical record" means a record in a system of records maintained for statistical research or reporting purposes only and not used in whole or in part in making any determination about an identifiable individual, except as provided by section 8 of Title 13;

(7) the term "routine use" means, with respect to the disclosure of a record, the use of such record for a purpose which is compatible with the purpose for which it was collected;

(8) the term "matching program"—

(A) means any computerized comparison of—

(i) two or more automated systems of records or a system of records with non-Federal records for the purpose of—

(I) establishing or verifying the eligibility of, or continuing compliance with statutory and regulatory requirements by, applicants for, recipients or beneficiaries of, participants in, or providers of services with respect to, cash or in-kind assistance or payments under Federal benefit programs, or

(II) recouping payments or delinquent debts under such Federal benefit programs, or

       (ii) two or more automated Federal personnel or payroll systems of records or a system of Federal personnel or payroll records with non-Federal records,

(B) but does not include—

       (i) matches performed to produce aggregate statistical data without any personal identifiers;

      (ii) matches performed to support any research or statistical project, the specific data of which may not be used to make decisions concerning the rights, benefits, or privileges of specific individuals;

     (iii) matches performed, by an agency (or component thereof) which performs as its principal function any activity pertaining to the enforcement of criminal laws, subsequent to the initiation of a specific criminal or civil law enforcement investigation of a named person or persons for the purpose of gathering evidence against such person or persons;

     (iv) matches of tax information (I) pursuant to section 6103(d) of the Internal Revenue Code of 1986, (II) for purposes of tax administration as defined in section 6103(b)(4) of such Code, (III) for the purpose of intercepting a tax refund due an individual under authority granted by section 404(e), 464, or 1137 of the Social Security Act; or (IV) for the purpose of intercepting a tax refund due an individual under any other tax refund intercept program authorized by statute which has been determined by the Director of the Office of Management and Budget to contain verification, notice, and hearing requirements that are substantially similar to the procedures in section 1137 of the Social Security Act;

      (v) matches—

         (I) using records predominantly relating to Federal personnel, that are performed for routine administrative purposes (subject to guidance provided by the Director of the Office of Management and Budget pursuant to subsection (v)); or

        (II) conducted by an agency using only records from systems of records maintained by that agency;

        if the purpose of the match is not to take any adverse financial, personnel, disciplinary, or other adverse action against Federal personnel; or

> (vi) matches performed for foreign counterintelligence purposes or to produce background checks for security clearances of Federal personnel or Federal contractor personnel;
>
> (vii) matches performed incident to a levy described in section 6103(k)(8) of the Internal Revenue Code of 1986; or
>
> (viii) matches performed pursuant to section 202(x)(3) or 1611(e)(1) of the Social Security Act (42 U.S.C. § 402(x)(3), § 1382(e)(1));

(9) the term "recipient agency" means any agency, or contractor thereof, receiving records contained in a system of records from a source agency for use in a matching program;

(10) the term "non-Federal agency" means any State or local government, or agency thereof, which receives records contained in a system of records from a source agency for use in a matching program;

(11) the term "source agency" means any agency which discloses records contained in a system of records to be used in a matching program, or any State or local government, or agency thereof, which discloses records to be used in a matching program;

(12) the term "Federal benefit program" means any program administered or funded by the Federal Government, or by any agent or State on behalf of the Federal Government, providing cash or in-kind assistance in the form of payments, grants, loans, or loan guarantees to individuals; and

(13) the term "Federal personnel" means officers and employees of the Government of the United States, members of the uniformed services (including members of the Reserve Components), individuals entitled to receive immediate or deferred retirement benefits under any retirement program of the Government of the United States (including survivor benefits).

(b) Conditions of disclosure. No agency shall disclose any record which is contained in a system of records by any means of communication to any person, or to another agency, except pursuant to a written request by, or with the prior written consent of, the individual to whom the record pertains, unless disclosure of the record would be—

(1) to those officers and employees of the agency which maintains the record who have a need for the record in the performance of their duties;

(2) required under section 552 of this title;

(3) for a routine use as defined in subsection (a)(7) of this section and described under subsection (e)(4)(D) of this section;

(4) to the Bureau of the Census for purposes of planning or carrying out a census or survey or related activity pursuant to the provisions of Title 13;

(5) to a recipient who has provided the agency with advance adequate written assurance that the record will be used solely as a statistical research or reporting record, and the record is to be transferred in a form that is not individually identifiable;

(6) to the National Archives and Records Administration as a record which has sufficient historical or other value to warrant its continued preservation by the United States Government, or for evaluation by the Archivist of the United States or the designee of the Archivist to determine whether the record has such value;

(7) to another agency or to an instrumentality of any governmental jurisdiction within or under the control of the United States for a civil or criminal law enforcement activity if the activity is authorized by law, and if the head of the agency or instrumentality has made a written request to the agency which maintains the record specifying the particular portion desired and the law enforcement activity for which the record is sought;

(8) to a person pursuant to a showing of compelling circumstances affecting the health or safety of an individual if upon such disclosure notification is transmitted to the last known address of such individual;

(9) to either House of Congress, or, to the extent of matter within its jurisdiction, any committee or subcommittee thereof, any joint committee of Congress or subcommittee of any such joint committee;

(10) to the Comptroller General, or any of his authorized representatives, in the course of the performance of the duties of the General Accounting Office;

(11) pursuant to the order of a court of competent jurisdiction; or

(12) to a consumer reporting agency in accordance with section 3711(e) of Title 31.

(c) Accounting of Certain Disclosures. Each agency, with respect to each system of records under its control, shall—

(1) except for disclosures made under subsections (b)(1) or (b)(2) of this section, keep an accurate accounting of—

(A) the date, nature, and purpose of each disclosure of a record to any person or to another agency made under subsection (b) of this section; and

(B) the name and address of the person or agency to whom the disclosure is made;

(2) retain the accounting made under paragraph (1) of this subsection for at least five years or the life of the record, whichever is longer, after the disclosure for which the accounting is made;

(3) except for disclosures made under subsection (b)(7) of this section, make the accounting made under paragraph (1) of this subsection available to the individual named in the record at his request; and

(4) inform any person or other agency about any correction or notation of dispute made by the agency in accordance with subsection (d) of this section of any record that has been disclosed to the person or agency if an accounting of the disclosure was made.

(d) Access to records. Each agency that maintains a system of records shall—

(1) upon request by any individual to gain access to his record or to any information pertaining to him which is contained in the system, permit him and upon his request, a person of his own choosing to accompany him, to review the record and have a copy made of all or any portion thereof in a form comprehensible to him, except that the agency may require the individual to furnish a written statement authorizing discussion of that individual's record in the accompanying person's presence;

(2) permit the individual to request amendment of a record pertaining to him and—

(A) not later than 10 days (excluding Saturdays, Sundays, and legal public holidays) after the date of receipt of such request, acknowledge in writing such receipt; and

(B) promptly, either—

(i) make any correction of any portion thereof which the individual believes is not accurate, relevant, timely, or complete; or

(ii) inform the individual of its refusal to amend the record in accordance with his request, the reason for the refusal, the procedures established by the agency for the individual to request a review of that refusal by the head of the agency or an officer designated by the head of the agency, and the name and business address of that official;

(3) permit the individual who disagrees with the refusal of the agency to amend his record to request a review of such refusal, and not later than 30 days (excluding Saturdays, Sundays, and legal public holidays) from the date on which the individual requests such review, complete such review and make a final determination unless, for good cause shown, the head of the

agency extends such 30-day period; and if, after his review, the reviewing official also refuses to amend the record in accordance with the request, permit the individual to file with the agency a concise statement setting forth the reasons for his disagreement with the refusal of the agency, and notify the individual of the provisions for judicial review of the reviewing official's determination under subsection (g)(1)(A) of this section;

(4) in any disclosure, containing information about which the individual has filed a statement of disagreement, occurring after the filing of the statement under paragraph (3) of this subsection, clearly note any portion of the record which is disputed and provide copies of the statement and, if the agency deems it appropriate, copies of a concise statement of the reasons of the agency for not making the amendments requested, to persons or other agencies to whom the disputed record has been disclosed; and

(5) nothing in this section shall allow an individual access to any information compiled in reasonable anticipation of a civil action or proceeding.

(e) Agency requirements. Each agency that maintains a system of records shall—

(1) maintain in its records only such information about an individual as is relevant and necessary to accomplish a purpose of the agency required to be accomplished by statute or by Executive order of the President;

(2) collect information to the greatest extent practicable directly from the subject individual when the information may result in adverse determinations about an individual's rights, benefits, and privileges under Federal programs;

(3) inform each individual whom it asks to supply information, on the form which it uses to collect the information or on a separate form that can be retained by the individual—

(A) the authority (whether granted by statute, or by Executive order of the President) which authorizes the solicitation of the information and whether disclosure of such information is mandatory or voluntary;

(B) the principal purpose or purposes for which the information is intended to be used;

(C) the routine uses which may be made of the information, as published pursuant to paragraph (4)(D) of this subsection; and

(D) the effects on him, if any, of not providing all or any part of the requested information;

(4) subject to the provisions of paragraph (11) of this subsection, publish in the Federal Register upon establishment or revision a notice of the existence and character of the system of records, which notice shall include—

    (A) the name and location of the system;

    (B) the categories of individuals on whom records are maintained in the system;

    (C) the categories of records maintained in the system;

    (D) each routine use of the records contained in the system, including the categories of users and the purpose of such use;

    (E) the policies and practices of the agency regarding storage, retrievability, access controls, retention, and disposal of the records;

    (F) the title and business address of the agency official who is responsible for the system of records;

    (G) the agency procedures whereby an individual can be notified at his request if the system of records contains a record pertaining to him;

    (H) the agency procedures whereby an individual can be notified at his request how he can gain access to any record pertaining to him contained in the system of records, and how he can contest its content; and

    (I) the categories of sources of records in the system;

(5) maintain all records which are used by the agency in making any determination about any individual with such accuracy, relevance, timeliness, and completeness as is reasonably necessary to assure fairness to the individual in the determination;

(6) prior to disseminating any record about an individual to any person other than an agency, unless the dissemination is made pursuant to subsection (b)(2) of this section, make reasonable efforts to assure that such records are accurate, complete, timely, and relevant for agency purposes;

(7) maintain no record describing how any individual exercises rights guaranteed by the First Amendment unless expressly authorized by statute or by the individual about whom the record is maintained or unless pertinent to and within the scope of an authorized law enforcement activity;

(8) make reasonable efforts to serve notice on an individual when any record on such individual is made available to any person under compulsory legal process when such process becomes a matter of public record;

(9) establish rules of conduct for persons involved in the design, development, operation, or maintenance of any system of records, or in maintaining any record, and instruct each such person with respect to such rules and the requirements of this section, including any other rules and procedures adopted pursuant to this section and the penalties for noncompliance;

(10) establish appropriate administrative, technical and physical safeguards to insure the security and confidentiality of records and to protect against any anticipated threats or hazards to their security or integrity which could result in substantial harm, embarrassment, inconvenience, or unfairness to any individual on whom information is maintained;

(11) at least 30 days prior to publication of information under paragraph (4)(D) of this subsection, publish in the Federal Register notice of any new use or intended use of the information in the system, and provide an opportunity for interested persons to submit written data, views, or arguments to the agency; and

(12) if such agency is a recipient agency or a source agency in a matching program with a non-Federal agency, with respect to any establishment or revision of a matching program, at least 30 days prior to conducting such program, publish in the Federal Register notice of such establishment or revision.

(f) Agency rules. In order to carry out the provisions of this section, each agency that maintains a system of records shall promulgate rules, in accordance with the requirements (including general notice) of section 553 of this title, which shall—

(1) establish procedures whereby an individual can be notified in response to his request if any system of records named by the individual contains a record pertaining to him;

(2) define reasonable times, places, and requirements for identifying an individual who requests his record or information pertaining to him before the agency shall make the record or information available to the individual;

(3) establish procedures for the disclosure to an individual upon his request of his record or information pertaining to him, including special procedure, if deemed necessary, for the disclosure to an individual of medical records, including psychological records, pertaining to him;

(4) establish procedures for reviewing a request from an individual concerning the amendment of any record or information pertaining to the individual, for making a determination on the

request, for an appeal within the agency of an initial adverse agency determination, and for whatever additional means may be necessary for each individual to be able to exercise fully his rights under this section; and

(5) establish fees to be charged, if any, to any individual for making copies of his record, excluding the cost of any search for and review of the record.

The Office of the Federal Register shall biennially compile and publish the rules promulgated under this subsection and agency notices published under subsection (e)(4) of this section in a form available to the public at low cost.

(g)

(1) Civil remedies. Whenever any agency

(A) makes a determination under subsection (d)(3) of this section not to amend an individual's record in accordance with his request, or fails to make such review in conformity with that subsection;

(B) refuses to comply with an individual request under subsection (d)(1) of this section;

(C) fails to maintain any record concerning any individual with such accuracy, relevance, timeliness, and completeness as is necessary to assure fairness in any determination relating to the qualifications, character, rights, or opportunities of, or benefits to the individual that may be made on the basis of such record, and consequently a determination is made which is adverse to the individual; or

(D) fails to comply with any other provision of this section, or any rule promulgated thereunder, in such a way as to have an adverse effect on an individual, the individual may bring a civil action against the agency, and the district courts of the United States shall have jurisdiction in the matters under the provisions of this subsection.

(2)

(A) In any suit brought under the provisions of subsection (g)(1) (A) of this section, the court may order the agency to amend the individual's record in accordance with his request or in such other way as the court may direct. In such a case the court shall determine the matter de novo.

(B) The court may assess against the United States reasonable attorney fees and other litigation costs reasonably incurred in any case under this paragraph in which the complainant has substantially prevailed.

(3)

    (A) In any suit brought under the provisions of subsection (g)(1)(B) of this section, the court may enjoin the agency from withholding the records and order the production to the complainant of any agency records improperly withheld from him. In such a case the court shall determine the matter de novo, and may examine the contents of any agency records in camera to determine whether the records or any portion thereof may be withheld under any of the exemptions set forth in subsection (k) of this section, and the burden is on the agency to sustain its action.

    (B) The court may assess against the United States reasonable attorney fees and other litigation costs reasonably incurred in any case under this paragraph in which the complainant has substantially prevailed.

(4) In any suit brought under the provisions of subsection (g)(1) (C) or (D) of this section in which the court determines that the agency acted in a manner which was intentional or willful, the United States shall be liable to the individual in an amount equal to the sum of—

    (A) actual damages sustained by the individual as a result of the refusal or failure, but in no case shall a person entitled to recovery receive less than the sum of $1,000; and

    (B) the costs of the action together with reasonable attorney fees as determined by the court.

(5) An action to enforce any liability created under this section may be brought in the district court of the United States in the district in which the complainant resides, or has his principal place of business, or in which the agency records are situated, or in the District of Columbia, without regard to the amount in controversy, within two years from the date on which the cause of action arises, except that where an agency has materially and willfully misrepresented any information required under this section to be disclosed to an individual and the information so misrepresented is material to establishment of the liability of the agency to the individual under this section, the action may be brought at any time within two years after discovery by the individual of the misrepresentation. Nothing in this section shall be construed to authorize any civil action by reason of any injury sustained as the result of a disclosure of a record prior to September 27, 1975.

(h) Rights of legal guardians. For the purposes of this section, the parent of any minor, or the legal guardian of any individual who has been declared to be incompetent due to physical or mental incapacity or age by a court of competent jurisdiction, may act on behalf of the individual.

(i)

   (1) Criminal penalties. Any officer or employee of an agency, who by virtue of his employment or official position, has possession of, or access to, agency records which contain individually identifiable information the disclosure of which is prohibited by this section or by rules or regulations established thereunder, and who knowing that disclosure of the specific material is so prohibited, willfully discloses the material in any manner to any person or agency not entitled to receive it, shall be guilty of a misdemeanor and fined not more than $5000.

   (2) Any officer or employee of any agency who willfully maintains a system of records without meeting the notice requirements of subsection (e)(4) of this section shall be guilty of a misdemeanor and fined not more than $5000.

   (3) Any person who knowingly and willfully requests or obtains any record concerning an individual from an agency under false pretenses shall be guilty of a misdemeanor and fined not more than $5000.

(j) General exemptions. The head of any agency may promulgate rules, in accordance with the requirements (including general notice) of sections 553(b)(1), (2), and (3), (c), and (e) of this title, to exempt any system of records within the agency from any part of this section except subsections (b), (c)(1) and (2), (e)(4)(A) through (F), (e)(6), (7), (9), (10), and (11), and (i) if the system of records is—

   (1) maintained by the Central Intelligence Agency; or

   (2) maintained by an agency or component thereof which performs as its principal function any activity pertaining to the enforcement of criminal laws, including police efforts to prevent, control, or reduce crime or to apprehend criminals, and the activities of prosecutors, courts, correctional, probation, pardon, or parole authorities, and which consists of (A) information compiled for the purpose of identifying individual criminal offenders and alleged offenders and consisting only of identifying data and notations of arrests, the nature and disposition of criminal charges, sentencing, confinement, release, and parole and probation status; (B) information compiled for the purpose

of a criminal investigation, including reports of informants and investigators, and associated with an identifiable individual; or (C) reports identifiable to an individual compiled at any stage of the process of enforcement of the criminal laws from arrest or indictment through release from supervision.

At the time rules are adopted under this subsection, the agency shall include in the statement required under section 553(c) of this title, the reasons why the system of records is to be exempted from a provision of this section.

(k) Specific exemptions

The head of any agency may promulgate rules, in accordance with the requirements (including general notice) of sections 553(b)(1), (2), and (3), (c), and (e) of this title, to exempt any system of records within the agency from subsections (c)(3), (d), (e)(1), (e)(4)(G), (H), and (I) and (f) of this section if the system of records is—

(1) subject to the provisions of section 552(b)(1) of this title;

(2) investigatory material compiled for law enforcement purposes, other than material within the scope of subsection (j)(2) of this section: *Provided, however,* that if any individual is denied any right, privilege, or benefit that he would otherwise be entitled by Federal law, or for which he would otherwise be eligible, as a result of the maintenance of such material, such material shall be provided to such individual, except to the extent that the disclosure of such material would reveal the identity of a source who furnished information to the Government under an express promise that the identity of the source would be held in confidence, or, prior to the effective date of this section, under an implied promise that the identity of the source would be held in confidence;

(3) maintained in connection with providing protective services to the President of the United States or other individuals pursuant to section 3056 of Title 18;

(4) required by statute to be maintained and used solely as statistical records;

(5) investigatory material compiled solely for the purpose of determining suitability, eligibility, or qualifications for Federal civilian employment, military service, Federal contracts, or access to classified information, but only to the extent that the disclosure of such material would reveal the identity of a source who furnished information to the Government under an express promise that the identity of the source would be held in confidence, or, prior to the effective date of this section, under an

implied promise that the identity of the source would be held in confidence;

(6) testing or examination material used solely to determine individual qualifications for appointment or promotion in the Federal service the disclosure of which would compromise the objectivity or fairness of the testing or examination process; or

(7) evaluation material used to determine potential for promotion in the armed services, but only to the extent that the disclosure of such material would reveal the identity of a source who furnished information to the Government under an express promise that the identity of the source would be held in confidence, or, prior to the effective date of this section, under an implied promise that the identity of the source would be held in confidence.

At the time rules are adopted under this subsection, the agency shall include in the statement required under section 553(c) of this title, the reasons why the system of records is to be exempted from a provision of this section.

(l) Archival records

(1) Each agency record which is accepted by the Archivist of the United States for storage, processing, and servicing in accordance with section 3103 of Title 44 shall, for the purposes of this section, be considered to be maintained by the agency which deposited the record and shall be subject to the provisions of this section. The Archivist of the United States shall not disclose the record except to the agency which maintains the record, or under rules established by that agency which are not inconsistent with the provisions of this section.

(2) Each agency record pertaining to an identifiable individual which was transferred to the National Archives of the United States as a record which has sufficient historical or other value to warrant its continued preservation by the United States Government, prior to the effective date of this section, shall, for the purposes of this section, be considered to be maintained by the National Archives and shall not be subject to the provisions of this section, except that a statement generally describing such records (modeled after the requirements relating to records subject to subsections (e)(4) (A) through (G) of this section) shall be published in the Federal Register.

(3) Each agency record pertaining to an identifiable individual which is transferred to the National Archives of the United States as a record which has sufficient historical or other value to warrant its continued preservation by the United States Government, on

or after the effective date of this section, shall, for the purposes of this section, be considered to be maintained by the National Archives and shall be exempt from the requirements of this section except subsections (e)(4)(A) through (G) and (e)(9) of this section.

(m) Government contractors

(1) When an agency provides by a contract for the operation by or on behalf of the agency of a system of records to accomplish an agency function, the agency shall, consistent with its authority, cause the requirements of this section to be applied to such system. For purposes of subsection (i) of this section any such contractor and any employee of such contractor, if such contract is agreed to on or after the effective date of this section, shall be considered to be an employee of an agency.

(2) A consumer reporting agency to which a record is disclosed under section 3711(e) of Title 31 shall not be considered a contractor for the purposes of this section.

(n) Mailing lists. An individual's name and address may not be sold or rented by an agency unless such action is specifically authorized by law. This provision shall not be construed to require the withholding of names and addresses otherwise permitted to be made public.

(o) Matching agreements

(1) No record which is contained in a system of records may be disclosed to a recipient agency or non-Federal agency for use in a computer matching program except pursuant to a written agreement between the source agency and the recipient agency or non-Federal agency specifying—

(A) the purpose and legal authority for conducting the program;

(B) the justification for the program and the anticipated results, including a specific estimate of any savings;

(C) a description of the records that will be matched, including each data element that will be used, the approximate number of records that will be matched, and the projected starting and completion dates of the matching program;

(D) procedures for providing individualized notice at the time of application, and notice periodically thereafter as directed by the Data Integrity Board of such agency (subject to guidance provided by the Director of the Office of Management and Budget pursuant to subsection (v)), to—

(i) applicants for and recipients of financial assistance or payments under Federal benefit programs, and

      (ii) applicants for and holders of positions as Federal personnel, that any information provided by such applicants, recipients, holders, and individuals may be subject to verification through matching programs;

(E) procedures for verifying information produced in such matching program as required by subsection (p);

(F) procedures for the retention and timely destruction of identifiable records created by a recipient agency or non-Federal agency in such matching program;

(G) procedures for ensuring the administrative, technical, and physical security of the records matched and the results of such programs;

(H) prohibitions on duplication and redisclosure of records provided by the source agency within or outside the recipient agency or the non-Federal agency, except where required by law or essential to the conduct of the matching program;

(I) procedures governing the use by a recipient agency or non-Federal agency of records provided in a matching program by a source agency, including procedures governing return of the records to the source agency or destruction of records used in such program;

(J) information on assessments that have been made on the accuracy of the records that will be used in such matching program; and

(K) that the Comptroller General may have access to all records of a recipient agency or a non-Federal agency that the Comptroller General deems necessary in order to monitor or verify compliance with the agreement.

(2)

    (A) A copy of each agreement entered into pursuant to paragraph (1) shall—

      (i) be transmitted to the Committee on Governmental Affairs of the Senate and the Committee on Government Operations of the House of Representatives; and

      (ii) be available upon request to the public.

    (B) No such agreement shall be effective until 30 days after the date on which such a copy is transmitted pursuant to subparagraph (A)(i).

    (C) Such an agreement shall remain in effect only for such period, not to exceed 18 months, as the Data Integrity Board of the agency determines is appropriate in light of the purposes, and length of time necessary for the conduct, of the matching program.

(D) Within 3 months prior to the expiration of such an agreement pursuant to subparagraph (C), the Data Integrity Board of the agency may, without additional review, renew the matching agreement for a current, ongoing matching program for not more than one additional year if—

    (i)   such program will be conducted without any change; and

    (ii) each party to the agreement certifies to the Board in writing that the program has been conducted in compliance with the agreement.

(p) Verification and Opportunity to Contest Findings

  (1) In order to protect any individual whose records are used in a matching program, no recipient agency, non-Federal agency, or source agency may suspend, terminate, reduce, or make a final denial of any financial assistance or payment under a Federal benefit program to such individual, or take other adverse action against such individual, as a result of information produced by such matching program, until—

    (A) (i) the agency has independently verified the information; or

        (ii) the Data Integrity Board of the agency, or in the case of a non-Federal agency the Data Integrity Board of the source agency, determines in accordance with guidance issued by the Director of the Office of Management and Budget that—

            (I) the information is limited to identification and amount of benefits paid by the source agency under a Federal benefit program; and

            (II) there is a high degree of confidence that the information provided to the recipient agency is accurate;

    (B) the individual receives a notice from the agency containing a statement of its findings and informing the individual of the opportunity to contest such findings; and

    (C) (i) the expiration of any time period established for the program by statute or regulation for the individual to respond to that notice; or

        (ii) in the case of a program for which no such period is established, the end of the 30-day period beginning on the date on which notice under subparagraph (B) is mailed or otherwise provided to the individual.

  (2) Independent verification referred to in paragraph (1) requires investigation and confirmation of specific information relating to an individual that is used as a basis for an adverse action

against the individual, including where applicable investigation and confirmation of—

(A) the amount of any asset or income involved;

(B) whether such individual actually has or had access to such asset or income for such individual's own use; and

(C) the period or periods when the individual actually had such asset or income.

(3) Notwithstanding paragraph (1), an agency may take any appropriate action otherwise prohibited by such paragraph if the agency determines that the public health or public safety may be adversely affected or significantly threatened during any notice period required by such paragraph.

(q) Sanctions

(1) Notwithstanding any other provision of law, no source agency may disclose any record which is contained in a system of records to a recipient agency or non-Federal agency for a matching program if such source agency has reason to believe that the requirements of subsection (p), or any matching agreement entered into pursuant to subsection (o), or both, are not being met by such recipient agency.

(2) No source agency may renew a matching agreement unless—

(A) the recipient agency or non-Federal agency has certified that it has complied with the provisions of that agreement; and

(B) the source agency has no reason to believe that the certification is inaccurate.

(r) Report on new systems and matching programs. Each agency that proposes to establish or make a significant change in a system of records or a matching program shall provide adequate advance notice of any such proposal (in duplicate) to the Committee on Government Operations of the House of Representatives, the Committee on Governmental Affairs of the Senate, and the Office of Management and Budget in order to permit an evaluation of the probable or potential effect of such proposal on the privacy or other rights of individuals.

(s) [Biennial report] Repealed by the Federal Reports Elimination and Sunset Act of 1995, Pub. L. No. 104-66, § 3003, 109 Stat. 707, 734-36 (1995), *amended by* Pub. L. No. 106–113, § 236, 113 Stat. 1501, 1501A-302 (1999) (changing effective date to May 15, 2000).

(t) Effect of other laws

(1) No agency shall rely on any exemption contained in section 552 of this title to withhold from an individual any record which is otherwise accessible to such individual under the provisions of this section.

(2) No agency shall rely on any exemption in this section to withhold from an individual any record which is otherwise accessible to such individual under the provisions of section 552 of this title.

(u) Data Integrity Boards

   (1) Every agency conducting or participating in a matching program shall establish a Data Integrity Board to oversee and coordinate among the various components of such agency the agency's implementation of this section.

   (2) Each Data Integrity Board shall consist of senior officials designated by the head of the agency, and shall include any senior official designated by the head of the agency as responsible for implementation of this section, and the inspector general of the agency, if any. The inspector general shall not serve as chairman of the Data Integrity Board.

   (3) Each Data Integrity Board—

      (A) shall review, approve, and maintain all written agreements for receipt or disclosure of agency records for matching programs to ensure compliance with subsection (o), and all relevant statutes, regulations, and guidelines;

      (B) shall review all matching programs in which the agency has participated during the year, either as a source agency or recipient agency, determine compliance with applicable laws, regulations, guidelines, and agency agreements, and assess the costs and benefits of such programs;

      (C) shall review all recurring matching programs in which the agency has participated during the year, either as a source agency or recipient agency, for continued justification for such disclosures;

      (D) shall compile an annual report, which shall be submitted to the head of the agency and the Office of Management and Budget and made available to the public on request, describing the matching activities of the agency, including—

         (i) matching programs in which the agency has participated as a source agency or recipient agency;

         (ii) matching agreements proposed under subsection (o) that were disapproved by the Board;

         (iii) any changes in membership or structure of the Board in the preceding year;

         (iv) the reasons for any waiver of the requirement in paragraph (4) of this section for completion and submission of a cost-benefit analysis prior to the approval of a matching program;

        (v) any violations of matching agreements that have been alleged or identified and any corrective action taken; and

        (vi) any other information required by the Director of the Office of Management and Budget to be included in such report;

   (E) shall serve as a clearinghouse for receiving and providing information on the accuracy, completeness, and reliability of records used in matching programs;

   (F) shall provide interpretation and guidance to agency components and personnel on the requirements of this section for matching programs;

   (G) shall review agency recordkeeping and disposal policies and practices for matching programs to assure compliance with this section; and

   (H) may review and report on any agency matching activities that are not matching programs.

(4)

   (A) Except as provided in subparagraphs (B) and (C), a Data Integrity Board shall not approve any written agreement for a matching program unless the agency has completed and submitted to such Board a cost-benefit analysis of the proposed program and such analysis demonstrates that the program is likely to be cost effective.

   (B) The Board may waive the requirements of subparagraph (A) of this paragraph if it determines in writing, in accordance with guidelines prescribed by the Director of the Office of Management and Budget, that a cost-benefit analysis is not required.

   (C) A cost-benefit analysis shall not be required under subparagraph (A) prior to the initial approval of a written agreement for a matching program that is specifically required by statute. Any subsequent written agreement for such a program shall not be approved by the Data Integrity Board unless the agency has submitted a cost-benefit analysis of the program as conducted under the preceding approval of such agreement.

(5)

   (A) If a matching agreement is disapproved by a Data Integrity Board, any party to such agreement may appeal the disapproval to the Director of the Office of Management and Budget. Timely notice of the filing of such an appeal shall be provided by the Director of the Office of Management and

Budget to the Committee on Governmental Affairs of the Senate and the Committee on Government Operations of the House of Representatives.

(B) The Director of the Office of Management and Budget may approve a matching agreement notwithstanding the disapproval of a Data Integrity Board if the Director determines that—

    (i) the matching program will be consistent with all applicable legal, regulatory, and policy requirements;

    (ii) there is adequate evidence that the matching agreement will be cost-effective; and

    (iii) the matching program is in the public interest.

(C) The decision of the Director to approve a matching agreement shall not take effect until 30 days after it is reported to committees described in subparagraph (A).

(D) If the Data Integrity Board and the Director of the Office of Management and Budget disapprove a matching program proposed by the inspector general of an agency, the inspector general may report the disapproval to the head of the agency and to the Congress.

(6) The Director of the Office of Management and Budget shall, annually during the first 3 years after the date of enactment of this subsection and biennially thereafter, consolidate in a report to the Congress the information contained in the reports from the various Data Integrity Boards under paragraph (3)(D). Such report shall include detailed information about costs and benefits of matching programs that are conducted during the period covered by such consolidated report, and shall identify each waiver granted by a Data Integrity Board of the requirement for completion and submission of a cost-benefit analysis and the reasons for granting the waiver.

(7) In the reports required by paragraphs (3)(D) and (6), agency matching activities that are not matching programs may be reported on an aggregate basis, if and to the extent necessary to protect ongoing law enforcement or counterintelligence investigations.

(v) Office of Management and Budget Responsibilities

The Director of the Office of Management and Budget shall—

(1) develop and, after notice and opportunity for public comment, prescribe guidelines and regulations for the use of agencies in implementing the provisions of this section; and

(2) provide continuing assistance to and oversight of the implementation of this section by agencies.

The following section originally was part of the Privacy Act but was not codified; it may be found at § 552a (note).

§. 7(a)

(1) It shall be unlawful for any Federal, State or local government agency to deny to any individual any right, benefit, or privilege provided by law because of such individual's refusal to disclose his social security account number.

(2) The provisions of paragraph (1) of this subsection shall not apply with respect to—

   (A) any disclosure which is required by Federal statute, or

   (B) any disclosure of a social security number to any Federal, State, or local agency maintaining a system of records in existence and operating before January 1, 1975, if such disclosure was required under statute or regulation adopted prior to such date to verify the identity of an individual.

(b)   Any Federal, State or local government agency which requests an individual to disclose his social security account number shall inform that individual whether that disclosure is mandatory or voluntary, by what statutory or other authority such number is solicited, and what uses will be made of it.

The following sections originally were part of P.L. 100-503, the Computer Matching and Privacy Protection Act of 1988; they may be found at § 552a (note).

§. 6 Functions of the Director of the Office of Management and Budget

(b)   Implementation Guidance for Amendments—The Director shall, pursuant to section 552a(v) of Title 5, United States Code, develop guidelines and regulations for the use of agencies in implementing the amendments made by this Act not later than 8 months after the date of enactment of this Act.

§. 9 Rules of Construction

Nothing in the amendments made by this Act shall be construed to authorize—

(1) the establishment or maintenance by any agency of a national data bank that combines, merges, or links information on individuals maintained in systems of records by other Federal agencies;

(2) the direct linking of computerized systems of records maintained by Federal agencies;

(3) the computer matching of records not otherwise authorized by law; or

(4) the disclosure of records for computer matching except to a Federal, State, or local agency.

§. 10 Effective Dates

(a) *In General*—Except as provided in subsection (b), the amendments made by this Act shall take effect 9 months after the date of enactment of this Act.

(b) *Exceptions*—The amendment made by sections 3(b) [Notice of Matching Programs—Report to Congress and the Office of Management and Budget], 6 [Functions of the Director of the Office of Management and Budget], 7 [Compilation of Rules and Notices], and 8 [Annual Report] of this Act shall take effect upon enactment.

Privacy Protection Act of 1980 (42 U.S.C. 2000aa)

Title 42 2000 Privacy Protection Act of 1980

    Subchapter I—First Amendment Privacy Protection
    Subchapter II—Attorney General Guidelines

Subchapter I—First Amendment Privacy Protection

    Part A—Unlawful Acts
    Part B—Remedies, Exceptions, and Definitions

§ 2000aa. Searches and Seizures by Government Officers and Employees in Connection with Investigation or Prosecution of Criminal Offenses

(a) Work Product Materials

Notwithstanding any other law, it shall be unlawful for a government officer or employee, in connection with the investigation or prosecution of a criminal offense, to search for or seize any work product materials possessed by a person reasonably believed to have a purpose to disseminate to the public a newspaper, book, broadcast, or other similar form of public communication in or affecting interstate or foreign commerce, but this provision shall not impair or affect the ability of any government officer or employee, pursuant to otherwise applicable law, to search for or seize such materials, if

(1) There is probable cause to believe that the person possessing such materials has committed or is committing the criminal offense to which the materials relate, provided, however, that a government officer or employee may not search for or seize such materials under the provisions of this paragraph if the offense to which the materials relate consists of the receipt, possession, communication, or withholding of such materials or the information contained therein (but such a search or seizure may be conducted under the provisions of this paragraph if the offense consists of the receipt, possession, or communication of information relating to the national defense, classified information, or restricted data under the provisions of Section 793, 794, 797, or 798 of Title 18, or Section 2274, 2275, or 2277 of this title, or Section 783 of Title 50, or if the offense involves the production, possession, receipt, mailing, sale, distribution, shipment, or transportation of child pornography, the sexual exploitation of children, or the sale or purchase of children under Section 2251, 2251A, 2252, or 2252A of Title 18)

(2) There is reason to believe that the immediate seizure of such materials is necessary to prevent the death of, or serious bodily injury to, a human being

(b) Other Documents

Notwithstanding any other law, it shall be unlawful for a government officer or employee, in connection with the investigation or prosecution of a criminal offense, to search for or seize documentary materials, other than work product materials, possessed by a person in connection with a purpose to disseminate to the public a newspaper, book, broadcast, or other similar form of public communication in or affecting interstate or foreign commerce, but this provision shall not impair or affect the ability of any government officer or employee, pursuant to otherwise applicable law, to search for or seize such materials, if

(1) There is probable cause to believe that the person possessing such materials has committed or is committing the criminal offense to which the materials relate, provided, however, that a government officer or employee may not search for or seize such materials under the provisions of this paragraph if the offense to which the materials relate consists of the receipt, possession, communication, or withholding of such materials or the information contained therein (but such a search or seizure may be conducted under the provisions of this paragraph if the offense consists of the receipt, possession, or communication of information relating to the national defense, classified information,

or restricted data under the provisions of Section 793, 794, 797, or 798 of Title 18, or Section 2274, 2275, or 2277 of this title, or Section 783 of Title 50, or if the offense involves the production, possession, receipt, mailing, sale, distribution, shipment, or transportation of child pornography, the sexual exploitation of children, or the sale or purchase of children under Section 2251, 2251A, 2252, or 2252A of title 18)

(2) There is reason to believe that the immediate seizure of such materials is necessary to prevent the death of, or serious bodily injury to, a human being

(3) There is reason to believe that the giving of notice pursuant to a subpoena duces tecum would result in the destruction, alteration, or concealment of such materials

(4) Such materials have not been produced in response to a court order directing compliance with a subpoena duces tecum

   (A) All appellate remedies have been exhausted

   (B) There is reason to believe that the delay in an investigation or trial occasioned by further proceedings relating to the subpoena would threaten the interests of justice

(c) Objections to Court-Ordered Subpoenas; Affidavits

In the event a search warrant is sought pursuant to paragraph (4)(B) of subsection (b) of this section, the person possessing the materials shall be afforded adequate opportunity to submit an affidavit setting forth the basis for any contention that the materials sought are not subject to seizure.

§ 2000aa-5. Border and Customs Searches

This chapter shall not impair or affect the ability of a government officer or employee, pursuant to otherwise applicable law, to conduct searches and seizures at the borders of, or at international points of, entry into the United States in order to enforce the customs laws of the United States.

§ 2000aa-6. Civil Actions by Aggrieved Persons

(a) Right of Action

A person aggrieved by a search for or seizure of materials in violation of this chapter shall have a civil cause of action for damages for such search or seizure

(1) Against the United States, against a state that has waived its sovereign immunity under the Constitution to a claim for damages resulting from a violation of this chapter, or against any other governmental unit, all of which shall be liable for violations of this chapter by their officers or employees while acting within the scope or under color of their office or employment

(2) Against an officer or employee of a state who has violated this chapter while acting within the scope or under color of his office or employment, if such state has not waived its sovereign immunity as provided in paragraph (1)

(b) Good Faith Defense

It shall be a complete defense to a civil action brought under paragraph (2) of subsection (a) of this section that the officer or employee had a reasonable good faith belief in the lawfulness of his conduct.

(c) Official Immunity

The United States, a state, or any other governmental unit liable for violations of this chapter under subsection (a)(1) of this section may not assert as a defense to a claim arising under this chapter the immunity of the officer or employee whose violation is complained of or his reasonable good faith belief in the lawfulness of his conduct, except that such a defense may be asserted if the violation complained of is that of a judicial officer.

(d) Exclusive Nature of Remedy

The remedy provided by subsection (a)(1) of this section against the United States, a state, or any other governmental unit is exclusive of any other civil action or proceeding for conduct constituting a violation of this chapter against the officer or employee whose violation gave rise to the claim or against the estate of such officer or employee.

(e) Admissibility of Evidence

Evidence otherwise admissible in a proceeding shall not be excluded on the basis of a violation of this chapter.

(f) Damages; Costs and Attorneys' Fees

A person having a cause of action under this section shall be entitled to recover actual damages but not less than liquidated damages of $1000, and such reasonable attorneys' fees and other litigation costs reasonably incurred as the court, in its discretion, may award, provided, however, that the United States, a state, or any other governmental unit shall not be liable for interest prior to judgment.

(g) Attorney General; Claims Settlement; Regulations

The attorney general may settle a claim for damages brought against the United States under this section and shall promulgate regulations to provide for the commencement of an administrative inquiry following a determination of a violation of this chapter by an officer or employee of the United States and for the imposition of administrative sanctions against such officer or employee, if warranted.

(h) Jurisdiction
     The district courts shall have original jurisdiction of all civil actions
     arising under this section.

§ 2000aa-7. Definitions

(a) "Documentary materials," as used in this chapter, means materials
     upon which information is recorded and includes, but is not limited
     to, written or printed materials, photographs, motion picture films,
     negatives, video tapes, audio tapes, and other mechanically, magneti-
     cally, or electronically recorded cards, tapes, or disks, but does not
     include contraband or the fruits of a crime or things otherwise crimi-
     nally possessed, or property designed or intended for use, or which is
     or has been used as, the means of committing a criminal offense.
(b) "Work product materials," as used in this chapter, means materials,
     other than contraband or the fruits of a crime or things otherwise crim-
     inally possessed, or property designed or intended for use, or which is
     or has been used, as the means of committing a criminal offense, and
     (1) In anticipation of communicating such materials to the public,
          are prepared, produced, authored, or created, whether by the
          person in possession of the materials or by any other person
     (2) Are possessed for the purposes of communicating such materi-
          als to the public
     (3) Include mental impressions, conclusions, opinions, or theories
          of the person who prepared, produced, authored, or created
          such material
(c) *Any other governmental unit,* as used in this chapter, includes the
     District of Columbia, the Commonwealth of Puerto Rico, any ter-
     ritory or possession of the United States, and any local government,
     unit of local government, or any unit of state government.

Subchapter II—Attorney General Guidelines

§ 2000aa-11. Guidelines for Federal Officers and Employees
§ 2000aa-12. Binding Nature of Guidelines, Disciplinary Actions for
Violations, and Legal Proceedings for Noncompliance Prohibited

§ 2000aa-11. Guidelines for Federal Officers and Employees

(a) Procedures to Obtain Documentary Evidence; Protection of Certain
     Privacy Interests
     The attorney general shall, within six months of October 13, 1980,
     issue guidelines for the procedures to be employed by any federal offi-
     cer or employee, in connection with the investigation or prosecution

of an offense, to obtain documentary materials in the private possession of a person when the person is not reasonably believed to
be a suspect in such offense or related by blood or marriage to such
a suspect and when the materials sought are not contraband or the
fruits or instrumentalities of an offense. The attorney general shall
incorporate in such guidelines

(1) A recognition of the personal privacy interests of the person in
    possession of such documentary materials
(2) A requirement that the least intrusive method or means of
    obtaining such materials be used, which do not substantially
    jeopardize the availability or usefulness of the materials sought
    to be obtained
(3) A recognition of special concern for privacy interests in cases
    in which a search or seizure for such documents would intrude
    upon a known confidential relationship such as that which may
    exist between clergyman and parishioner, lawyer and client, or
    doctor and patient
(4) A requirement that an application for a warrant to conduct a
    search governed by this subchapter be approved by an attorney
    for the government, except that in an emergency situation, the
    application may be approved by another appropriate supervisory
    official if, within 24 hours of such emergency, the appropriate
    United States Attorney is notified

(b) Use of Search Warrants; Reports to Congress
    The attorney general shall collect and compile information on and
    report annually to the committees on the judiciary of the Senate and
    the House of Representatives on the use of search warrants by fed-
    eral officers and employees for documentary materials described in
    subsection (a)(3) of this section.

§ 2000aa-12. Binding Nature of Guidelines; Disciplinary Actions for Violations; Legal Proceedings for Noncompliance Prohibited

Guidelines issued by the attorney general under this subchapter shall have
the full force and effect of Department of Justice regulations, and any
violation of these guidelines shall make the employee or officer involved
subject to appropriate administrative disciplinary action. However, an
issue relating to the compliance, or the failure to comply, with guidelines
issued pursuant to this subchapter may not be litigated, and a court may
not entertain such an issue as the basis for the suppression or exclusion of
evidence.

Employee Polygraph Protection Act (EPPA) (29 U.S.C. 2001–2009)

§ 2001. Definitions

As used in this chapter,

(1) *Commerce*

The term *commerce* has the meaning provided by Section 203 (b) of this title.

(2) *Employer*

The term *employer* includes any person acting directly or indirectly in the interest of an employer in relation to an employee or prospective employee.

(3) *Lie detector*

The term *lie detector* includes a polygraph, deceptograph, voice stress analyzer, psychological stress evaluator, or any other similar device (whether mechanical or electrical) that is used, or the results of which are used, for the purpose of rendering a diagnostic opinion regarding the honesty or dishonesty of an individual.

(4) *Polygraph*

The term *polygraph* means an instrument that

(A) Records continuously, visually, permanently, and simultaneously changes in cardiovascular, respiratory, and electrodermal patterns as minimum instrumentation standards

(B) Is used, or the results of which are used, for the purpose of rendering a diagnostic opinion regarding the honesty or dishonesty of an individual

(5) *Secretary*

The term *Secretary* means the Secretary of Labor.

§ 2002. Prohibitions on Lie Detector Use

Except as provided in Sections 2006 and 2007 of this title, it shall be unlawful for any employer engaged in or affecting commerce or in the production of goods for commerce

(1) Directly or indirectly, to require, request, suggest, or cause any employee or prospective employee to take or submit to any lie detector test

(2) To use, accept, refer to, or inquire concerning the results of any lie detector test of any employee or prospective employee

(3) To discharge, discipline, discriminate against in any manner, deny employment or promotion to, or threaten to take any such action against

    (A)   Any employee or prospective employee who refuses, declines, or fails to take or submit to any lie detector test

    (B)   Any employee or prospective employee on the basis of the results of any lie detector test

(4) To discharge, discipline, discriminate against in any manner, deny employment or promotion to, or threaten to take any such action against any employee or prospective employee because

    (A)   Such employee or prospective employee has filed any complaint or instituted or caused to be instituted any proceeding under or related to this chapter

    (B)   Such employee or prospective employee has testified or is about to testify in any such proceeding

    (C)   Of the exercise by such employee or prospective employee, on behalf of such employee or another person, of any right afforded by this chapter

§ 2003. Notice of Protection

The Secretary shall prepare, have printed, and distribute a notice setting forth excerpts from, or summaries of, the pertinent provisions of this chapter. Each employer shall post and maintain such notice in conspicuous places on its premises where notices to employees and applicants to employment are customarily posted.

§ 2004. Authority of Secretary

(a) *In general*

The Secretary shall

    (1)   Issue such rules and regulations as may be necessary or appropriate to carry out this chapter

    (2)   Cooperate with regional, state, local, and other agencies and cooperate with and furnish technical assistance to employers, labor organizations, and employment agencies to aid in effectuating the purposes of this chapter

    (3)   Make investigations and inspections and require the keeping of records necessary or appropriate for the administration of this chapter

(b) *Subpoena authority*

For the purpose of any hearing or investigation under this chapter, the Secretary shall have the authority contained in Sections 49 and 50 of Title 15.

§ 2005. Enforcement Provisions

(a) *Civil penalties*

    (1) In general

        Subject to paragraph (2), any employer who violates any provision of this chapter may be assessed a civil penalty of not more than $10,000.

    (2) Determination of amount

        In determining the amount of any penalty under paragraph (1), the Secretary shall take into account the previous record of the person in terms of compliance with this chapter and the gravity of the violation.

    (3) Collection

        Any civil penalty assessed under this subsection shall be collected in the same manner as is required by subsections (b)–(e) of Section 1853 of this title with respect to civil penalties assessed under subsection (a) of such section.

(b) *Injunctive actions by Secretary*

    The Secretary may bring an action under this section to restrain violations of this chapter. The Solicitor of Labor may appear for and represent the Secretary in any litigation brought under this chapter. In any action brought under this section, the district courts of the United States shall have jurisdiction, for cause shown, to issue temporary or permanent restraining orders and injunctions to require compliance with this chapter, including such legal or equitable relief incident thereto as may be appropriate, including, but not limited to, employment, reinstatement, promotion, and the payment of lost wages and benefits.

(c) *Private civil actions*

    (1) Liability

        An employer who violates this chapter shall be liable to the employee or prospective employee affected by such violation. Such employer shall be liable for such legal or equitable relief as may be appropriate, including, but not limited to, employment, reinstatement, promotion, and the payment of lost wages and benefits.

    (2) Court

        An action to recover the liability prescribed in paragraph (1) may be maintained against the employer in any federal or state court of competent jurisdiction by an employee or prospective employee for or on behalf of such employee, prospective employee, and other employees or prospective employees similarly situated. No such action may be commenced more than 3 years after the date of the alleged violation.

(3) Costs
The court, in its discretion, may allow the prevailing party (other than the United States) reasonable costs, including attorney's fees.

(d) *Waiver of rights prohibited*
The rights and procedures provided by this chapter may not be waived by contract or otherwise, unless such waiver is part of a written settlement agreed to and signed by the parties to the pending action or complaint under this chapter.

§ 2006. Exemptions

(a) *No application to governmental employers*
This chapter shall not apply with respect to the U.S. Government, any state or local government, or any political subdivision of a state or local government.

(b) *National defense and security exemption*
(1) National defense
Nothing in this chapter shall be construed to prohibit the administration, by the federal government, in the performance of any counterintelligence function, of any lie detector test to
(A) Any expert or consultant under contract to the Department of Defense or any employee of any contractor of such department
(B) Any expert or consultant under contract with the Department of Energy in connection with the atomic energy defense activities of such department or any employee of any contractor of such department in connection with such activities

(2) Security
Nothing in this chapter shall be construed to prohibit the administration, by the federal government, in the performance of any intelligence or counterintelligence function, of any lie detector test to
(A) (i) Any individual employed by, assigned to, or detailed to the National Security Agency, the Defense Intelligence Agency, the National Geospatial-Intelligence Agency, or the Central Intelligence Agency
(ii) Any expert or consultant under contract to any such agency

           (iii)   Any employee of a contractor to any such agency

           (iv)   Any individual applying for a position in any such agency

           (v)   Any individual assigned to a space where sensitive cryptologic information is produced, processed, or stored for any such agency

      (B)   Any expert or consultant (or employee of such expert or consultant) under contract with any federal government department, agency, or program whose duties involve access to information that has been classified at the level of top secret or designated as being within a special access program under Section 4.2(a) of Executive Order 12356 (or a successor executive order)

(c) *FBI contractors' exemption*

Nothing in this chapter shall be construed to prohibit the administration, by the federal government, in the performance of any counterintelligence function, of any lie detector test to an employee of a contractor of the Federal Bureau of Investigation of the Department of Justice who is engaged in the performance of any work under the contract with such bureau.

(d) *Limited exemption for ongoing investigations*

Subject to Sections 2007 and 2009 of this title, this chapter shall not prohibit an employer from requesting an employee to submit to a polygraph test if

(1)   The test is administered in connection with an ongoing investigation involving economic loss or injury to the employer's business, such as theft, embezzlement, misappropriation, or an act of unlawful industrial espionage or sabotage

(2)   The employee had access to the property that is the subject of the investigation

(3)   The employer has a reasonable suspicion that the employee was involved in the incident or activity under investigation

(4)   The employer executes a statement, provided to the examinee before the test, that

    (A)   Sets forth with particularity the specific incident or activity being investigated and the basis for testing particular employees

    (B)   Is signed by a person (other than a polygraph examiner) authorized to legally bind the employer

    (C)   Is retained by the employer for at least 3 years

    (D)   Contains at a minimum

        (i)   An identification of the specific economic loss or injury to the business of the employer

        (ii)   A statement indicating that the employee had access to the property that is the subject of the investigation

        (iii)   A statement describing the basis of the employer's reasonable suspicion that the employee was involved in the incident or activity under investigation

(e) *Exemption for security services*

    (1) In general

        Subject to paragraph (2) and Sections 2007 and 2009 of this title, this chapter shall not prohibit the use of polygraph tests on prospective employees by any private employer whose primary business purpose consists of providing armored car personnel; personnel engaged in the design, installation, and maintenance of security alarm systems; or other uniformed or plainclothes security personnel and whose function includes protection of

        (A)   Facilities, materials, or operations having a significant impact on the health or safety of any state or political subdivision thereof, or the national security of the United States, as determined under rules and regulations issued by the Secretary within 90 days after June 27, 1988, including

           (i)   Facilities engaged in the production, transmission, or distribution of electric or nuclear power

           (ii)   Public water supply facilities

           (iii) Shipments or storage of radioactive or other toxic waste materials

           (iv) Public transportation

        (B)   Currency, negotiable securities, precious commodities or instruments, or proprietary information

    (2) Access

        The exemption provided under this subsection shall not apply if the test is administered to a prospective employee who would not be employed to protect facilities, materials, operations, or assets referred to in paragraph (1).

(f) *Exemption for drug security, drug theft, or drug diversion investigations*

    (1) In general

        Subject to paragraph (2) and Sections 2007 and 2009 of this title, this chapter shall not prohibit the use of a polygraph test by any employer authorized to manufacture, distribute, or dispense a controlled substance listed in schedule I, II, III, or IV of Section 812 of Title 21.

    (2) Access

        The exemption provided under this subsection shall apply

(A) If the test is administered to a prospective employee who would have direct access to the manufacture, storage, distribution, or sale of any such controlled substance

(B) In the case of a test administered to a current employee, if

  (i) The test is administered in connection with an ongoing investigation of criminal or other misconduct involving, or potentially involving, loss or injury to the manufacture, distribution, or dispensing of any such controlled substance by such employer

  (ii) The employee had access to the person or property that is the subject of the investigation

§ 2007. Restrictions on Use of Exemptions

(a) *Test as basis for adverse employment action*

  (1) Under ongoing investigations' exemption
  Except as provided in paragraph (2), the exemption under subsection (d) of Section 2006 of this title shall not apply if an employee is discharged, disciplined, denied employment or promotion, or otherwise discriminated against in any manner on the basis of the analysis of a polygraph test chart or the refusal to take a polygraph test, without additional supporting evidence. The evidence required by such subsection may serve as additional supporting evidence.

  (2) Under other exemptions
  In the case of an exemption described in subsection (e) or (f) of such section, the exemption shall not apply if the results of an analysis of a polygraph test chart are used, or the refusal to take a polygraph test is used, as the sole basis upon which an adverse employment action described in paragraph (1) is taken against an employee or prospective employee.

(b) *Rights of examinee*
  The exemptions provided under subsections (d)–(f) of Section 2006 of this title shall not apply unless the requirements described in the following paragraphs are met:

  (1) All phases
  Throughout all phases of the test,

    (A) The examinee shall be permitted to terminate the test at any time

    (B) The examinee is not asked questions in a manner designed to degrade, or needlessly intrude on, such examinee

    (C) The examinee is not asked any question concerning

      (i) Religious beliefs or affiliations

      (ii) Beliefs or opinions regarding racial matters

      (iii)   Political beliefs or affiliations

      (iv)   Any matter relating to sexual behavior

      (v)   Beliefs, affiliations, opinions, or lawful activities regarding unions or labor organizations

  (D)   The examiner does not conduct the test if there is sufficient written evidence by a physician that the examinee is suffering from a medical or psychological condition or undergoing treatment that might cause abnormal responses during the actual testing phase

(2) Pretest phase

During the pretest phase, the prospective examinee

  (A)   Is provided with reasonable written notice of the date, time, and location of the test and of such examinee's right to obtain and consult with legal counsel or an employee representative before each phase of the test

  (B)   Is informed in writing of the nature and characteristics of the tests and of the instruments involved

  (C)   Is informed in writing

      (i)   Whether the testing area contains a two-way mirror, a camera, or any other device through which the test can be observed

      (ii)   Whether any other device, including any device for recording or monitoring the test, will be used

      (iii)   That the employer or the examinee may (with mutual knowledge) make a recording of the test

  (D)   Is read and signs a written notice informing such examinee

      (i)   That the examinee cannot be required to take the test as a condition of employment

      (ii)   That any statement made during the test may constitute additional supporting evidence for the purposes of an adverse employment action described in subsection (a) of this section

      (iii)   Of the limitations imposed under this section

      (iv)   Of the legal rights and remedies available to the examinee if the polygraph test is not conducted in accordance with this chapter

      (v)   Of the legal rights and remedies of the employer under this chapter (including the rights of the employer under Section 2008(c)(2) of this title)

  (E)   Is provided an opportunity to review all questions to be asked during the test and is informed of the right to terminate the test at any time

(3) Actual testing phase

During the actual testing phase, the examiner does not ask such examinee any question relevant during the test that was not presented in writing for review to such examinee before the test.

(4) Posttest phase

Before any adverse employment action, the employer shall

    (A) Further interview the examinee on the basis of the results of the test

    (B) Provide the examinee with

        (i) A written copy of any opinion or conclusion rendered as a result of the test

        (ii) A copy of the questions asked during the test along with the corresponding charted responses

(5) Maximum number and minimum duration of tests

The examiner shall not conduct and complete more than five polygraph tests on a calendar day on which the test is given and shall not conduct any such test for less than a 90 minute duration.

(c) *Qualifications and requirements of examiners*

The exemptions provided under subsections (d)–(f) of Section 2006 of this title shall not apply unless the individual who conducts the polygraph test satisfies the requirements under the following paragraphs:

(1) Qualifications

The examiner

    (A) Has a valid and current license granted by licensing and regulatory authorities in the state in which the test is to be conducted, if so required by the state

    (B) Maintains a minimum of a $50,000 bond or an equivalent amount of professional liability coverage

(2) Requirements

The examiner

    (A) Renders any opinion or conclusion regarding the test

        (i) In writing and solely on the basis of an analysis of polygraph test charts

        (ii) That does not contain information other than admissions, information, case facts, and interpretation of the charts relevant to the purpose and stated objectives of the test

        (iii) That does not include any recommendation concerning the employment of the examinee

    (B) Maintains all opinions, reports, charts, written questions, lists, and other records relating to the test for a minimum period of 3 years after administration of the test

§ 2008. Disclosure of Information

(a) *In general*
A person, other than the examinee, may not disclose information obtained during a polygraph test, except as provided in this section.

(b) *Permitted disclosures*
A polygraph examiner may disclose information acquired from a polygraph test only to
(1) The examinee or any other person specifically designated in writing by the examinee
(2) The employer that requested the test
(3) Any court, governmental agency, arbitrator, or mediator, in accordance with due process of law, pursuant to an order from a court of competent jurisdiction

(c) *Disclosure by employer*
An employer (other than an employer described in subsection (a), (b), or (c) of Section 2006 of this title) for whom a polygraph test is conducted may disclose information from the test only to
(1) A person in accordance with subsection (b) of this section
(2) A governmental agency, but only insofar as the disclosed information is an admission of criminal conduct

§ 2009. Effect on Other Law and Agreements

Except as provided in subsections (a), (b), and (c) of Section 2006 of this title, this chapter shall not preempt any provision of any state or local law or of any negotiated collective bargaining agreement that prohibits lie detector tests or is more restrictive with respect to lie detector tests than any provision of this chapter.

Fair Credit Reporting Act (15 U.S.C. 1681)

§ 1681. Congressional Findings and Statement of Purpose

(a) Accuracy and fairness of credit reporting
The Congress makes the following findings:
(1) The banking system is dependent upon fair and accurate credit reporting. Inaccurate credit reports directly impair the efficiency of the banking system, and unfair credit reporting methods undermine the public confidence which is essential to the continued functioning of the banking system.
(2) An elaborate mechanism has been developed for investigating and evaluating the credit worthiness, credit standing, credit capacity, character, and general reputation of consumers.

(3) Consumer reporting agencies have assumed a vital role in assembling and evaluating consumer credit and other information on consumers.

(4) There is a need to insure that consumer reporting agencies exercise their grave responsibilities with fairness, impartiality, and a respect for the consumer's right to privacy.

(b) Reasonable procedures

It is the purpose of this subchapter to require that consumer reporting agencies adopt reasonable procedures for meeting the needs of commerce for consumer credit, personnel, insurance, and other information in a manner which is fair and equitable to the consumer, with regard to the confidentiality, accuracy, relevancy, and proper utilization of such information in accordance with the requirements of this subchapter.

§ 1681a. Definitions; Rules of Construction

(a) Definitions and rules of construction set forth in this section are applicable for the purposes of this subchapter.

(b) The term "person" means any individual, partnership, corporation, trust, estate, cooperative, association, government or governmental subdivision or agency, or other entity.

(c) The term "consumer" means an individual.

(d) Consumer Report.

(1) *In general:* The term "consumer report" means any written, oral, or other communication of any information by a consumer reporting agency bearing on a consumer's credit worthiness, credit standing, credit capacity, character, general reputation, personal characteristics, or mode of living which is used or expected to be used or collected in whole or in part for the purpose of serving as a factor in establishing the consumer's eligibility for

(A) credit or insurance to be used primarily for personal, family, or household purposes;

(B) employment purposes; or

(C) any other purpose authorized under section 1681b of this title.

(2) *Exclusions:* Except as provided in paragraph (3), the term "consumer report" does not include

(A) subject to section 1681s–3 of this title, any—

(i) report containing information solely as to transactions or experiences between the consumer and the person making the report;

        (ii)   communication of that information among persons related by common ownership or affiliated by corporate control; or

        (iii)   communication of other information among persons related by common ownership or affiliated by corporate control, if it is clearly and conspicuously disclosed to the consumer that the information may be communicated among such persons and the consumer is given the opportunity, before the time that the information is initially communicated, to direct that such information not be communicated among such persons;

  (B)   any authorization or approval of a specific extension of credit directly or indirectly by the issuer of a credit card or similar device;

  (C)   any report in which a person who has been requested by a third party to make a specific extension of credit directly or indirectly to a consumer conveys his or her decision with respect to such request, if the third party advises the consumer of the name and address of the person to whom the request was made, and such person makes the disclosures to the consumer required under section 1681m of this title; or

  (D)   a communication described in subsection (o) or (x) of this section.

  (3) Restriction on sharing of medical information—Except for information or any communication of information disclosed as provided in section 1681b (g)(3) of this title, the exclusions in paragraph (2) shall not apply with respect to information disclosed to any person related by common ownership or affiliated by corporate control, if the information is—

  (A)   medical information;

  (B)   an individualized list or description based on the payment transactions of the consumer for medical products or services; or

  (C)   an aggregate list of identified consumers based on payment transactions for medical products or services.

(e) The term "investigative consumer report" means a consumer report or portion thereof in which information on a consumer's character, general reputation, personal characteristics, or mode of living is obtained through personal interviews with neighbors, friends, or associates of the consumer reported on or with others with whom he is acquainted or who may have knowledge concerning any such items of information. However, such information shall not include specific factual information on a consumer's credit record obtained directly from a creditor of the consumer or from a consumer reporting agency when such information was obtained directly from a creditor of the consumer or from the consumer.

(f) The term "consumer reporting agency" means any person which, for monetary fees, dues, or on a cooperative nonprofit basis, regularly engages in whole or in part in the practice of assembling or evaluating consumer credit information or other information on consumers for the purpose of furnishing consumer reports to third parties, and which uses any means or facility of interstate commerce for the purpose of preparing or furnishing consumer reports.

(g) The term "file," when used in connection with information on any consumer, means all of the information on that consumer recorded and retained by a consumer reporting agency regardless of how the information is stored.

(h) The term "employment purposes" when used in connection with a consumer report means a report used for the purpose of evaluating a consumer for employment, promotion, reassignment or retention as an employee.

(i) *Medical Information:* The term "medical information"—
  (1) means information or data, whether oral or recorded, in any form or medium, created by or derived from a health care provider or the consumer, that relates to—
    (A) the past, present, or future physical, mental, or behavioral health or condition of an individual;
    (B) the provision of health care to an individual; or
    (C) the payment for the provision of health care to an individual.
  (2) does not include the age or gender of a consumer, demographic information about the consumer, including a consumer's residence address or e-mail address, or any other information about a consumer that does not relate to the physical, mental, or behavioral health or condition of a consumer, including the existence or value of any insurance policy.

(j) **Definitions Relating to Child Support Obligations.**
  (1) *Overdue support:* The term "overdue support" has the meaning given to such term in section 666 (e) of title 42.
  (2) *State or local child support enforcement agency:* The term "State or local child support enforcement agency" means a State or local agency which administers a State or local program for establishing and enforcing child support obligations.

(k) **Adverse Action.**
  (1) *Actions included:* The term "adverse action"
    (A) has the same meaning as in section 1691 (d)(6) of this title; and
    (B) means
      (i) a denial or cancellation of, an increase in any charge for, or a reduction or other adverse or unfavorable change in the terms of coverage or amount of, any insurance, existing or applied for, in connection with the underwriting of insurance;
      (ii) a denial of employment or any other decision for employment purposes that adversely affects any current or prospective employee;
      (iii) a denial or cancellation of, an increase in any charge for, or any other adverse or unfavorable change in the terms of, any license or benefit described in section 1681b (a)(3)(D) of this title; and
      (iv) an action taken or determination that is
        (I) made in connection with an application that was made by, or a transaction that was initiated by, any consumer, or in connection with a review of an account under section 1681b (a)(3)(F)(ii) of this title; and
        (II) adverse to the interests of the consumer.
  (2) *Applicable findings, decisions, commentary, and orders:* For purposes of any determination of whether an action is an adverse action under paragraph (1)(A), all appropriate final findings, decisions, commentary, and orders issued under section 1691 (d)(6) of this title by the Board of Governors of the Federal Reserve System or any court shall apply.
(l) **Firm Offer of Credit or Insurance.** The term "firm offer of credit or insurance" means any offer of credit or insurance to a consumer that will be honored if the consumer is determined, based on information in a consumer report on the consumer, to meet the specific criteria used to select the consumer for the offer, except that the offer may be further conditioned on one or more of the following:
  (1) The consumer being determined, based on information in the consumer's application for the credit or insurance, to meet specific criteria bearing on credit worthiness or insurability, as applicable, that are established—
    (A) before selection of the consumer for the offer; and
    (B) for the purpose of determining whether to extend credit or insurance pursuant to the offer.

(2) Verification
   (A) that the consumer continues to meet the specific criteria used to select the consumer for the offer, by using information in a consumer report on the consumer, information in the consumer's application for the credit or insurance, or other information bearing on the credit worthiness or insurability of the consumer; or
   (B) of the information in the consumer's application for the credit or insurance, to determine that the consumer meets the specific criteria bearing on credit worthiness or insurability.
(3) The consumer furnishing any collateral that is a requirement for the extension of the credit or insurance that was
   (A) established before selection of the consumer for the offer of credit or insurance; and
   (B) disclosed to the consumer in the offer of credit or insurance.

(m) **Credit or Insurance Transaction That Is Not Initiated by the Consumer.** The term "credit or insurance transaction that is not initiated by the consumer" does not include the use of a consumer report by a person with which the consumer has an account or insurance policy, for purposes of
(1) reviewing the account or insurance policy; or
(2) collecting the account.

(n) **State.** The term "State" means any State, the Commonwealth of Puerto Rico, the District of Columbia, and any territory or possession of the United States.

(o) **Excluded Communications.** A communication is described in this subsection if it is a communication—
(1) that, but for subsection (d)(2)(D) of this section, would be an investigative consumer report;
(2) that is made to a prospective employer for the purpose of—
   (A) procuring an employee for the employer; or
   (B) procuring an opportunity for a natural person to work for the employer;
(3) that is made by a person who regularly performs such procurement;
(4) that is not used by any person for any purpose other than a purpose described in subparagraph (A) or (B) of paragraph (2); and
(5) with respect to which—
   (A) the consumer who is the subject of the communication—
     (i) consents orally or in writing to the nature and scope of the communication, before the collection of any information for the purpose of making the communication;

(ii)   consents orally or in writing to the making of the communication to a prospective employer, before the making of the communication; and

(iii) in the case of consent under clause (i) or (ii) given orally, is provided written confirmation of that consent by the person making the communication, not later than 3 business days after the receipt of the consent by that person;

(B) the person who makes the communication does not, for the purpose of making the communication, make any inquiry that if made by a prospective employer of the consumer who is the subject of the communication would violate any applicable Federal or State equal employment opportunity law or regulation; and

(C) the person who makes the communication

(i)   discloses in writing to the consumer who is the subject of the communication, not later than 5 business days after receiving any request from the consumer for such disclosure, the nature and substance of all information in the consumer's file at the time of the request, except that the sources of any information that is acquired solely for use in making the communication and is actually used for no other purpose, need not be disclosed other than under appropriate discovery procedures in any court of competent jurisdiction in which an action is brought; and

(ii) notifies the consumer who is the subject of the communication, in writing, of the consumer's right to request the information described in clause (i).

(p) **Consumer Reporting Agency That Compiles and Maintains Files on Consumers on a Nationwide Basis.** The term "consumer reporting agency that compiles and maintains files on consumers on a nationwide basis" means a consumer reporting agency that regularly engages in the practice of assembling or evaluating, and maintaining, for the purpose of furnishing consumer reports to third parties bearing on a consumer's credit worthiness, credit standing, or credit capacity, each of the following regarding consumers residing nationwide:

(1) Public record information

(2) Credit account information from persons who furnish that information regularly and in the ordinary course of business

(q) **Definitions Relating to Fraud Alerts.**
   (1) *Active duty military consumer:* The term "active duty military consumer" means a consumer in military service who
      (A) is on active duty (as defined in section 101 (d)(1) of title 10) or is a reservist performing duty under a call or order to active duty under a provision of law referred to in section 101 (a)(13) of title 10; and
      (B) is assigned to service away from the usual duty station of the consumer.
   (2) *Fraud alert; active duty alert:* The terms "fraud alert" and "active duty alert" mean a statement in the file of a consumer that—
      (A) notifies all prospective users of a consumer report relating to the consumer that the consumer may be a victim of fraud, including identity theft, or is an active duty military consumer, as applicable; and
      (B) is presented in a manner that facilitates a clear and conspicuous view of the statement described in subparagraph (A) by any person requesting such consumer report.
   (3) *Identity theft:* The term "identity theft" means a fraud committed using the identifying information of another person, subject to such further definition as the Commission may prescribe, by regulation.
   (4) *Identity theft report:* The term "identity theft report" has the meaning given that term by rule of the Commission, and means, at a minimum, a report—
      (A) that alleges an identity theft;
      (B) that is a copy of an official, valid report filed by a consumer with an appropriate Federal, State, or local law enforcement agency, including the United States Postal Inspection Service, or such other government agency deemed appropriate by the Commission; and
      (C) the filing of which subjects the person filing the report to criminal penalties relating to the filing of false information if, in fact, the information in the report is false.
   (5) *New credit plan:* The term "new credit plan" means a new account under an open end credit plan (as defined in section 1602 (i) of this title) or a new credit transaction not under an open end credit plan.
(r) **Credit and Debit Related Terms.**
   (1) *Card issuer:* The term "card issuer" means
      (A) a credit card issuer, in the case of a credit card; and
      (B) a debit card issuer, in the case of a debit card.
   (2) *Credit card:* The term "credit card" has the same meaning as in section 1602 of this title.

Appendix D: Consumer and Credit Data Privacy Laws

(3) *Debit card:* The term "debit card" means any card issued by a financial institution to a consumer for use in initiating an electronic fund transfer from the account of the consumer at such financial institution, for the purpose of transferring money between accounts or obtaining money, property, labor, or services.

(4) *Account and electronic fund transfer:* The terms "account" and "electronic fund transfer" have the same meanings as in section 1693a of this title.

(5) *Credit and creditor:* The terms "credit" and "creditor" have the same meanings as in section 1691a of this title.

(s) **Federal Banking Agency.** The term "Federal banking agency" has the same meaning as in section 1813 of title 12.

(t) **Financial Institution.** The term "financial institution" means a State or National bank, a State or Federal savings and loan association, a mutual savings bank, a State or Federal credit union, or any other person that, directly or indirectly, holds a transaction account (as defined in section 461 (b) of title 12) belonging to a consumer.

(u) **Reseller.** The term "reseller" means a consumer reporting agency that—

(1) assembles and merges information contained in the database of another consumer reporting agency or multiple consumer reporting agencies concerning any consumer for purposes of furnishing such information to any third party, to the extent of such activities; and

(2) does not maintain a database of the assembled or merged information from which new consumer reports are produced.

(v) **Commission.** The term "Commission" means the Federal Trade Commission.

(w) **Nationwide Specialty Consumer Reporting Agency.** The term "nationwide specialty consumer reporting agency" means a consumer reporting agency that compiles and maintains files on consumers on a nationwide basis relating to

(1) medical records or payments;

(2) residential or tenant history;

(3) check writing history;

(4) employment history; or

(5) insurance claims.

(x) **Exclusion of Certain Communications for Employee Investigations.**

(1) *Communications described in this subsection:* A communication is described in this subsection if

(A) but for subsection (d)(2)(D) of this section, the communication would be a consumer report;

    (B) the communication is made to an employer in connection with an investigation of
- (i) suspected misconduct relating to employment; or
- (ii) **compliance** with Federal, State, or local laws and regulations, the rules of a self-regulatory organization, or any preexisting written policies of the employer;

    (C) the communication is not made for the purpose of investigating a consumer's credit worthiness, credit standing, or credit capacity; and

    (D) the communication is not provided to any person except
- (i) to the employer or an agent of the employer;
- (ii) to any Federal or State officer, agency, or department, or any officer, agency, or department of a unit of general local government;
- (iii) to any self-regulatory organization with regulatory authority over the activities of the employer or employee;
- (iv) as otherwise required by law; or
- (v) pursuant to section 1681f of this title.

(2) *Subsequent disclosure.* After taking any adverse action based in whole or in part on a communication described in paragraph (1), the employer shall disclose to the consumer a summary containing the nature and substance of the communication upon which the adverse action is based, except that the sources of information acquired solely for use in preparing what would be but for subsection (d)(2)(D) of this section an investigative consumer report need not be disclosed.

(3) *Self-regulatory organization defined.* For purposes of this subsection, the term "self-regulatory organization" includes any self-regulatory organization (as defined in section 78c (a)(26) of this title), any entity established under title I of the Sarbanes-Oxley Act of 2002 [15 U.S.C. 7211 et seq.], any board of trade designated by the Commodity Futures Trading Commission, and any futures association registered with such Commission.

§ 1681b. Permissible Purposes of Consumer Reports

(a) **In general**

Subject to subsection (c) of this section, any consumer reporting agency may furnish a consumer report under the following circumstances and no other:

(1) In *response* to the order of a court having jurisdiction to issue such an order, or a subpoena issued in connection with proceedings before a Federal grand jury.

(2) In *accordance* with the written instructions of the consumer to whom it relates.

(3) To a *person* which it has reason to believe—

(A) intends to use the information in connection with a credit transaction involving the consumer on whom the information is to be furnished and involving the extension of credit to, or review or collection of an account of, the consumer; or

(B) intends to use the information for employment purposes; or

(C) intends to use the information in connection with the underwriting of insurance involving the consumer; or

(D) intends to use the information in connection with a determination of the consumer's eligibility for a license or other benefit granted by a governmental instrumentality required by law to consider an applicant's financial responsibility or status; or

(E) intends to use the information, as a potential investor or servicer, or current insurer, in connection with a valuation of, or an assessment of the credit or prepayment risks associated with, an existing credit obligation; or

(F) otherwise has a legitimate business need for the information—

(i) in connection with a business transaction that is initiated by the consumer; or

(ii) to review an account to determine whether the consumer continues to meet the terms of the account.

(G) executive departments and agencies in connection with the issuance of government-sponsored individually billed travel charge cards.

(4) In *response* to a request by the head of a State or local child support enforcement agency (or a State or local government official authorized by the head of such an agency), if the person making the request certifies to the consumer reporting agency that

(A) the consumer report is needed for the purpose of establishing an individual's capacity to make child support payments or determining the appropriate level of such payments;

(B) the paternity of the consumer for the child to which the obligation relates has been established or acknowledged by the consumer in accordance with State laws under which the obligation arises (if required by those laws);

(C) the person has provided at least 10 days' prior notice to the consumer whose report is requested, by certified or registered mail to the last known address of the consumer, that the report will be requested; and

(D) the consumer report will be kept confidential, will be used solely for a purpose described in subparagraph (A), and will not be used in connection with any other civil, administrative, or criminal proceeding, or for any other purpose.

(5) To an agency administering a State plan under section 654 of title 42 for use to set an initial or modified child support award.

(6) To the Federal Deposit Insurance Corporation or the National Credit Union Administration as part of its preparation for its appointment or as part of its exercise of powers, as conservator, receiver, or liquidating agent for an insured depository institution or insured credit union under the Federal Deposit Insurance Act [12 U.S.C. 1811 et seq.] or the Federal Credit Union Act [12 U.S.C. 1751 et seq.], or other applicable Federal or State law, or in connection with the resolution or liquidation of a failed or failing insured depository institution or insured credit union, as applicable.

(b) **Conditions for furnishing and using consumer reports for employment purposes**

(1) **Certification from user**

A consumer reporting agency may furnish a consumer report for employment purposes only if—

(A) the person who obtains such report from the agency certifies to the agency that—

(i) the person has complied with paragraph (2) with respect to the consumer report, and the person will comply with paragraph (3) with respect to the consumer report if paragraph (3) becomes applicable; and

(ii) information from the consumer report will not be used in violation of any applicable Federal or State equal employment opportunity law or regulation; and

(B) the consumer reporting agency provides with the report, or has previously provided, a summary of the consumer's rights under this subchapter, as prescribed by the Federal Trade Commission under section 1681g (c)(3) of this title.

(2) **Disclosure to consumer**

(A) **In general**

Except as provided in subparagraph (B), a person may not procure a consumer report, or cause a consumer report to be procured, for employment purposes with respect to any consumer, unless—

  (i) a clear and conspicuous disclosure has been made in writing to the consumer at any time before the report is procured or caused to be procured, in a document that consists solely of the disclosure, that a consumer report may be obtained for employment purposes; and

  (ii) the consumer has authorized in writing (which authorization may be made on the document referred to in clause (i)) the procurement of the report by that person.

(B) **Application by mail, telephone, computer, or other similar means**

If a consumer described in subparagraph (C) applies for employment by mail, telephone, computer, or other similar means, at any time before a consumer report is procured or caused to be procured in connection with that application—

  (i) the person who procures the consumer report on the consumer for employment purposes shall provide to the consumer, by oral, written, or electronic means, notice that a consumer report may be obtained for employment purposes, and a summary of the consumer's rights under section 1681m (a)(3) of this title; and

  (ii) the consumer shall have consented, orally, in writing, or electronically to the procurement of the report by that person.

(C) **Scope**

Subparagraph (B) shall apply to a person procuring a consumer report on a consumer in connection with the consumer's application for employment only if

  (i) the consumer is applying for a position over which the Secretary of Transportation has the power to establish qualifications and maximum hours of service pursuant to the provisions of section 31502 of title 49, or a position subject to safety regulation by a State transportation agency; and

  (ii) as of the time at which the person procures the report or causes the report to be procured the only interaction between the consumer and the person in connection with that employment application has been by mail, telephone, computer, or other similar means.

(3) **Conditions on use for adverse actions**
(A) **In general**
Except as provided in subparagraph (B), in using a consumer report for employment purposes, before taking any adverse action based in whole or in part on the report, the person intending to take such adverse action shall provide to the consumer to whom the report relates—
(i) a copy of the report; and
(ii) a description in writing of the rights of the consumer under this subchapter, as prescribed by the Federal Trade Commission under section 1681g (c)(3) of this title.
(B) **Application by mail, telephone, computer, or other similar means**
(i) If a consumer described in subparagraph (C) applies for employment by mail, telephone, computer, or other similar means, and if a person who has procured a consumer report on the consumer for employment purposes takes adverse action on the employment application based in whole or in part on the report, then the person must provide to the consumer to whom the report relates, in lieu of the notices required under subparagraph (A) of this section and under section 1681m (a) of this title, within 3 business days of taking such action, an oral, written or electronic notification—
(I)   that adverse action has been taken based in whole or in part on a consumer report received from a consumer reporting agency;
(II) of the name, address and telephone number of the consumer reporting agency that furnished the consumer report (including a toll-free telephone number established by the agency if the agency compiles and maintains files on consumers on a nationwide basis);
(III) that the consumer reporting agency did not make the decision to take the adverse action and is unable to provide to the consumer the specific reasons why the adverse action was taken; and
(IV) that the consumer may, upon providing proper identification, request a free copy of a report and may dispute with the consumer

reporting agency the accuracy or completeness of any information in a report.

(ii) If, under clause (B)(i)(IV), the consumer requests a copy of a consumer report from the person who procured the report, then, within 3 business days of receiving the consumer's request, together with proper identification, the person must send or provide to the consumer a copy of a report and a copy of the consumer's rights as prescribed by the Federal Trade Commission under section 1681g (c)(3) of this title.

(C) **Scope**

Subparagraph (B) shall apply to a person procuring a consumer report on a consumer in connection with the consumer's application for employment only if

(i) the consumer is applying for a position over which the Secretary of Transportation has the power to establish qualifications and maximum hours of service pursuant to the provisions of section 31502 of title 49, or a position subject to safety regulation by a State transportation agency; and

(ii) as of the time at which the person procures the report or causes the report to be procured the only interaction between the consumer and the person in connection with that employment application has been by mail, telephone, computer, or other similar means.

(4) **Exception for national security investigations**

(A) **In general**

In the case of an agency or department of the United States Government which seeks to obtain and use a consumer report for employment purposes, paragraph (3) shall not apply to any adverse action by such agency or department which is based in part on such consumer report, if the head of such agency or department makes a written finding that—

(i) the consumer report is relevant to a national security investigation of such agency or department;

(ii) the investigation is within the jurisdiction of such agency or department;

(iii) there is reason to believe that compliance with paragraph (3) will—

(I) *endanger* the life or physical safety of any person;

(II) result in flight from prosecution;

(III) result in the destruction of, or tampering with, evidence relevant to the investigation;

(IV) result in the intimidation of a potential witness relevant to the investigation;

(V) result in the compromise of classified information; or

(VI) otherwise seriously jeopardize or unduly delay the investigation or another official proceeding.

(B) **Notification of consumer upon conclusion of investigation**

Upon the conclusion of a national security investigation described in subparagraph (A), or upon the determination that the exception under subparagraph (A) is no longer required for the reasons set forth in such subparagraph, the official exercising the authority in such subparagraph shall provide to the consumer who is the subject of the consumer report with regard to which such finding was made—

(i) a copy of such consumer report with any classified information redacted as necessary;

(ii) notice of any adverse action which is based, in part, on the consumer report; and

(iii) the identification with reasonable specificity of the nature of the investigation for which the consumer report was sought.

(C) **Delegation by head of agency or department**

For purposes of subparagraphs (A) and (B), the head of any agency or department of the United States Government may delegate his or her authorities under this paragraph to an official of such agency or department who has personnel security responsibilities and is a member of the Senior Executive Service or equivalent civilian or military rank.

(D) **Definitions**

For purposes of this paragraph, the following definitions shall apply:

(i) Classified information The term "classified information" means information that is protected from unauthorized disclosure under Executive Order No. 12958 or successor orders.

(ii) National security investigation The term "national security investigation" means any official inquiry by an agency or department of the United States Government to determine the eligibility of a consumer to receive access or continued access to classified information or to determine whether classified information has been lost or compromised.

(c) **Furnishing reports in connection with credit or insurance transactions that are not initiated by consumer**

(1) **In general**

A consumer reporting agency may furnish a consumer report relating to any consumer pursuant to subparagraph (A) or (C) of subsection (a)(3) of this section in connection with any credit or insurance transaction that is not initiated by the consumer only if—

(A) the consumer authorizes the agency to provide such report to such person; or

(B)

(i) the transaction consists of a firm offer of credit or insurance;

(ii) the consumer reporting agency has complied with subsection (e) of this section;

(iii) there is not in effect an election by the consumer, made in accordance with subsection (e) of this section, to have the consumer's name and address excluded from lists of names provided by the agency pursuant to this paragraph; and

(iv) the consumer report does not contain a date of birth that shows that the consumer has not attained the age of 21, or, if the date of birth on the consumer report shows that the consumer has not attained the age of 21, such consumer consents to the consumer reporting agency to such furnishing.

(2) **Limits on information received under paragraph (1)(B)**

A person may receive pursuant to paragraph (1)(B) only—

(A) the name and address of a consumer;

(B) an identifier that is not unique to the consumer and that is used by the person solely for the purpose of verifying the identity of the consumer; and

(C) other information pertaining to a consumer that does not identify the relationship or experience of the consumer with respect to a particular creditor or other entity.

(3) **Information regarding inquiries**

Except as provided in section 1681g (a)(5) of this title, a consumer reporting agency shall not furnish to any person a record of inquiries in connection with a credit or insurance transaction that is not initiated by a consumer.

(d) **Reserved**

(e) **Election of consumer to be excluded from lists**

   (1) **In general**

   A consumer may elect to have the consumer's name and address excluded from any list provided by a consumer reporting agency under subsection (c)(1)(B) of this section in connection with a credit or insurance transaction that is not initiated by the consumer, by notifying the agency in accordance with paragraph (2) that the consumer does not consent to any use of a consumer report relating to the consumer in connection with any credit or insurance transaction that is not initiated by the consumer.

   (2) **Manner of notification**

   A consumer shall notify a consumer reporting agency under paragraph (1)—

   (A) through the notification system maintained by the agency under paragraph (5); or

   (B) by submitting to the agency a signed notice of election form issued by the agency for purposes of this subparagraph.

   (3) **Response of agency after notification through system**

   Upon receipt of notification of the election of a consumer under paragraph (1) through the notification system maintained by the agency under paragraph (5), a consumer reporting agency shall—

   (A) inform the consumer that the election is effective only for the 5-year period following the election if the consumer does not submit to the agency a signed notice of election form issued by the agency for purposes of paragraph (2)(B); and

   (B) provide to the consumer a notice of election form, if requested by the consumer, not later than 5 business days after receipt of the notification of the election through the system established under paragraph (5), in the case of a request made at the time the consumer provides notification through the system.

   (4) **Effectiveness of election**

   An election of a consumer under paragraph (1)

   (A) shall be effective with respect to a consumer reporting agency beginning 5 business days after the date on which

the consumer notifies the agency in accordance with
paragraph (2);

(B) shall be effective with respect to a consumer reporting
agency—

(i) subject to subparagraph (C), during the 5-year period
beginning 5 business days after the date on which
the consumer notifies the agency of the election, in
the case of an election for which a consumer notifies the agency only in accordance with paragraph
(2)(A); or

(ii) until the consumer notifies the agency under subparagraph (C), in the case of an election for which a
consumer notifies the agency in accordance with paragraph (2)(B);

(C) shall not be effective after the date on which the consumer notifies the agency, through the notification system
established by the agency under paragraph (5), that the
election is no longer effective; and

(D) shall be effective with respect to each affiliate of the agency.

(5) **Notification system**

(A) **In general**

Each consumer reporting agency that, under subsection (c)(1)(B)
of this section, furnishes a consumer report in connection with a
credit or insurance transaction that is not initiated by a consumer,
shall—

(i) establish and maintain a notification system,
including a toll-free telephone number, which
permits any consumer whose consumer report is
maintained by the agency to notify the agency,
with appropriate identification, of the consumer's
election to have the consumer's name and address
excluded from any such list of names and addresses
provided by the agency for such a transaction; and

(ii) publish by not later than 365 days after September 30,
1996, and not less than annually thereafter, in a publication of general circulation in the area served by the
agency—

(I) a *notification* that information in consumer
files maintained by the agency may be used in
connection with such transactions; and

(II) the *address* and toll-free telephone number for
consumers to use to notify the agency of the
consumer's election under clause (i).

(B) **Establishment and maintenance as compliance**
Establishment and maintenance of a notification system (including a toll-free telephone number) and publication by a consumer reporting agency on the agency's own behalf and on behalf of any of its affiliates in accordance with this paragraph is deemed to be compliance with this paragraph by each of those affiliates.

(6) **Notification system by agencies that operate nationwide**
Each consumer reporting agency that compiles and maintains files on consumers on a nationwide basis shall establish and maintain a notification system for purposes of paragraph (5) jointly with other such consumer reporting agencies.

(f) **Certain use or obtaining of information prohibited**
A person shall not use or obtain a consumer report for any purpose unless—

(1) the consumer report is obtained for a purpose for which the consumer report is authorized to be furnished under this section; and

(2) the purpose is certified in accordance with section 1681e of this title by a prospective user of the report through a general or specific certification.

(g) **Protection of medical information**

(1) Limitation *on consumer reporting agencies*
A consumer reporting agency shall not furnish for employment purposes, or in connection with a credit or insurance transaction, a consumer report that contains medical information (other than medical contact information treated in the manner required under section 1681c (a)(6) of this title) about a consumer, unless—

(A) if furnished in connection with an insurance transaction, the consumer affirmatively consents to the furnishing of the report;

(B) if furnished for employment purposes or in connection with a credit transaction

    (i) the information to be furnished is relevant to process or effect the employment or credit transaction; and

    (ii) the consumer provides specific written consent for the furnishing of the report that describes in clear and conspicuous language the use for which the information will be furnished; or

(C) the information to be furnished pertains solely to transactions, accounts, or balances relating to debts arising from the receipt of medical services, products, or devises, where such information, other than account status or amounts, is restricted or reported using codes that do not identify, or do not provide information sufficient to infer, the specific provider or the nature of such services, products, or devices, as provided in section 1681c (a)(6) of this title.

(2) **Limitation on creditors**

Except as permitted pursuant to paragraph (3)(C) or regulations prescribed under paragraph (5)(A), a creditor shall not obtain or use medical information (other than medical information treated in the manner required under section 1681c (a)(6) of this title) pertaining to a consumer in connection with any determination of the consumer's eligibility, or continued eligibility, for credit.

(3) **Actions authorized by Federal law, insurance activities and regulatory determinations**

Section 1681a (d)(3) of this title shall not be construed so as to treat information or any communication of information as a consumer report if the information or communication is disclosed—

(A) in connection with the business of insurance or annuities, including the activities described in section 18B of the model Privacy of Consumer Financial and Health Information Regulation issued by the National Association of Insurance Commissioners (as in effect on January 1, 2003);

(B) for any purpose permitted without authorization under the Standards for Individually Identifiable Health Information promulgated by the Department of Health and Human Services pursuant to the Health Insurance Portability and Accountability Act of 1996, or referred to under section 1179 of such Act, or described in section 6802 (e) of this title; or

(C) as otherwise determined to be necessary and appropriate, by regulation or order and subject to paragraph (6), by the Commission, any Federal banking agency or the National Credit Union Administration (with respect to any financial institution subject to the jurisdiction of such agency or Administration under paragraph (1), (2), or (3) of section 1681s (b) of this title, or the applicable State insurance authority (with respect to any person engaged in providing insurance or annuities).

(4) **Limitation on redisclosure of medical information**

Any person that receives medical information pursuant to paragraph (1) or (3) shall not disclose such information to any other person, except as necessary to carry out the purpose for which the information was initially disclosed, or as otherwise permitted by statute, regulation, or order.

(5) **Regulations and effective date for paragraph (2)**
  (A) **Regulations required**
  Each Federal banking agency and the National Credit Union Administration shall, subject to paragraph (6) and after notice and opportunity for comment, prescribe regulations that permit transactions under paragraph (2) that are determined to be necessary and appropriate to protect legitimate operational, transactional, risk, consumer, and other needs (and which shall include permitting actions necessary for administrative verification purposes), consistent with the intent of paragraph (2) to restrict the use of medical information for inappropriate purposes.
  (B) **Final regulations required**
  The Federal banking agencies and the National Credit Union Administration shall issue the regulations required under subparagraph (A) in final form before the end of the 6-month period beginning on December 4, 2003.
(6) **Coordination with other laws**
  No provision of this subsection shall be construed as altering, affecting, or superseding the applicability of any other provision of Federal law relating to medical confidentiality.

§ 1681c. Requirements relating to information contained in consumer reports
§ 1681c-1. Identity theft prevention; fraud alerts and active duty alerts
§ 1681c-2. Block of information resulting from identity theft
§ 1681d. Disclosure of investigative consumer reports
§ 1681e. Compliance procedures
§ 1681f. Disclosures to governmental agencies
§ 1681g. Disclosures to consumers
§ 1681h. Conditions and form of disclosure to consumers
§ 1681i. Procedure in case of disputed accuracy
§ 1681j. Charges for certain disclosures
§ 1681k. Public record information for employment purposes
§ 1681l. Restrictions on investigative consumer reports
§ 1681m. Requirements on users of consumer reports
§ 1681n. Civil liability for willful noncompliance
§ 1681o. Civil liability for negligent noncompliance
§ 1681p. Jurisdiction of courts; limitation of actions
§ 1681q. Obtaining information under false pretenses
§ 1681r. Unauthorized disclosures by officers or employees
§ 1681s. Administrative enforcement
§ 1681s-1. Information on overdue child support obligations

Federal Trade Commission Act of 1914 (15 U.S.C. §§ 41–51)

Subchapter I: Federal Trade Commission

Any person who shall neglect or refuse to attend and testify, or to answer any lawful inquiry, or to produce any documentary evidence, if in his power to do so, in obedience to an order of a district court of the United States directing compliance with the subpoena or lawful requirement of the commission, shall be guilty of an offense and upon conviction thereof by a court of competent jurisdiction shall be punished by a fine of not less than $1000 nor more than $5000, or by imprisonment for not more than 1 year, or by both such fine and imprisonment.

Any person who shall willfully make, or cause to be made, any false entry or statement of fact in any report required to be made under this subchapter; or who shall willfully make, or cause to be made, any false entry in any account, record, or memorandum kept by any person, partnership, or corporation subject to this subchapter; or who shall willfully neglect or fail to make, or to cause to be made, full, true, and correct entries in such accounts, records, or memoranda of all facts and transactions appertaining to the business of such person, partnership, or corporation; or who shall willfully remove out of the jurisdiction of the United States, or willfully mutilate, alter, or by any other means falsify any documentary evidence of such person, partnership, or corporation; or who shall willfully refuse to submit to the commission or to any of its authorized agents, for the purpose of inspection and taking copies, any documentary evidence of such person, partnership, or corporation in his possession or within his control shall be deemed guilty of an offense against the United States and shall be subject, upon conviction in any court of the United States of competent jurisdiction, to a fine of not less than $1000 nor more than $5000, or to imprisonment for a term of not more than 3 years, or to both such fine and imprisonment.

If any person, partnership, or corporation required by this subchapter to file any annual or special report shall fail to do so within the time fixed by the commission for filing the same, and such failure shall continue for 30 days after notice of such default, the corporation shall forfeit to the United States the sum of $100 for each and every day of the continuance of such failure, which forfeiture shall be payable into the treasury of the United States and shall be recoverable in a civil suit in the name of the United States brought in the case of a corporation or partnership in the district where the corporation or partnership has its principal office or in any district in which it shall do business, and in the case of any person in the district where such person resides or has his principal place of business. It shall be the duty of the various United States attorneys, under the direction of the attorney general of the United States, to prosecute for the recovery of the forfeitures. The costs and expenses of such prosecution shall be paid out of the appropriation for the expenses of the courts of the United States.

Any officer or employee of the commission who shall make public any information obtained by the commission without its authority, unless directed by a court, shall be deemed guilty of a misdemeanor and, upon conviction thereof, shall be punished by a fine not exceeding $5000, or by imprisonment not exceeding 1 year, or by fine and imprisonment, in the discretion of the court.

§ 51. Effect on Other Statutory Provisions
§ 52. Dissemination of False Advertisements
§ 53. False Advertisements; Injunctions and Restraining Orders
§ 54. False Advertisements; Penalties
§ 55. Additional Definitions
§ 56. Commencement, Defense, Intervention, and Supervision of Litigation and Appeal by Commission or Attorney General
§ 57. Separability Clause
§ 57a. Unfair or Deceptive Acts or Practices Rulemaking Proceedings

§ 57a-1. Omitted

§ 57b. Civil Actions for Violations of Rules and Cease and Desist Orders Respecting Unfair or Deceptive Acts or Practices

§ 57b-1. Civil Investigative Demands

§ 57b-2. Confidentiality

§ 57b-2a. Confidentiality and Delayed Notice of Compulsory Process for Certain Third Parties

§ 57b-2b. Protection for Voluntary Provision of Information

§ 57b-3. Rulemaking Process

§ 57b-4. Good Faith Reliance on Actions of Board of Governors

§ 57b-5. Agricultural Cooperatives

§ 57c. Authorization of Appropriations

§ 57c-1. Staff Exchanges

§ 57c-2. Reimbursement of Expenses

§ 58. Short Title

Health Insurance Portability and Accountability Act (HIPAA)

HIPAA is found in 29 U.S.C. 1181, 42 U.S.C. 1320, and 42 U.S.C. 1395. The Privacy Rule is located at 45 C.F.R. Part 160 and Subparts A and E of Part 164 (the Code of Federal Regulations).

The *HIPAA Privacy Rule* establishes national standards to protect individuals' medical records and other personal health information and applies to health plans, health-care clearinghouses, and those health-care providers that conduct certain health-care transactions electronically. The rule requires appropriate safeguards to protect the privacy of personal health information and sets limits and conditions on the uses and disclosures that may be made of such information without patient authorization. The rule also gives patients rights over their health information, including rights to examine and obtain a copy of their health records and to request corrections.

Jencks Act (18 U.S.C. 3500)

Jencks Act 18 U.S.C. 3500 and 3504

§ 3500. Demands for Production of Statements and Reports of Witnesses

(a) In any criminal prosecution brought by the United States, no statement or report in the possession of the United States, which was made by a government witness or prospective government witness (other than the defendant), shall be the subject of subpoena, discovery, or inspection until the said witness has testified on direct examination in the trial of the case.

(b) After a witness called by the United States has testified on direct examination, the court shall, on motion of the defendant, order the United States to produce any statement (as hereinafter defined) of the witness in the possession of the United States, which relates to the subject matter as to which the witness has testified. If the entire contents of any such statement relate to the subject matter of the testimony of the witness, the court shall order it to be delivered directly to the defendant for his examination and use.

(c) If the United States claims that any statement ordered to be produced under this section contains matter that does not relate to the subject matter of the testimony of the witness, the court shall order the United States to deliver such statement for the inspection of the court in camera. Upon such delivery, the court shall excise the portions of such statement that do not relate to the subject matter of the testimony of the witness. With such material excised, the court shall then direct delivery of such statement to the defendant for his use. If, pursuant to such procedure, any portion of such statement is withheld from the defendant and the defendant objects to such withholding, and the trial is continued to an adjudication of the guilt of the defendant, the entire text of such statement shall be preserved by the United States and, in the event the defendant appeals, shall be made available to the appellate court for the purpose of determining the correctness of the ruling of the trial judge. Whenever any statement is delivered to a defendant pursuant to this section, the court in its discretion, upon application of the said defendant, may recess proceedings in the trial for such time as it may determine to be reasonably required for the examination of such statement by the said defendant and his preparation for its use in the trial.

(d) If the United States elects not to comply with an order of the court under subsection (b) or (c) hereof to deliver to the defendant any such statement, or such portion thereof as the court may direct, the court shall strike from the record the testimony of the witness, and the trial shall proceed unless the court in its discretion shall determine that the interests of justice require that a mistrial be declared.

(e) The term *statement*, as used in subsections (b)–(d) of this section in relation to any witness called by the United States, means

 (1) A written statement made by the said witness and signed or otherwise adopted or approved by him

(2) A stenographic, mechanical, electrical, or other recording, or a transcription thereof, which is a substantially verbatim recital of an oral statement made by the said witness and recorded contemporaneously with the making of such oral statement

(3) A statement, however, taken or recorded, or a transcription thereof, if any, made by the said witness to a grand jury

§ 3504. Litigation Concerning Sources of Evidence

(a) In any trial, hearing, or other proceeding in or before any court, grand jury, department, officer, agency, regulatory body, or other authority of the United States,

(1) Upon a claim by a party aggrieved that evidence is inadmissible because it is the primary product of an unlawful act or because it was obtained by the exploitation of an unlawful act, the opponent of the claim shall affirm or deny the occurrence of the alleged unlawful act

(2) Disclosure of information for a determination if evidence is inadmissible because it is the primary product of an unlawful act occurring prior to June 19, 1968, or because it was obtained by the exploitation of an unlawful act occurring prior to June 19, 1968, shall not be required unless such information may be relevant to a pending claim of such inadmissibility

(3) No claim shall be considered that evidence of an event is inadmissible on the ground that such evidence was obtained by the exploitation of an unlawful act occurring prior to June 19, 1968, if such event occurred more than 5 years after such allegedly unlawful act

(b) As used in this section, *unlawful act* means any act of use of any electronic, mechanical, or other device (as defined in Section 2510 (5) of this title) in violation of the Constitution or laws of the United States or any regulation or standard promulgated pursuant thereto.

Law Enforcement Officer Safety Act of 2004 (18 U.S.C. 926B and 926C)

18 U.S.C.A § 926. Rules and regulations

The attorney general may prescribe only such rules and regulations as are necessary to carry out the provisions of this chapter

(a) Relating to Federal Firearms Licenses, that is, dealers' licenses and prohibition on national registries

(b) Relating to public notice for new regulations

(c) Relating to purchasers of black powder

Amendments: 2002 Amendments. Pub. L. 107-296, § 1112(f)(6), struck out "Secretary" and inserted "Attorney General," throughout the section.

§ 926A. Interstate transportation of firearms

Notwithstanding any other provision of any law or any rule or regulation of a state or any political subdivision thereof, any person who is not otherwise prohibited by this chapter from transporting, shipping, or receiving a firearm shall be entitled to transport a firearm for any lawful purpose from any place where he may lawfully possess and carry such firearm to any other place if, during such transportation, the firearm is unloaded, and neither the firearm nor any ammunition being transported is readily accessible or is directly accessible from the passenger compartment of such transporting vehicle, provided that in the case of a vehicle without a compartment separate from the driver's compartment, the firearm or ammunition shall be contained in a locked container other than the glove compartment or console.

18 U.S.C.A § 926B

§ 926B. Carrying of concealed firearms by qualified law enforcement officers (Effective: July 22, 2004)

(a) Notwithstanding any other provision of the law of any state or any political subdivision thereof, an individual who is a qualified law enforcement officer and who is carrying the identification required by subsection (d) may carry a concealed firearm that has been shipped or transported in interstate or foreign commerce, subject to subsection (b).

(b) This section shall not be construed to supersede or limit the laws of any state that
   (1) Permit private persons or entities to prohibit or restrict the possession of concealed firearms on their property
   (2) Prohibit or restrict the possession of firearms on any state or local government property, installation, building, base, or park

(c) As used in this section, the term *qualified law enforcement officer* means an employee of a governmental agency who
   (1) Is authorized by law to engage in or supervise the prevention, detection, investigation, or prosecution of, or the incarceration of any person for, any violation of law and has statutory powers of arrest
   (2) Is authorized by the agency to carry a firearm
   (3) Is not the subject of any disciplinary action by the agency
   (4) Meets standards, if any, established by the agency, which require the employee to regularly qualify in the use of a firearm

    (5) Is not under the influence of alcohol or another intoxicating or hallucinatory drug or substance

    (6) Is not prohibited by federal law from receiving a firearm

(d) The identification required by this subsection is the photographic identification issued by the governmental agency for which the individual is employed as a law enforcement officer.

(e) As used in this section, the term *firearm* does not include

    (1) Any machine gun (as defined in *Section* 5845 of the *National Firearms Act*)

    (2) Any firearm silencer (as defined in Section921 of this title)

    (3) Any destructive device (as defined in Section921 of this title)

References in text: Section 5845 of the *National Firearms Act*, referred to in subsection (e)(1), is 26 U.S.C.A § 5845.

18 U.S.C.A § 926C

§ 926C. Carrying of concealed firearms by qualified retired law enforcement officers

(a) Notwithstanding any other provision of the law of any state or any political subdivision thereof, an individual who is a qualified retired law enforcement officer and who is carrying the identification required by subsection (d) may carry a concealed firearm that has been shipped or transported in interstate or foreign commerce, subject to subsection (b).

(b) This section shall not be construed to supersede or limit the laws of any state that

    (1) Permit private persons or entities to prohibit or restrict the possession of concealed firearms on their property

    (2) Prohibit or restrict the possession of firearms on any state or local government property, installation, building, base, or park

(c) As used in this section, the term *qualified retired law enforcement officer* means an individual who

    (1) Retired in good standing from service with a public agency as a law enforcement officer, other than for reasons of mental instability

    (2) Before such retirement, was authorized by law to engage in or supervise the prevention, detection, investigation, or prosecution of, or the incarceration of any person for, any violation of law and had statutory powers of arrest

Pub. L. 99-570, Pub. L. 100-690, and Pub. L. 101-647), are utilized in conformance with the privacy and constitutional rights of individuals.

§ 23.2 Background   It is recognized that certain criminal activities including, but not limited to, loan sharking, drug trafficking, trafficking in stolen property, gambling, extortion, smuggling, bribery, and corruption of public officials often involve some degree of regular coordination and permanent organization involving a large number of participants over a broad geographical area. The exposure of such ongoing networks of criminal activity can be aided by the pooling of information about such activities. However, because the collection and exchange of intelligence data necessary to support control of serious criminal activity may represent potential threats to the privacy of individuals to whom such data relate, policy guidelines for federally funded projects are required.

§ 23.3 Applicability

(a) These policy standards are applicable to all criminal intelligence systems operating through support under the Omnibus Crime Control and Safe Streets Act of 1968, 42 U.S.C. 3711, et seq., as amended (Pub. L. 90-351, as amended by Pub. L. 91-644, Pub. L. 93-83, Pub. L. 93-415, Pub. L. 94-430, Pub. L. 94-503, Pub. L. 95-115, Pub. L. 96-157, Pub. L. 98-473, Pub. L. 99-570, Pub. L. 100-690, and Pub. L. 101-647).

(b) As used in these policies:

(1) Criminal intelligence system or intelligence system means the arrangements, equipment, facilities, and procedures used for the receipt, storage, interagency exchange or dissemination, and analysis of criminal intelligence information.

(2) Interjurisdictional intelligence system means an intelligence system that involves two or more participating agencies representing different governmental units or jurisdictions.

(3) Criminal intelligence information means data that have been evaluated to determine that it

(i) Is relevant to the identification of and the criminal activity engaged in by an individual who or organization that is reasonably suspected of involvement in criminal activity

(ii) Meets criminal intelligence system submission criteria

(4) Participating agency means an agency of local, county, state, federal, or other governmental unit that exercises law enforcement or criminal investigation authority and that is authorized to submit and receive criminal intelligence information through an interjurisdictional intelligence system. A participating agency may be a member or a nonmember of an interjurisdictional intelligence system.

(5) Intelligence project or project means the organizational unit that operates an intelligence system on behalf of and for the benefit of a single agency or the organization that operates an interjurisdictional intelligence system on behalf of a group of participating agencies.

(6) Validation of information means the procedures governing the periodic review of criminal intelligence information to assure its continuing compliance with system submission criteria established by regulation or program policy.

§ 23.20 Operating Principles

(a) A project shall collect and maintain criminal intelligence information concerning an individual only if there is reasonable suspicion that the individual is involved in criminal conduct or activity and the information is relevant to that criminal conduct or activity.

(b) A project shall not collect or maintain criminal intelligence information about the political, religious, or social views, associations, or activities of any individual or any group, association, corporation, business, partnership, or other organization unless such information directly relates to criminal conduct or activity and there is reasonable suspicion that the subject of the information is or may be involved in criminal conduct or activity.

(c) Reasonable suspicion or criminal predicate is established when information exists, which establishes sufficient facts to give a trained law enforcement or criminal investigative agency officer, investigator, or employee a basis to believe that there is a reasonable possibility that an individual or organization is involved in a definable criminal activity or enterprise. In an interjurisdictional intelligence system, the project is responsible for establishing the existence of reasonable suspicion of criminal activity either through examination of supporting information submitted by a participating agency or by delegation of this responsibility to a properly trained participating agency, which is subject to routine inspection and audit procedures established by the project.

(d) A project shall not include in any criminal intelligence system information that has been obtained in violation of any applicable federal, state, or local law or ordinance. In an interjurisdictional intelligence system, the project is responsible for establishing that no information is entered in violation of federal, state, or local laws, either through examination of supporting information submitted by a participating agency or by delegation of this responsibility to a properly trained participating agency, which is subject to routine inspection and audit procedures established by the project.

(e) A project or authorized recipient shall disseminate criminal intelligence information only where there is a need to know and a right to know the information in the performance of a law enforcement activity.

(f) (1) Except as noted in paragraph (f) (2) of this section, a project shall disseminate criminal intelligence information only to law enforcement authorities who shall agree to follow procedures regarding information receipt, maintenance, security, and dissemination, which are consistent with these principles.

   (2) Paragraph (f) (1) of this section shall not limit the dissemination of an assessment of criminal intelligence information to a government official or to any other individual, when necessary, to avoid imminent danger to life or property.

(g) A project maintaining criminal intelligence information shall ensure that administrative, technical, and physical safeguards (including audit trails) are adopted to ensure against unauthorized access and against intentional or unintentional damage. A record indicating who has been given information, the reason for release of the information, and the date of each dissemination outside the project shall be kept. Information shall be labeled to indicate levels of sensitivity, levels of confidence, and the identity of submitting agencies and control officials. Each project must establish written definitions for the need to know and right to know standards for dissemination to other agencies as provided in paragraph (e) of this section. The project is responsible for establishing the existence of an inquirer's need to know and right to know the information being requested either through inquiry or by delegation of this responsibility to a properly trained participating agency, which is subject to routine inspection and audit procedures established by the project. Each intelligence project shall assure that the following security requirements are implemented:

   (1) Where appropriate, projects must adopt effective and technologically advanced computer software and hardware designs to prevent unauthorized access to the information contained in the system.

   (2) The project must restrict access to its facilities, operating environment, and documentation to organizations and personnel authorized by the project.

   (3) The project must store information in the system in a manner such that it cannot be modified, destroyed, accessed, or purged without authorization.

   (4) The project must institute procedures to protect criminal intelligence information from unauthorized access, theft, sabotage, fire, flood, or other natural or manmade disaster.

(5) The project must promulgate rules and regulations based on good cause for implementing its authority to screen, reject for employment, transfer, or remove personnel authorized to have direct access to the system.

(6) A project may authorize and utilize remote (off-premises) system databases to the extent that they comply with these security requirements.

(h) All projects shall adopt procedures to assure that all information, which is retained by a project, has relevancy and importance. Such procedures shall provide for the periodic review of information and the destruction of any information that is misleading, obsolete, or otherwise unreliable and shall require that any recipient agencies be advised of such changes, which involve errors or corrections. All information retained as a result of this review must reflect the name of the reviewer, date of review, and explanation of decision to retain. Information retained in the system must be reviewed and validated for continuing compliance with system submission criteria before the expiration of its retention period, which in no event shall be longer than 5 years.

(i) If funds awarded under the act are used to support the operation of an intelligence system, then

(1) No project shall make direct remote terminal access to intelligence information available to system participants, except as specifically approved by the Office of Justice Programs (OJP) based on a determination that the system has adequate policies and procedures in place to ensure that it is accessible only to authorized system users

(2) A project shall undertake no major modifications to system design without prior grantor agency approval

(j) A project shall notify the grantor agency prior to initiation of formal information exchange procedures with any federal, state, regional, or other information systems not indicated in the grant documents as initially approved at time of award.

(k) A project shall make assurances that there will be no purchase or use in the course of the project of any electronic, mechanical, or other device for surveillance purposes that is in violation of the provisions of the Electronic Communications Privacy Act of 1986; Public Law 99-508; 18 U.S.C. 2510-2520, 2701-2709, and 3121-3125; or any applicable state statute related to wiretapping and surveillance.

(l) A project shall make assurances that there will be no harassment or interference with any lawful political activities as part of the intelligence operation.

(m) A project shall adopt sanctions for unauthorized access, utilization, or disclosure of information contained in the system.

(n) A participating agency of an interjurisdictional intelligence system must maintain in its agency files information that documents each submission to the system and supports compliance with project entry criteria. Participating agency files supporting system submissions must be made available for reasonable audit and inspection by project representatives. Project representatives will conduct participating agency inspection and audit in such a manner so as to protect the confidentiality and sensitivity of participating agency intelligence records.

(o) The attorney general or designee may waive, in whole or in part, the applicability of a particular requirement or requirements contained in this part with respect to a criminal intelligence system, or for a class of submitters or users of such system, upon a clear and convincing showing that such waiver would enhance the collection, maintenance, or dissemination of information in the criminal intelligence system while ensuring that such system would not be utilized in violation of the privacy and constitutional rights of individuals or any applicable state or federal law.

§ 23.30 *Funding Guidelines* The following funding guidelines shall apply to all Crime Control Act–funded discretionary assistance awards and Bureau of Justice Assistance (BJA) formula grant program subgrants, the purpose of which is to support the operation of an intelligence system. Intelligence systems shall only be funded where a grantee/subgrantee agrees to adhere to the principles set forth previously and the project meets the following criteria:

(a) The proposed collection and exchange of criminal intelligence information have been coordinated with and will support ongoing or proposed investigatory or prosecutorial activities relating to specific areas of criminal activity.

(b) The areas of criminal activity for which intelligence information is to be utilized represent a significant and recognized threat to the population and

   (1) Are either undertaken for the purpose of seeking illegal power or profits or pose a threat to the life and property of citizens

   (2) Involve a significant degree of permanent criminal organization

   (3) Are not limited to one jurisdiction

(c) The head of a government agency or an individual with general policy-making authority who has been expressly delegated such control and supervision by the head of the agency will retain control and supervision of information collection and dissemination for the criminal intelligence system. This official shall certify in writing that he or she takes full responsibility and will be accountable for the information maintained by and disseminated from the system and that the operation of the system will be in compliance with the principles set forth in § 23.20.

(d) Where the system is an interjurisdictional criminal intelligence system, the governmental agency, which exercises control and supervision over the operation of the system, shall require that the head of that agency or an individual with general policy-making authority who has been expressly delegated such control and supervision by the head of the agency

 (1) Assume official responsibility and accountability for actions taken in the name of the joint entity

 (2) Certify in writing that the official takes full responsibility and will be accountable for ensuring that the information transmitted to the interjurisdictional system or to participating agencies will be in compliance with the principles set forth in § 23.20

The principles set forth in § 23.20 shall be made part of the by-laws or operating procedures for that system. Each participating agency, as a condition of participation, must accept in writing those principles that govern the submission, maintenance, and dissemination of information included as part of the interjurisdictional system.

(e) Intelligence information will be collected, maintained, and disseminated primarily for state and local law enforcement efforts, including efforts involving federal participation.

§ 23.40 Monitoring and Auditing of Grants for the Funding of Intelligence Systems

(a) Awards for the funding of intelligence systems will receive specialized monitoring and audit in accordance with a plan designed to ensure compliance with operating principles as set forth in § 23.20. The plan shall be approved prior to award of funds.

(b) All such awards shall be subject to a special condition requiring compliance with the principles set forth in § 23.20.

(c) An annual notice will be published by OJP that will indicate the existence and the objective of all systems for the continuing interjurisdictional exchange of criminal intelligence information, which are subject to the 28 C.F.R. Part 23 Criminal Intelligence Systems Policies.

Laurie Robinson, Acting Assistant Attorney General, Office of Justice Programs (FR Doc. 93-22614 Filed 9-15-93; 8:45 a.m.) Criminal Intelligence Sharing Systems; Policy Clarification [Federal Register: December 30, 1998 (Volume 63, Number 250)] [Pages 71752–71753] from the Federal Register online via GPO access [wais.access.gpo.gov], Department of Justice, 28 C.F.R. Part 23 [OJP(BJA)-1177B] RIN 1121-ZB40.

1993 Revision and Commentary

28 C.F.R. Part 23 Final Revision to the Office of Justice Programs, Criminal Intelligence Systems Operating Policies

----

Agency: OJP, Justice

Action: Final rule

Summary: The regulation governing criminal intelligence systems operating through support under Title I of the Omnibus Crime Control and Safe Streets Act of 1968, as amended, is being revised to update basic authority citations and nomenclature, to clarify the applicability of the regulation, to define terms, and to modify a number of the regulation's operating policies and funding guidelines.

Effective date: September 16, 1993

For further information, contact: Paul Kendall, Esquire, General Counsel, *Office of Justice Programs*, 633 Indiana Ave., NW, Suite 1245-E, Washington, DC, 20531, Telephone (202) 307-6235.

Supplementary information: The rule, which this rule supersedes, had been in effect and unchanged since September 17, 1980. A notice of proposed rulemaking for 28 C.F.R. Part 23 was published in the *Federal Register* on February 27, 1992 (57 FR 6691). The statutory authorities for this regulation are Section 801(a) and Section 812(c) of Title I of the Omnibus Crime Control and Safe Streets Act of 1968, as amended, the Act, 42 U.S.C. 3782(a) and 3789g(c). 42 U.S.C. 3789g (c) and (d) provide as follows:

Confidentiality of Information
Section 812

(c) All criminal intelligence systems operating through support under this title shall collect, maintain, and disseminate criminal intelligence information in conformance with policy standards, which are prescribed by the OJP and which are written to assure that the funding and operation of these systems further the purpose of this title and to assure that such systems are not utilized in violation of the privacy and constitutional rights of individuals.

(d) Any person violating the provisions of this section, or of any rule, regulation, or order issued thereunder, shall be fined not to exceed $10,000, in addition to any other penalty imposed by law.

This statutory provision and its implementing regulation apply to intelligence systems funded under Title I of the act, whether the system is operated by a single law enforcement agency, is an interjurisdictional intelligence system, is funded with discretionary grant funds, or is funded by a state with formula grant funds awarded under the act's Drug Control and System Improvement Grant Program pursuant to part E, subpart 1 of the act, 42 U.S.C. 3751-3759. The need for change to 28 C.F.R. Part 23 grew out of the program experience of the OJP and its component agency, the BJA, with the regulation and the changing and expanding law enforcement agency need to respond to criminal mobility, the national drug program, the increased complexity of criminal networks and conspiracies, and the limited funding available to state and local law enforcement agencies. In addition, law enforcement's capability to perform intelligence database and analytical functions has been enhanced by technological advancements and sophisticated analytical techniques.

28 C.F.R. Part 23 governs the basic requirements of the intelligence system process. The process includes

1. Information submission or collection
2. Secure storage
3. Inquiry and search capability
4. Controlled dissemination
5. Purge and review process

Information systems that receive, store, and disseminate information on individuals or organizations based on reasonable suspicion of their involvement in criminal activity are criminal intelligence systems under the regulation. The definition includes both systems that store detailed intelligence or investigative information on the suspected criminal activities of subjects and those that store only information designed to identify individuals or organizations that are the subject of an inquiry or analysis (a so-called *pointer system*). It does not include criminal history record information (CHRI) or identification (fingerprint) systems. There are nine significant areas of change to the regulation:

(1) Nomenclature changes (authority citations, organizational names) are included to bring the regulation up to date.
(2) Definitions of terms (28 C.F.R. 23.3(b)) are modified or added as appropriate. The term *intelligence system* is redefined to clarify the fact that historical telephone toll files, analytical information, and work products that are not either retained, stored, or exchanged and CHRI or identification (fingerprint) systems are excluded from the definition and hence are not covered by the regulation; the terms

interjurisdictional intelligence system, criminal intelligence information, participating agency, intelligence project, and *validation of information* are key terms that are defined in the regulation for the first time.

(3) The operating principles for intelligence systems (28 C.F.R. 23.20) are modified to define the term *reasonable suspicion* or *criminal predicate.* The finding of reasonable suspicion is a threshold requirement for entering intelligence information on an individual or organization into an intelligence database (28 C.F.R. 23.20(c)). This determination, as well as determinations that information was legally obtained (28 C.F.R. 23.20(d)) and that a recipient of the information has a need to know and a right to know the information in the performance of a law enforcement function (28 C.F.R. 23.20(e)), is established as the responsibility of the project for an interjurisdictional intelligence system. However, the regulation permits these responsibilities to be delegated to a properly trained participating agency, which is subject to project inspection and audit (28 C.F.R. 23.20(c),(d),(g)).

(4) Security requirements are established to protect the integrity of the intelligence database and the information stored in the database (28 C.F.R. 23.20(g)(1)(i)–(vi)).

(5) The regulation provides that information retained in the system must be reviewed and validated for continuing compliance with system submission criteria within a 5-year retention period. Any information not validated within that period must be purged from the system (28 C.F.R. 23.20(h)).

(6) Another change continues the general prohibition of direct remote terminal access to intelligence information in a funded intelligence system but provides an exception for systems that obtain express OJP approval based on a determination that the system has adequate policies and procedures in place to ensure that access to system intelligence information is limited to authorized system users (28 C.F.R. 23.20(i)(1)). OJP will carefully review all requests for exception to assure that a need exists and that system integrity will be provided and maintained (28 C.F.R. 23.20(i)(1)).

(7) The regulation requires participating agencies to maintain backup files for information submitted to an interjurisdictional intelligence system and provide for inspection and audit by project staff (28 C.F.R. 23.20(h)).

(8) The final rule also includes a provision allowing the attorney general or the attorney general's designee to authorize a departure from the specific requirements of this part, in those cases where it is clearly shown that such waiver would promote the purposes and effectiveness of a criminal intelligence system while at the same time ensuring compliance with all applicable laws and protection for the

privacy and constitutional rights of individuals. The department recognizes that other provisions of federal law may be applicable to (or may be adopted in the future with respect to) certain submitters or users of information in criminal intelligence systems. Moreover, as technological developments unfold over time in this area, experience may show that particular aspects of the requirements in this part may no longer be needed to serve their intended purpose or may even prevent desirable technological advances. Accordingly, this provision grants the flexibility to make such beneficial adaptations in particular cases or classes without the necessity to undertake a new rulemaking process. This waiver authority could only be exercised by the attorney general or designee, in writing, upon a clear and convincing showing (28 C.F.R. 23.20 (o)).

(9) The funding guidelines (28 C.F.R. 23.30) are revised to permit funded intelligence systems to collect information either on organized criminal activity that represents a significant and recognized threat to the population or on criminal activity that is multijurisdictional in nature.

Rulemaking History

On February 27, 1992, the Department of Justice, OJP, published a notice of proposed rulemaking in the Federal Register (57 FR 6691). The OJP received a total of 11 comments on the proposed regulation, 7 from state agencies, 2 from Regional Information Sharing Systems (RISS) program fund recipients, 1 from a federal agency, and 1 from the RISS Project Directors Association. Comments will be discussed in the order in which they address the substance of the proposed regulation.

Discussion of Comments

Title—Part 23 comment: One commentor suggested reinserting the word *Operating* in the title of the regulation to read *Criminal Intelligence Systems Operating Policies* to reflect that the regulation applies only to policies governing system operations.

Response: Agreed. The title has been changed.

Applicability: Section 23.3(a)   *Comment*: A question was raised by one respondent as to whether the applicability of the regulation under Section 23.3(a) to systems *operating through support* under the Crime Control Act included agencies receiving any assistance funds and who operated an intelligence system *or* only those who received assistance funds for the specific purpose of funding the operation of an intelligence system.

Response: The regulation applies to grantees and subgrantees who receive and use the Crime Control Act funds to fund the operation of an intelligence system.

Comment: Another commentor asked whether the purchase of software and office equipment or the payment of staff salaries for a criminal intelligence system would constitute *operating through support* under the Crime Control Act.

Response: Any direct Crime Control Act fund support that contributes to the operation of a criminal intelligence system would subject the system to the operation of the policy standards during the period of fund support.

Comment: A third commentor inquired whether an agency's purchase of a telephone pen register or computer equipment to store and analyze pen register information would subject the agency or its information systems to the regulation.

Response: No. Neither a pen register nor equipment to analyze telephone toll information falls under the definition of a criminal intelligence system even though it may assist an agency to produce investigative or other information for an intelligence system.

Applicability: Section 23.3(b) *Comment*: Several commentors questioned whether information systems that are designed to collect information on criminal suspects for purposes of inquiry and analysis and that provide for dissemination of such information qualify as *criminal intelligence systems*. One pointed out that the information qualifying for system submission could not be *unconfirmed* or *soft* intelligence. Rather, it would generally have to be investigative file-based information to meet the *reasonable suspicion* test.

Response: The character of an information system as a criminal intelligence system does not depend upon the source or categorization of the underlying information as *raw* or *soft* intelligence, preliminary investigation information, or investigative information, findings, or determinations. It depends upon the purpose for which the information system exists and the type of information it contains. If the purpose of the system is to collect and share information with other law enforcement agencies on individuals reasonably suspected of involvement in criminal activity, and the information is identifying or descriptive information about the individual and the suspected criminal activity, then the system is a criminal intelligence system for purposes of the regulation. Only those criminal intelligence systems that receive, store, and provide for the interagency exchange and analysis of criminal intelligence information in a manner consistent with this regulation are eligible for funding support with Crime Control Act funds.

Comment: One respondent asked whether the definition of criminal intelligence system covered CHRI systems, fugitive files, or other want- or warrant-based information systems.

Response: No. A CHRI system contains information collected on arrests, detention, indictments, informations or other charges, dispositions, sentencing, correctional supervision, and release. It encompasses systems designed to collect, process, preserve, or disseminate such information.

CHRI is factual, historical, and objective information, which provides a criminal justice system *profile* of an individual's past and present involvement in the criminal justice system. A fugitive file is designed to provide factual information to assist in the arrest of individuals for whom there is an outstanding want or warrant. Criminal intelligence information, by contrast, is both factual and conjectural (reasonable suspicion), current and subjective. It is intended for law enforcement use only, to provide law enforcement officers and agencies with useful information on criminal suspects and to foster interagency coordination and cooperation. A criminal intelligence system can have CHRI in it as an identifier, but a CHRI system would not contain the suspected criminal activity information contained in a criminal intelligence system.

This distinction provides the basis for the limitations on criminal intelligence systems set forth in the operating policies. Because criminal intelligence information is both conjectural and subjective in nature, may be widely disseminated through the interagency exchange of information, and cannot be accessed by criminal suspects to verify that the information is accurate and complete, the protections and limitations set forth in the regulation are necessary to protect the privacy interests of the subjects and potential subjects of a criminal intelligence system.

Comment: Another commentor asked whether a law enforcement agency's criminal intelligence information unit, located at headquarters, which authorizes no outside access to information in its intelligence system, would be subject to the regulation.

Response: No. The sharing of investigative or general file information on criminal subjects within an agency is a practice that takes place on a daily basis and is necessary for the efficient and effective operation of a law enforcement agency. Consequently, whether such a system is described as a case management or intelligence system, the regulation is not intended to apply to the exchange or sharing of such information when it takes place within a single law enforcement agency or organizational entity. For these purposes, an operational multijurisdictional task force would be considered a single organizational entity provided that it is established by and operates under a written memorandum of understanding or interagency agreement. The definition of *criminal intelligence system* has been modified to clarify this point. However, if a single agency or entity system provides access to system information to outside agencies on an inquiry or request basis, as a matter of either policy or practice, the system would qualify as a criminal intelligence system and be subject to the regulation.

Comment: A commentor questioned whether the proposed exclusion of *analytical information and work products* from the definition of *intelligence system* was intended to exclude all dissemination of analytical results from coverage under the regulation.

Response: No. The exceptions in the proposed definition of *intelligence system* of modus operandi files, historical telephone toll files, and analytical information and work products are potentially confusing. The exceptions reflect types of data that may or may not qualify as *criminal intelligence information* depending on particular facts and circumstances. Consequently, these exceptions have been deleted from the definition of *intelligence system* in the final rule. For example, analytical information and work products that are derived from unevaluated or bulk data (i.e., information that has not been tested to determine that it meets intelligence system submission criteria) are not intelligence information if they are returned to the submitting agency. This information and its products cannot be retained, stored, or made available for dissemination in an intelligence system unless and until the information has been evaluated and determined to meet system submission criteria. The proposed definition of *analytical information and work products* in Section 23.3(b) has also been deleted.

To address the aforementioned issues, the definition of *intelligence system* has been modified to define a *criminal intelligence system or intelligence system* to mean "the arrangements, equipment, facilities, and procedures used for the receipt, storage, interagency exchange or dissemination, and analysis of criminal intelligence information."

Comment: Several commentors raised questions regarding the concept of *evaluated data* in the definition of *criminal intelligence information*, requesting guidance on what criteria to use in evaluating data. Another questioned whether there needed to be an active investigation as the basis for information to fall within the definition and whether information on an individual who or organization that is not the primary subject or target of an investigation or other data source, for example, a criminal associate or coconspirator, can qualify as *criminal intelligence information*.

Response: The definition of *criminal intelligence information* has been revised to reflect that data are evaluated for two purposes related to criminal intelligence system submissions: (1) to determine that it is relevant in identifying a criminal suspect and the criminal activity involved and (2) to determine that the data meet criminal intelligence system submission criteria, including reasonable suspicion of involvement in criminal activity. As rewritten, there is no requirement that an *active investigation* is necessary. Further, the revised language makes it clear that individuals or organizations that are not primary subjects or targets can be identified in the criminal intelligence information, provided that they independently meet system submission criteria.

Comment: One commentor requested clarification of the role of the *project* in the operation of an intelligence system, that is, is the project required to have physical control (possession) of the information in an intelligence system or will authority over the system (operational control) suffice?

Response: Operational control over an intelligence system's intelligence information is sufficient. The regulation seeks to establish a single locus of authority and responsibility for system information. Once that principle is established, the regulation permits, for example, the establishment of remote (off-premises) databases that meet applicable security requirements.

Operating Principles: Section 23.20(c) *Comment*: One respondent took the position that *reasonable suspicion*, as defined in Section 23.20(c), is not necessary to the protection of individual privacy and constitutional rights, suggesting instead that information in a funded intelligence system need only be *necessary and relevant to an agency's lawful purposes.*

Response: While it is agreed that the standard suggested is appropriate for investigative or other information files maintained for use by or within an agency, the potential for national dissemination of information in intelligence information systems, coupled with the lack of access by subjects to challenge the information, justifies the reasonable suspicion standard as well as other operating principle restrictions set forth in this regulation. Also, the quality and utility of *hits* in an information system are enhanced by the reasonable suspicion requirement. Scarce resources are not wasted by agencies in coordinating information on subjects for whom information is vague, incomplete, and conjectural.

Comment: The prior commentor also criticized the proposed definition of reasonable suspicion for its specific reference to an *investigative file* as the source of intelligence system information, the potential inconsistency between the concepts of *infer* and *conclude* as standards for determining whether reasonable suspicion is justified by the information available and the use of *reasonable possibility* rather than *articulable* or *sufficient* facts as the operative standard to conclude that reasonable suspicion exists.

Response: The reference to an *investigative file* as the information source has been broadened to encompass any information source. The information available must provide a basis for the submitter to *believe* there is a reasonable possibility of the subject's involvement in the criminal activity or enterprise.

The concept of a *basis to believe* requires reasoning and logic coupled with sound judgment based on experience in law enforcement rather than a mere hunch, whim, or guess. The belief that is formed that there is a *reasonable possibility* of criminal involvement has been retained because the proposed standard is appropriately less restrictive than that which is required to establish probable cause.

Operating Principles: Section 23.20(d)   *Comment*: Section 23.20(d) prohibits the inclusion in an intelligence system of information obtained in violation of federal, state, or local law or ordinance. Would a project be potentially liable for accepting, maintaining, and disseminating such information even if it did not know that the information was illegally obtained?

Response: In addition to protecting the rights of individuals and organizations that may be subjects in a criminal intelligence system, this prohibition serves to protect a project from liability for disseminating illegally obtained information. A clear project policy that prohibits the submission of illegally obtained information, coupled with an examination of supporting information to determine that the information was obtained legally or the delegation of such authority to a properly trained participating agency, and the establishment and performance of routine inspection and audit of participating agency records should be sufficient to shield a project from potential liability based on negligence in the performance of its intelligence information screening function.

Operating Principles: Section 23.20(h)   *Comment*: One commentor requested clarification of the *periodic review* requirement in Section 23.20(h) and what constitutes an *explanation of decision to retain* information.

Response: The periodic review requirement is designed to ensure that system information is accurate and as up-to-date as reasonably possible. When a review has occurred, the record is appropriately updated and notated. The explanation of decision to retain can be a variety of reasons including *active investigation, preliminary review in progress*, and *subject believed still active in jurisdiction*. When information that has been reviewed or updated and a determination made that it continues to meet system submission criteria, the information has been *validated* and begins a new retention period. The regulation limits the retention period to a maximum of 5 years without a review and validation of the information.

Operating Principles: Section 23.20(i)   *Comment*: One commentor requested a definition of *remote terminal* and asked how OJP would determine whether *adequate policies and procedures* are in place to ensure the continued integrity of a criminal intelligence system.

Response: A *remote terminal* is hardware that enables a participating agency to input into or access information from a project's criminal intelligence database without the intervention of project staff. While the security requirements set forth in Section 23.20(g)(1)–(5) should minimize the threat to system integrity from unauthorized access to and the use of system information, special measures are called for when direct remote terminal access is authorized.

The OJP will expect any request for approval of remote terminal access to include information on the following system protection measures:

1. Procedures for identification of authorized remote terminals and security of terminals
2. Authorized access officer (remote terminal operator) identification and verification procedures
3. Provisions for the levels of dissemination of information as directed by the submitting agency
4. Provisions for the rejection of submissions unless critical data fields are completed
5. Technological safeguards on system access, use, dissemination, and review and purge
6. Physical security of the system
7. Training and certification of system-participating agency personnel
8. Provisions for the audit of system-participating agencies, to include file data supporting submissions to the system, security of access terminals, and policy and procedure compliance
9. Documentation for audit trails of the entire system operation

Moreover, a waiver provision has been added to ensure flexibility in adapting quickly to technological and legal changes, which may impact any of the requirements contained in this regulation (see Section 23.20(o)).

Comment: Related to the aforementioned discussion, another commentor asked whether restrictions on direct remote terminal access would prohibit remote access to an *index* of information in the system.

Response: Yes. The ability to obtain all information directly from a criminal intelligence system through the use of hardware based outside the system constitutes direct remote terminal access contrary to the provisions of Section 23.20(i)(1), except as specifically approved by OJP. Thus, a hit/no-hit response, if gleaned from an index, would bring a remote terminal within the scope of the requirement for OJP approval of direct remote terminal access.

Comment: One commentor pointed out that the requirement for prior OJP approval of *modifications to system design* was overly broad and could be read to require that even minor changes be submitted for approval. The commentor proposed a substitute that would limit the requirement to those modifications *that alter the system's identified goals in a way contrary to the requirements of this regulation.*

Response: While it is agreed that the language is broad, the proposed limitation is too restrictive. The intent was that *modifications to system design* refer to *major* changes to the system, such as the nature of the information collected, the place or method of information storage, the authorized uses of information in the system, and the provisions for access to system information by authorized participating agencies. This clarification has been incorporated in the regulation. In order to decentralize responsibility for approval of system design modifications, the proposed regulation has been revised to provide for approval of such modifications by the grantor agency rather than OJP. A similar change has been made to Section 23.20(j).

Operating Principles: Section 23.20(n)   *Comment*: Several commentors expressed concern with the verification procedures set forth in Section 23.20(n). One suggested that file information cannot *verify* the correctness of submissions but instead serves to *document* or *substantiate* its correctness. Another proposed deleting the requirements that (1) files maintained by participating agencies to support system submissions be subject to the operating principles and (2) participating agencies are authorized to maintain such files separately from other agency files. The first requirement conflicts with the normal investigative procedures of a law enforcement agency in that all information in agency source files cannot meet the operating principles, particularly the reasonable suspicion and relevancy requirements. The important principle is that the information, which is gleaned from an agency's source files and submitted to the system, meets the operating principles. The second requirement has no practical value. At most, it results in the creation of duplicative files or in submission information being segregated from source files.

Response: OJP agrees with both comments. The word *documents* has been substituted for *verifies*, and the provisions subjecting participating agency source files to the operating principles and authorizing maintenance of separate files have been deleted. Projects should use their audit and inspection access to agency source files to document the correctness of participating agency submissions on a sample basis.

Funding Guidelines: Section 23.30(b)   *Comment*: One commentor asked: Who defines the areas of criminal activity that *represent a significant and recognized threat to the population*?

Response: The determination of areas of criminal activity focus and priority is a matter for projects, project policy boards, and member agencies to determine, provided that the additional regulatory requirements set forth in Section 23.30(b) are met.

Monitoring and Auditing of Grants: Section 23.40(a)   *Comment*: One commentor asked: *Who is responsible for developing the specialized monitoring and audit of awards for intelligence systems to ensure compliance with the operating principles?*

Response: The grantor agency (the agency awarding a subgrant to support an intelligence system) shall establish and approve a plan for specialized monitoring and audit of subawards prior to award. For the BJA Formula Grant Program, the state agency receiving the award from BJA is the grantor agency. Technical assistance and support in establishing a monitoring and audit plan is available through BJA.

Information on Juveniles   *Comment*: Can intelligence information pertaining to a juvenile who otherwise meets criminal intelligence system submission criteria be entered into an intelligence database?

Response: There is no limitation or restriction on entering intelligence information on juvenile subjects set forth in federal law or regulation. However, state law may restrict or prohibit the maintenance or dissemination of such information by its law enforcement agencies. Therefore, state laws should be carefully reviewed to determine their impact on this practice and appropriate project policies adopted.

Executive Order 12291

These regulations are not a *major rule* as defined by Section 1(b) of Executive Order No. 12291, 3 C.F.R. Part 127 (1981), because they do not result in (a) an effect on the economy of $100 million or more, (b) a major increase in any costs or prices, or (c) adverse effects on competition, employment, investment, productivity, or innovation among American enterprises.

Regulatory Flexibility Act

These regulations are not a rule within the meaning of the Regulatory Flexibility Act, 5 U.S.C. 601-612. These regulations, if promulgated, will not have a *significant* economic impact on a substantial number of small *entities*, as defined by the Regulatory Flexibility Act.

Paperwork Reduction Act

There are no collection of information requirements contained in the proposed regulation.

List of Subjects in 28 C.F.R. Part 23

Administrative practice and procedure, grant programs, intelligence, law enforcement. For the reasons set out in the preamble, Title 28, Part 23, of the Code of Federal Regulations is revised to read as follows:

Part 23: Criminal Intelligence Systems Operating Policies Section
23.1. Purpose
23.2. Background
23.3. Applicability
23.20 Operating Principles
23.30 Funding Guidelines
23.40 Monitoring and Auditing of Grants for the Funding of Intelligence
    Systems

Authority: 42 U.S.C. 3782(a); 42 U.S.C. 3789g(c)

§ 23.1 Purpose   The purpose of this regulation is to assure that all criminal intelligence systems operating through support under the Omnibus Crime Control and Safe Streets Act of 1968, 42 U.S.C. 3711, et seq., as amended (Pub. L. 90-351, as amended by Pub. L. 91-644, Pub. L. 93-83, Pub. L. 93-415, Pub. L. 94-430, Pub. L. 94-503, Pub. L. 95-115, Pub. L. 96-157, Pub. L. 98-473, Pub. L. 99-570, Pub. L. 100-690, and Pub. L. 101-647), are utilized in conformance with the privacy and constitutional rights of individuals.

§ 23.2 Background   It is recognized that certain criminal activities including, but not limited to loan, sharking, drug trafficking, trafficking in stolen property, gambling, extortion, smuggling, bribery, and corruption of public officials often involve some degree of regular coordination and permanent organization involving a large number of participants over a broad geographical area. The exposure of such ongoing networks of criminal activity can be aided by the pooling of information about such activities. However, because the collection and exchange of intelligence data necessary to support control of serious criminal activity may represent potential threats to the privacy of individuals to whom such data relate, policy guidelines for federally funded projects are required.

§ 23.3 Applicability
(a) These policy standards are applicable to all criminal intelligence systems operating through support under the Omnibus Crime Control and Safe Streets Act of 1968, 42 U.S.C. 3711, et seq., as amended (Pub. L. 90-351, as amended by Pub. L. 91-644, Pub. L. 93-83, Pub. L. 93-415, Pub. L. 94-430, Pub. L. 94-503, Pub. L. 95-115, Pub. L. 96-157, Pub. L. 98-473, Pub. L. 99-570, Pub. L. 100-690, and Pub. L. 101-647).
(b) As used in these policies, (1) *criminal intelligence system* or *intelligence system* means the arrangements, equipment, facilities, and procedures used for the receipt, storage, interagency exchange or dissemination, and analysis of criminal intelligence information; (2) *interjurisdictional intelligence system* means an intelligence system that involves two or more participating agencies representing

different governmental units or jurisdictions; (3) *criminal intelligence information* means data that have been evaluated to determine that it (i) is relevant to the identification of and the criminal activity engaged in by an individual who or organization that is reasonably suspected of involvement in criminal activity and (ii) meets criminal intelligence system submission criteria; (4) *participating agency* means an agency of local, county, state, federal, or other governmental unit, which exercises law enforcement or criminal investigation authority and which is authorized to submit and receive criminal intelligence information through an interjurisdictional intelligence system (a participating agency may be a member or a nonmember of an interjurisdictional intelligence system); (5) *intelligence project* or *project* means the organizational unit that operates an intelligence system on behalf of and for the benefit of a single agency or the organization that operates an interjurisdictional intelligence system on behalf of a group of participating agencies; and (6) *validation of information* means the procedures governing the periodic review of criminal intelligence information to assure its continuing compliance with system submission criteria established by regulation or program policy.

§ 23.20 Operating Principles

(a) A project shall collect and maintain criminal intelligence information concerning an individual only if there is reasonable suspicion that the individual is involved in criminal conduct or activity and the information is relevant to that criminal conduct or activity.

(b) A project shall not collect or maintain criminal intelligence information about the political, religious, or social views, associations, or activities of any individual or any group, association, corporation, business, partnership, or other organization unless such information directly relates to criminal conduct or activity and there is reasonable suspicion that the subject of the information is or may be involved in criminal conduct or activity.

(c) *Reasonable suspicion* or *criminal predicate* is established when information exists, which establishes sufficient facts to give a trained law enforcement or criminal investigative agency officer, investigator, or employee a basis to believe that there is a reasonable possibility that an individual or organization is involved in a definable criminal activity or enterprise. In an interjurisdictional intelligence system, the project is responsible for establishing the existence of reasonable suspicion of criminal activity either through examination of supporting information submitted by a participating agency or by delegation of this responsibility to a properly trained participating agency, which is subject to routine inspection and audit procedures established by the project.

(d) A project shall not include in any criminal intelligence system information, which has been obtained in violation of any applicable federal, state, or local law or ordinance. In an inter-jurisdictional intelligence system, the project is responsible for establishing that no information is entered in violation of federal, state, or local laws, either through examination of supporting information submitted by a participating agency or by delegation of this responsibility to a properly trained participating agency, which is subject to routine inspection and audit procedures established by the project.

(e) A project or authorized recipient shall disseminate criminal intelligence information only where there is a need to know and a right to know the information in the performance of a law enforcement activity.

(f) (1) Except as noted in paragraph (f) (2) of this section, a project shall disseminate criminal intelligence information only to law enforcement authorities who shall agree to follow procedures regarding information receipt, maintenance, security, and dissemination, which are consistent with these principles.

(2) Paragraph (f) (1) of this section shall not limit the dissemination of an assessment of criminal intelligence information to a government official or to any other individual, when necessary, to avoid imminent danger to life or property.

(g) A project maintaining criminal intelligence information shall ensure that administrative, technical, and physical safeguards (including audit trails) are adopted to ensure against unauthorized access and against intentional or unintentional damage. A record indicating who has been given information, the reason for release of the information, and the date of each dissemination outside the project shall be kept. Information shall be labeled to indicate levels of sensitivity, levels of confidence, and the identity of submitting agencies and control officials. Each project must establish written definitions for the need to know and right to know standards for dissemination to other agencies as provided in paragraph (e) of this section. The project is responsible for establishing the existence of an inquirer's need to know and right to know the information being requested either through inquiry or by delegation of this responsibility to a properly trained participating agency, which is subject to routine inspection and audit procedures established by the project. Each intelligence project shall assure that the following security requirements are implemented:

(1) Where appropriate, projects must adopt effective and technologically advanced computer software and hardware designs to prevent unauthorized access to the information contained in the system.

(2) The project must restrict access to its facilities, operating environment, and documentation to organizations and personnel authorized by the project.

(3) The project must store information in the system in a manner such that it cannot be modified, destroyed, accessed, or purged without authorization.

(4) The project must institute procedures to protect criminal intelligence information from unauthorized access, theft, sabotage, fire, flood, or other natural or manmade disaster.

(5) The project must promulgate rules and regulations based on good cause for implementing its authority to screen, reject for employment, transfer, or remove personnel authorized to have direct access to the system.

(6) A project may authorize and utilize remote (off-premises) system databases to the extent that they comply with these security requirements.

(h) All projects shall adopt procedures to assure that all information, which is retained by a project, has relevancy and importance. Such procedures shall provide for the periodic review of information and the destruction of any information that is misleading, obsolete, or otherwise unreliable and shall require that any recipient agencies be advised of such changes, which involve errors or corrections. All information retained as a result of this review must reflect the name of the reviewer, date of review, and explanation of decision to retain. Information retained in the system must be reviewed and validated for continuing compliance with system submission criteria before the expiration of its retention period, which in no event shall be longer than 5 years.

(i) If funds awarded under the act are used to support the operation of an intelligence system, then

(1) No project shall make direct remote terminal access to intelligence information available to system participants, except as specifically approved by the OJP based on a determination that the system has adequate policies and procedures in place to ensure that it is accessible only to authorized system users

(2) A project shall undertake no major modifications to system design without prior grantor agency approval

(j) A project shall notify the grantor agency prior to initiation of formal information exchange procedures with any federal, state, regional, or other information systems not indicated in the grant documents as initially approved at time of award.

(k) A project shall make assurances that there will be no purchase or use in the course of the project of any electronic, mechanical, or other device for surveillance purposes that is in violation of the provisions of the Electronic Communications Privacy Act of 1986; Public Law 99-508; 18 U.S.C. 2510-2520, 2701-2709, and 3121-3125; or any applicable state statute related to wiretapping and surveillance.

(l) A project shall make assurances that there will be no harassment or interference with any lawful political activities as part of the intelligence operation.

(m) A project shall adopt sanctions for unauthorized access, utilization, or disclosure of information contained in the system.

(n) A participating agency of an interjurisdictional intelligence system must maintain in its agency files information that documents each submission to the system and supports compliance with project entry criteria. Participating agency files supporting system submissions must be made available for reasonable audit and inspection by project representatives. Project representatives will conduct participating agency inspection and audit in such a manner so as to protect the confidentiality and sensitivity of participating agency intelligence records.

(o) The attorney general or designee may waive, in whole or in part, the applicability of a particular requirement or requirements contained in this part with respect to a criminal intelligence system, or for a class of submitters or users of such system, upon a clear and convincing showing that such waiver would enhance the collection, maintenance, or dissemination of information in the criminal intelligence system while ensuring that such system would not be utilized in violation of the privacy and constitutional rights of individuals or any applicable state or federal law.

§ 23.30 *Funding Guidelines*   The following funding guidelines shall apply to all Crime Control Act–funded discretionary assistance awards and BJA formula grant program subgrants, the purpose of which is to support the operation of an intelligence system. Intelligence systems shall only be funded where a grantee/subgrantee agrees to adhere to the principles set forth previously and the project meets the following criteria:

(a) The proposed collection and exchange of criminal intelligence information have been coordinated with and will support ongoing or proposed investigatory or prosecutorial activities relating to specific areas of criminal activity.

(b) The areas of criminal activity for which intelligence information is to be utilized represent a significant and recognized threat to the population and

    (1) Are either undertaken for the purpose of seeking illegal power or profits or pose a threat to the life and property of citizens

    (2) Involve a significant degree of permanent criminal organization

    (3) Are not limited to one jurisdiction

(c) The head of a government agency or an individual with general policy-making authority who has been expressly delegated such control and supervision by the head of the agency will retain control and supervision of information collection and dissemination for the criminal intelligence system. This official shall certify in writing that he or she takes full responsibility and will be accountable for the information maintained by and disseminated from the system and that the operation of the system will be in compliance with the principles set forth in § 23.20.

(d) Where the system is an interjurisdictional criminal intelligence system, the governmental agency, which exercises control and supervision over the operation of the system, shall require that the head of that agency or an individual with general policy-making authority who has been expressly delegated such control and supervision by the head of the agency

    (1) Assume official responsibility and accountability for actions taken in the name of the joint entity

    (2) Certify in writing that the official takes full responsibility and will be accountable for ensuring that the information transmitted to the interjurisdictional system or to participating agencies will be in compliance with the principles set forth in § 23.20

The principles set forth in § 23.20 shall be made part of the by-laws or operating procedures for that system. Each participating agency, as a condition of participation, must accept in writing those principles that govern the submission, maintenance, and dissemination of information included as part of the interjurisdictional system.

(e) Intelligence information will be collected, maintained, and disseminated primarily for state and local law enforcement efforts, including efforts involving federal participation.

§ 23.40 *Monitoring and Auditing of Grants for the Funding of Intelligence Systems*

(a) Awards for the funding of intelligence systems will receive specialized monitoring and audit in accordance with a plan designed to ensure compliance with operating principles as set forth in § 23.20. The plan shall be approved prior to award of funds.

(b) All such awards shall be subject to a special condition requiring compliance with the principles set forth in § 23.20.

(c) An annual notice will be published by OJP that will indicate the existence and the objective of all systems for the continuing inter-jurisdictional exchange of criminal intelligence information, which are subject to the 28 C.F.R. Part 23 Criminal Intelligence Systems Policies.

Laurie Robinson, Acting Assistant Attorney General, Office of Justice Programs (FR Doc. 93-22614 Filed 9-15-93; 8:45 a.m.)

1998 Policy Clarification

Agency: BJA, OJP, Justice

Action: Clarification of policy

Summary: The current policy governing the entry of identifying information into criminal intelligence sharing systems requires clarification. This policy clarification is to make clear that the entry of individuals, entities and organizations, and locations that do not otherwise meet the requirements of reasonable suspicion is appropriate when it is done solely for the purposes of criminal identification or is germane to the criminal subject's criminal activity. Further, the definition of *criminal intelligence system* is clarified.

Effective date: This clarification is effective on December 30, 1998.

For further information, contact: Paul Kendall, General Counsel, Office of Justice Programs, 810 7th Street NW, Washington, DC, 20531, (202) 307-6235.

Supplementary information: The operation of criminal intelligence information systems is governed by 28 C.F.R. Part 23. This regulation was written both to protect the privacy rights of individuals and to encourage and expedite the exchange of criminal intelligence information between and among law enforcement agencies of different jurisdictions. Frequent interpretations of the regulation, in the form of policy guidance and correspondence, have been the primary method of ensuring that advances in technology did not hamper its effectiveness.

Comments

The clarification was opened to public comment. Comments expressing unreserved support for the clarification were received from two RISS and five states. A comment from the chairperson of a RISS, relating to the use of identifying information to begin new investigations, has been incorporated. A single negative comment was received, but was not addressed to the subject of this clarification.

Use of Identifying Information

28 C.F.R. 23.3(b)(3) states that criminal intelligence information that can be put into a criminal intelligence sharing system is "information relevant to the identification of and the criminal activity engaged in by an individual who or organization which is reasonably suspected of involvement in criminal activity, and... meets criminal intelligence system submission criteria." Further, 28 C.F.R. 23.20(a) states that a system shall only collect information on an individual if "there is reasonable suspicion that the individual is involved in criminal conduct or activity and the information is relevant to that criminal conduct or activity." 28 C.F.R. 23.20(b) extends that limitation to [page 71753] collecting information on groups and corporate entities.

In an effort to protect individuals and organizations from the possible taint of having their names in intelligence systems (as defined at 28 C.F.R. Section 23.3(b)(1)), the OJP has previously interpreted this section to allow information to be placed in a system only if that information independently meets the requirements of the regulation. Information that might be vital to identifying potential criminals, such as favored locations and companions or names of family members, has been excluded from the systems. This policy has hampered the effectiveness of many criminal intelligence sharing systems.

Given the swiftly changing nature of modern technology and the expansion of the size and complexity of criminal organizations, the BJA has determined that it is necessary to clarify this element of 28 C.F.R. Part 23. Many criminal intelligence databases are now employing "Comment" or "Modus Operandi" fields whose value would be greatly enhanced by the ability to store more detailed and wide-ranging identifying information. This may include names and limited data about people and organizations that are not suspected of any criminal activity or involvement but merely aid in the identification and investigation of a criminal suspect who independently satisfies the reasonable suspicion standard.

Therefore, BJA issues the following clarification to the rules applying to the use of identifying information. Information that is relevant to the identification of a criminal suspect or to the criminal activity in which the suspect is engaged may be placed in a criminal intelligence database, provided that (1) appropriate disclaimers accompany the information noting that is strictly identifying information, carrying no criminal connotations; (2) identifying information may not be used as an independent basis to meet the requirement of reasonable suspicion of involvement in criminal activity necessary to create a record or file in a criminal intelligence system; and (3) the individual who is the criminal suspect identified by this information otherwise meets all requirements of 28 C.F.R. Part 23. This information may be a searchable field in the intelligence system.

For example, a person reasonably suspected of being a drug dealer is known to conduct his criminal activities at the fictional "Northwest Market."

An agency may wish to note this information in a criminal intelligence database, as it may be important to future identification of the suspect. Under the previous interpretation of the regulation, the entry of "Northwest Market" would not be permitted, because there was no reasonable suspicion that the "Northwest Market" was a criminal organization. Given the current clarification of the regulation, this will be permissible, provided that the information regarding the "Northwest Market" was clearly noted to be noncriminal in nature. For example, the data field in which "Northwest Market" was entered could be marked "non-criminal identifying information," or the words "Northwest Market" could be followed by a parenthetical comment such as "This organization has been entered into the system for identification purposes only - it is not suspected of any criminal activity or involvement." A criminal intelligence system record or file could not be created for "Northwest Market" solely on the basis of information provided, for example, in a comment field on the suspected drug dealer. Independent information would have to be obtained as a basis for the opening of a new criminal intelligence file or record based on reasonable suspicion on "Northwest Market." Further, the fact that other individuals frequent "Northwest Market" would not necessarily establish reasonable suspicion for those other individuals, as it relates to criminal intelligence systems.

Definition of a Criminal Intelligence System

The definition of a *criminal intelligence system* is given in 28 C.F.R. 23.3(b) (1) as the "arrangements, equipment, facilities, and procedures used for the receipt, storage, interagency exchange or dissemination, and analysis of criminal intelligence information…." Given the fact that cross-database searching techniques are now commonplace and that multiple databases may be contained on the same computer system, BJA has determined that this definition needs clarification, specifically to differentiate between criminal intelligence systems and nonintelligence systems.

The comments to the 1993 revision of 28 C.F.R. Part 23 noted that "the term 'intelligence system' is redefined to clarify the fact that historical telephone toll files, analytical information, and work products that are not either retained, stored, or exchanged and criminal history record information or identification (fingerprint) systems are excluded from the definition, and hence are not covered by the regulation…" 58 FR 48448–48449 (September 16, 1993). The comments further noted that materials that "may assist an agency to produce investigative or other information for an intelligence system…" do not necessarily fall under the regulation. Id.

The aforementioned rationale for the exclusion of nonintelligence information sources from the definition of *criminal intelligence system* suggests now that, given the availability of more modern nonintelligence information sources such as the Internet, newspapers, motor vehicle administration records, and other public record information online, such sources shall not be considered part of criminal intelligence systems and shall not be covered by this regulation, even if criminal intelligence systems access such sources during searches on criminal suspects. Therefore, criminal intelligence systems may conduct searches across the spectrum of nonintelligence systems without those systems being brought under 28 C.F.R. Part 23. There is also no limitation on such nonintelligence information being stored on the same computer system as criminal intelligence information, provided that sufficient precautions are in place to separate the two types of information and to make it clear to operators and users of the information that two different types of information are being accessed.

Such precautions should be consistent with the aforementioned clarification of the rule governing the use of identifying information. This could be accomplished, for example, through the use of multiple windows, differing colors of data, or clear labeling of the nature of information displayed.

Additional guidelines will be issued to provide details of the aforementioned clarifications as needed.

Dated: December 22, 1998

Nancy Gist
Director, Bureau of Justice Assistance
[FR Doc. 98-34547 Filed 12-29-98; 8:45 a.m.]
Billing Code 4410-18-P

Appendix E: Lists of Most Common Languages

List of Official Languages by Language and Area Spoken

Abkhaz

- Abkhazia (independence disputed)
- Georgia, on the territory of Abkhazia

Afrikaans

- South Africa (with English, Ndebele, Northern Sotho, Sotho, Swati, Tsonga, Tswana, Venda, Xhosa, and Zulu)

Albanian

- Albania
- Kosovo (independence disputed)
- Montenegro (with Montenegrin, Serbian, Bosnian, and Croatian)
- Serbia (in Kosovo and several municipalities in Central Serbia)

Amharic

- Ethiopia

Arabic

- Algeria
- Bahrain (with English)
- Chad (with French)
- Comoros (with French and Comorian)
- Djibouti (with French)
- Egypt
- Eritrea (with Tigrignan)
- Iraq (with Kurdish)
- Israel (with Hebrew)

- Jordan
- Kuwait
- Lebanon (with French and English)
- Libya
- Mauritania
- Morocco (with French and Spanish)
- Oman
- Palestinian Authority
- Qatar
- Saudi Arabia
- Somalia (with Somali)
- Sudan
- Syria
- Tunisia
- United Arab Emirates
- Western Sahara
- Yemen

Armenian

- Armenia

Assamese

- India (with 22 other official languages)
  - Assam

Aymara

- Bolivia (with Spanish and Quechua)
- Peru (with Spanish and Quechua)

Azeri

- Azerbaijan

Basque

- Spain (co-official in Basque autonomous community)

Belarusian

- Belarus (with Russian)

Bengali

- Bangladesh
- India (with 22 other official languages)
  - Tripura
  - West Bengal

Bislama

- Vanuatu

Bosnian

- Bosnia and Herzegovina (with Croatian and Serbian)
- Montenegro (with Montenegrin, Serbian, Albanian, and Croatian)
- Serbia (in the region of Sandžak)

Bulgarian

- Bulgaria

Burmese

- Myanmar

Catalan

- Andorra
- Spain (co-official in Catalonia, the Balearic Islands, and the Valencian Community)

Chinese (Sinitic languages)

- Republic of China in Taiwan (Mandarin is spoken, traditional Chinese is written, Mandarin is designated as national language.)
- People's Republic of China (Varieties of Chinese languages are spoken, simplified Chinese is written, Mandarin is designated as national language.)
  - Hong Kong (The Sino-British Joint Declaration and Hong Kong Basic Law do not explicitly specify the standard for *Chinese*, but de facto Cantonese is spoken and traditional Chinese is written, co-official with English.)

- Macau (Cantonese is spoken de facto, traditional Chinese is written, co-official with Portuguese.)
- Singapore (Mandarin is spoken, simplified Chinese is written, with English, Malay, and Tamil.)

Croatian

- Part of Austria
  - Burgenland (with German and Hungarian)
- Bosnia and Herzegovina (with Bosnian and Serbian)
- Croatia
- Part of Italy
  - Molise
- Part of Serbia
  - Vojvodina (with Serbian, Hungarian, Romanian, Slovak, and Ruthenian)
- Montenegro (with Montenegrin, Serbian, Bosnian, and Albanian)

Czech

- Czech Republic

Danish

- Denmark
  - Faroe Islands (with Faroese)
  - Greenland (with Kalaallisut)

Dari

- Afghanistan (with Pashto)

Dhivehi

- Maldives

Dutch

- Belgium (sole official language in Flanders, with French in Brussels)
- The Netherlands (sole official language in every province except Friesland, where West Frisian is co-official)
  - Aruba (with Papiamento)

- Netherlands Antilles (with English and Papiamento)
- Suriname

Dzongkha

- Bhutan

English

- Antigua and Barbuda
- Australia (considered de facto as no official language is mentioned in the Australian Constitution)
- Bahamas
- Barbados
- Belize
- Botswana (but the national language is Tswana)
- Canada (with French)
- Cameroon (with French)
- Dominica
- Fiji (with Bau Fijian and Hindustani)
- Hong Kong (with Chinese)
- The Gambia
- Ghana
- Grenada (with French Creole)
- Guernsey (with French)
- Guyana
- India (with 22 other official languages)
- Republic of Ireland (with Irish)
- Jamaica
- Jersey (with French)
- Kenya (with Swahili)
- Kiribati
- Lesotho (with Sotho)
- Liberia
- Madagascar (with Malagasy and French)
- Malawi (with Chichewa)
- Malta (with Maltese)
- Isle of Man (with Manx Gaelic)
- Marshall Islands (with Marshallese)
- Mauritius
- Micronesia
- Namibia (Afrikaans, German, and Oshiwambo are regional spoken.)
- Nauru (with Nauruan)

- Netherlands Antilles (with Dutch and Papiamento)
- New Zealand (with Māori and New Zealand Sign Language)
- Nigeria
- Pakistan (with Urdu as the national language)
- Philippines (with Filipino)
- Palau (with Palauan and Japanese)
- Papua New Guinea (with Tok Pisin and Motu)
- Rwanda (with French and Kinyarwanda)
- St. Kitts and Nevis
- St. Lucia (with French Creole)
- St. Vincent and the Grenadines (with French Creole)
- Samoa (with Samoan)
- Seychelles (with Creole, French)
- Sierra Leone
- Singapore (with Chinese, Malay, and Tamil)
- Solomon Islands
- South Africa (with Afrikaans, Ndebele, Northern Sotho, Sotho, Swati, Tsonga, Tswana, Venda, Xhosa, and Zulu)
- Sudan (with Arabic)
- Swaziland (with Swati)
- Tanzania (with Swahili)
- Tonga
- Trinidad and Tobago
- Tuvalu
- Uganda (with Swahili)
- United Kingdom
- United States
- Vanuatu (with Bislama and French)
- Zambia
- Zimbabwe

Estonian

- Estonia

Fijian

- Fiji (with English and Hindustani)

Filipino

- Philippines (with English)

Finnish

- Finland (with Swedish)

French

- Belgium (with Dutch and German)
- Benin
- Burkina Faso
- Burundi (with Kirundi)
- Cameroon (with English)
- Canada (with English)
- Central African Republic
- Chad (with Arabic)
- Comoros (with Arabic and Comorian)
- Côte d'Ivoire
- Democratic Republic of the Congo
- Djibouti (with Arabic)
- Equatorial Guinea (with Spanish)
- France
  - French Guyana
  - French Polynesia
  - French Loyalty Islands
  - French Southern and Antarctic Lands
  - Scattered islands in the Indian Ocean
  - Guadeloupe
  - Martinique
  - Mayotte
  - Morocco
  - New Caledonia
  - Réunion
  - Saint Barthélemy
  - Saint Martin
  - Saint Pierre et Miquelon
  - Wallis and Futuna
  - Adelie Land
  - Clipperton Island
- Gabon
- Guernsey (with English)
- Guinea
- Haiti (with Haitian Creole)
- Part of Italy
  - The Aosta Valley with Italian

- Jersey (with English)
- Luxembourg (with German and Luxembourgish)
- Madagascar (with Malagasy and English)
- Mali
- Monaco
- Niger
- Republic of the Congo
- Rwanda (with English and Kinyarwanda)
- Senegal
- Seychelles (with English)
- Saint Lucia (French Patois with English)
- Switzerland (with German, Italian, and Rhaeto-Romansch)
  - Geneva
  - Vaud
  - Jura
  - Neuchâtel
  - Fribourg (with German)
  - Bern (with German)
  - Valais (with German)
- Togo
- Vanuatu (with Bislama and English)

Frisian (West)

- The Netherlands (with Dutch)

Gagauz

- Moldova (with Moldovan, Russian, and Ukrainian)

Georgian

- Georgia
- South Ossetia (with Russian and Ossetian—independence disputed)

German

- Austria
- Belgium (with Dutch and French)
- Germany
- Liechtenstein

- Luxembourg (with French and Luxembourgish)
- Italy
  - Province of Bolzano-Bozen (together with Italian and Ladin)
- Namibia national language (regional spoken)
- Switzerland (with French, Italian, and Rhaeto-Romansch)
  - 17 of the 26 cantons (monolingual German)
  - Graubünden (with Italian and Romansh)
  - Bern (with French)
  - Fribourg (with French)
  - Valais (with French)

Greek

- Greece
- Cyprus (with Turkish)
- Parts of south Italy
  - Salento (Grecia Salentina, together with Italian)
  - Calabria (Bovesia, together with Italian)

Guaraní

- Paraguay (with Spanish)

Gujarati

- India (with 22 other official languages)
  - Dadra and Nagar Haveli
  - Daman and Diu
  - Gujarat

Haitian Creole

- Haiti (with French)

Hebrew

- Israel (with Arabic)

Hindi

- India (with 22 other official languages)
- Fiji (with English and Bau Fijian; known constitutionally as *Hindustani* as an umbrella term to cover Urdu, as well as Hindi)

Hiri Motu

- Papua New Guinea (with English and Tok Pisin)

Hungarian

- Hungary
- Part of Serbia
  - Vojvodina (with Croatian, Serbian, Romanian, Slovak, and Ruthenian)
- Part of Romania
- Part of Austria

Icelandic

- Iceland

Indonesian

- Indonesia

Irish

- Ireland (with English)
- Northern Ireland (along with English and Ulster-Scots)

Italian

- Italy
- Switzerland (with German and French)
  - Ticino
  - Graubünden (with German and Rhaeto-Romansh)
- San Marino
- Vatican City (with Latin and French)
- Part of Croatia
  - Istria County (with Croatian)
- Part of Slovenia
  - Izola, Koper, and Piran municipalities (with Slovene)

Japanese

- Japan (de facto)
- Part of Palau
  - Angaur (with Angaur and English)

Kannada

- India (with 22 other official languages)
  - Karnataka

Kashmiri

- India (with 22 other official languages)
  - Jammu and Kashmir

Kazakh

- Kazakhstan (with Russian)
- Part of the People's Republic of China
  - Ili, with Chinese (Mandarin)
  - Barkol, with Chinese (Mandarin)
  - Mori, with Chinese (Mandarin)

Khmer

- Cambodia (with French)

Korean

- Democratic People's Republic of Korea
- Republic of Korea
- Part of the People's Republic of China with Chinese (Mandarin)
  - Changbai (Jangbaek, Changbaek)
  - Yanbian (Yeonbyeon, Yŏnbyŏn)

Kurdish

- Iraq (with Arabic)

Kyrgyz

- Kyrgyzstan (with Russian)
- Part of the People's Republic of China
  - Kizilsu (with Chinese [Mandarin])

Lao

- Laos

Latvian

- Latvia

Lithuanian

- Lithuania

Luxembourgish

- Luxembourg (with French and German)

Macedonian

- Republic of Macedonia
- Part of Albania
  - Korçë (with Albanian)

Malagasy

- Madagascar (with French and English)

Malay

- Malaysia
- Brunei
- Singapore (with English, Chinese, and Tamil)

Malayalam

- India (with 22 other official languages)
  - Kerala
  - Pondicherry
  - Lakshadweep

Maltese

- Malta (with English)

Manx Gaelic

- Isle of Man (with English)

Māori

- New Zealand (with English and New Zealand Sign Language)

Marathi

- India (with 22 other official languages)—Maharashtra

Mayan

- Mexico (with Spanish and Náhuatl)

Moldovan (identical to Romanian according to the law of Moldova)

- Moldova

Mongolian

- Mongolia
- Part of the People's Republic of China
  - Inner Mongolia, with Chinese (Mandarin)
  - Haixi, with Tibetan and Chinese (Mandarin)
  - Bortala, with Chinese (Mandarin)
  - Bayin'gholin, with Chinese (Mandarin)
  - Dorbod, with Chinese (Mandarin)
  - Qian Gorlos, with Chinese (Mandarin)
  - Harqin Left, with Chinese (Mandarin)
  - Fuxin, with Chinese (Mandarin)
  - Weichang, with Chinese (Mandarin)
  - Subei, with Chinese (Mandarin)
  - Henan, with Chinese (Mandarin)

Montenegrin

- Montenegro (with Bosnian, Albanian, and Croatian)

Náhuatl

- Mexico (with Spanish and Mayan)

Ndebele

- South Africa (with Afrikaans, English, Northern Sotho, Sotho, Swati, Tsonga, Tswana, Venda, Xhosa, and Zulu)
- Zimbabwe (with English and Shona)

Nepali

- Nepal
- India (with 22 other official languages)
  - Sikkim
  - West Bengal

New Zealand Sign Language

- New Zealand (alongside Māori and English)

Northern Sotho

- South Africa (with Afrikaans, English, Ndebele, Sotho, Swati, Tsonga, Tswana, Venda, Xhosa, and Zulu)

Norwegian

- Norway (two official written forms—*Bokmål* and *Nynorsk*)

Occitan

- Spain (Aranese is co-official in the Aran Valley and in Catalonia)

Oriya

- India (with 22 other official languages)
  - Orissa

Ossetian

- South Ossetia (with Russian and Georgian—independence disputed)

Papiamento

- Aruba (with Dutch)
- Netherlands Antilles (with English and Dutch)

Pashto

- Afghanistan (with Dari)
- Pakistan (majority language of the NWFP but has no official status)

Persian (Farsi)

- Iran
- Afghanistan (called Dari Persian in Afghanistan, with Pashto)
- Tajikistan (called Tajik Persian in Tajikistan)

Polish

- Poland

Portuguese

- Angola
- Brazil
- Cape Verde
- East Timor (with Tetum)
- Guinea-Bissau
- Part of the People's Republic of China
  - Macau (with Chinese)
- Mozambique
- Portugal
- São Tomé and Príncipe

Punjabi

- India (with 22 other official languages)
  - Punjab
  - Delhi
- Pakistan (with English, Pothowari, Urdu, Kashmiri [Koshur], Pashto, Sindhi, Saraiki, Balochi, and Brahui; Dogri is also spoken in part of the Rawalpindi district)

Quechua

- Bolivia (with Spanish and Aymara)
- Peru (with Spanish and Aymara)

Romanian

- Romania
- Moldova (officially called Moldovan, although identical to Romanian according to the law of Moldova)

- Part of Serbia
  - Vojvodina (with Croatian, Hungarian, Serbian, Slovak, and Ruthenian)

Rhaeto-Romansh

- Switzerland (with German, French, and Italian)—Graubünden (with German and Italian)

Russian

- Russia (in some regions together with regional languages)
- Abkhazia (with Abkhaz—independence disputed)
- Belarus (with Belarusian)
- Kazakhstan (with Kazakh)
- Kyrgyzstan (with Kyrgyz)
- Moldova (with Moldovan, Ukrainian, and Gagauz)
- South Ossetia (with Ossetian and Georgian—independence disputed)

Sanskrit

- India (with 22 other official languages)

Serbian

- Bosnia and Herzegovina (with Bosnian, Croatian)
- Serbia
- Kosovo (independence disputed, with Albanian)

Shona

- Zimbabwe (with English and Ndebele)

Sindhi

- India (with 22 other official languages)
- Pakistan (official language in the province of Sindh along with Urdu and English)

Sinhala

- Sri Lanka (with Tamil and with English as a link language)

Slovak

- Slovakia
- Part of Serbia
  - Vojvodina (with Croatian, Serbian, Hungarian, Romanian, and Ruthenian)

Slovene

- Slovenia
- Part of Italy
  - Friuli–Venezia Giulia (with Italian)
- Part of Austria
  - Carinthia (with German)

Somali

- Somalia

Sotho

- Lesotho (with English)
- South Africa (with Afrikaans, English, Ndebele, Northern Sotho, Swati, Tsonga, Tswana, Venda, Xhosa, and Zulu)

Spanish

- Argentina
- Bolivia (with Aymara and Quechua)
- Chile
- Colombia
- Costa Rica
- Cuba
- Dominican Republic
- Ecuador
- El Salvador
- Equatorial Guinea (with French and Portuguese)
- Guatemala
- Honduras
- Mexico (de facto) (with Mayan and Náhuatl)
- Nicaragua
- Panama

- Paraguay (with Guaraní)
- Peru (with Aymara and Quechua)
- Puerto Rico (with English)
- Spain (Aranese, Basque, Catalan, and Galician are co-official in some regions)
- Uruguay
- Venezuela

Swahili

- Kenya (with English)
- Tanzania (de facto)
- Uganda (since 2005, with English)

Swati

- Swaziland (with English)
- South Africa (with Afrikaans, English, Ndebele, Northern Sotho, Sotho, Tsonga, Tswana, Venda, Xhosa, and Zulu)

Swedish

- Sweden
- Finland (with Finnish)
  - Åland (monolingual Swedish) (an autonomous province under Finnish sovereignty)

Tajik

- Tajikistan
- Part of the People's Republic of China
  - Taxkorgan (with Chinese [Mandarin])

Tamil

- India (with 22 other official languages)
  - Andaman and Nicobar Islands
  - Pondicherry
  - Tamil Nadu
- Singapore (with English, Chinese, and Malay)
- Sri Lanka (with Sinhala and with English as a link language)

Telugu

- India (with 22 other official languages)
  - Andhra Pradesh
  - Pondicherry

Tetum

- East Timor (with Portuguese)

Thai

- Thailand

Tok Pisin

- Papua New Guinea (with English and Hiri Motu)

Tsonga

- South Africa (with Afrikaans, English, Ndebele, Northern Sotho, Sotho, Swati, Tswana, Venda, Xhosa, and Zulu)

Tswana

- Botswana (with English)
- South Africa (with Afrikaans, English, Ndebele, Northern Sotho, Sotho, Swati, Tsonga, Venda, Xhosa, and Zulu)

Turkish

- Turkey
- Cyprus (with Greek)

Turkmen

- Turkmenistan

Ukrainian

- Ukraine
- Moldova (with Moldovan, Russian, and Gagauz)

Urdu

- India (with 22 other official languages)
  - Jammu and Kashmir
  - Delhi territory
  - Uttar Pradesh state
- Pakistan (with English, Pothowari, Punjabi, Kashmiri [Koshur], Pashto, Sindhi, Saraiki, Balochi, and Brahui)
- Fiji (with English and Bau Fijian; known constitutionally as *Hindustani* as an umbrella term to cover Urdu, as well as Hindi)

Uzbek

- Uzbekistan

Venda

- South Africa (with Afrikaans, English, Ndebele, Northern Sotho, Sotho, Swati, Tsonga, Tswana, Xhosa, and Zulu)

Vietnamese

- Vietnam

Welsh

- United Kingdom (Wales, with English)

Xhosa

- South Africa (with Afrikaans, English, Ndebele, Northern Sotho, Sotho, Swati, Tsonga, Tswana, Venda, and Zulu)

Yiddish

- Russia (only in Jewish autonomous Oblast, with Russian)

Zulu

- South Africa (with Afrikaans, English, Ndebele, Northern Sotho, Sotho, Swati, Tsonga, Tswana, Venda, and Xhosa)

List of Languages by State and Language Spoken

Recognized States

- Afghanistan
  - Pashto (statewide; official)
  - Dari (statewide; official)
  - Uzbek (statewide; third official language in areas where spoken by majority of population)
  - Turkmen (statewide; third official language in areas where spoken by majority of population)
  - Pashai (statewide; third official language in areas where spoken by majority of population)
  - Nuristani (statewide; third official language in areas where spoken by majority of population)
  - Balochi (statewide; third official language in areas where spoken by majority of population)
  - Pamiri (statewide; third official language in areas where spoken by majority of population)
- Albania: Albanian (based on Tosk dialect)
- Algeria
  - Arabic (official and national)
  - Tamazight (national)
  - French (de facto official)
- Andorra (languages of Andorra): Catalan
- Angola: Portuguese
- Antigua and Barbuda: English (de facto official)
- Argentina
  - Spanish
  - Guarani (Corrientes)
- Armenia: Armenian
- Australia: No official language; English is the de facto official language
- Austria
  - German (official statewide)
  - Croatian (official in Burgenland in areas where live Austrians of the Croat minority; statewide minority language)
  - Slovene (official in Carinthia and Styria in areas where live Austrians of the Slovene minority; statewide minority language)
  - Czech (statewide minority language)
  - Hungarian (in Burgenland; statewide minority language)
  - Slovak (statewide minority language)
  - Romani (statewide minority language)

- Azerbaijan: Azerbaijani
- Bahamas: English
- Bahrain: Arabic
- Bangladesh: Bengali
- Barbados: English
- Belarus
  - Belarusian
  - Russian
- Belgium (languages of Belgium)
  - Dutch
  - French
  - German
- Belize: English
- Benin: French
- Bhutan: Dzongkha
- Bolivia
  - Spanish
  - Aymara
  - Quechua
- Bosnia and Herzegovina
  - Bosnian
  - Croatian
  - Serbian
- Botswana
  - English
  - Tswana (national)
- Brazil: Portuguese
- Brunei: Malay
- Bulgaria: Bulgarian
- Burkina Faso
  - French
  - Fula (national)
  - Jula (national)
  - More (national)
- Burundi
  - French
  - Kirundi
- Cambodia: Khmer
- Cameroon
  - English
  - French

- Canada
  - English (national)
    - Official provincial language of New Brunswick
  - French (national)
    - Official provincial language of Quebec and New Brunswick
  - Chipewyan (Dëne Sųłiné) (in the Northwest Territories)
  - Cree (in the Northwest Territories)
  - Dogrib (Tłįchǫ) (in the Northwest Territories)
  - Gwich'in (in the Northwest Territories)
  - Inuinnaqtun (in the Northwest Territories and Nunavut)
  - Inuktitut (in the Northwest Territories and Nunavut)
  - Inuvialuktun (in the Northwest Territories)
  - Slavey (in the Northwest Territories)
- Cape Verde
  - Portuguese (official)
  - Cape Verdean Creole (national)
- Central African Republic
  - French
  - Sango (national)
- Chad
  - Arabic
  - French
- Chile: Spanish
- People's Republic of China
  - Chinese
    - Written: Simplified Chinese statewide, traditional Chinese de facto in Hong Kong and Macau
    - Spoken: Mandarin statewide, Cantonese de facto in Hong Kong and Macau
  - English (in Hong Kong)
  - Portuguese (in Macau)
  - Kazakh (in Ili Kazakh, Xinjiang)
  - Korean (in Changbai and Yanbian, Jilin)
  - Mongolian (in Inner Mongolia)
  - Tajik (in Taxkorgan, Xinjiang)
  - Tibetan (in Tibet)
  - Uyghur (in Xinjiang)
  - Zhuang (in Guangxi)
- Colombia: Spanish (The languages and dialects of ethnic groups are also official in their territories)
- Comoros
  - Arabic

- Comorian
- French
- Democratic Republic of the Congo
  - French
  - Lingala (national)
  - Kikongo (national)
  - Swahili (national)
  - Tshiluba (national)
- Republic of the Congo
  - French
  - Lingala (national)
  - Munukutuba (national)
- Costa Rica: Spanish
- Côte d'Ivoire: French
- Croatia
  - Croatian (statewide)
  - Italian (in Istria)
- Cuba: Spanish
- Cyprus
  - Greek
  - Turkish
- Czech Republic: Czech
- Denmark
  - Danish (statewide)
  - Faroese (in the Faroe Islands)
  - German (protected minority language in South Jutland)
  - Kalaallisut (in Greenland)
- Djibouti
  - Arabic
  - French
- Dominica: English
- Dominican Republic: Spanish
- East Timor
  - Portuguese
  - Tetum
- Ecuador: Spanish (Quechua or Kichwa and Shuar are official languages of intercultural relations; ancient languages are official in their territories)
- Egypt: Arabic
- El Salvador: Spanish
- Equatorial Guinea
  - Spanish
  - French

- Eritrea
  - Arabic (working language)
  - Tigrinya (working language)
- Estonia: Estonian
- Ethiopia: Amharic
- Fiji
  - English
  - Fijian
  - Hindustani
- Finland
  - Finnish (statewide, except in the Åland Islands)
  - Swedish (statewide; in the Åland Islands where Swedish is spoken monolingually)
  - Sami (minority language in Enontekiö, Inari, Sodankylä, and Utsjoki)
- France (and overseas departments and territories): French
- Gabon: French
- Gambia: English
- Georgia
  - Abkhaz (in Abkhazia)
  - Georgian (statewide, except in Abkhazia and South Ossetia)
  - Ossetic (in South Ossetia)
  - Russian (in Abkhazia and South Ossetia)
- Germany
  - No official language nationwide; German is the de facto official language and the national language
  - Danish (in Schleswig-Holstein; minority language)
  - Lower Sorbian (in Brandenburg; minority language)
  - North Frisian (in Schleswig-Holstein; minority language)
  - Romani (in Hesse)
  - Saterland Frisian (in Lower Saxony; minority language)
  - Upper Sorbian (in Saxony) (minority language)
- Ghana
  - Adangme (in Greater Accra)
  - Dagaare (in the Upper Western Region)
  - Dagbani (in the Northern Region)
  - English (statewide)
  - Ewe (in the Volta Region)
  - Ga (in Greater Accra)
  - Gonja (in the Northern Region)
  - Kasem (in the Upper Eastern Region)
  - Nzema (in the Western Region)
  - Twi (in Akuapem, Akyem, Ashanti, Fanteakwa, Fante, and Kwahu)

- Greece: Greek
- Grenada: English
- Guatemala: Spanish
- Guinea
  - French
  - Fula (national)
  - Maninka (national)
  - Susu (national)
- Guinea-Bissau: Portuguese
- Guyana: English
- Haiti
  - French
  - Haitian Creole
- Honduras: Spanish
- Hungary: Hungarian
- Iceland: Icelandic
- India
  - Assamese (in Assam)
  - Bengali (in Tripura and West Bengal)
  - Bhojpuri (in Bihar)
  - Bodo (in Assam)
  - Chhattisgarhi (in Chhattisgarh)
  - Dogri (in Jammu and Kashmir)
  - English (statewide)
  - French (in Pondicherry)
  - Garo (in Meghalaya)
  - Gujarati (in Dadra and Nagar Haveli, Daman and Diu, and Gujarat)
  - Hindi (central government and most of the states)
  - Kannada (in Karnataka)
  - Karbi (in Assam)
  - Kashmiri (in Jammu and Kashmir)
  - Khasi (in Meghalaya)
  - Kokborok (in Tripura)
  - Konkani (in Goa)
  - Magadhi (only in Bihar)
  - Maithili (in Bihar)
  - Malayalam (in Kerala, Pondicherry, and Lakshadweep)
  - Meitei (in Manipur)
  - Marathi (in Maharashtra, Goa)
  - Mizo (in Mizoram)
  - Nepali (in Sikkim)
  - Nicobarese (in Andaman and Nicobar Islands)
  - Oriya (in Orissa)

- Pahari (in Himachal Pradesh)
- Portuguese (in Diu and Goa)
- Punjabi (in Punjab, Haryana, and Chandigarh)
- Rajasthani (in Rajasthan)
- Sanskrit (statewide)
- Santali (in Jharkhand)
- Sindhi (Sindhi community/people dependent)
- Tamil (in Tamil Nadu, Andaman and Nicobar Islands, and Pondicherry)
- Telugu (in Andhra Pradesh and Pondicherry)
- Urdu (in Jammu and Kashmir)
- Indonesia: Indonesian
- Iran: Persian
- Iraq
  - Arabic (statewide)
  - Kurdish (in the Kurdish autonomous region)
  - Assyrian Neo-Aramaic (in Assyrian areas)
  - Iraqi Turkmen (in Turkmen areas)
- Ireland (Languages of Ireland)
  - Irish (national)
  - English (national)
- Israel
  - Hebrew
  - English
  - Arabic
- Italy
  - Italian (statewide)
  - Albanian (in some parts of Southern Italy)
  - Catalan (in Alghero, Sardinia)
  - Croatian (in Montemitro and Acquaviva Collecroce and San Felice, Molise)
  - French (in Aosta Valley)
  - Friulian (in Friuli)
  - German (in Alto Adige/Südtirol)
  - Greek (in some parts of Apulia and Calabria)
  - Ladin (in some parts of Trentino-Alto Adige/Südtirol)
  - Slovene (in some parts of Friuli-Venezia Giulia)
- Jamaica: English
- Japan
  - Japanese
  - Ryukyuan (minority language)
  - Ainu (minority language)
  - Korean (minority language)

- Jordan: Arabic
- Kazakhstan
  - Kazakh (national)
  - Russian
- Kenya
  - English
  - Swahili (national)
- Kiribati
  - English
  - Kiribati (national)
- North Korea: Korean
- South Korea: Korean
- Kuwait: Arabic
- Kyrgyzstan
  - Kirghiz (national)
  - Russian
- Laos: Lao
- Latvia
  - Latvian
  - Latgalian
- Lebanon
  - Arabic
  - French
  - English
  - Armenian
- Lesotho
  - English
  - Sotho (national)
- Liberia: English
- Libya: Arabic
- Liechtenstein: German
- Lithuania: Lithuanian
- Luxembourg
  - French
  - German
  - Luxembourgish (national)
- Macedonia
  - Macedonian (statewide)
  - Albanian
  - Turkish
- Madagascar
  - French
  - English

- Malagasy (national)
- Malawi
  - Chichewa (national)
  - English
- Malaysia: Malay (national)
- Maldives: Dhivehi
- Mali: French
- Malta
  - Maltese (national)
  - English
  - Italian
- Marshall Islands
  - English
  - Marshallese (national)
- Mauritania
  - Arabic (national)
  - French
  - Fula (national)
  - Soninke (national)
  - Wolof (national)
- Mauritius
  - English
  - French (de facto, lingua franca)
  - Mauritian Creole
- Mexico: No official language; Spanish is the de facto official language
- Federated States of Micronesia
  - Chuukese (in Chuuk)
  - English (statewide except in Kosrae, where it has a constitutionally protected associate status)
  - Kosraean (in Kosrae)
  - Pohnpeian (in Pohnpei)
  - Ulithian (in Yap)
  - Yapese (in Yap)
- Moldova
  - Gagauz (in Gagauzia)
  - Moldovan (or Romanian; statewide)
  - Russian (in Gagauzia and Transnistria)
  - Ukrainian (in Transnistria)
- Monaco: French
- Mongolia: Mongolian
- Montenegro
  - Montenegrin (national)
  - Bosnian

- Croatian (in Tivat)
- Serbian (in Herceg Novi)
- Albanian (in Ulcinj)
- Morocco: Arabic
- Mozambique: Portuguese
- Myanmar (Burma): Burmese
- Namibia: English
- Nauru
  - English
  - Nauruan
- Nepal: Nepali
- Netherlands
  - No official language nationwide; Dutch is the de facto official language and the national language
  - English (on Netherlands Antilles)
  - West Frisian (in Friesland)
  - Limburgish (regional language)
  - Low Saxon (regional language)
  - Papiamento (on Aruba, Netherlands Antilles)
- New Zealand
  - English is a de facto official language (statewide)
  - Maori (statewide)
  - NZSL (New Zealand deaf community)
  - Cook Islands Maori (in the Cook Islands)
  - Niuean (in Niue)
  - Tokelauan (in Tokelau)
- Nicaragua: Spanish
- Niger: French
- Nigeria
  - English
  - Hausa (national)
  - Yoruba (national)
  - Igbo (national)
- Norway (languages of Norway)
  - Norwegian (statewide; Bokmål and Nynorsk are the official forms, and municipalities choose between them or a neutral stance)
  - Sami (indigenous language in vast areas from Engerdal to the Russian border, official administrative language in Kautokeino, Karasjok, Gáivuotna-Kåfjord, Nesseby, Porsanger, Tana, Tysfjord, and Snåsa)
  - Kven (national minority language, administrative language in Porsanger)

- Romani (national minority language)
  - Scandoromani (national minority language)
- Oman: Arabic
- Pakistan
  - Urdu (national language)
  - English (official language)
  - Balochi (provincial language)
  - Pashto (provincial language)
  - Punjabi (provincial language)
  - Sindhi (provincial language)
- Palau
  - English (statewide)
  - Palauan (statewide)
  - Sonsorolese (in Sonsorol)
  - Tobian (in Hatohobei)
  - Angaur (in Angaur)
  - Japanese (in Angaur)
- Palestinian Authority: Arabic
- Panama: Spanish
- Papua New Guinea
  - English
  - Hiri Motu
  - Tok Pisin
- Paraguay
  - Spanish
  - Guaraní
- Peru
  - Spanish
  - Aymara
  - Quechua
  - All native languages in areas where they are spoken by the majority of people
- Philippines
  - Arabic (recognized as *voluntary and optional* statewide)
  - Bikol Central (in Luzon)
  - Cebuano (in Visayas and Mindanao)
  - English (statewide)
  - Filipino (statewide) (national)
  - Hiligaynon (in Visayas and Mindanao)
  - Ilokano (in Luzon)
  - Kapampangan (in Luzon)
  - Kinaray-a (in the Visayas)

- Maranao (in Mindanao)
- Maguindanao (in Mindanao)
- Pangasinan (in Luzon)
- Spanish (recognized as *voluntary and optional* statewide)
- Tagalog (in Luzon)
- Tausug (in Mindanao)
- Waray-Waray (in the Visayas)
- Poland
  - Polish (sole official language of state)
  - Kashubian (recognized regional language and auxiliary language in part of Pomeranian Voivodeship)
  - German (minority language and auxiliary language in part of Opole Voivodeship)
  - Lithuania (minority language and auxiliary language in Puńsk commune, Podlaskie Voivodeship)
  - Belorussian (minority language and auxiliary language in Hajnówka commune, Podlaskie Voivodeship)
- Portugal (languages of Portugal)
  - Portuguese
  - Mirandese (regional, in Miranda do Douro)
- Qatar: Arabic
- Romania: Romanian
- Russia (languages of Russia)
  - Russian (federal)
  - Abaza (in the Karachay-Cherkess Republic)
  - Adyghe (in the Republic of Adygea)
  - Agul (in the Republic of Dagestan)
  - Altay (in the Altai Republic)
  - Avar (in the Republic of Dagestan)
  - Azerbaijani (in the Republic of Dagestan)
  - Bashkir (in the Republic of Bashkortostan)
  - Buryat (in Buryat Republic)
  - Chechen (in the Chechen Republic and Republic of Dagestan)
  - Chuvash (in the Chuvash Republic)
  - Dargin (in the Republic of Dagestan)
  - Erzya (in the Republic of Mordovia)
  - Ingush (in the Republic of Ingushetia)
  - Kabardian (in the Kabardino-Balkar Republic and Karachay-Cherkess Republic)
  - Kalmyk (in the Republic of Kalmykia)
  - Karachay-Balkar (in the Kabardino-Balkar Republic and Karachay-Cherkess Republic)
  - Khakas (in the Republic of Khakassia)

- Komi-Zyrian (in the Komi Republic)
- Kumyk (in the Republic of Dagestan)
- Lak (in the Republic of Dagestan)
- Lezgian (in the Republic of Dagestan)
- Mari (in the Mari El Republic)
- Moksha (in the Republic of Mordovia)
- Nogai (in the Karachay-Cherkess Republic and in the Republic of Dagestan)
- Ossetic (in the Republic of North Ossetia–Alania)
- Rutul (in the Republic of Dagestan)
- Sakha (in the Sakha Republic)
- Tabasaran (in the Republic of Dagestan)
- Tatar (in the Republic of Tatarstan)
- Tati (in the Republic of Dagestan)
- Tsakhur (in the Republic of Dagestan)
- Tuvin (in the Tuva Republic)
- Udmurt (in the Republic of Udmurtia)
- Rwanda
  - English
  - French
  - Kinyarwanda
- Saint Kitts and Nevis: English
- Saint Lucia: English
- Saint Vincent and the Grenadines: English
- Samoa
  - English
  - Samoan (national)
- San Marino: Italian
- São Tomé and Príncipe: Portuguese
- Saudi Arabia: Arabic
- Senegal
  - French
  - Jola-Fogny (national)
  - Malinke (national)
  - Mandinka (national)
  - Pulaar (national)
  - Serer-Sine (national)
  - Wolof (national)
- Serbia
  - Serbian (statewide)
  - Albanian (in Kosovo and some municipalities in southern Serbia)
  - Bosniak (in municipalities of Sandzak)
  - Croatian (in Vojvodina)

- Hungarian (in Vojvodina)
- Romanian (in Vojvodina)
- Rusyn (in Vojvodina)
- Slovak (in Vojvodina)
- Seychelles
  - English
  - French
  - Seychellois Creole
- Sierra Leone: English
- Singapore
  - English
  - Malay (national)
  - Chinese (*written*: simplified Chinese; *spoken*: Mandarin)
  - Tamil
- Slovakia
  - Slovak
  - Hungarian (minority, in southern Slovakia)
- Slovenia
  - Hungarian (*minority language in* Dubrovnik, Hodoš, and Lendava)
  - Italian (minority language in Izola, Koper, and Piran)
  - Slovene (statewide)
- Solomon Islands: English
- Somalia
  - Somali is the de facto official language and the national language
  - Italian spoken by dying few
  - Arabic not spoken, only to read Quran
- South Africa
  - Afrikaans
  - English
  - Ndebele
  - Northern Sotho
  - Sotho
  - Swazi
  - Tsonga
  - Tswana
  - Venda
  - Xhosa
  - Zulu
- Spain
  - Spanish (statewide)
  - Catalan (in the Balearic Islands, Catalonia, and Valencia)
  - Galician (in Galicia)

- Basque (in Basque Country and Navarre)
- Occitan (in Catalonia)
- Sri Lanka
  - Sinhala
  - Tamil
- Sudan
  - Arabic
  - English
- Suriname: Dutch
- Swaziland
  - English
  - Swazi
- Sweden
  - No official language statewide; Swedish is the de facto official language. As of July 1, 2009, Swedish is the official language de jure
  - Finnish (in Gällivare, Haparanda, Kiruna, Pajala, Övertorneå, and the surrounding areas; minority language)
  - Meänkieli (in Gällivare, Haparanda, Kiruna, Pajala, Övertorneå, and the surrounding areas; minority language)
  - Romani (historical minority language)
  - Sami (in Arjeplog, Gällivare, Jokkmokk, Kiruna, and the surrounding areas; minority language)
  - Yiddish (historical minority language)
- Switzerland
  - German (in Aargau, Appenzell Ausserrhoden, Appenzell Innerrhoden, Basel-Landschaft, Basel-Stadt, Bern, Fribourg, Glarus, Graubünden, Lucerne, Nidwalden, Obwalden, St. Gallen, Schaffhausen, Schwyz, Solothurn, Thurgau, Uri, Valais, Zug, and Zürich)
  - French (in Bern, Fribourg, Geneva, Jura, Neuchâtel, Valais, and Vaud)
  - Italian (in Ticino and Graubünden)
  - Romansh (in Graubünden)
- Syria: Arabic
- Tajikistan: Tajik
- Tanzania: Swahili (national)
- Thailand: Thai
- Togo: French
- Tonga
  - English
  - Tongan (national)
- Trinidad and Tobago: English

- Tunisia
  - Arabic (national)
  - French
- Turkey: Turkish
- Turkmenistan: Turkmen
- Tuvalu
  - English
  - Tuvaluan (national)
- Uganda
  - English
  - Swahili (national)
- Ukraine
  - Ukrainian
  - Russian (regional in Donetsk Oblast, Luhansk, Kherson, Mykolaiv, Odessa Oblasts, and the Autonomous Republic of Crimea)
  - Hungarian (regional in parts of Zakarpattia Oblast)
- United Arab Emirates: Arabic
- United Kingdom
  - English, with the following specifications:
    - English (in Anguilla, Bermuda, the British Indian Ocean Territory, the British Virgin Islands, the Cayman Islands, the Falkland Islands, Gibraltar, Guernsey, Jersey, Montserrat, Northern Ireland [de facto], the Pitcairn Islands, Saint Helena, and Turks and Caicos Islands)
    - Cornish (minority language in Cornwall)
    - Dgèrnésiais (in Guernsey)
    - French (in Guernsey and Jersey)
    - Irish (in Northern Ireland)
    - Jèrriais (in Jersey)
    - Pitcairnese (in the Pitcairn Islands)
    - Scots (minority language in Northern Ireland and Scotland)
    - Scottish Gaelic (in Scotland)
    - Welsh (in Wales)
- United States
  - No official language nationwide; English is the de facto official language
    - Carolinian (regional language in the Northern Mariana Islands)
    - Chamorro (regional language in Guam and the Northern Mariana Islands)
    - French (regional language in parts of Louisiana and Maine)
    - Hawaiian (regional language in Hawaii)
    - Samoan (regional language in American Samoa)
    - Spanish (regional language in Puerto Rico and New Mexico)

- Uruguay: Spanish
- Uzbekistan: Uzbek
- Vanuatu
  - Bislama (national)
  - English
  - French
- Vatican City: No official language; Italian is the de facto official language
- Venezuela: Spanish
- Vietnam: Vietnamese
- Western Sahara (SADR) (Western Sahara): Arabic
- Yemen: Arabic
- Zambia: English
- Zimbabwe
  - English
  - Shona
  - Ndebele

Partially Recognized States

- Abkhazia
  - Abkhazian (statewide; official)
  - Russian (statewide; official)
- Kosovo
  - Albanian (territory wide)
  - Serbian (territory wide)
  - English (territory wide, during the NATO occupation of the territory on behalf of the UN)
  - Turkish (territory wide, upon request)
- South Ossetia
  - Ossetian (statewide; official)
  - Russian (statewide; official)
  - Georgian (in Georgian-speaking areas)

References

Anonymous (1978). *Technique of safe & vault manipulation.* Cornville, AZ: Desert Publications.

BrainyQuote.com, "Bill Gates Quotes." Available at http://www.brainyquote.com/quotes/authors/b/bill_gates.html. Retrieved June 5, 2013.

BrainyQuote.com, "Carl Sagan Quotes" Available at http://www.brainyquote.com/quotes/authors/c/carl_sagan.html. Retrieved June 5, 2013.

BrainyQuote.com, "Stephen Hawking Quotes." Available at http://www.brainyquote.com/quotes/authors/s/stephen_hawking.html. Retrieved June 5, 2013.

BrainyQuote.com, "Steve Jobs Quotes." Available at http://www.brainyquote.com/quotes/authors/s/steve_jobs.html. Retrieved June 5, 2013.

U.S. Army Field Manual FM 30-17 Counterintelligence Operations (1972) (Not Classified)

U.S. Army Field Manual FM 31-20 Special Forces Operational Techniques (1971) (Not Classified)

Foster, R. E. (2005). *Police technology.* Upper Saddle River, NJ: Pearson Prentice Hall.

Girod, R. J. (2009). *Infamous Murders and Mysteries: Cold Case Files and Who-Done-Its.* iUniverse. ISBN 978-0-595-63183-4.

Hough, H. (1991). *Satellite surveillance.* Port Townsend, WA: Loompanics Unlimited.

Memorandum from FBI to Senate select Committee, January 13, 1976.

Morris, J. (1982). *Crime analysis charting: An introduction to visual investigative analysis.* Orangevale, CA: Palmer Publishing.

Russell, J. L., III. (1979). *Involuntary repossession or in the steal of the night.* Boulder, CO: Paladin Press.

Schmidt, E. & Cohen, J. (2013). *The new digital age: Reshaping the future of people, nations, and business.* New York: Alfred A. Knopf.

Select Committee to Study Governmental Operations, Supplementary Detailed Staff Reports on Intelligence Activities and the Rights of Americans, April 23, 1976.

Index

Index